Deathsong of the River

DEATHSONG

OF THE RIVER

A Reader's Guide
to the Chinese TV Series
Heshang

Su Xiaokang
Wang Luxiang

Introduced, translated, and annotated by
Richard W. Bodman
Pin P. Wan

East Asia Program
Cornell University
Ithaca, New York 14853

●

The *Cornell East Asia Series* publishes manuscripts on a wide variety of scholarly topics pertaining to East Asia. Manuscripts are published on the basis of camera-ready copy provided by the volume author or editor.

Inquiries should be addressed to Editorial Board, Cornell East Asia Series, East Asia Program, Cornell University, 140 Uris Hall, Ithaca, New York 14853.

The calligraphy on the title page is by Sha Menghai

OCLC #24839362

© 1991 Richard W. Bodman and Pin P. Wan
Second printing 1992
ISSN 8756-5293
ISBN 0-939657-54-6

tla 00-486

Table of Contents

Translators' Foreword

We have translated <u>Deathsong of the River</u> in order to introduce the English-speaking public to what is probably modern China's most innovative and controversial television documentary series, one which provides both a fresh look at the long history of Chinese civilization, as well as a reflection on the forty years of the People's Republic of China. It also provides a useful key for understanding the past decade of economic and political reform in China as well as the thinking of a cross-section of liberal intellectuals in the year leading up to the events of June 4th, 1989.

In Section One, Introductory Notes, we have each contributed an essay providing some of the context the non-Chinese reader needs. R. Bodman's essay, "From History to Allegory to Art" begins with a summary of the intellectual content of the series and a study of its use of symbols. He then puts the series in the context of the past decade and in the tradition of history writing in China. A brief biography of Su Xiaokang suggests connections between the author's life experience and other writings and the text of <u>Heshang</u>. A final section explores how the text creates allegorical meaning through the use of literary devices. Pin P. Wan's essay, "A Second Wave of Enlightenment? Or an Incomplete Nirvana?" discusses <u>Heshang</u> in relation to three topics: 1. the mood and motivations of its makers; 2. the debate over the role of the intellectual in Chinese society; and 3. the relationship of contemporary intellectuals to the May 4th heritage.

Section Two, A Reader's Guide, is an annotated translation of the first published edition of the script as published by the Xiandai chubanshe in June, 1988. Some readers may wonder why our annotation is as extensive as it is, and how a slim volume of 100 pages in Chinese could become so fat in English. We felt that the film script deserved several different sorts of annotation in order to serve the different needs of readers. 1. For readers unfamiliar with Chinese history and historical figures, we provide basic identification, dates of birth and death, and references to biographical sources. 2. Due to the controversial nature of the text and the fact that its critics have spent a great deal of effort pointing out historical mistakes, ranging from errors of fact to ideological errors, we have felt it important to identify the sources of <u>Heshang</u>'s ideas and information, where possible. We also note what we believe to be examples of literary language in the script, where it suggests a critique of contemporary China through the use of allusions, puns, etc. 3. Because the published text of the filmscript is not identical with the version broadcast on television, we have felt it important to point out those differences also, as described below. 4. Because some of the ideas in the script are developed at greater length in other writings by the authors, we include references and quotations as appropriate.

There are two principal sources of difference: first, the printed script includes lengthy interviews with a number of scholars. All of these were cut or trimmed to some degree, even eliminated in one case, by Director Xia Jun before the first broadcast. Hence when we refer to the "broadcast version," we mean the televised version of the interviews. Second, the authors of the script made a number of revisions in the narration for the second national broadcast in August of 1988; these are not reflected in the published version, yet an examination of the changes gives valuable clues as to what were sensitive topics.

Section Three, A Viewer's Guide, gives the reader some idea of the relationship between the narration and the images on the television screen. For two selected episodes, Part Four and Part Six, the text of the narrative is presented in the left-hand column, while a detailed inventory of the images on the screen appears in the right-hand column. A comparison of the two columns should give the reader an idea of how images on the screen were used to emphasize or amplify ideas in the narrative; such a comparison also reveals how the selection of images can provide much ironic commentary, both on the script and on contemporary history. The text of the narrative used in this section is the text of the second broadcast of August, 1988, which we have transcribed as necessary from the videotape. The commercially available videotape represents the August, 1988 version, despite being dated June. A second reason for providing this section is the fact that an English-dubbed version of the videotape is not yet available. We hope that this version will help to fill the gap and will be especially useful in college classes.

Section Four, Commentary, provides perspective on the film and the controversy from three different points of view. Su Xiaokang's "The Distress of a Dragon Year" describes the process of writing the script as well as the various reactions to the broadcast, from viewers within and without China, and from China's conservative establishment. His commentary identifies many ideas that are only hinted at in the script. Prof. Wei-ming Tu's essay was chosen to represent the views of many Chinese scholars outside of China, who felt that <u>Deathsong of the River</u> improperly attacked traditional Chinese culture. His essay thus provides a balance to the many statements in the script critical of the Confucian tradition. Finally,

"Historians in the Capital Criticize Heshang: a summary" is an article published in Lishi yanjiu in November, 1989, representing the views of mainland scholars in the wake of the events of June 4th, 1989. This article clearly points out the many ways in which the script of Heshang deviates from the accepted view of Chinese history on the mainland; a careful study of it also reveals what some of the more outrageous statements in Heshang were, in the eyes of conservative critics.

Finally, we include a bibliography, a table of Chinese historical chronology, and a number of maps. The bibliography is by no means a complete record of everything we read or that has been published about Heshang. It also does not reflect many of the sources which we have mentioned in our annotated translation. It does contain what we think should be the core of any reference collection on Heshang: a list of the published editions of the script; a list of articles about Heshang by the makers of the film, including published interviews with them; a list of articles published in book form; and a listing of articles in languages other than Chinese. Of particular interest are a full translation and study in German and two translations into Japanese.

We have written this book both for our professional colleagues in the field of Chinese studies as well as for students in classes on Chinese culture or history. To our professional colleagues, we must first apologize for attempting a subject which requires much expertise we do not possess. Both of us received our graduate training in Chinese literature: R. Bodman at Cornell, specializing in Tang poetry and criticism; and Pin P. Wan at the University of Washington, Seattle, in traditional fiction. In order to annotate this text we have hastily acquired a smattering of economics and political science; we hope colleagues will be forgiving and offer corrections toward a second edition.

We believe that this can be a useful text for students in a variety of classes, from Chinese civilization and history to contemporary China, especially if used in conjunction with the videotape. It has been used, in a trial version, by students at St. Olaf College in R. Bodman's course on East Asian civilization, and at Cornell, in Edward Gunn's class on Chinese civilization. The experience of using this text with students has underlined the importance of preparing students adequately for dealing with a complex text, one that requires some basic knowledge of Chinese history as well as a willingness to think about theories of historical development. Hence it would be best used as a supplementary textbook.

The videotape of Heshang is available mail-order from Cheng & Tsui, 25-31 West Street, Boston, MA 02111. Telephone (617) 426-6074.

This translation project has occupied most of our free time over the past two years, starting in the fall of 1989. By the spring of 1990, we had a working translation of the text and had started on providing annotations. It was not until the end of 1990 that we felt we had detected a second, literary level of meaning. By the spring of 1991, when our translation and annotation were nearly complete, we were fortunate to meet Su Xiaokang and Yuan Zhiming, who were kind enough to confirm some of our guesses. We should note, however, that the long distance between Princeton and Northfield has not allowed us much opportunity for exchanging views, and the time and effort that would have been required to translate our work from English back into Chinese has made it impossible for Su Xiaokang or Yuan Zhiming to comment in any detail on our ideas. Our introductions, translations and annotations essentially represent our own views, for which we bear all the responsibility.

We would like to call the reader's attention to two forthcoming publications on Heshang. First, the Bulletin of Concerned Asian Scholars is devoting a special issue to Heshang, edited by Mark Selden, to be published this fall. Second, the papers presented at the conference at Princeton this May [Cultural China: from May 4th to River Elegy] will be published in Chinese and will include contributions on Heshang by Su Xiaokang, Yuan Zhiming, and R. Bodman.

Acknowledgements. First of all, we would like to thank Su Xiaokang, for graciously giving permission to translate both Heshang and his essay entitled "Longnian de beichuang" [The Distress of a Dragon Year]. Important thanks are also due to Prof. Wei-ming Tu for permission to translate his article entitled: "Heshang: Whither Chinese Culture?" We would also like to thank the organizers of several conferences for the opportunity to present our ideas in preliminary form and to receive helpful feedback. R. Bodman presented a paper entitled "Decoding the Rhetoric of Deathsong of the River" at a conference sponsored by Cornell's East Asia Program on April 27th, 1991. He also delivered a paper entitled "Heshang shi yige liti de wenxue zuopin" [Heshang is a multi-dimensional literary work] at Princeton on May 3rd this year, as part of a conference entitled "Cultural China: from May 4th to River Elegy," jointly sponsored by Princeton and the East-West Center. Pin P. Wan gave a preliminary version of his essay "A Second Wave of Enlightenment? Or an Illusory Nirvana?" at the June 1991 ASPAC conference.

Many people have assisted us in understanding and interpreting Heshang, as well as in commenting on our work in draft. Those who have read and commented on the draft included: Robert Entenmann, Edward Gunn,

Kristina Huber, Yvonne Klinnert, and Dian Murray. Rachel Huener helped us skim through the text of the German translation, as well as providing a tutorial in film criticism. Chonghae Chung assisted with the transliteration of Japanese names and titles in the bibliography. James Walker and Irina Walter provided their expertise on Soviet matters. In addition, valuable bibliographic citations were provided by Marc Blecher, Jill Cheng, David S.K. Chu, Robert Entenmann, Janet Goff, Erling Jorstad, Su Xiaokang, and Dali Yang. Connie Gunderson's assistance in arranging inter-library loan of books, periodicals, microfilms, and newspapers was invaluable. We would also like to thank Dr. Richard Howard for his help in locating materials at the Library of Congress.

The production of camera-ready copy was also the result of collective labor. Kirsten Grinde scanned and manipulated the graphics files for the maps, the title-page calligraphy, and for the illustration of the title page of the first edition. Additional scanning and printing services were provided by Artform Communications, Inc. and by Northfield Printing. Tom White designed the title page, did additional graphics work, and massaged our original text-files into final form. Karen Smith at the East Asia Program at Cornell provided expert long-distance consulting on matters of book layout and format.

To all of the above, we express our heartfelt gratitude. We would also like to thank our families and friends who have put up with our frequent absences during these two years while providing strong encouragement to finish.

Richard Bodman
Pin P. Wan
Northfield, MN
August, 1991

From History to Allegory to Art:

A Personal Search for Interpretation

by Richard W. Bodman

Deathsong of the River is one of the more creative, maverick, and controversial works to emerge from China since the founding of the People's Republic in 1949. In proclaiming the death of traditional Chinese civilization, this 1988 TV documentary series set off a debate comparable in nature to the Death of God controversy in the West—for technically atheist China has many worshippers at the altar of national greatness—and with all the intensity and invective of a religious war. Yet the Death of God in the West did not produce a single autodafe, while the makers of this film series have had to face the full wrath of a modern inquisition.

Yet the foreign reader, before being able to appreciate the theological niceties of this televised heresy, is in need of basic information and may be allowed a few naive questions. For example: What is it? And what does it say?

Deathsong of the River [Chinese title: Heshang] is a six-part TV documentary series that was aired twice on national television, in June and August, 1988; it is also the published text of the narration, which is similar but not identical to the film. Beyond that, the question "What is it?" becomes increasingly complicated. The next few steps should be to place it within a genre; to explain its rhetorical strategy for expressing meaning; and to provide comparisons for the Western reader. The reader will want to know: Is the film rigorous scholarship, or inspired synthesis? Is it history, or allegory? Is it a work of art, or a political tract? As a study of culture, is it a Chinese version of The Closing of the American Mind, or of The Chariot of the Gods? As a work of art, is it closer to Ansel Adams, or to Robert Mapplethorpe? For only when we know what it is and is not can we attempt to judge it fairly. Surely it would be a waste of breath to criticize the historical accuracy of 1984 or the Christian existentialism of Fear and Loathing in Las Vegas; yet the majority of critics of this series have done exactly this, by refusing to see it as anything going beyond their own

1

discipline. This essay is thus devoted to providing a number of contexts—historical, biographical, literary and artistic—which may help the reader come to his or her own conclusions.

Su Xiaokang, one of the script's principal authors, has already given his own reply to the above question: *"Heshang is neither an editorial, nor a scholarly article, nor a political manifesto; it is only a television film."*[1] He has also said: *"Of course we must first of all blame the fact that Heshang is neither fish nor fowl, so that both the world of art and of scholarship regard it as a freak. But I think, whenever something new appears, most people in the world will want to critique its head and feet. Don't these two kinds of criticism go to show that at the present we lack the appropriate aesthetic criteria to judge this new genre of television?"*[2]

My own response is perhaps best given as a question: If as its critics say Deathsong of the River is an ugly duckling, then who laid the egg? Can we find its missing Mom in China? Can we find her by looking at the historical context of recent Chinese history? The role of history writing in the tradition? The personal life and biography of Su Xiaokang, one of the principal writers? Or in the "environment of discourse" of Chinese society, past and present? These are the various contexts which this essay will present.

If there is some doubt as to what the film is, there is less as to what it says, little of which is pleasant reading for a Chinese patriot. Some have found it ugly because of its message that traditional Chinese culture is dead and cannot bring China into the modern world, or its hint that forty years of socialism are a failure. Others have found it ugly for asserting that the Great Wall, the Yellow River, and the dragon are themselves morally ugly, that they symbolize the sickness of China's collective soul and not the greatness of her history or people. Yet others have found it ugly in terms of its effect on youth, holding it responsible in part for the "turmoil and counter-revolutionary rebellion" of 1989 at Tian'anmen Square. Yet ugliness is in the eye of the beholder, and ugly ducklings have a way of growing up. When I first read it, I found it ugly also, for its account of history impressed me as highly emotional, exaggerated, and factually suspect. Yet after incubating it in my mind's eye for quite some time, the film metamorphosed into a swan and flew away. As a reader, your task will be to find the context which best explains why it is as it is. In other words, you must find out: Who laid the egg?

---

[1] Su Xiaokang, "Heshang de shangque" in Longnian de beichuang, Hong Kong: Sanlian shudian, April 1989, p. 176.

[2] Ibid., p. 174.

Topical Outline:

I.   The Film and the Phenomenon

  1. The content of the film
  2. The symbolism of the film
  3. The significance of the film
  4. The film as a cultural "phenomenon"

II. The History of Reform and Reforming History

  1. Reform from the top down
  2. Truth from the bottom up
  3. History and allegory

III. Su Xiaokang: Criticism and Self-criticism

  1. Character and early life
  2. A writer of reportage literature, 1983-87
  3. 1988: Attacking the dragon in the dragon year
  4. 1989: The Democracy Movement
  5. Thoughts in exile

IV. Discourse and Language

  1. The Chinese environment of discourse
  2. Heshang's use of language

V.   Concluding Remarks

I. The Film and the Phenomenon

1. **The content of the film.** The Chinese title of the series is Heshang. He means river, and especially the Yellow River, considered the cradle of China's ancient civilization. Shang means to die ahead of one's time. The title as a whole incorporates an allusion to the "Guoshang," a poem of the third century B.C. ascribed to the poet-statesman Qu Yuan. The "Guoshang" is a lament for soldiers who died in battle, while Qu Yuan is a Cassandra figure, the archetype of the loyal minister whose prophecies of doom go unheeded by his king. The authors of the script may well see themselves as latter-day Qu Yuan figures, foretelling the doom of their civilization to an unresponsive leadership. The title has been translated as River Elegy by Leo Lee, as River Dirge by Frederick Wakeman and as The River Dies Young by the editors of Beijing Review.[3] All of these renditions have considerable

---

[3] See Leo Ou-fan Lee,"Towards an Azure Culture," Times Literary Supplement, April 28-May 4, 1989, pp. 454 & 458; Frederick Wakeman, "All the Rage in China," New York

merit but suffer from being too elegant, too beautiful. As translators, we wanted a title that would convey at least a suggestion of the shock the series caused, and so we chose one incorporating the ugly word "death." In translating the title as <u>Deathsong</u>, we also took the liberty of interpretation, by transforming a lament for the dead into a song sung by those about to die. In many cultures, the hero aware of his imminent death (such as Xiang Yu surrounded on all four sides by the troops of Han) sings his own deathsong, which is at once a lament and an act of defiance. This is precisely how we as translators understand <u>Heshang</u>. The "deathsong" of the river is not merely a lament for the doom of traditional Chinese civilization. To no small degree it is also a defiant "call to arms," a summons to Chinese to take up the challenge provided by the modern world and become part of it. It found a receptive audience among young people who in the past ten years of increasing openness in Chinese society have been able to see just how backwards China still is in contrast with the industrialized West and who have been given, in grudging amounts, greater and greater latitude to doubt the wisdom of official ideology.

The film series was the result of "collective labor," as one of its authors would later say.[4] The collaborative nature of the project goes far towards explaining both the complexity of the work as well as the occasional error that crept in. The original scenario or outline for the film was drafted by Su Xiaokang, a well-known writer of reportage literature,[5] in cooperation with Xia Jun, the film's young director. Parts One and Five were drafted by Su Xiaokang. Parts Two and Three were drafted by Wang Luxiang, a young critic on the staff of the Beijing Normal College. Part Four was drafted by Su Xiaokang in collaboration with Zhang Gang, a member of the Research Institute on the Reform of the Economic Structure, a government think-tank. Part Six was drafted jointly by Xie Xuanjun, a scholar of comparative mythology and cultures, and by Yuan Zhiming, a doctoral candidate in political theory at People's University in Beijing. Ideas and advice were provided by two principal advisors: economist Li Yining and historian Jin Guantao, whose ideas find expression in Parts Four and Five respectively. There were also a host of other advisors, many of whom were interviewed on screen as part of the series. All of the episodes were finally edited by Su Xiaokang, who was concerned to produce a text suitable for spoken narration, one that would read smoothly and which would work well when matched with film images. Xia Jun undertook the arduous task of translating

---

Review of Books, March 2, 1989, pp. 19-21; Yi Jiayan [pseud.], "What Does 'The River Dies Young' Advocate?," <u>Beijing Review</u>, August 21, 1989, pp.14-21.

[4] Wang Luxiang, "Huiyi yu sikao" in <u>Heshang lun</u>, pp. 91-97.

[5] "Reportage literature" is <u>baogao wenxue</u>, a genre on the border between journalistic exposé and fiction. It frequently concentrates on the exposure of social problems.

the ideas of the script into images on film. He was hampered by a very low budget which restricted the amount of original filming he could do. But he had the advantage of access to CCTV's extensive television and film archives, on which he drew broadly. He created a film which was visually innovative but sometimes difficult to follow, in which he turned images into symbols of ideas, in which most shots were extremely short, and where his skill as an editor in juxtaposing images was crucial. His experiment may remind viewers of Soviet documentarist Dziga Vertov, who advocated the art of montage and who saw the film artist as a poet skilled in fusing images.[6] Continuity was provided not by the camera, as in many film documentaries, but by the voice of the narrator, as in many TV documentaries. In many ways the film takes ideas from the script and amplifies them or goes beyond them.

The film series is particularly hard to summarize because it is not organized in a strict chronological fashion, as we might normally expect for a work of history. Rather, its structure is developed thematically, and within each thematic episode the narrative thread can jump around both in time and space. Within each episode, the historical narrative is leavened with the presentation of historical theories, studio interviews with experts, and topics of contemporary interest. The various themes are unified visually through the use of repeated symbolic images, but the script makes no attempt at a structured exposition of ideas. Many of the script's ideas are coded and lie beneath the surface. While the written script puts more emphasis on ancient history, the images on the screen provide constant references to the recent past, and especially to the political turmoil of the Cultural Revolution. It is also clear that the discussion of the past is motivated in large part by the concerns of the present. Any attempt at a summary, therefore, is bound to be interpretive and represent only one possible reading.

Part One: "Searching for a Dream." Here Su Xiaokang attempts to characterize the complex psychology of a nation, as well as the social structure which gave rise to it. China is in pursuit of a dream, a dream of national greatness, a search made all the more intense by a realization of her backwardness. This dream motivates her participation in international sports, the only field in which China can still compete with the world. As an agricultural civilization, China matured extremely early and has changed little since. China was a state founded on the need for water control, as described by Marx and Engels in their theory of the "Asiatic Mode of Production." Yet since the 17th century, Chinese civilization has declined. Her decline was due not to imperialism but to her own internal failure to respond to the challenge represented by Western industrial civilization.

---

[6] Vertov's approach is summarized in Louis Gianetti, <u>Understanding Movies</u>, 4th edition, pp. 313-317.

"History has proven countless times that the decline of a civilization is not caused by attack from external forces, but rather by the degeneration of its internal system." [116] China—like ancient Egypt and Babylon before her—still remains an agricultural civilization, one which exhibits a pyramidal structure of power in society, fostering a kind of oriental despotism inimical to democracy, freedom and equality. Even within the very recent past, this society continued to engender a nearly religious reverence for cruel and inhuman rulers, as represented by the dragon. It is time to wake up, the script says. *"Now the most important thing is not to cheat ourselves anymore."* [115]

Part Two: "Destiny." Wang Luxiang here describes another aspect of the national character—its attachment to the soil, its resistance to outside culture, its lack of a spirit of aggression or exploration—as arising from China's unique geography. China's geography isolated it from the rest of the world, except on its northern frontier, where the farmers of the plains came into constant contact with the horsemen of the grasslands. Chinese chose a defensive strategy based upon building walls, of which the Great Wall was the final expression. Yet the Wall never stopped the invading horsemen and only served to exhaust the human and financial resources of the state. *"And yet, if the Great Wall could speak, it would very frankly tell its Chinese grandchildren that it is a great and tragic gravestone forged by historical destiny. It can by no means represent strength, initiative and glory; it can only represent an isolationist, conservative and incompetent defence and a cowardly lack of aggression."* [130] While the Ming dynasty sponsored Zheng He's voyages of exploration in the Pacific and Indian Oceans even before the arrival of the Europeans, the Chinese were motivated by political vanity and not by trade, and before long they retreated behind their walls again. China's naval defeat by Japan in 1894 and 1895 was presaged long ago at the time of Zheng He. To protect itself from foreign invasion, China's first thought has always been to keep her doors shut; yet to save her civilization from decline, she needs to throw her gates open to receive the new culture of science and democracy. *"These extremely contradictory antiphonal themes of national salvation and modernization have taken turns over the past century in writing China's abnormally-shaped history..."* [134]

Part Three: "The Light of the Spirit." This episode is devoted to the fate of China's scholars and intellectuals throughout history. Wang Luxiang develops his theme by asking a series of questions: Why is it that the light of Chinese civilization—her art, science, and technology—dimmed after the 17th century? Why did the four great inventions of paper, printing, gunpowder and the compass, all of which originated in China, produce a scientific and an industrial revolution in Europe but leave China unchanged? The answer is that the primacy of politics and ethics have always severely limited the Chinese scholar's free pursuit of knowledge. The ordered ranks of terra-cotta horses and warriors from the First Emperor's tomb suggest the theme of heavy-handed control: "*Ever since the First Emperor of Qin burnt the books... China has never again re-enacted such a grand historical drama as the competition among the Hundred Philosophical Schools. From these large square military formations, in addition to hearing the melodies of war and dictatorship, can we not also discern the repression of individuals caused by expelling unorthodox opinions, confining people's knowledge, and forcefully unifying thought?*" [141] The Han, the Tang, and the Sung dynasties in contrast show the level of artistic and of technological sophistication to which China could reach when she opened her gates to other cultures; the statue of the Vairocana Buddha at Longmen, a fusion of Chinese and Greek ideas of beauty, is a masterpiece of cultural fusion that China never succeeded in replicating. A comparison of the posthumous treatment of three historical figures shows that bureaucratic rank has always been considered superior to scientific achievement. The grave of Zhuge Liang, who served as a Prime Minister, is grandest of all. Next is that of Zhang Zhongjing, who served as a local administrator in addition to being a famous doctor. Most forlorn is the grave of Zhang Heng, China's foremost astronomer in antiquity, the inventor of the world's first seismograph, and a talented poet. The episode closes with a lament for intellectuals today, who live and work under such difficult conditions that many of them die young. "*The old generation has burned down their candles ... yet the new generation will refuse to follow in their footsteps. The educational crisis has become China's most urgent crisis.*" [156]

Part Four: "The New Era." China's economic reform process and its concomitant problems are the major focus of this episode. Authors Zhang Gang and Su Xiaokang begin by asking: "*Why had Industrial Civilization with its promise of vast wealth never appeared in Chinese history?*" [162] The answer: China was always a society of peasants with small landholdings who never had the social cohesiveness to challenge authority. Commerce existed, but the emperor and his officials skimmed off all the surplus wealth, and there was never a concept of a commodity [i.e. market] economy. Further, China's excessive population ensured that labor-saving devices and efficiency would never be important values; rather, the labor force would be characterized by "*a weak spirit of enterprise, a very low ability to accept risk, a deep psychology of dependency, and a strong sense of passive acceptance of fate.*" [169] This type of thinking in turn made the Chinese peasant an easy victim for the political and economic folly of the Great Leap Forward and Cultural Revolution. As a result of that folly, China now ranks 20th from the bottom in per capita GNP amongst nations of the world. She wants to join the world market, but her own market is unhealthy. "*As long as competition exists without the prerequisite of equal opportunity, then the loosening of price controls, which would seem to be appropriate to the rules of a commodity economy... will necessarily make*

the people apprehensive, even to the point of fomenting social unrest."
[175] Another problem is the unevenness of economic development, in which the rich areas get richer and the poor get poorer. The episode highlights General Secretary Zhao Ziyang's policies designed to promote a commodity economy, to develop China's coastal areas, and to pursue a change in the system of ownership, but it also warns that reform is not a piece of cake: *"Reform is rather a great burst of pain in which a civilization is transformed, a task fraught with danger..."* [162]

Part Five: "Sorrow and Worry." In this installment, Su Xiaokang develops broad analogies between natural and man-made disasters, and particularly between the recurring floods of the Yellow River and the periodic outbreaks of turmoil in Chinese history. These outbreaks of peasant rebellion were destructive, and were not, as Chairman Mao had written, the motive force of Chinese history. *"This kind of collapse of the social structure does not possess any revolutionary significance... No, it merely demonstrates a startling destructive force and cruelty."* [187] History did not advance with each outbreak of rebellion but rather kept returning to a stable state. *"Why has our feudal age lasted as long as the endless Yellow River floods? This is an even greater nightmare. It keeps oozing out from the imperial tomb [of the First Emperor] at Li Mountain and has spread all over, filling two thousand years of historical space. Over the past century, no matter how many times the Chinese people have tried to put it back into its tomb, it has never truly died."* [184] Is it possible then, that the same turmoil could re-occur? If the Yellow River represents the destructive forces of history, then the thousand-li long great dikes that hem it in represent China's social structure of "great unification." The tremendous power that bound together a society made up of disorganized peasants was its Confucian bureaucracy. Yet such a bureaucracy also had an irresistible tendency to corruption, leading that same society to periodic collapse. Two historical sites in Kaifeng provide food for thought. The newly-restored Shrine of Judge Bao shows that the Chinese people still revere the idea of justice, which they worship in the form of this deified Song dynasty bureaucrat. Yet the site of Liu Shaoqi's death[7] is a chilling reminder that justice cannot depend on the grace of gods; it must depend on the supremacy of law. *"The fate of a President of the Republic is sufficient to represent the fate of an age. But looking at it from another angle, when the law could no longer protect an ordinary citizen, it ultimately could not even protect the President of the Republic."* [200]

---

[7] Liu Shaoqi [1898-1969], President of the People's Republic from 1959 to 1969, died in Kaifeng, Henan, on November 12, 1969. At the time Liu Shaoqi was the principal political target of the Cultural Revolution, accused of promoting capitalism. He died of ill-health and medical neglect while in prison.

Part Six: "Blueness." This is the most "political" of all the episodes. Drawing on the discussion of China as a land-based, inward-looking civilization already developed in Part Two, authors Xie Xuanjun and Yuan Zhiming here propose the bold hypothesis that world civilizations can be classed as either "yellow" or "blue." "Yellow" civilizations, like China's, are agricultural, continental, inward-looking and defensive. "Blue" civilizations, like that of ancient Greece or modern Europe, are industrial, seafaring, outward-looking and aggressive. "Yellow" civilizations are characterized by political despotism and by a monistic, ethical creed that forbids diversity. "Blue" civilizations are marked by the liberation of the new productive forces of industry, which in turn require democracy, science, and the promotion of diversity. They conclude that *"The distinguishing marks of a despotic government are secrecy, rule by an individual, and the fickleness of his temperament. The marks of a democratic government should be transparency, responsiveness to popular will, and a scientific approach."* [221] Chinese have lost many past opportunities to follow the path of "blueness" and need to seize another opportunity today, in terms of Zhao Ziyang's policy of promoting seaboard economic development, already introduced in Part Four. China's intellectuals should play a major role in making the transition to a new "blue" culture, despite their historic weaknesses. Harking back to the discussion of traditional intellectuals in Part Three, the script declares that Chinese intellectuals have never been able to stand up to political power. *"Their talents can be manipulated by others, their wills can be twisted, their souls emasculated, their backbones bent and their flesh destroyed. And yet, they hold in their hands the weapon to destroy ignorance and superstition. It is they who can conduct a direct dialogue with 'sea-faring' civilization. It is they who can channel the 'blue' sweetwater spring of science and democracy onto our yellow earth!"* [218] The episode concludes with a hymn to the union of the Yellow River with the sea, where new land will be created from the old sediment.

While heavy on historical interpretation, the script did not shrink from contemporary issues, mentioning the increasing poverty of the countryside [178], the problems of over-population [167], and the crisis in education [156]. The script touches on the taboo topics of special privilege and corruption [168], of the 1986 student demonstrations [219], and of the unprecedented "no" votes in the 7th National People's Congress of 1988 [201]. Further, the narrative conveys a prevailing sense of unease, a fear that the reforms might not work, and that social turmoil might result. A primary subtext of the film, enhanced by contemporary footage, is the reflection on the lesson to be learned from the Cultural Revolution: when will China substitute the rule of law for the arbitrary rule of an individual?

2. The symbolism of the film. The series is unified by a number of repeated visual images: the dragon; the Great Wall; Yan'an and the yellow-soil plateau; the turbulent, muddy Yellow River; the blue Pacific; and finally the blue earth seen from outer space against a background of stars. All of these have symbolic meanings which help to link the varied themes of the film series together. The first four of these are symbols of China as a nation and a culture. While some have long histories as symbols, all of them have been used at different times over the past forty years to create a national cult of patriotism. Heshang's iconoclastic attack on these symbols is hence a reaction against the state-supported cult of nationalism.

The dragon. In traditional Chinese culture, the dragon figures as a symbol on at least two levels. At the level of folk-culture, the dragon appears in the dragon dance, performed at the lunar new year; and in the dragon-boat race on the fifth of the fifth lunar month. The dragon is associated with water: oceans and rivers each have their respective dragons, in charge of bringing rain. Hence it is quite understandable that there should be cults to the dragon spirit in north China where rainfall is so fitful. As a dragon, the Yellow River can demand a cruel price in return for its services. The biography of Ximen Bao in the Historical Records, for example, records the story of the annual sacrifice of a virgin bride to the spirit of the Yellow River. At the national level, the dragon is the symbol of the emperor, and dragon motifs covered imperial robes, architecture, and the imperial flag as well. But since the downfall of the Qing dynasty in 1911, dragons have not played a strongly symbolic role in national life until recently. In the late 80s, the song "Descendants of the Dragon" by Taiwan pop singer Hou Dejian achieved tremendous popularity on both sides of the Taiwan straits and could be seen as a welcome attempt to provide a new national identity at a time when other symbols had lost their magic. As 1988 was a "dragon year" in the twelve-year cycle as well as being "The International Year of Tourism," all of a sudden the panda was reincarnated as a dragon and plastered everywhere.

But attempts to discredit the dragon as a national symbol were not lacking either. In 1981, Sun Jingxuan's poem "A Spectre is Haunting China" had already used the dragon to symbolize the despotism and terror of Cultural Revolution politics.[8] In 1988, sociologist Yan Jiaqi took up the sword of St. George and created a furor by proclaiming that "*China is no*

---

[8] Translated by Geremie Barmé and John Minford in Seeds of Fire: Chinese Voices of Conscience, Hong Kong: Far Eastern Economic Review, 1986, pp. 121-130, under the title: "A Spectre Prowls Our Land."

longer a dragon."[9] He understood the modern cult of the dragon in two ways. First, it was a conceited national self-image, one appropriate perhaps for an isolationist empire but not for a republic trying to open up to the world. *"The image of the dragon reveals completely the mentality of self-centeredness, self-conceit, of regarding oneself as being in a special position in the world rather than as being an ordinary member of the international community. What the 'dragon culture' expresses is a self-consciousness that regards China as the center of the world, with other countries as mere embellishments, barbarians, and ordinary and undeifiable bears, eagles, cows, and elephants..."*[10] Second, the cult of the dragon represented the very reverence for charismatic, personal political authority that had led to the cult of Mao and which needed to be replaced by a reverence for impersonal authority embodied in law. *"This ferocious and omnipotent dragon hanging over the heads of millions makes people abandon their initiative and abstain from decision making even when they should make decisions; instead, people bathe in the hope for imperial favors and God-given fulfillments. We ought to change the concept of authority worship as represented by the 'dragon culture,' and make all levels of government and all enterprises and individuals shoulder their decision-making powers within their respective domains and make their own decisions when the legal 'rules of choice' permit. Only in so doing can we reduce, to a bare minimum, the number of mistakes in decision making. ... The idealization of the dragon amounts to the indoctrination among the people of the idea that there is a master over all humans. Religion needs intoxication, needs to make people content amid equivocation and speciousness. The idealized dragon satisfies this sort of human psychological need."*[11]

Deathsong of the River continued in the same iconoclastic vein. Director Xia Jun made clear visual comparisons between imperial palace architecture, featuring dragon-emblazoned marble staircases, with the temple of Confucius in Qufu, whose pillars feature coiling dragons, thus linking Confucian ideology with the tradition of political despotism. The script in turn emphasized that dragons represented inhuman monsters, and hinted that China's rulers, past and present, were also inhuman. The worship of the dragon in popular festivals could be interpreted as the worship of supreme political authority, and the worship of Mao during the Cultural Revolution

---

[9] The article first appeared in Shanghai's Shijie jingji daobao [World Economic Herald] on March 21st, 1988, and was excerpted in Renmin ribao [People's Daily] on March 23rd. An English translation of the excerpted version is published in Yan Jiaqi and China's Struggle for Democracy, trans. and edited by David Bachman and Dali L. Yang, Armonk, N.Y.: M.E. Sharpe, 1991, pp. 77-82.

[10] Ibid., p. 79.

[11] Ibid, pp. 81-82.

would thus be only the most recent example of this ancient tradition. Chairman Mao in a symbolic sense was the inheritor of the dragon throne and also happened to die in a dragon year: 1976. By 1988, when the series was broadcast, another cycle of twelve years had rolled around, and it was a dragon year once again. Did the authors fear that China was due for another tumultuous change?

The Great Wall. In contrast to the dragon, the Great Wall is not an ancient symbol of national or cultural identity. In traditional times it symbolized only the cruelty and despotism of the First Emperor of Qin, who had drafted armies of conscripts to build the wall, many of whom died on the job. Historian Arthur Waldron has shown rather convincingly that **a.** the historical evidence is lacking to prove the existence of a massive Great Wall functioning effectively throughout Chinese history; **b.** that the Great Wall as a symbol of China traces its origin to European writers of the 17th and 18th centuries; and **c.** that the myth of the Great Wall is not thoroughly transplanted to China until the middle of the 20th century.[12] "The Song of the Volunteers," a song popular during the Anti-Japanese War [1937-1945], and now the national anthem of the People's Republic, may have been responsible for canonizing the Wall. It reads in part: *"Rise up, ye people who refuse to be slaves, let us use our flesh and blood to construct a new Great Wall..."* Later, the People's Liberation Army became known as a "Great Wall of Iron" for defending the country. In the latter half of the Cultural Revolution, the campaign to criticize Confucius had as its ideological corollary a campaign to praise the First Emperor of Qin and his works. The archaeological discoveries of the terra-cotta soldiers and the symbolism of the Great Wall both served to bolster the cult of Mao, who was understood as a new First Emperor. As Waldron notes, Nixon's pilgrimage to the Great Wall set a precedent for other foreign leaders to pay obeisance to a new national symbol, one which was profoundly appealing to ordinary Chinese. In 1984, Deng Xiaoping called on the nation to "Love our Great Wall and repair it," launching a patriotic campaign which attracted donations from ordinary people on a large scale. The spring of 1988 witnessed the appearance of a television documentary entitled The 10,000 li Great Wall devoted to the positive interpretation of the Wall as an expression of *"mankind's vast creativity,"* and of *"the Chinese people's extraordinary intelligence and untiring spirit of self-strengthening."* The film appears to have de-emphasized the First Emperor of Qin in order to stress the continuity of wall-building under a long series of dynasties, both Han and non-Han. The Wall was interpreted as protecting Chinese civilization as

---

[12] Arthur Waldron, The Great Wall of China: From History to Myth, Cambridge, Cambridge University Press, 1990. The myth of the Great Wall is traced in Chapter 11, "The Wall Acquires New Meanings," pp. 194-226.

well as the Silk Road.[13] At a time when other symbols of national identity had become discredited, the Great Wall seems to have taken its place in the hearts of many Chinese as the principal representative of China's historic greatness, one recognized and paid homage to by world leaders and floods of happy tourists. Its unexamined claim to be the only man-made structure visible from the moon had become a new article of faith.

As with the dragon, iconoclasts had also arisen to make chinks in its wall of symbolic authority. Earlier in the century, the writer Lu Xun had already criticized the Great Wall: "*Actually, it never did more than kill the many workers who labored on it; nor did it ever stop the northern barbarians...*" He went on to liken the Great Wall to a psychological barrier hemming people in: "*I have always felt there was a Great Wall enclosing me. The material making up this Great Wall consists both of ancient bricks and of newly added ones. These two things have joined together to create the wall which surrounds us. When will we ever stop adding new bricks to the Great Wall? ...*"[14] Over sixty years later, in the spring of 1988, two PLA soldiers published an account of their trek along the wall entitled "The Great Wall Dialogues," a narrative full of philosophical asides: "*The Great Wall is truly the symbol of China. ... Building great walls has long been the standard psychology of the Chinese people. ... When have people ever stopped building defensive walls between each other? Beijing's four-sided courtyards; the surrounding walls and guardhouses at every work unit; and even the institutions of higher education imported from western civilization are all surrounded by imposing walls and guards. While in the modern west, with the exception of places of worship, not even homes have walls, let alone universities... One could say that if you can't understand the Great Wall, you can't understand China.*"[15]

In Heshang, the Great Wall receives both historical and metaphorical treatment. It is depicted first of all as a tragic tombstone commemorating those who died building it, an unanswered question mark vanishing in the desert sands, the typical expression of an isolationist mentality. Why, the script asks, was the Great Wall so ineffective in preventing foreign invasion, yet so ingrained in the national psyche that Chinese keep erecting

---

[13] The film was made cooperatively by a consortium of ten television stations, under the general supervision of Wu Yingcai and with academic support from Luo Zhewen. See the review in Zhongguo qingnian bao, March 6, 1988, p. 4. Appearing so close in time to Heshang, this film presumably provided it both with a convenient source of footage and with a foil to work against.

[14] Lu Xun, "Chang cheng" in Lu Xun quan ji, Beijing: Renmin wenxue chubanshe, 1973, vol. 3, pp. 63-64. His essay is dated May 11th, 1925.

[15] See Liu Fangwei and Jin Hui, "Chang cheng duihua lu" in Hua cheng, April 1988, pp. 54-80.

barriers to foreign culture? And why have the Chinese never had the guts to reach beyond their defensive walls to attack? Next, the script emphasized the Wall's function in creating a centralized power and a psychology of unity and submission: "*This sort of lay-out clearly highlights the psychology of uniting towards the center. .. With the existence of defensive walls, one could resist the attacks of herding peoples from the outside, while at the same time one could produce a sort of cohesive force on the inside, forcing the people within the walls towards the nucleus of power. Thus whoever rebuilt the Great Wall would then possess the land, the territory, and the people within it, and the Great Wall would become the wall of his family compound.*" [124] Finally, the text presents the Wall as a symbol of the spiritual constraints binding Chinese intellectuals: "*If you affixed a black cross to their spirits or weighed them down under a grey Great Wall, then the light of the spirit would never become the sun!*" [156]

Yan'an and the yellow-soil plateau. The yellow or loess-soil plateau was the home of many of China's most significant neolithic and bronze age cultures, as well as the site of the capitals of dynasties from the Qin to Northern Song. Yan'an in the middle of this plateau was Mao Zedong's capital during the Anti-Japanese War. Hence Yan'an and the yellow soil plateau together symbolize both the origins of the Chinese revolution as well as the origins of Chinese civilization.[16]

The makers of the film are able to play on this identity, by concealing a critique of Communism within a critique of traditional culture. There was a long period in the literature of the People's Republic when it was obligatory to hail the richness of rural life, the nobility of the peasant, and the transforming effect of work in the countryside on the petit bourgeois intellectual. The actual truth was far different. Many rural areas in China remained desperately poor, and the yellow soil plateau in northern Shaanxi was among the poorest, devastated not only by soil erosion, but also by a long history of mistaken agricultural policies, and by "blood transfusions" of governmental aid that fostered laziness and dependency. Even in the more relaxed climate of the early '80s, a former dissident such as Wang Meng, rehabilitated after spending two decades in rural exile, would continue to paint a picture of idyllic rural life, while portraying the cities as sources of

---

[16] Mao Zedong himself was well aware of the symbolic associations of China's landscape. In his most famous poem, "Snow," written in 1936, Mao used the backdrop of the Great Wall and the Yellow River to bear witness to his imperial ambitions, declaring that the past founders of great dynasties were no match for the man of the hour: "*Yet the emperors Shih Wang Ti and Wu Ti were barely able to write./The first emperors of the Tang and Sung dynasties were crude./ Genghis Khan, man of his epoch and favored by heaven, knew only how to hunt the great eagle./ They are all gone. /Only today are we men of feeling.*" Willis Barnstone, The Poems of Mao Tse-tung, Bantam Books, 1972, pp. 85-87.

moral corruption.[17] Since 1985 onwards, however, one of the main tendencies in both reportage literature and fiction has been to rediscover the poverty of the countryside, and to ask the embarrassing question why. Wang Luxiang, one of Heshang's principal authors, wrote in a wry vein: *"Yan'an is very poor—all of the old revolutionary base areas are very poor; this common phenomenon is worth looking into, the connection between poverty, backwardness and revolution gives much food for thought..."* [213n] The makers of the film all found considerable irony in the fact that the Yan'an pagoda, once the symbol of revolution, is now in juxtaposition with a lively street full of shops. Forty years after the leaders of the revolution had abandoned Yan'an for the cities, the ghost of capitalism had come back to haunt the forlorn shrine of the revolution.

The Yellow River. Throughout the Chinese tradition, there was a presumed relationship between the moral quality of the ruler and the behavior of the Yellow River. The great sage Yu became emperor precisely because of his ability to tame the Yellow River's floods. It was prophesied that only when a sage ruler appeared that the Yellow River would yield up a magic chart inscribed on the back of a tortoise or dragon; it was only when a sage appeared that the Yellow River would run clear. Monarchs throughout history had to continually devote resources to controlling the Yellow River and repairing its dikes, or a disastrous flood would be the result.

The Yellow River attained patriotic significance in the Anti-Japanese War, when the Great Bend formed the demarcation line between Japanese-occupied territory in Shanxi and Inner Mongolia and Mao's revolutionary base area centered in Shaanxi. The river was ennobled as the subject of "The Yellow River Concerto" and the "Yellow River Chorale."[18] Most recently, the Yellow River was the subject of a television documentary jointly produced by China and Japan entitled The Yellow River. Both Xia Jun and Su Xiaokang had worked on the film, and it was their dissatisfaction with it that led them to seek the deeper meaning of the Yellow River in Heshang and to rework its footage.

The Yellow River receives the most complex development as a metaphor in Heshang. Its pattern of cyclical floods is compared to the cyclical outbreak of turmoil and rebellion in Chinese history. Its heavy yellow sediment is the oppressive weight of Confucian and "feudal" tradition

---

[17] Wang Meng's novelette The Butterfly was a path-breaking technical experiment in Chinese fiction as well as a somewhat critical reflection on the history of the People's Republic as seen through the eyes of a rehabilitated cadre and reformer, still loyal to the system despite the mistakes of the past. The countryside is portrayed as an idyllic paradise, a sort of "Peach-blossom Spring" in which the main character found spiritual renewal. His short story, "The Eyes of Night" suggests the corruption of cadres living in the cities.

[18] See Su Xiaokang,"Heshang de shangque," in Longnian de beichuang, p. 175.

which still hinders China's progress. Its journey from the yellow soil plateau in the west to the Pacific ocean in the east mimics the path of Chinese history, from its beginnings as a land-locked agricultural civilization, to its hoped-for future as a modern, industrial and sea-faring civilization, a full participant in the international world.

Its journey is also a metaphor for the recent history of China, which has also been a pilgrimage from the yellow soil plateau to the ocean: from Mao's revolutionary base in Yan'an, now a poverty-stricken backwater, to Hainan Island, the centerpiece of ex-General Secretary Zhao Ziyang's plan of seaboard economic development.[19] Its twists and turns thus suggest the twists and turns of government policy in the attempt to bring China into the modern world. Its yellow color becomes a metaphor for China's traditional civilization, just as the blueness of the ocean takes on the meaning of modernity, democracy, and trade. The murkiness of its waters suggest the difficulty of seeing what is really going on in Chinese society and government, just as the transparent blue waters of the Pacific suggest a model of government conducted in the light of day.

Blueness and the planet earth. Neither the color blue nor the earth seen from outer space have any standing in the Chinese tradition of symbols. They have to be seen, in the first instance, as anti-symbols, in which the color blue stands in opposition to the color red, and in which the earth stands in opposition to the sun. As I shall explain in greater detail in a later section [IV.2], red stands equally for revolution and for blood, while the sun stands for Chairman Mao and the cult of personality. It is not an accident that Heshang shows so many scenes of sunset, or that occasionally it reverses the color balance, turning the sun blue-green. Naturally, the film also invests these images with new symbolic significance: blue becomes shorthand for Western civilization, for democracy, openness, etc., while the planet earth suggests both the future and the possibility of a China freed from parochialism that becomes a full world citizen.

The overall message is clear: just as the Yellow River must flow into the sea and its murky yellow waters merge with the clear blue ocean, so too must China abandon isolation, open up to the world, eliminate the "sediment" of its traditional culture, and seek for more "transparency" in the workings of society and government.

3. **The significance of the film.** The filmscript's authors were concerned that the series was overly intellectual, that only those with a college degree or higher would be interested in it or could understand it. Yet

---

[19] For the interpretation of the Yellow River as history, I am indebted to Professor Frederick Wakeman's article, "All the Rage in China" in New York Review of Books, March 2nd, 1989, pp. 19-21.

there is much of interest for all kinds of viewers: for viewers interested in theories of history and cultural change, to those troubled by real-life issues of inflation and poverty, to those curious to view their history and political leadership in a different and sometimes irreverent light. Director Xia Jun had produced a film with a highly-varied format, alternating historical narrative, interviews with experts, archival footage of Chinese leaders long gone or disgraced, excerpts from prize-winning films, and images of the modern West.

The contrast between east and west was heightened by Xia Jun's editing, which often juxtaposed color scenes of an affluent, scientifically-advanced modern world with jerky, black-and-white scenes of Chinese poverty or political struggle. As Peter Zarrow points out in his film review for the American Historical Review, there are no scenes of Western social problems, while there are plenty of scenes contrasting the modern West with a backwards China.[20]

For a host of reasons—its advocacy of democracy and popularity among young people, in particular—Deathsong of the River is essential viewing and reading for those wanting to understand the thinking of Chinese young people and intellectuals in the period leading up to the Democracy Movement of 1989. Yet for the non-Chinese reader, Deathsong of the River is not easy to understand. It abounds with references to historical events and figures unfamiliar to the foreign reader, who cannot tell the good guys from the bad guys. Some of its facts appear to be wrong. It gives little hint of the sources of its ideas. The Western authorities it does cite by name, such as Hegel and Toynbee, may strike the Western viewer as out-of-date. Its spoken narration may impress a Western audience as emotional, preachy, nation-alistic and even anti-foreign; yet many Chinese viewers would find the same narration profoundly moving, for daring to express their own unvoiced feelings and thoughts. Finally, its style of rhetoric or argument employs a degree of indirection to which Westerners are unaccustomed. What to a Chinese reader would be daring innuendo is frequently invisible to the untutored foreigner.

The series provides much food for thought. For foreign scholars wishing to understand China, it provides a capsule view of the debate within China over the past decade on a host of issues such as economic reform, political reform, as well as the reevaluation of capitalism, Marxism, and traditional Chinese culture. It does so in an entirely novel way. Eschewing familiar Marxist explanations of China's poverty and backwardness, it attempts to provide what Su Xiaokang called *"a many-layered and*

---

[20] American Historical Review, vol. 95, no. 4 (October 1990), pp. 1122-24.

pluralistic" perspective, [95] one which western academics might term integrated, cross-cultural and interdisciplinary.

For the professional sinologist or China watcher outside of China, the task of understanding the ideas broached and questions raised by this series requires a breadth of study and degree of integration that goes counter to the practice of specialization in a single discipline of Chinese studies. Yet these questions are important for future interdisciplinary study of China as well as for the comparative study of China and the rest of the developed and developing world. In studying these issues, foreign scholars have a unique opportunity to go beyond the traditional bounds of their disciplines. They bear a responsibility as well, bequeathed to them by Chinese intellectuals who at present cannot easily carry out this debate at home. Perhaps outside the highly-charged atmosphere of China, some of these questions can be depoliticized and better understood.

One of the problems raised by Heshang may be particularly suitable for discussion by scholars outside China able to provide a broader, comparative context: the relationship between cultural change and economic and political change in a developing country. Part Four of Heshang refers several times to an important study of rural poverty in Guizhou by Wang Xiaoqiang and Bai Nanfeng where they attempt to relate problems of economic development to cultural and psychological attitudes towards work and making money. They state that one of the greatest obstacles to reform comes from ordinary people mentally unprepared to engage in business, to compete, or to stand up for their rights vis-à-vis authority. If this is the case, then China's reformers may find that the route to modernization is more than just one of institutional reform and moral exhortation. Their book, Furao de pinkun: Zhongguo luohou diqu de jingji kaocha [The Poverty of Wealth: An Economic Investigation of China's Backwards Areas], represents a new departure in Chinese social science and deserves to be better known. Their discussion is framed, however, in terms of a concept many Westerners would not find "politically correct." They say that China is backwards because of a deficiency in ordinary people's suzhi, i.e. their psychological makeup or character. Social scientists outside of China, drawing on experience in other developing countries, may be able to divert Chinese intellectuals from what seems a fixation on the Western model of development, allowing them to consider other possible models.

For contemporary Chinese intellectuals, patriots and critics whose identity is tied to a profound sense of concern for their country's fate, its modernization and international reputation, the questions raised by Deathsong of the River were far more than academic. They were not particularly concerned with the sociological or anthropological approach to culture. For them, the crucial question proposed by Heshang was that of a choice of culture. In this context, the term culture itself became highly symbolic, for to redefine Chinese culture was to redefine the national identity. Hence they were asking: What kind of culture and what cultural values can unite the Chinese people in their current crisis of faith and carry them into the modern world? What definition of Chineseness can give legitimacy to a government? By joining in this debate, intellectuals were looking for a confirmation of their historic role in Chinese society and for a plan of action. Yet such a debate over culture was bound to have strong political overtones, signalling the emergence of intellectuals as an increasingly organized [and hence threatening] pressure group.

4. **The film as a cultural "phenomenon."** Though broadcast only twice,[21] Heshang was seen by millions of viewers, perhaps by as many as several hundred millions. Its script was first published in abridged form in several national newspapers with circulations of several millions,[22] and it subsequently sold over seven hundred thousand copies in book form in 1988 alone, since which time it has gone through multiple editions in Hong Kong and Taiwan. The series has inspired a storm of books and articles, both critical and favorable, plus a multitude of conferences at home and abroad.[23]

In selecting the general topic of Chinese culture, the makers of the series could not have found a better vehicle for broadening their audience to include Chinese outside of mainland China. For this audience, which in general lived in industrial, developed societies with all their concomitant problems, traditional culture still had a strong appeal and represented a possible alternative to the dominant western culture. Moreover, the topic of culture was one that the conservative mainland establishment had to take seriously, especially as they tried to persuade Hong Kong and Taiwan to come back to the fold. One of the most ironic about-faces in recent Chinese history is the fact that China's leaders, who started out by opposing the Confucian and feudal traditions at the time of May Fourth, should find

---

[21] The first set of broadcasts started June 11th, 1988; the second set started August 15th, 1988.

[22] Abridged versions of the filmscript were published on the literary supplement pages of various major newspapers as follows: Part One was published in Renmin ribao, June 12th; Part Two was published in Wenhui bao, June 28th; Parts Three, Four, Five and Six were published in Guangming ribao on June 21, June 26, and July 1 respectively. While these preliminary published versions cut large portions, presumably for reasons of space, the text that did appear is basically the same as the later published version, with only minor changes in stage directions, etc. Other newspapers also published versions of the script: Zhongguo qingnianbao published Parts Five and Six on June 30th, 1988; other newspapers and periodicals included: Jingji ribao; Guoji shangbao; Beijing qingnianbao; and Xinhua wenzhai.

[23] See the bibliography in this volume, pp. 329-342.

themselves in the ideological crisis of the 1980s as supporters of traditional Chinese culture. Perhaps in reaction to this attempt to use traditional culture as a symbol of national identity, the younger generation of intellectuals responded with a renewed assault against tradition, which was in itself a veiled critique of the establishment. The debate that emerged was peculiar because each of the different parties to the debate—China's young intellectuals, China's conservative establishment, and overseas Chinese intellectuals—appeared to mean something different by culture. For instance, overseas intellectuals tended to take Heshang's critique of traditional culture at face value, not recognizing the many references to contemporary China and not sharing the general feeling of anxiety in society. They felt that a blanket critique of traditional culture was mistaken, that a critique of the political system was required. Conservative establishment intellectuals probably realized exactly what Heshang's authors were trying to say but could not publicly admit it for reasons of national face, especially since Chinese outside of China were involved in the debate. Hence they concentrated either on finding errors of historical fact or branding Heshang's authors as unpatriotic. Ordinary viewers and readers within China presumably shared the film series' prevailing mood of anxiety, understood the general drift of its satire and sympathized as well with its focus on topics of contemporary concern such as inflation and corruption. But they may have missed many of the fine points.

While reaction from young people and intellectuals was generally favorable, official circles were divided. Before broadcast, the series had been approved by China Central TV but had not been sent to higher authorities for review; this was unusual but reflected a policy set by General Secretary Zhao Ziyang of non-interference in literary matters.[24] Zhao Ziyang is said to have praised the series, even recommending it to a visiting head of state, Singapore Prime Minister Lee Kuan Yew. Vice-president Wang Zhen, on the other hand, reportedly condemned it strongly, claiming that it slandered the Chinese people and their ancestors, that it was worse than Taiwan dissident Bo Yang's The Ugly Chinese. Wang is reported to have complained: *Intellectuals are dangerous. If the Japanese were to invade, these assistant professors and graduate students would all be on the welcoming committee. ... If things continue in this fashion, the Party and the State will be finished.*[25] Enraged, the series' authors struck back in the press, with

---

[24] The story of the composition of the script and its approval by CCTV is told by Wang Luxiang in "Huiyi yu sikao" [Remembering and Pondering], Heshang lun, pp. 91-97; and by Su Xiaokang in "Longnian de beichuang" [The Distress of a Dragon Year] in Longnian de beichuang, pp. 1-44, and in this volume, pp. 271-299.

[25] Vice-President Wang Zhen holds the rank of General. His critique of Deathsong of the River was first publicly launched in the Ningxia Daily on Sept. 27, 1988 when he led a

Su Xiaokang quoting a rhyming proverb that "*a scholar who's in the right/ Can't beat a soldier in a fight.*"[26] During the summer and early autumn of 1988, Zhao Ziyang apparently successfully shielded the series from outright censorship and permitted a lively debate in the press. Afterwards, the debate died down on the mainland due to political pressures from the conservatives, but the controversy continued to be waged in the Hong Kong and overseas Chinese press.[27] Later, most of the authors and on-camera guests of the series were involved to a greater or lesser degree in the Spring 1989 Democracy Movement, signing petitions and open letters and seeking to protect the students by invoking the Constitution.[28] The crackdown of June 4th was in turn followed by a spate of books and articles attacking the creators of the series for diverse sins, from propagating cultural nihilism to preparing the way for counter-revolutionary turmoil. The series is now banned in China, several of its principal writers have found asylum abroad, while two of their interviewees have received stiff sentences for political crimes.

This would not be the first time in recent Chinese history that a literary controversy had preceded the eruption of political and social tumult. Both the anti-rightist movement of 1957 and the Great Proletarian Cultural Revolution of 1966-76 were prefaced by debates over film and drama. And indeed, the split in China's leadership over <u>Deathsong of the River</u>

---

delegation to celebrate the 40th anniversary of the Ningxia Hui Autonomous Region. These remarks, however, come from a conversation with Tan Wenrui, editor-in-chief of <u>Renmin ribao</u>, as reported by Liu Yanying in Hong Kong's <u>Jingbao yuekan</u>, November, 1988, pp. 44-45. Su Xiaokang cited them in "The Distress of a Dragon Year" first published in November, 1988; see p. 296 in this volume.

[26] <u>Xiucai yuzhi bing, you li shuo bu qing</u>. Su Xiaokang used this saying in his "The Distress of a Dragon Year"; see p. 297 in this volume. The implication of the saying is that the soldier is uneducated and only understands the use of force in a dispute. Wang Zhen apparently did not see much action at the front. During the Yan'an period, he was in charge of transforming Nanniwan into a productive agricultural area; in the early 1950s, he led a "construction brigade" to Xinjiang. See Su Xiaokang, <u>Longnian de beichuang</u>, p. 43; Hua Yan, ed., <u><Heshang> pipan</u>, p.24.

[27] A number of articles highly critical of Wang Zhen were published in the Hong Kong journal <u>Zheng ming</u>; see esp. Nov., 1988, pp. 44-45;Dec., 1988, pp. 12-13. The other side of the story, alleging that the authors of the series were deliberately creating favorable propaganda for Zhao Ziyang's "New Order of the Socialist Commodity Economy" and that Zhao actively suppressed adverse criticism of the series was told by Jin Ren in his article, "Zhao Ziyang tongzhi de jieru shuo he <u>Heshang</u> de <xin jiyuan>" [Comrade Zhao Ziyang's involvement and <u>Heshang</u>'s <New Era>], originally published in <u>Guangming ribao</u>, August 14th, 1989; reprinted in <u>Heshang pipan</u>, pp. 20-25.

[28] See Section III.4 below for examples of Su Xiaokang's political activity during this period.

paralleled in some ways the split that evolved in the Spring of 1989, between Zhao Ziyang and party conservatives.[29]

In advocating these changes, were the creators of the series going beyond the limits of acceptable criticism? Were they being rebels, or reformers within the system? The answer to that question depends in part on your political point of view and in part on seeing Heshang in the historical context of the last decade.

For a culture which still values "correctness" over pluralism and debate, only one answer is possible: they were rebels. They are accused of a lack of patriotism, of ethnic and cultural nihilism, of fawning on foreigners and foreign culture, and of a host of intellectual sins: geographical determinism, a theory of historical cycles, the failure to be guided by a correct and scientific [read Marxist] view of history, as well as basic errors of fact.

Yet in the summer of 1988, before the democracy movement of 1989 was born, most of the views presented in the film series could be seen as the natural outcome of a decade of an increasingly liberal climate of opinion, while its views on economic development could be seen as echoing those of Zhao Ziyang and his liberal brain trust.

II. The History of Reform and the Reforming of History

The history of the decade from 1978 to 1988 in China is one of a dialectical progress towards greater and greater openness, punctuated by a series of short-lived official attempts to reassert control over ideology, and to substitute faith in the nation for faith in Marxism.

1. **Reform from the top down.** In 1978, the Chinese government initially took a leading role in restoring the civil rights of intellectuals and expanding their freedom of speech, after more than a decade in which they had been the object of unremitting "class struggle." Deng Xiaoping's ascension to power was warmly welcomed because of his pledge to "seek truth from facts," rather than from the orthodox texts of Maoism. He initially supported the Democracy Wall Movement of 1978-79 for its critique of the Cultural Revolution. In the fall of 1980, he supported open elections to local peoples' congresses. In June of 1981, Deng led the effort to rewrite party history, concluding with the unprecedented "Resolution on Certain Questions in the History of our Party" which assigned Chairman

---

[29] Joining Wang Zhen in opposition to the series were Song Renqiong, Bo Yibo, Peng Zhen, Hu Qili and Wang Renzhi. See Zheng Ming, December, 1988, p. 12.

Mao a judicious portion of the blame for the past excesses of the "Great Leap Forward" and the "Cultural Revolution."[30]

Other confidence-building measures undertaken by the authorities were the re-opening of religious and educational institutions. China's Buddhists, Muslims and Daoists, as well as Catholics and Protestants, were free for the first time in years to worship in public, to open schools to train the next generation of religious leaders, and to publish religious literature. The Banchan Lama was freed from house arrest, and a dialogue was opened with the Dalai Lama in exile. Religious property that had been confiscated was gradually returned, and the state spent large sums on the refurbishing of places of worship. The Chinese constitution was re-written to give stronger guarantees of religious freedom. By Easter of 1988, the Amity Press in Nanjing was issuing the first simplified-character edition of the Bible to an enthusiastic welcome. Yet greater religious freedom in Tibet was accompanied by increasing calls for Tibetan autonomy and clashes between police and demonstrators.

Institutions of higher education were re-opened, competitive entrance examinations were re-instituted, and academic degrees were re-introduced. The classes that entered college in 1977 and 78 consisted of many students who had been forced to wait ten years for the opportunity, and the entrance examinations were particularly competitive. Ten years later it would be this group of graduate students and young professors who would be most active in the movement to reevaluate traditional Chinese culture and from whom many of the authors and advisors of Heshang would be drawn. Student activism increased among college students. The Fall of 1986 witnessed widespread demonstrations in which students called for better living conditions, for dialogue with the authorities, and for the media to tell the truth.

But the momentum towards political reform was slowed or checked in each instance: by the closing down of Democracy Wall in 1979; by interference with the 1980 elections; by the 1983 campaigns to combat crime and "spiritual pollution"; and finally by the movement to combat "bourgeois liberalization" in early 1987.

The hopes of political reformers were raised once again with Zhao Ziyang's accession to the post of General Secretary in the Fall of 1987. Zhao called for greater consultation and dialogue within Chinese society and gave the media greater freedom. The 13th Party Congress in October, 1987

---

[30] See the Resolution on Certain Questions in the History of Our Party Since the Founding of the People's Republic of China [Adopted by the Sixth Plenary Session of the Eleventh Central Committee of the Communist Party of China on June 27, 1981], Foreign Languages Press, Beijing, 1981, 126 pp. On the evaluation of Mao's leftist errors in fomenting the "Great Leap Forward" and the "Cultural Revolution," see pp. 27-47.

and the meetings of the 7th National People's Congress and the 7th National Political Consultative Assembly in March and April of 1988 were fully open to both the Chinese and the foreign press. Chinese TV gave live coverage to press conferences and to delegates' speeches. For the first time in the history of the People's Republic, some delegates cast "no" votes.

The same decade witnessed considerable developments in economic theory and development strategy. Deng's approach was characteristically pragmatic: socialism would be defined by whatever policies would work to revive the economy, whether or not tainted by capitalism. [*"It doesn't matter if the cat is black or white, as long as it catches mice, it's a good cat."*] By 1987, Zhao Ziyang had managed to convince the Party that China was still in a "preliminary stage of socialism" appropriate for the development of a "commodity economy" [read market economy]; that this was a necessary historical stage—and a long one—through which China would have to pass. The way was thus open for more and more experimentation with policies of economic development that were not Marxist but which had worked, notably in Asia's "four small dragons"—Singapore, Hong Kong, Taiwan, and South Korea.

Deng's pragmatism had paid off first of all in rural economic reforms. His highly-popular "responsibility system" dismantled the communes and allowed the re-emergence of family farms and rural entrepreneurs, bringing about a doubling of rural income in some areas. Policies for the revitalization of urban industry were slower to evolve. Many of them started out as experiments in the various special economic zones set up along the coast. Yet by 1987, a host of daring decisions signalled the transition from a centrally-planned economy to a market economy: the transformation of many government enterprises into semi-private corporations, the granting of greater power to enterprise managers, the gradual elimination of state subsidies for industry, and the end of price-setting for almost all commodities. As China's prescription for economic development relied more and more on foreign investment and earnings from export trade, development strategy increasingly concentrated on China's coastal cities and provinces.

But there was a price to pay for economic reform in terms of popular discontent. Reform in general meant that people felt less secure than before, even though more goods were available. For urban consumers, commodity prices that had been unchanging for years all of a sudden exhibited inflation, at rates conservatively estimated between 20-30%. Surplus labor from poor areas of the countryside poured into the cities looking for work, increasing rates of crime and prostitution, and creating a lumpenproletariat that could not be easily controlled. All of a sudden the disparities in wealth between occupational groups and between rich and poor areas became increasingly apparent. Intellectuals found that they made less than cabdrivers. Many college students, disappointed by their prospects for a good work assignment after graduation, turned either to playing mahjongg or gambling on the prospect of studying abroad. Some farmers found that they couldn't get enough chemical fertilizer from the government store, while others found that in some situations they were paid for their grain in non-redeemable chits. Urban workers discovered their salaries docked for "voluntary" purchases of state bonds and contributions to the 1990 Asian Games. Price reform had put the economy in disarray, increasing opportunities for official corruption and nepotism. By 1988 there was a general psychology of frustration and unease.

2. **Truth from the bottom up.** While economic and especially political reforms came slowly, there had been a notable relaxation in ideological control, and a wider tolerance for new subjects of research and publication. A number of disparate social groups were involved in testing the new limits of thought and of expression. These groups included the think-tanks and research institutes involved in forming policy; academics with a sense of social conscience; writers; film-makers; journalists; publishers; and television producers. They would all be vocal constituencies for reform, though their boldness would normally vary in inverse ratio to the size of their public. The main problem that they faced was that their increased latitude of expression was not protected by law and could be canceled at any time.

Think-tanks. The cause of reform was institutionalized in a number of think-tanks, both public and private, and their proposals and research were widely published in a number of newspapers and journals. The Research Institute for the Reform of the Economic Structure [RIRES], led by Chen Yizi, the Research Center for the Reform of the Political Structure, and the China Rural Development Research Center were directly under the State Council. A government-owned corporation, the China International Trust and Investment Corporation [CITIC], had its own Institute of International Studies. In addition, there were at least two privately-founded institutes: the Research and Development Institute of the Stone Corporation, headed by Cao Siyuan, and the Beijing Social and Economic Sciences Research Institute [SERI] headed by Chen Xiaoping and Wang Juntao.[31] These think-tanks conducted some pioneering research into Chinese social conditions. Wang Xiaoqiang of RIRES composed a major report entitled Poverty Amidst Plenty: An Economic Survey of China's Backwards Areas,[32] focussing primarily on Guizhou. Wang Juntao, Min Qi and others from SERI conducted a nation-wide questionnaire survey in the summer of 1987

---

[31] For a history of these think-tanks, see News from Asia Watch, Rough Justice in Beijing, January 17, 1991.

[32] Furao de pinkun: Zhongguo luohou diqu de jingji kaocha. Part Four uses excerpts from this. See notes 24, 31, 32, 55, 58, 60.

focussing on China's "political culture," that led to the publication in February 1989 of <u>China's Political Culture: Social-psychological Factors in the Delayed Birth of Democratic Politics</u>.[33] Part Six of <u>Heshang</u> would draw on this survey as proof of most citizens' reluctance to participate in politics.

Social Science. During this time as well, a number of new book series were founded to bring the results of social research, comparative cultural studies, and foreign social science to the Chinese public. Two of the best known were the <u>Zouxiang weilai congshu</u> [<u>Towards the Future Series</u>, edited by Jin Guantao; and the <u>Wenhua zhexue congshu</u> [<u>Philosophy of Culture Series</u>], edited by Bao Zunxin. A study of the membership of the editorial boards of these two books series would reveal a cross-section of China's reformist intellectuals.

Chinese intellectuals were particularly drawn to the writings of overseas Chinese scholars able to reinterpret the Chinese tradition from new perspectives. The works of archaeologist Zhang Guangzhi, Confucian apologist Weiming Tu, and historian Ray Huang all were reprinted in Chinese editions and snapped up as ammunition in the growing scholarly debate over the reevaluation of Chinese culture.

Systems theory and cybernetics caught the imagination of China's economic planners, as did futurist Alvin Toffler's <u>The Third Wave</u>, with its prediction of a new society transformed by the information revolution and supplanting the societies formed by the two earlier "waves" of the agrarian and industrial revolution[34] Max Weber's <u>The Religion of China</u> was read for its contrast of charismatic versus legal-rational authority, one which helped China's intellectuals make sense of the Cultural Revolution and the cult of Mao in particular. Fairbank's <u>The U.S. and China</u> and <u>China's Great Revolution</u> both aroused critical interest.

Just as China's thinkers were attracted to adopting the works of Western social science, so too were they engaged in a re-evaluation of Marxist theory. Jin Guantao, already well-known for his study of capitalism's failure to appear in China, published an article entitled: "The Deep Structure of Confucian Culture and its Influence on the Sinicization of Marxism."[35] Li Honglin, a political philosopher, evaluated the history of Marxism in China

---

[33] <u>Zhongguo zhengzhi wenhua: minzhu zhengzhi nan chan de shehui xinli yinsu,</u> Kunming: Yunnan renmin chubanshe.

[34] For the reception of future studies and Toffler's book in China, see Carol Lee Hamrin, <u>China and the Challenge of the Future: Changing Political Patterns</u>, Westview Press, 1990, pp. 75-80.

[35] "Rujia wenhua de shenceng jiegou dui Makesizhuyi Zhongguo hua de yingxiang," in <u>Xin qimeng 2: Weiji yu gaige</u>, December, 1988, pp. 22-36.

as follows: "...*Capitalism, due to its internal contradictions, will someday be replaced by an even more highly advanced socialism. But first, a socialist society more highly advanced than it is yet to be created by the people, and there is no ready-made model to follow... The socialist theories of Marxism have been around for more than one hundred years, and yet there has not yet been a single case of the socialist revolution they predicted. As for the time and the conditions under which a future socialist revolution will occur, as well as the path that such a revolution will follow, traditional socialist theory has no answers. ... Socialist states have indeed appeared in the world. And yet not one of them has entered socialism according to the rules that scientific socialism originally proclaimed. Revolution did not occur because the level of productive forces was too high for the old relations of production to contain. It was the precise opposite: the levels of their productivity were all rather low...*"[36]

Literature. In the decade from 1978 to 1988, many previously forbidden areas were opened up in literature, with authors writing not merely about the excesses of the Cultural Revolution but also about the abuse of official power and privilege in contemporary China. The first such literature to appear was called "Scar Literature" [shanghen wenxue], in reference to the physical and psychological scars left by the Cultural Revolution. Zheng Yi's short story entitled "Maple" broached the subject of armed struggle between Red Guard factions. Zhang Xianliang's Half of Man is Woman appearing in 1986 explored the subject of prison labor camps during the Cultural Revolution and titillated his young readership with its frank description of sex and its clever analogies between sexual and political impotence.

A new genre of poetry entitled "Misty Poetry" [menglong shi] experimented with modern techniques and was the first to challenge traditional symbols of Chinese identity. Gu Cheng's poem "All is Finished" was a reflection on the recent past that presented the Yellow River in an unaccustomed fashion: "*In a twinkling—/ The landslide ceased,/ The riverside was piled high with skulls of giants./ The junk in mourning,/ Slowly passes by,/ And unfolds the dull-yellow shroud...*"[37] Here, the Yellow River is no longer the mother of the nation, but rather the undertaker who receives the dead of the Cultural Revolution.

---

[36] Li Honglin, "Weiji yu gaige" [Crisis and Reform] in Xin qimeng 2: Weiji yu gaige, December, 1988, pp. 37-57. Draft translation by Richard Bodman.

[37] See Michael S. Duke, ed., Contemporary Chinese Literature: An Anthology of Post-Mao Fiction and Poetry, Armonk, N.Y.: M.E. Sharpe, 1985, p. 49. My thanks to Su Xiaokang for providing this reference.

Another major genre was reportage literature [baogao wenxue], which straddled the boundary between journalism and fiction. Liu Binyan, a member of the generation of writers who had been silenced by the Anti-Rightist movement, now took up his pen again and wrote a number of pieces indicting corruption in present-day China, such as <u>People or Monsters?</u>[38] and <u>A Second Kind of Loyalty</u>.[39] His work met with considerable resistance because he wrote in detail about individual cases, thus mobilizing local authorities to fight back. Younger writers in the same genre took up the topic of social problems. Qian Gang's <u>The Great Tangshan Earthquake</u> explored both the natural catastrophe caused by the great quake of July 28, 1976, as well as the further catastrophes caused by human error and bureaucratic bungling. Other famous pieces in this genre included <u>Shijie da chuanlian</u>, about the exodus of Chinese students overseas; Zhao Yu's reports on China's failure at the Olympics, <u>Qiang guo meng</u> and <u>Bing bai Hancheng</u>; and Kang Jian's "Xingbing zai Zhongguo,"[40] about the growing incidence of sexually-transmitted diseases.

Before 1988, perhaps the largest furor of all had been caused by the publication of <u>The Ugly Chinese</u>, a book of satirical essays lampooning the national character by Taiwan dissident Bo Yang. It was reprinted on the mainland in 1986 and quickly became a cult item amongst young people. The controversy caused by his book, with its contention that the Chinese national character was "ugly," has only been matched by that over <u>Deathsong of the River</u>, with its declaration that Chinese culture is dead. To a greater degree than <u>Heshang</u>, <u>The Ugly Chinese</u> is preoccupied with the <u>suzhi</u> of the Chinese people: why are Chinese noisy, dirty and quarrelsome? Why can't they cooperate? Why is there so much infighting? Why can't Chinese admit when they are wrong? But Bo Yang is also concerned with reflecting on why traditional culture—i.e., Confucianism—has made it difficult for democracy to be adopted in China:

> "*This culture, from the time of Confucius onwards, hasn't produced a single thinker! Everyone who can read is occupied in annotating the theories of Confucius or those of his followers; they don't have their own independent opinions because our culture doesn't allow them to, and so they can only try to survive somehow in this pool of stagnant water. This pool,*

---

[38] See Liu Binyan, <u>People or Monsters? And Other Stories and Reportage from China after Mao</u>, edited by Perry Link, Indiana University Press, 1983, pp. 11-68.

[39] Published as "Di er zhong zhongcheng" in <u>Kaituozhe</u>, no. 1, 1985. A French translation by Jean-Phillipe Béja, "La deuxième forme de loyauté" may be found in Liu Binyan, <u>La cauchemar des mandarins rouges</u>, Gallimard, 1989, pp. 195-254.

[40] <u>Beijing wenxue</u>, September, 1988, pp. 33-52.

this stagnant water, is the soy-bean paste vat[41] in which Chinese culture is brewed. Whenever the vat emits a stink, it makes Chinese look ugly. And it's because this vat is so deep, so deep that there are many problems we cannot solve by thinking on our own, that we can only rely on the thinking of others to guide us. This stagnant water, this paste vat is such that, if dropped in it, even a honey peach would come out a turd ball. When things from the outside come to China, they always turn sour. Other people have democracy; we've got democracy, too. Our democracy is: 'You are the demos, I am the crat!'[42] Other people have the rule of law; we've got the rule of law, too. Other people have freedom; we've got freedom too. Whatever you've got, we've got, too. You've got zebra-striped crosswalks? We've got 'em too—of course, our zebra-stripe crossings are for the purpose of tempting you into being run over by a car."[43]

The Ugly Chinese differs greatly from Heshang. It is primarily anecdotal and does not draw broadly on scholarly theories and research. But its concern with the national character was reflected in the debate during the next few years in mainland China over the nature of Chinese intellectuals. Did Chinese intellectuals have a tradition of independence or of subservience to political authority?[44] While Heshang does not make specific references to The Ugly Chinese, it shares with it a serious questioning of tradition combined with an irreverent spirit.

Film. Other writers, embarked in a search for their cultural roots, wrote about the unattractive realities of the poverty-stricken countryside. Two such novels, The Yellow Earth[45] and The Old Well,[46] were turned into

---

41 "Soy-bean paste vat" translates jiang gang. These are hermetically-sealed jars in which bean-paste is fermented.

42 This is a pun on the word for democracy [minzhu], made up of the two elements, min or "people" and "zhu," which has the double meanings of "to rule" and "ruler."

43 For the original text, see Bo Yang [Guo Yidong], Choulou de Zhongguo ren, #12 in the Daoyu wenku series, Taibei: Linbai chubanshe, 1985, pp. 15-39, esp. 36-37. Draft translation by R. Bodman. The mainland China edition was issued by the Hunan wenyi chubanshe.

44 For a detailed account of this discussion, see Pin P. Wan's essay in this volume, "A Second Wave of Enlightenment? Or an Illusory Nirvana?," especially section two: "Intellectuals, Cultural Crisis, and the May Fourth Legacy," pp. 70-85.

45 Directed by Chen Kaige and released in Hong Kong for the 1985 International Film Festival. For details see Geremie Barmé and John Minford, eds., Seeds of Fire: Chinese Voices of Conscience, Far Eastern Economic Review, Hong Kong, 1986, pp. 252-270.

46 Based on the novel Lao jing by author Zheng Yi, the film directed by Wu Tianming won top prize at the Tokyo International Film Festival. See Zheng Yi, Old Well, translated by David Kwan with an introduction by Anthony P. Kane, China Books and Periodicals, San Francisco, 1989.

films which won prizes in international competitions, and from which Deathsong of the River has borrowed footage. Other film-makers explored the tragedies of the Cultural Revolution. The final scene from the film adaptation of Gu Hua's novel A Village called Hibiscus is drawn upon by Heshang for its ominous suggestion that the turmoil of the Cultural Revolution could still reoccur.

The Press. Among the more liberal publications during this period were newspapers such as Shanghai's World Economic Herald; the Shenzhen Youth News; China Youth News; and Economic Studies Weekly, from Beijing, owned by SERI; and magazines such as Xin guancha [The New Observer] from Beijing and Hainan jishi. A journal that bridged the gap between the Chinese mainland and overseas scholars was Zhishi fenzi [The Chinese Intellectual], edited by Liang Heng in New York; it accepted contributions from mainland, Taiwan and U.S. academics and was distributed on the mainland.

Book Publishing. The translation of foreign works of all sorts was another area in which broad tolerance was allowed, as publishing houses and eager young translators sought to find profitable best-sellers in the absence of international copyright. In 1988 and the first half of 1989, China's bookstores and street-corner stands overflowed with translations of foreign books, from Nancy Reagan's Now Its My Turn to George Bush's campaign biography, from Sidney Sheldon to James Bond, from George Orwell's 1984 to thinly-disguised color albums of erotic art. Detailed manuals for newly-weds hit the shelves with alluring covers. Western formulas for success and happiness abounded, from Lee Iacocca to L. Ron Hubbard. Popular works on China by Western authors and Chinese in exile was another best-selling category, including Sterling Seagrave's The Soong Dynasty, Liang Heng's Son of the Revolution, as well as four separate translations of Cheng Nian's Life and Death in Shanghai.

Television. As the medium with the greatest public impact, television was one of the most important organs of government and party policy and was used as a major tool for promoting patriotic awareness. Hence television was rather slow to take on a critical role, or even to discuss government-sponsored policies of reform. Yet China's accelerated process of opening up to the outside world was inevitably reflected in what television viewers saw, giving them a broadening window on the world.

The television viewing audience grew rapidly over the decade, as provincial governments realized the profits to be made from the sale of sets. Television ownership in Jiangsu province rose almost nine-fold, from 4.5 million sets in 1979 to 35.9 million sets in 1989. It was estimated that China had 112 million television sets in 1987 and a total viewing audience of 600 million. In 1985 alone, China sold over 21 million television sets, representing 4% of total consumer spending. Televisions had thus become one of the most desirable consumer goods. The number of television stations also increased, from 38 stations in 1979, to 292 stations in 1986, to 422 in 1989. As the new stations began to produce their own programs, control of programming also began to shift away from the national network to local stations.[47]

The content of television programming also changed. While national television news still featured foreign leaders paying ritual obeisance to China, it also included many segments borrowed from foreign newscasts. It began to report plane crashes. Press conferences in which foreign reporters would ask probing questions of the leaders would be broadcast unedited. A number of foreign programs were adopted for broadcast in China. These included the Walt Disney hour on Sunday evenings; foreign soap operas, such as the long-playing Mexican series Infamia [Feibang in Chinese]; and detective dramas, such as Hunter. Live and delayed broadcasts of Olympic competition probably attracted the largest viewing audience of all.

Documentaries made for television gained increasing sophistication. A favorite subject was the exploration of the Chinese landscape, as a repository both of history and of folk culture. Multi-part series were devoted to The Story of the Yangtze, The Story of the Grand Canal, The Silk Road, and the Ten-thousand li Great Wall, the largest project of which was the thirty-part series entitled the Yellow River, jointly produced by China Central TV and Japan's NHK. The majority of these were made without a detailed shooting script, and the text of the narration was made to fit the edited film. A film entitled Let the Past Tell the Future [Rang lishi gaosu weilai] provided the first example of a documentary made from a detailed shooting script, in which the narrative was created before the editing. It was said to have been the first Chinese documentary to break the taboo on using archival footage of past political leaders. Examples of well-made foreign documentaries shown on Chinese TV included Alvin Toffler's The Third Wave and a French production entitled Earth—The Dark Shadow of Mankind representing an ecological critique. In terms of the primacy of the script, choice of editing techniques, and a thoughtful focus on contemporary problems these documentaries provided a precedent for making Heshang.[48]

---

[47] See Zhongguo guangbo dianshi nianjian 1989, Beijing: Guangbo xueyuan chubanshe, 1990, esp. pp. 147, 321, 330-333 and 499.

[48] For a brief history of television documentaries in China, see Cui Wenhua, "Heshang dui Zhongguo dianshi de qishi he zai?" [What is the lesson of Heshang for Chinese television?] in Cui Wenhua, ed., Heshang lun, pp. 123-142, esp. 123-127.

Hence by 1988, even though economic reform was progressing slowly, and political reform advancing glacially, a number of different constituencies for reform had developed whose expectations were being raised. These included the above-mentioned think tanks; publishers and the media; intellectuals; and a broad spectrum of the urban reading public.

3. **History and allegory.** In retrospect, the viewpoints of <u>Deathsong of the River</u> did not appear to be out of line, while the views it expressed on economic reform were remarkably close to the officially-accepted policy of the Zhao administration. Yet the film-makers were still treading on dangerous ground: In traditional China, history writing was the prerogative of the government; each new dynasty would write the history of the previous one, with the assumption that its downfall had been due to a decline in the moral character of the ruling elite. In People's China, this prerogative was inherited by the Party, and it was assumed that all history writing would be done in the framework of Marxism-Leninism-Mao Zedong thought. In fact, for both Confucianists and Marxists alike, history was viewed as the way in which the Tao or dialectic was revealed, and the keepers of history were necessarily politically legitimate and morally correct.

Yet in China the study of historical texts could also be a means of social criticism, albeit somewhat oblique. In contrast, for the Western reader the same sort of oblique social criticism has often been expressed through the genre of the fictional travelogue, represented by <u>Gulliver's Travels</u>, Oliver Goldsmith's <u>A Citizen of the World</u> or Montesquieu's <u>Persian Letters</u>, one which has continued into the late twentieth century in the form of science fiction travels, ranging from <u>Planet of the Apes</u> to <u>The Left Hand of Darkness</u>. In the Western literary tradition, however, it is hard to think of a good example of social criticism cast in the form of history. While China has also employed the genre of the fictional travelogue, most notably in the Qing novel <u>Jinghua yuan</u> [<u>Flowers in the Mirror</u>], the study of history has been a favorite mode for critical thinkers in China's past. One historical classic in particular, the <u>Spring and Autumn Annals</u>, has been the subject of much creative exegesis, perhaps due to its attribution to Confucius. The Gongyang Commentary on the classic started with the assumption that the extremely laconic statements of the text incorporated through their choice of wording the Sage's moral judgements on historical events and persons. Qing reformers such as Gong Zizhen and Kang Yuwei were heavily influenced by the Gongyang school of interpretation, leading Kang Yuwei to reinterpret Confucius as a reformer. Perhaps the special relationship of history writing to reform in the Chinese tradition was one reason why the makers of <u>Heshang</u> chose to cast their film in the guise of history rather than fiction.

The moral seriousness of history made it no accident that the Museum of History was erected on the east side of Tian'anmen Square, at the symbolic center of China's universe. But the keepers of the past were unable to write or reflect adequately on their own. The Museum's extensive displays began with the skulls of Peking Man and Lantian Man but ended in 1949 with a decorative display of the flag of the new republic, as if to warn would-be historians, "*Abandon hope, ye who enter here.*" It was the need to reflect on the forty years of the People's Republic that primarily motivated the makers of Heshang, but their reflection could not be explicit. It could only be developed as a critique of traditional culture, an approach which in theory should have been safe, for the Party acknowledged its inheritance of the May Fourth Movement's debunking of the feudal past. Hence Heshang was destined to be better read as allegory than as history.

The makers of the film were aided by the fact that the reading of the past as an allegory for the present was standard practice in the People's Republic. Everyone knew that the film Secrets of the Qing Court as well as Wu Han's play Hai Rui Dismissed from Office[49] had gotten into trouble precisely on account of their allegorical significance. Similarly, the campaign to "Criticize Lin Biao and Confucius" had a target in Zhou Enlai, the supposed reincarnation of the Duke of Zhou.

Hence an allegorical reading of Heshang is relatively fruitful: The mythical figure Gun, who was unable to control the Yellow River's floods, can be seen as a modern Mao, unable to control the turmoil of the Cultural Revolution; the First Emperor of Qin, as well as Zhu Yuanzhang, the first Ming Emperor, can also be read as stand-ins for the founder of the People's Republic. Song Meiling, wife of former President Chiang Kaishek, can be seen as Mao's infamous wife Jiang Qing. So much for the villains. As for positive heroes, Qu Yuan, the ancient statesman full of concern for his nation's crisis, can be seen as a modern Yan Fu or Chen Tianhua; Zhang Heng, the Han astronomer neglected by history can be seen as cosmologist Fang Lizhi, China's best-known advocate of human rights, who was dismissed from the Party a year before the broadcast of Heshang. At the extreme limit of allegory, even the description of the English revolution of 1649 might be read as a capsule history of the People's Republic: "*A one-man dictatorship gave way to joint rule by a group of men.*" [164] The problem posed by an allegorical reading is this: once you admit the existence of allegory, how do you tell the difference between what is allegorical and what is intended as genuine history?

---

[49] See James R. Pusey, Wu Han: attacking the present through the past, Cambridge, Mass., East Asian Research Center, 1969. The dismissal of Hai Rui was an allusion to Mao's dismissal of Marshal Peng Dehuai.

The problem of identifying a core of historical ideas that were taken seriously is complicated by the fact that Heshang's authors did not claim to present one set of correct ideas. Rather they saw as their task the presentation of a variety of different opinions and different points of view in order to start a dialogue with the audience. In his preface to the published edition, Su Xiaokang wrote that the film "*should propose to bring information about all sorts of theories and thinking to the TV screen in large volume... enabling it to offer people all sorts of ideas and to create the effect of a two-way dialogue with the audience and society...*" [95]

Nevertheless, a small number of ideas are repeated sufficiently often that we can be confident of their importance. "*The culture of the Yellow River was a sort of culture that matured very early, and it was a very appropriate culture during mankind's agricultural period. But after the 17th century, the West witnessed the phenomenon of rapid change marked by industrial civilization, so that all of a sudden this sort of agricultural civilization paled in comparison and could not withstand its attack. For all sorts of reasons, this early-maturing civilization lacked a mechanism for rebirth and was unable to transform itself in time into a new civilization; that is to say, what should have died off did not in fact die off.*"[50] In his choice of images to accompany the narration, Xia Jun took pains to emphasize the connection between an agricultural society and its final result: the cult of the leader. In Part One, to illustrate the decline of Chinese civilization, Xia Jun superimposes scenes of Red Guards hailing Mao over a farmer plowing his field. In Part Four, the photograph of a peasant girl sitting on a haystack immediately precedes the colossal white statue of Mao Zedong used in a parade at Tian'anmen.

While the film-makers did not entirely abandon the Marxist approach to history, they could definitely be described as revisionists. A study of their quotations shows that they were particularly interested in the early Marx, in his notion of the "Asiatic mode of production," in his emphasis on the development of productive forces, and in his analysis of the particular kind of autocracy to which an economy of peasant small holders gives rise. What they have abandoned is Lenin's emphasis on imperialism and Mao's theory of peasant rebellions as the motive force of history. Instead of pointing out the evils of capitalism, the script asks why capitalism failed to develop in China. Marx, Lenin, Mao and even Deng each receive a carefully-measured share of subtle mockery. For a television series to assume the prerogative to write Chinese history from a non-Marxist perspective and to proclaim the decline of Chinese civilization comes dangerously close to saying that the Party has lost the mandate to rule.

---

[50] See Mai Tianshu's interview with Su Xiaokang published in Qingnian bao, August 16th, 1988, p. 1.

III. Su Xiaokang: Criticism and Self-criticism

As we have said above, while Heshang's script criticizes the tradition, it explicitly supports China's current reform program. Its oblique statements are not aimed against reform, either, but rather against symbols of the pre-reform order of politics. The authors of Deathsong of the River have denied that they had ulterior political motives in creating the series.[51] Yet to contest their statement, the current regime can easily point at the record of their involvement in the Democracy Movement of 1989. How do we evaluate this charge?

While not as well-known outside of China as the student leaders of the Democracy Movement, many of the people involved in this TV film project were amongst an active group of Beijing intellectuals who in the spring of 1989 first called for the release of political prisoners, then attempted to mobilize public support behind the students, and finally tried to invoke provisions of the Chinese constitution to cancel the martial law declaration of May 19th. This group included principal writers Su Xiaokang and Wang Luxiang; co-authors Xie Xuanjun, Yuan Zhiming and Zhang Gang; one of their principal advisors, Jin Guantao; and a number of the experts they interviewed on screen, such as Bao Zunxin, Wang Juntao and Zheng Yi.[52]

Since June of 1989, the mainland press has charged Su Xiaokang with a heavy responsibility for the events of Tian'anmen: *"In a certain sense, Su Xiaokang's vigorous plotting in back-rooms and repeated activities on the scene are tied with Heshang and inseparable from the 'Heshang phenomenon.' If we may regard Su Xiaokang's high-handed and overbearing manner in the Heshang affair as a result of the tolerance and support of Zhao Ziyang, then his frenetic participation in plotting and inciting the turmoil, in which he transformed his bourgeois liberalism into political action, was a continuation and development of the 'Heshang phenomenon,' it was the last blow struck in the attempt to make the 'new order' supported by Zhao Ziyang into a political reality..."[53]*

No one disputes the fact of Su Xiaokang's participation in signing petitions and sending telegrams; what is disputed are his intentions. Hence

---

[51] See for example, Su Xiaokang, "Heshang de shangque" in Longnian de beichuang, p. 169.

[52] Their activities in this period can be gathered from observing the various open letters and public declarations that they signed; most of these documents are reprinted with signatures in Tian'anmen: 1989, Lianjing chuban shiye gongsi, Taiwan, August 1989, pp. 320-347. Principal advisor Li Yining did not find himself in this group; evidence suggests he was on a scholarly visit to Hong Kong in the Spring of 1989.

[53] Kuang Pingxin in Heshang pipan, pp. 91-97, esp. 96-97.

we need to take a look at Su Xiaokang's life and writings in order to form a better judgement of his character, his thinking, and his intent.[54]

1. Character and early life. A fellow writer has given the following personal sketch of Su Xiaokang:

"It's hard to give my impression of Su Xiaokang. Is he a political essayist, concerned for the country and the people? Is he a searcher in tireless pursuit of spiritual beliefs? Is he a dancing partner with a good sense of rhythm on the dance floor? Or is he just a 'rebel red guard'? Ultimately it is very difficult to understand a person and even superficial impressions are hard to grasp. Thus when I first met Su Xiaokang four or five years ago in Nanjing, I only saw that he was like me in having some Sichuanese spice in his blood... In his own words, he just pursues sensational effects in his writing. While this may sound very selfish, but under circumstances in which journalism, literature and theory are all under many restrictions, a person who dares to write this sort of risky literature is actually acting on behalf of self-denying, moral values..."[55]

Su Xiaokang was born in Hangzhou in August, 1949, the year of the founding of the People's Republic. His family came originally from Chengdu, Sichuan; his grandfather was a capitalist, while his father Su Xing was a high-ranking cadre in China's official press. He grew up in Hangzhou and Beijing, as his father worked first for the Zhejiang Daily and later for Red Flag magazine, long considered the Party's principal theoretical mouthpiece. At the age of sixteen he left his privileged environment and went to school in Henan, where he quickly learned of the hardships of the peasants faced with famine and hungry bureaucrats.

"Someone has said, either playfully or seriously, that Su Xiaokang's father rebelled against his capitalist grandfather, while Su Xiaokang rebelled against his revolutionary father. The reason for saying this is because during the 'Cultural Revolution' Su Xiaokang joined the 'rebel faction' [zaofanpai].

---

[54] Material for this sketch is drawn from the article by Ji Wei, "Guanyu yige ren—guanyu Su Xiaokang" [About a man—about Su Xiaokang] appearing first in Wenhui bao, May, 1988, pp. 25-26 and reprinted in Heshang jiwaiji, pp. 227-233; from Wang Luxiang, "Huiyi yu sikao" in Heshang lun, pp. 91-97; from Xie Yong, "Kexue yu minzhu jingshen de zhangyang—cong Liu Binyan dao Su Xiaokang" [The Advocacy of Science and Democracy—from Liu Binyan to Su Xiaokang] in Wenxue pinlun, no. 5, 1988, reprinted in Su Xiaokang, Ziyou beiwanglu, Hong Kong: Sanlian shudian, 1989, pp. 302-311; from two articles in Heshang pipan, pp. 20-25 and 231-242. Additional information comes from Chen Xitong, "Report on Checking the Turmoil and Quelling the Counter-Revolutionary Rebellion," Beijing Review, July 17-23, 1989; Che Muqi, Beijing Turmoil: More Than Meets the Eye, Beijing Foreign Languages Press, 1990, esp. pp. 98-102.

[55] Ji Wei, "Guanyu yige ren—guanyu Su Xiaokang" in Wenhui yuekan, May, 1989, pp. 25-26.

Once when we were at Lushan, Su Xiaokang couldn't keep from crying in talking about the Cultural Revolution..."[56]

The Cultural Revolution appears to have been crucial in forming his character, both as a rebel against the establishment, and as a self-critical thinker. At the outbreak of the Cultural Revolution, he joined the Red Guards and went to Beijing to see the Chairman in Tian'anmen Square. He became a member of the Red Guard 'rebel' faction [zaofanpai] and briefly held the editorship of the Henan Red Guard newspaper. He is said to have been a leader of the "February 7th Commune." Then his father was "overthrown" in the political struggle, and the whole family suffered. Towards the end of the Cultural Revolution, he was working for the Henan Daily. As a young reporter he evidently thought that he could now speak for the people and help individuals seek redress for grievances. He was fired for a time as a result of an investigation of "factionalism" within the paper.

"Su Xiaokang had some friends who once committed some not particularly serious crimes during the Cultural Revolution; there are plenty of people around who did far worse and who are now blithely getting rich in their official positions. But they went to prison and are still there. They are paying for the mistakes they once made... In comparison to them, Su Xiaokang was much luckier. But he is still paying back his debt. Dipping his pen into the blood squeezed out from his soul by reflecting on the past, he is recording the past and the present; he is recording the conflict of this generation between their disillusionment in the present and their search for faith; their agony and their struggle. Not long ago in Beijing, one day at dusk Su Xiaokang and I took a taxi together on some business, and the young cabdriver started talking about the Cultural Revolution. 'Let's have another Great Cultural Revolution, so that I can be a rebel too.' Startled, Su Xiaokang asked him: 'You're making lots of money, and yet you still hope for a Cultural Revolution?' The young driver explained: 'I hear that there were plenty of people who got rich then, that you could even pick gold out of the garbage cans. Too bad I was born fifteen years too late, otherwise I definitely would've rebelled.' Su Xiaokang and I were struck dumb, as if we had been slapped. The winter sunset was dull and cold. It hadn't been all that long since the Cultural Revolution, had it? Most people, whether intentionally or not, choose to forget or avoid thinking about that cruel decade full of blood and tears. But the coming generation and the one following it know nothing whatsoever about it, and so anything could reoccur. After being silent for a long time, Su Xiaokang said to me that it was precisely to avoid the repetition of such a tragedy, and also to redeem his own past, that

---

[56] Ibid.

he took such risks, that he urgently tried to understand the people and its history, that he critiqued those distorted beliefs and -isms. ..."[57]

2. **A writer of reportage literature, 1983-87.** He was back as a reporter at the Henan ribao by 1982 when he wrote his first piece of reportage literature, "Dongfang fodiao"[58] [The Buddhist Sculpture of the Orient], a piece about the Buddhist caves at Longmen and about the sufferings of a hard-working researcher and guide there named Guo Dazhong. While recent critics have not regarded it as highly as his later works, finding it to be too much in the tradition of "singing praises," this piece did win a national prize for reportage literature at the time. And, when he came to write Heshang, Su Xiaokang would draw on this piece for its description of the Vairocana Buddha.

Shortly thereafter, Su Xiaokang was admitted to the Beijing College of Broadcasting; and after graduation, he was assigned as a reporter with Central Broadcasting in Henan. While still a student, he returned to Henan during the summer vacation to write a piece of reportage on the flooding of the Hong and Ru rivers near Zhumadian in 1984, entitled "Honghuang qishi lu."[59] One critic wrote that in this piece he did more than just express his sympathy for the suffering of the peasants after the flood. For this first time he experimented with a comprehensive reflection on a large number of atypical cases as a way of understanding both the harm caused by the extreme leftist line in contemporary history, as well as the depth of feudal thinking; from this, he proceeded to the realization that the problems caused by an unhealthy political system are harder to avoid than those caused by natural disaster. What differentiated his reporting from Liu Binyan's was that he restrained his anger and chose a deliberately sober style.[60]

Subsequently, Su Xiaokang produced a whole series of investigative reports on subjects that attracted popular interest: "Ziyou beiwanglu" [The Freedom Memorandum], through a long list of incidents of infringements on civil rights, directly raised the question of the freedom of China's citizens and asked to what degree China's constitution protected her citizens.[61]

---

[57] Ibid.

[58] Renmin wenxue, October, 1983, pp. 81-92.

[59] Published in Zhongguo zuojia, February, 1986; reprinted in Su Xiaokang, Ziyou beiwanglu, Hong Kong: Sanlian shudian, 1989, pp. 1-35.

[60] Xie Yong, "Kexue yu minzhu jingshen de zhangyang - cong Liu Binyan dao Su Xiaokang," in Wenxue pinlun, May, 1988; reprinted in Ziyou beiwang lu: Su Xiaokang baogao wenxue jingxuan, Hong Kong: Sanlian shudian, 1989, pp. 302-312.

[61] Published in Tianjin wenxue, September, 1987; reprinted in Su Xiaokang, Ziyou beiwang lu, pp. 36-81.

"Shensheng yousi lu—zhong xiaoxue jiaoyu weijing jishi" [The Teachers Lament—on the crisis in elementary and secondary education][62] reported the results of his study of middle school teachers in Beijing, that many suffered from sickness and poor housing, while fewer and fewer young people were willing to start teaching careers. Both these two reports provided material used in Heshang. Other publications during this period included Yinyang da liebian [The Great Male-Female Fission], a book-length report on unhappy marriages, wife abuse, etc., which was awarded a national prize[63]; "Huoyu" [The Living Prison], on mental illness[64]; and "Zui hou de gu du" [The Last Ancient Capital], on the housing crisis in Beijing.[65] Critics have noted that one of the special features of his style is its frequent citation of scholarly research.

In 1987, he was back in Beijing as an instructor in the news department of the Beijing College of Broadcasting. He was already nationally-known as a writer. While he would continue to write reportage literature, he had already developed an interest in writing for television. He had written the narration for several installments of the Yellow River documentary, and he had written "Zui hou de gu du" in the form of a film script. He was ready to undertake a new project. By October of 1987, he had already written a detailed outline for a TV series on the Yellow River entitled The Great Artery, which subsequently became Deathsong of the River. Wang Luxiang recalled his first meeting with Su Xiaokang:

"He was not tall, but his face made a strong first impression. His eyes were deep-set, and though he wore glasses, his eyes were bright and full of spirit. A tall, straight nose with fine nostrils—these were the marks of a superior intelligence. The corners of his mouth were slightly drawn down, making the line of his lips into a bow. When he spoke it was with an unusual certainty and force—he was very self-confident. And yet he was also extremely relaxed. When he laughed, he would laugh out loud, gesturing with hands and feet, without restraint. And when he swore he was even less

---

[62] Published in Renmin wenxue, September, 1987; reprinted in Su Xiaokang, Ziyou beiwang lu, pp. 82-125.

[63] Published in Zhongguo zuojia, May, 1986; reprinted in Su Xiaokang quanjing baogao wenxue ji, Hong Kong: Shanghai shuju, June, 1989, pp. 140-206; and reprinted as a separate volume under the same title by the Nanyue chubanshe, Hong Kong, in February, 1989.

[64] Written in cooperation with Zhang Min, completed in late 1987. Reprinted in Su Xiaokang, Ziyou beiwanglu, pp. 126-156; and in Su Xiaokang quanjing baogao wenxue ji, pp. 207-241.

[65] Published in Hua cheng, June, 1987, pp. 12-39.

restrained than me—this was a person of a rare self-assurance, hard to find in academic circles, the sort of person I really like."

Filming for the series began at the end of October. Director Xia Jun, Su Xiaokang, and Wang Luxiang flew first to Yan'an in Shaanxi, then visited Mangshan and Kaifeng in Henan. Returning to Beijing, he started script-writing in earnest. In early 1988, he left the college to work at CCTV, after which he never returned to his teaching job, despite appeals from his school.

3. **1988: Attacking the dragon in the dragon year.** 1988 would be an extremely busy and productive year for Su Xiaokang. Not only would he complete the script of Heshang; he would also begin work on a script for a film to be called May Fourth; he would publish a book-length account of the 1959 Lushan Conference, at which Mao dismissed Peng Dehuai, entitled Sacrifice in Utopia; and he would publish an account of how Heshang came to be written and of the criticism it had received, entitled "The Distress of a Dragon Year." If for understandable reasons Su Xiaokang's indictment of China's current problems was muted in Heshang, his other publications reveal how sharp his pen could be.

In January 1988 Su Xiaokang published an essay entitled "My Views on 'A Sense of Mission,'" which may be seen as a reflection on the reportage literature he had published to date, as well as a philosophical statement of purpose:[66]

At present our great, ancient people is experiencing unprecedented pangs of disquiet. Our ancestors' temples have toppled, and the calling and articles of belief bequeathed us by the older generation now face a renewed investigation. The shock waves transmitted from the wealthy west have made lots of Orientals unable to feel at peace. ... In sum, everyone seems to realize that our situation on this planet is anything but reassuring.

Although we have come to our senses a little late, at least we are no longer continuing in ignorance. Their awakening has made Chinese so upset as to stamp their feet, to want to settle accounts with their ancestors, to find fault, to get mad at any trivial event—to tell the truth, for an ancient people whose vitality has declined so badly, to dare to get mad, to dare to laugh and to scold, to dare to look our ancestors in the eye, is a good thing. It's a pity that in this past century there have been too few people daring to laugh and scold like Lu Xun.

Some people have given this feeling a very weighty term: a "sense of sorrow and worry." [youhuan yishi]. Actually, I've skimmed through history and discovered that Chinese have never lacked a "sense of sorrow and

---

[66] Published in Qiu shi, no. 2, 1988, pp. 47-48. Qiu shi is the successor to Hong qi [Red Flag], the theoretical organ of the CCP published at the Central Party School.

worry." ... *Thus in my view, Chinese have possessed a "sense of sorrow and worry" since antiquity, but it has neither been continuous nor deeply rooted. It's always the case that it only appears when times are bad. But it is ultimately a pulse inherited from those scholar officials of ancient times...*

In China, this "sense of sorrow and worry" is much more intense and obvious in the world of thinkers than anywhere else. From their concern for real-life crises, to their critique of history, and even to their self-questioning of our entire culture, the world of thinkers has always been in the vanguard. In contrast, over the past ten years the literary world, which once had dazzled people and had a mass following, has seemed to be moving slowly with few accomplishments, to the point that at present people no longer have the patience to put up with the sort of mystification, smoothing over of problems and searching for roots that writers are pursuing.[67] The reason why literature has lost its sensational effect is perhaps due to the fact that writers haven't been able to find the Chinese people's pulse.

But that is not the case with reportage literature. Not only has it not lost its sensational effect but there are also some good pieces that continue to provide food for thought after the sensation is over, making those in both high and low position uncomfortable for a while. ...

Writers of fiction have their own reasons for striving for elegance. But does reportage literature want to follow in their footsteps? My view is precisely the opposite. Just as reportage literature is not necessarily subservient to politics, so too it is not necessarily the handmaid of fiction. We have to find our own place and role. At a time when most fiction has made life insipid, can reportage literature not come along and fill in the gap it has left?

These days reportage literature cannot do without a "sense of sorrow and worry." We have sung songs of praise for so long that the older writers have lost their teeth, while our readers' ears have been filled with cocoons; moreover, if you just open your eyes and look at the real world, can China's anguished soul be calmed down by hymns of praise? Even the great task of reform, which of all things most deserves hymns of praise, is it not also full of contradictions and anguish? Readers no longer want to hear reportage literature sing hymns of praise, just as they no longer have patience for fiction's mystification and smoothing over of problems. Perhaps it is in between these two that we can find our place. ...

Naturally, I'm not trying to make reportage literature into some sort of miracle drug that will save the world. Throughout history, literature can only be seen as the externalization of the soul. Yet one cannot expect it to

---

[67] The Chinese terms are <u>kongling</u>, <u>danhua</u>, and <u>xungen</u>. Su's point would seem to be that writers of fiction are no longer addressing the contemporary problems of society.

serve pragmatic goals. While it might perhaps have a curative effect on society, that is still a latent role. I fear that writers would find it very difficult to go all out honing its blade as a knife for slaughtering pigs. For this reason I do not much agree with those theories about [literature's] "sense of mission." While perhaps from the point of view of the public or of post-facto hindsight, one could apply this term to it, yet judging from the point of view of an author's motives for creativity, it might make him feel highly embarrassed.

I don't know why, but that is how I feel whenever someone says that my motives for writing those reportage pieces on social problems is due to my strong "sense of mission." ... I have often asked myself why I want to write about those suffering peasants, those ordinary people with nowhere to take their complaints, those intellectuals whose flame is about to burn out; could it really be that after hearing them tell their bitter tales I could proclaim to them like a messiah that "I have come to save you"? Even though my conscience and my sympathy constantly fill me with righteous anger, and I get so mad I grit my teeth, yet I clearly realize that the only thing I can do is to offer a few words of sympathy and consolation. Can the act of writing out their stories actually change their plight? Sometimes it does exactly the opposite and gets them in even worse trouble. ... Literature ultimately can never again be the tool of politics; it cannot affect our lives so concretely and so completely. Nor can society expect writers to be like politicians in having a direct and down-to-earth sense of mission.

For writers as intellectuals, to have a "sense of sorrow and worry" will be quite sufficient. No matter that this sense of sorrow and worry is not at all like gamma globulin for type A hepatitis, which can be injected into people from outside. These days, although young people in their twenties are full of an uneasy restlessness yet they are still unwilling to acknowledge that they are worried about something, while the older generation of intellectuals are full of depression in their hearts but dare not voice their bitterness...

Here I am only referring to this generation of ours that grew up in the gap—those right about forty years old. Today, those who are the most clearly concerned and most deeply worried are this generation. No matter whether they belong to the world of thinkers or of writers, or whether they are officials or ordinary people, this generation is perhaps the only one which dares not refuse to be concerned and whose worries moreover have reached the degree that philosophers call "ultimate concerns." In my view, this is the legacy that they have inherited, willing or not, from those past days of folly; it is the result of the fact that they must take the present seriously.

My own feeling is that the reason for the seriousness of this sense of social concern in this generation is perhaps due to a very strange motive:

they must find a rational explanation for the days of their youth that they had muddled through unconsciously—for that life made abnormal by fanaticism, by passion, naiveté, blindness, frankness, and even dedication. Even if it is not for noble purposes such as a sense of mission or for the sake of the next generation, we would still need to question ourselves. Otherwise we will have ruined ourselves without ever knowing why, and we would become a generation to be pitied and to be mocked. ... We must settle accounts with ourselves. But, you must excuse us, this settling of accounts cannot help but touch all those who came through those days, including even our ancestors. In my view, this is where our "sense of sorrow and worry" and where our "ultimate concerns" lie.

First of all, we must redeem ourselves. If we do have any sort of a sense of mission then we must first of all be responsible to ourselves. When our generation was growing up, life never taught us how to combine a responsibility for ourselves with one for the whole of society. We grew up in the midst of restrictions, suppressions, and inhibitions. We didn't have our own heads on our shoulders, which is why we were once so intemperate. We really were too cruelly deceived! Now that we are finally thinking for ourselves, how can we not help but feel a painful regret? ...

Of course, because umbilical cords still bind us to those past days, and because our 'six senses' are still unpurified, it is hard for us to become thoroughly aroused. And so perhaps we lack a certain extremism. This is our strong point as well as our weak point. This sort of in-between life has perhaps unconsciously given us some sort of mission and has determined that having been deceived ourselves we will never again deceive others, but only tell the truth. This is how I understand "a sense of mission."

Written at the same time as the script of Heshang, this statement is significant for emphasizing that he and his generation need to reflect on and accept responsibility for their behavior during the Cultural Revolution. While the Cultural Revolution is mentioned only elliptically in the script of Heshang, director Xia Jun makes use of scenes from the Cultural Revolution in many places, to illustrate the social turmoil that is the inevitable end of an agricultural civilization. Viewers wrote in saying that these were the scenes that affected them the most. In light of the above statement, it would seem fair to say that the makers of the series were not only critical but also self-critical. When Su Xiaokang says that Chinese must reflect on their history so that tragedies such as Liu Shaoqi's death can never be repeated, he is blaming his own generation as much as he is blaming China's system. He ends his article with a solemn vow not to deceive himself or others, but only to tell the truth. These two resolutions of his, to understand and accept responsibility for the tragedy of the Cultural Revolution, and to tell the truth, would be tested soon, in the spring of 1989.

In the spring of 1988, Su Xiaokang had left Beijing for several weeks to work on a new writing project, a book entitled Sacrifice in Utopia. The book was a semi-fictional recreation of a number of important characters, including Mao Zedong, who had never been written about in this way before. Due to the sensitivity of his subject, his original publisher, Baihuazhou magazine, had their press run of two hundred thousand copies all locked up in a warehouse. But in November of 1988 the book was finally published, with a prominent quotation from Zhao Ziyang on the inside:

"In a certain sense, if the Great Cultural Revolution had not turned everything upside down, then we could not be as enlightened as we are today and reflect on the problems arising since 1957. In that case we would have to waste even more time before reaching our current level of intellectual liberation." [68]

The late fall of 1988 also saw the appearance of Su Xiaokang's "The Distress of a Dragon Year," in which Su Xiaokang took the opportunity to strike back at his critics, including Vice President Wang Zhen. By the end of this year, his resolution to tell the truth had already had expensive consequences. Heshang had been banned, and he had become embroiled, willing or not, in political struggle at the highest level.

4. The Democracy Movement. Political events moved quickly in the Spring of 1989. In January, Chinese astrophysicist Fang Lizhi had published an open letter to Deng Xiaoping, calling for amnesty for Wei Jingsheng and other political prisoners, in order to mark the 40th anniversary of the People's Republic as well as the 70th anniversary of the May Fourth Movement. In February thirty-three other intellectuals, including Su Xiaokang, followed suit in a petition to the Standing Committee of the National Peoples' Congress [NPC] and the Central Committee of the Party. [69]

The death of ex-General Secretary Hu Yaobang on April 15th led quickly to student demonstrations. On April 21st, an "Open Letter" signed by two hundred intellectuals, including Su Xiaokang, called on the Central Committee, the Standing Committee of the NPC and the State Council not to ignore the students' demands.

The April 24th issue of Shanghai's World Economic Herald reported on a forum it had organized in Beijing to discuss Hu Yaobang's achievements,

---

[68] Su Xiaokang, Luo Shixu, and Chen Zheng, Wutuobang ji: 1959 nian Lushan zhi xia, Beijing, Zhongguo xinwen chubanshe, Nov. 1988. 409 pp. ISBN 7-80041-190-7\g.137.

[69] Chinese texts of these two letters are reproduced in Jiushi niandai, March, 1989, p. 18. English translations are provided in Han Minzhu, ed., Cries for Democracy, Princeton University Press, 1990, pp. 24-25.

leading the Shanghai Municipal Party Committee to close down the paper. On April 28th, Yan Jiaqi, Su Xiaokang and twenty-nine others published an open letter to the Shanghai authorities, protesting their decision and calling for protection of the freedom of the press.

The May 1989 issue of Shanghai's Wenhui bao carried a front-cover color photo of Su Xiaokang as well as an article in which Su described the new project that he and Xia Jun had been working on: a film entitled May Fourth. The article included lengthy reflections on the legacy of May Fourth thinkers such as Hu Shih and Chen Duxiu—neither of whom had yet been evaluated positively in Chinese Communist historiography of the movement—as well as Mao Zedong. The discussion of Mao Zedong gave Su Xiaokang an opportunity to reflect on Max Weber's concept of charismatic leadership. At its end, the article reveals that the film project had been canceled for political reasons: his signature on the February 13th letter. At the beginning of his article occurred a paragraph which a critic would later cite as an incitement to students to demonstrate:

"The year 1989 is destined to be a singular memorial year which meets many historical giants: It is the bicentenary of the French Revolution; the centenary of the founding of the Second International; the 70th anniversary of the May 4th movement; the 70th anniversary of the founding of the Third International; the 40th anniversary of the founding of the People's Republic of China; the 30th anniversary of the Lushan Conference; the 20th anniversary of the 9th National Congress of the Communist Party of China; the 20th anniversary of the death of Liu Shaoqi; and so on. No one can escape these coming days of the year which may make you happy or unhappy one way or the other." [70]

On May 14th, he joined with journalist Dai Qing and ten others in publishing "Our Urgent Appeal Regarding the Present Situation," declaring that students had opened up a new era in Chinese history, and calling on the government to recognize that theirs was a patriotic and democratic movement. [71]

Su Xiaokang was also among the prominent signers of the May 16th Declaration, written on the third day of the hunger strike in Tian'anmen Square, which called on the government to retract the People's Daily editorial of April 26th, which had deemed the student movement to be

---

[70] Translated in Che Muqi, op.cit., p. 102. For Su Xiaokang's article, "Shijimo huimou—guanyu Heshang xuji liuchan de jilu" [A Glance Back at the End of the Century—On the Miscarriage of Heshang's sequel], see Wenhui yuekan, May, 1988, pp. 16-24; reprinted in Heshang taolun ji, pp.195-227.

[71] For a translation, see Han Minzhu, Cries for Democracy, pp. 207-8.

"turmoil" [dongluan], and to recognize the legality of the new student organizations.[72]

On May 20th, he was among ten signers of "The Intellectuals' Vow" which swore that they would never pledge allegiance to the "last emperor" of the 1980s.

On May 21st, after the government had imposed martial law (apparently without consulting Wan Li, the head of the Standing Committee of the NPC who was then out of the country), Su Xiaokang joined Yan Jiaqi and others in sending a telegram to the Standing Committee of the NPC, urging them to call an emergency meeting.

One day in May, it is said, Su Xiaokang and his colleagues came to Tian'anmen Square bearing a big sign reading Heshang. This is the only example cited by his critics of his active participation in demonstrations.[73]

Subsequent to June 4th, the group of young intellectuals involved in making Heshang scattered to the winds. Su Xiaokang and Yuan Zhiming found their way out of China to Paris and then on to Princeton, where they are involved in editing the journal Minzhu Zhongguo [Democratic China]. Zhang Gang found his way first to Taiwan and then to the U.S. Wang Luxiang was imprisoned for several months but subsequently released, while Bao Zunxin, Wang Juntao, and Zheng Yi were all reported to have been arrested.[74] In trials held in January and February 1991, while world attention was focussed on the war in the Persian Gulf, Bao Zunxin was sentenced to five years, and Wang Juntao to thirteen years, on charges of counter-revolution. The participation of the authors and their guest experts in the events of the Beijing Spring of 1989 helps to explain the particularly vehement attacks that have been launched against Deathsong of the River since June of 1989. A host of articles were published to condemn Heshang, many of them finding their way into four books: Heshang pipan, Heshang baimiu, Heshang xuanyang le shenme?, and Chong ping Heshang.[75]

5. **Thoughts in exile**. Su Xiaokang's first publication after leaving China was a reflection both on the massacre at Tian'anmen Square and on Heshang, spurred by his initial impressions of Paris. While the events of Tian'anmen had produced a kind of unpredictable wildness in some of his colleagues in exile, it had produced in him a kind of spiritual numbness,

---

[72] For a translation see Han Minzhu, op.cit., pp. 218-221.

[73] See Kuang Pingxin in Heshang pipan, p. 95.

[74] The arrests are documented in Punishment Season: Human Rights in China after Martial Law, Asia Watch, 1990, pp. 89 & 103-104.

[75] See the bibliography in this volume, items #5, #32, #33, and #34.

leaving him unable to join his companions in singing and unable to respond to the noble sights of Paris. What struck him and depressed him at the same time, rather, were the city's pigeons, who had never known fear, and the calm and unworried expressions of its citizens. He wrote that on a visit to Sacre Coeur Cathedral in Montmartre he all of a sudden felt a need to kneel down and pray. Later he learned that the cathedral had been built by French President Louis Adolphe Thiers after having put down the uprising of the Paris Commune of May 1871; and that in turn reminded him of Tian'anmen Square.[76]

In the past, it was my admiration for the Western spirit of freedom which led me to admire Western culture; and, because our culture had been unable to produce this spirit of freedom, I could never forgive it. Heshang was perhaps the product of this way of thinking, as was its bias also. Many scholars in Hong Kong, Taiwan and the West constantly pointed out this bias, saying that the problem of today's China was principally one of the system and not one of culture. I did not agree with them on this point but rather thought that they were just a little too fond of Chinese culture. Ever since May 4th [1919], China's intellectuals have hated her backwardness and have always sought for its roots in culture.... Throughout this decade of reform and opening up to the outside, everyone also believed that there would be hope for China if only people would change their outlook and if the common people could learn to struggle for their rights. Everyone was under the illusion that "culture could save the country."

Of course there were good reasons to avoid discussing the system and to settle accounts with culture instead. In my view, rather than regarding this as a conscious plan on the part of intellectuals, it would be better to regard it as an expression of their carefulness and goodwill. Despite disasters such as the anti-rightist movement of 1957 and the Great Cultural Revolution, intellectuals on the mainland had still not completely given up hope in the political system which had brought about those disasters; on the contrary, due to Deng Xiaoping's reform policies, everybody even went so far as to feel that this system had a chance of gaining new life. Everyone sincerely wanted to help out in the perfection of this system; no one ever intended to overthrow it. This situation is reminiscent of the reformers of 1898, who wanted to assist the Guangxu Emperor in making reforms and who never intended to topple the Great Qing Empire. No matter whether it was the "think-tanks" directly involved in the reform of the economic and political structures, or the "luminaries" of academia who expounded the various problems of reform, or writers who sounded the call to arms for reform in

---

[76] Su Xiaokang, "Zai Bali xiangqi Caishikou—liuwang ganhuai" [Remembering Caishikou in Paris—feelings in Exile], Bai xing, Hong Kong, October 16th, 1989, pp. 3-4.

their own field of literary creativity—who of these was not more careful than Kang Yuwei, Liang Qichao, and Tan Sitong had been?

And yet the tragedy of Caishikou[77] repeated itself. At the outset of the student movement, [the authorities] maintained that there was a "graybeard" manipulating the students from off-stage; after the students had commenced the hunger-strike and the entire intellectual community had sounded appeals to Heaven and Earth, this was seen as "fanning the flames" or as "pouring oil on the fire." After the shootings of June 4th, the very first target to be "resolutely attacked" was none other than the intelligentsia. When we reckon up the tally on our fingers, of all those outstanding and accomplished individuals in various fields of endeavour who appeared over the past ten years, how many of them did not have warrants issued for their arrest? How many were not either arrested, denounced, or investigated?

That intellectuals were still the number one enemy of this system was something I only realized after June 4th. All [slogans] such as "respect for knowledge," "respect for intellectuals," "intellectuals are part of the working class" and so on and so on, were never anything but false masks. When we look back at the two political campaigns since the end of the Cultural Revolution—against "spiritual pollution" and against "bourgeois liberalization"—their targets were all intellectuals. To say that the authorities, failing to find the "black hand" behind the "turmoil," took out their anger on intellectuals would be one explanation. But in my view, ever since the Chinese Communist party gained power on the mainland, aside from regarding intellectuals as "enemies," they have been unable to find any other opponent.

Clearly, this is now a problem of the system and not one of culture. In traditional Chinese society, aside from the foolish last ruler of a dynasty, there have been very few dynasties which have been able to rule the empire successfully by regarding intellectuals as enemies and mistreating them. Yet in this regard, the Chinese communist party has exhibited a very clear tendency to oppose tradition. If one were to call this, too, a cultural phenomenon—a sort of extremely sick, anti-intellectual culture, for example—then we have an even greater need to seek for the roots of the illness in the system which brought this culture into being. ...

The historical connections between intellectuals and this system are worth reflecting on. On the one hand, from its sacrifice of Wang Shiwei[78] at

---

[77] Caishikou in Beijing is where Tan Sitong and other members of the 1898 reform movement were executed.

[78] On Wang Shiwei, see Gregor Benton, "Writers and the Party: The Ordeal of Wang Shiwei, Yanan, 1942" in Gregor Benton, ed., <u>Wild Lilies, Poisonous Weeds: Dissident Voices from People's China</u>, London: Pluto Press, 1982, pp. 168-186. Wang Shiwei

its very inception in Yan'an, this system revealed its antagonism to intellectuals; while on the other hand, it was precisely due to the loyal support of intellectuals that this system was able to gain power on the mainland forty years ago. As soon as this system was established, it brazenly proceeded to put intellectuals on the operating table and make them undergo castration. The problem was that intellectuals on the mainland basically accepted this operation without protest. They thus lost the ability to examine and critique this system; other than submitting to it, they could only flee it. After June 4th, this sort of situation must come to an end. ...

While one consequence of leaving China was that Su was now free to criticize China's political system much more directly, another consequence was a new ability to converse with Chinese intellectuals outside of China. Not a few of them had previously objected to the way in which Heshang had appeared to equate the Confucian tradition with the political tradition of despotism, and the rather cursory way in which Heshang had dismissed the possibility of a "third flowering of Confucianism." Tu Wei-ming's article "Heshang: Whither Chinese Culture?" which we have translated in this volume [301-309] was just such a criticism and made the case for employing elements of the Confucian tradition in pursuing modernization, as opposed to blindly copying everything western. In June 1990, Su Xiaokang wrote up an account of a recent conversation with Prof. Tu in which they discussed this very question.[79]

SU: *The generation of college students who launched the 1989 student movement had been influenced by the intellectual community and represented a new set of values opposed to the communist system, yet precisely because of this they had a very clear awareness of opposing tradition. And so overseas scholars will constantly discover the phenomenon that opposition to communism is tied to opposition to the tradition. Of course, this is not very helpful to making use of the resources of the tradition. ...*

At that time Mao did not rely, at least superficially, on terror and violence to maintain control, so I always wondered what force it was that could make people hold their tempers and keep quiet after

---

[1907-1947?] was among the urban intellectuals who made the pilgrimage to Yan'an; his two articles from 1942 in Yan'an, "Politicians, Artists" and "Wild Lily," reveal his thinking about problems within the party as well as the role of literature vis-à-vis politics. Even after Mao's definitive statements on the role of literature at the famous Yan'an Forum in May, 1942, Wang Shiwei refused to eat his words. He was put on trial and publicly humiliated. He is said to have been shot by security forces during the evacuation of Yan'an in 1947.

[79] Su Xiaokang, "Guanyu liyong chuantong ziyuan—yu Du Weiming jiaoshou zai Bali yixi tan" [On Making Use of the Resources of the Tradition—a Conversation in Paris with Prof. Tu Wei-ming], in Minzhu Zhongguo, June 1990, pp. 52-55.

having suffered such a great disaster? The formation of an "omnipotent' government is always founded on a high degree of conformity between all aspects of society, including the conformity of the tradition with the communist system. And so I feel that in terms of China's modernization, if we want to make use of resources from the tradition, the first thing is to undo the curse, the curse of communism and of Marxism; otherwise the barriers will be difficult to overcome. ...

TU: *Some on the mainland have criticized my point of view, saying that Chinese society is still in the pre-modern or modern stage, so who cares about [the problems of being] post-modern? And yet this view of the problem is both overly shallow and also no longer realistic. Because although we have not yet enjoyed the wealth of modern civilization, yet we have already suffered the destructive effects of post-modern society, such as pollution.*

SU: *This is how I used to counter the criticisms that others made of Heshang; I always felt that at present the most important thing was for China to modernize, that we should not trouble ourselves too much with the problems of being post-modern, or else we would be at a total loss. Because of this I never conceived of the issue of making use of the tradition, and had no qualms about opposing it. Only after having experienced the great debate aroused by Heshang did I discover the limitations of my vision. And especially after having come overseas, I have had all sorts of real experiences [shigan]; and moreover after having been to Taiwan and having seen the cultural crisis that they face in the wake of their economic development, I suddenly realized that what we are facing is an all-embracing sort of problem. The reason why those who come late to modernization are even worse off than those who achieved it first consists in that they must simultaneously overcome a two-fold barrier, of the difficulties that the latter has already overcome plus the ones it is now facing. This has made it especially important for us to discover how to transform tradition from a burden into a resource, to engage in what Prof. Lin Yusheng has called "creative transformation."* [80]

The need for China's intellectuals to reevaluate traditional culture was especially important if intellectuals were to play a future role in leading public opinion outside of their own limited circles. For China's intellectuals

---

[80] Lin Yusheng is Prof. of History at the University of Wisconsin in Madison. He is the author of a review of Heshang entitled: "Zhongguo yishi weiji he chuantong chuangzao de zhuanhua" [The Crisis of Chinese Consciousness and the Creative Transformation of the Tradition] in Longnian de beichuang, pp. 45-50.

were identified in the public mind with Western values and were effectively cut off from much contact either with workers or with peasants. At the same time, traditional culture was undergoing a renaissance in the countryside, with widespread rebuilding of clan temples and local shrines. By permitting the establishment of the Confucius Foundation in 1984 and by turning Qufu into a Chinese cultural mecca, the government had already gained the initiative in the quiet struggle to claim the symbols of political legitimacy.

IV. Discourse and Language

1. The Chinese environment of discourse. The creators of Deathsong of the River were in trouble for other reasons than merely presuming to write history. A second charge was *lèse-majesté*, for the meaning of their text is by no means as crystal-clear as the blue waters of the Pacific. In some places it is as deeply-layered as the sediments on the North China Plain. The writers of the script employ all the rich resources of the Chinese language, from allusions, to irony, to deliberate ambiguity and puns to suggest a critique of Chinese leaders past and present. Mao and Deng both come in for their full share of irreverent treatment. Yet the authors are masters of the indirect statement, whose meaning is always sufficiently ambiguous that the authors can claim innocence.

In fact, the Chinese literary tradition gives ample precedent and authority for writers to reproach authority by indirect means. Wei Hong's preface to The Book of Songs identifies one of the principal purposes of literature as feng, meaning to criticize or instruct:

> *Superiors use feng to transform their inferiors, and inferiors use feng to criticize their superiors. Since the main emphasis is placed on musical pattern and direct criticism is restrained, he who speaks it causes no offence, yet it is still sufficient for the listener to take heed from it. ...*[81]

Hence from an early period Chinese writers realized that they had two audiences: the common people, on whom literature was supposed to exert a civilizing influence; and their rulers, to whom literature delivered tactful reminders of problems in need of solution. Su Xiaokang and his colleagues in 1988 were also very aware of their two audiences. In his memoir entitled "The Distress of a Dragon Year," Su Xiaokang recalled an interview with the vice-director of CCTV, Chen Hanyuan. Chen found no fault with their proposal, but offered a bit of advice:

---

[81] The Book of Songs or Shi jing dates from the early Zhou dynasty and was supposedly edited by Confucius. As one of the Five Classics, it was memorized by schoolboys for centuries. Wei Hong dates from the first century A.D., and the text of his preface may be found in Xiao Tong, Wen xuan, ch. 45.

"You are more learned than I am. I believe that young people will surpass us, otherwise there is no hope for China. I have no demands to make of you, but only a little experience to offer for your consideration: To do TV in China, you need to observe a certain amount of tact, so that you can satisfy the 'two olds' [er lao]. One of these is the old comrades [lao tongzhi] in the central government, and the other is "the old hundred names' [laobaixing]. If one of these "two olds' is unsatisfied, then you'll be in trouble." [290]

Because of the existence of these two audiences, and because of the extreme sensitivity of the state-owned medium of television, the makers of Heshang had no choice but to choose indirection to make some of their more controversial points, as Su Xiaokang later admitted:

Leaving aside the question of how many restrictions there are in using the public media or tools of public opinion to analyze or critique real-life topics on the mainland today, haven't even the academics, the theorists, and the writers in their observation, research and probing of real-life questions been constantly guilty of hemming and hawing, equivocating, walking the tightrope, beating around the bush, chiming in to support someone else's view, and "hitting edge balls"? How many people are there who are not speaking tongue-in-cheek to attack via innuendo, according to the Chinese tradition of "investing great meaning in subtle words" or "writing in the style of the Spring and Autumn Annals"? Given the sort of cultural environment and scholarly foundation we have at present, how far could Heshang depart from the norm? Heshang did not fall down from Heaven, and it could not bypass what is really possible on the mainland in order to brazenly make criticisms as it pleased; everyone knows that.[82]

An "edge-ball" is a term from ping-pong, referring to a ball that barely grazes the extreme edge of the table. Technically such a shot is "in" and hence legal; thus it is a metaphor for statements in print which also try to test the limits of free expression. The need to resort to a certain degree of verbal subterfuge is underscored by popular sayings such as: *"The gun gets the bird that sticks out its neck"* [qiang da chutou niao] or *"Only tell others three-tenths of what you mean; never can you completely reveal your heart to anyone."* [jian ren zhi shuo san fen hua, wei ke quan pao yi pian xin]. Faced with such restrictions in public discourse, the ordinary person selects his friends wisely, choosing to tell the truth only to a few, while maintaining polite fictions with most people. The writer, however, cannot choose his audience; he must find a way of telling the truth and lying at the

---

[82] Su Xiaokang, "Heshang de shangque," in Longnian de beichuang, Hong Kong: Sanlian shudian, April 1989, pp. 168-177, esp. pp. 172-173.

same time. His solution is to code his language in such a way that either **a**. the target does not understand the code, while sensitive readers do; or **b**. the target understands the code but cannot admit it in public without losing face.

Presumably writers resort to these time-honored strategies of indirection for a number of reasons arising from the traditional political culture. First of all, the arena of public discourse has never been a free market of ideas; rather it has been what the Chinese call "yi yan tang," a *hall in which what one person says goes.*" The traditional scholar was willing to accept this situation, for he always saw his role in society as an advisor in government service, rather than as an eccentric academic with nothing to lose by speaking out freely. Hence it behooved him to maintain good relations with the authorities and to give them "face" even when he privately disagreed with them. He would almost never identify an opponent by name; rather, he would let his concerns be known by an indirect means, frequently through a literary work. The fact that intellectuals consider themselves as the public conscience and that literary works are often the only means through which they can express themselves helps to explain why revolutions in the cultural world are often harbingers of political storms to come.

But whether in past or in present, it was rare for someone to speak out, even indirectly, without a patron. It was normally expected that one way in which an official expressed loyalty to his superior was to express opinions on his behalf, opinions which for reasons of face it was impolitic for the leader to express or to publicly acknowledge. Hence public debates which on the surface appear to be scholarly debates on culture or literature might actually reflect a political struggle between factions in the leadership. When the leader of one faction won out, then his loyal retainers would also be rewarded, as expressed in the popular saying: "*When someone attains enlightenment, even his chickens and dogs ascend to heaven.*" [yi ren de dao, ji gou sheng tian]. Hence the making of critical statements, even indirectly, was normally perceived as motivated by political ambition, the desire to please or to do the bidding of someone in power. Thus, the scholarly critics serving the current leadership have interpreted Deathsong of the River as serving the personal political agenda of Zhao Ziyang, while Su Xiaokang complained that the critical attacks on him smacked of political skull-duggery.[83] In such a situation it is generally impossible for an outsider, let alone a foreign reader, to understand the factional infighting. Presumably this will always be an area in which "transparency" [toumingdu] is lacking.

---

[83] For the charges that Su Xiaokang was working in cahoots with Zhao Ziyang, see the articles by Jin Ren and by Guang Pingxin in Heshang pipan, pp. 20-25 and 91-97. For Su Xiaokang's suspicion that criticisms were politically motivated, see "Heshang de shangque" in Longnian de beichuang, p. 173.

The clever use of ambiguity serves several crucial functions for its author—it preserves "face" for both critic and his target; it preserves "deniability" for its author; and it creates a special link between an author and an audience trained to look for nuances of interpretation: the pleasure of detecting a concealed message, and the intimacy of a shared joke. Such coded speech has many precedents in Chinese literary history. A particularly good example is provided by Han Yu's poem entitled "Sent to Zhang the Registrar on the Night of the Harvest Moon." In the poem, Han Yu constructs a fictional dialogue with his friend Zhang, who was sent into exile under the former emperor and who has not yet been recalled by the present one. Han Yu first sets the scene: "*Fine clouds roll away, the Starry River dims/ A clear breeze sweeps the sky, the moon smooths out the waves.*" Han Yu is not describing an autumn evening; he is saying metaphorically that the political storm of the old administration is past, that the advent of the new emperor has smoothed out the waves. He then invites his friend to tell the sad story of his exile, which appears to be the story of a journey into the southern wilds: "*Dongting Lake stretched far and wide, Mt. Jiuyi rose tall/ Water dragons rose and sank, apes and squirrels screamed./ Of ten alive, nine of us died in reaching our exile posts / Then kept real still as prisoners will when they've escaped from jail./ We shied from snakes beneath our beds, feared poison in the food/ The lake's damp air was feverful and scented with a stink...*" Here the rise and fall of water dragons suggests the change of emperors, while the screaming of apes and squirrels is most likely the harsh rhetoric of the court officials who attacked him for their own benefit. Similarly, the fear of snakes and of poison suggests the veiled political attacks at court as much as it does the perils of exile.[84]

This same genre continues to be practiced and understood right up to the present. An example of such "edge-ball" literature, which needs no interpretation, comes from Shanghai's Liberation Daily of May 24th, 1989, a few days after the declaration of martial law in Beijing. The ostensible subject was the human brain.

A set of four-year-old female Siamese twins was sent to a big hospital in Moscow. These two girls shared the same heart and lungs and the same circulatory system. But they each had their own brains. Sometimes, one of them would be sleeping sweetly while the other would be looking around, wide-eyed; sometimes one would cry while the other laughed, so that despite sharing a common body, they each had different minds. The principal function of the brain is to think; if it can only think according to someone

---

[84] Han Yu, "Ba yue shiwu ye zeng Zhang gongcao" in Tang shi sanbai shou. Translated and interpreted by R. Bodman. Mainland author Yang Jiang alludes to the significance of this poem in her Six Chapters from a Life Downunder [Ganxiao liu ji], a memoir of life in a cadre school during the Cultural Revolution.

else's set pattern, or if one person's thinking is substituted for that of millions, then what use is it if their heads grow on their shoulders? ... An ordinary person after the age of thirty loses 100,000 brain cells every day and in a year loses 36 million. If he lives to be 100, then out of 14 trillion cells he loses 2.5 trillion, or about 20 percent. This large-scale loss of brain cells makes thinking sluggish, feelings stubborn, and memory foggy. In the past, people didn't understand the brain very well but just hoped that great men would never die and be their leaders forever. Did they ever realize what the results would be for the people if they made their helmsman an old man whose mental faculties were rapidly declining?

2. **Heshang's use of language**. With this technique of composition in mind, let us now examine how <u>Deathsong of the River</u> uses all the varied resources of language to point to a second level of meaning.

Allusions. Part Five yields an example of a double allusion. After mentioning the disappearance of the Confucian bureaucracy, the text states: *"Yet it seems that the spectre of great unification still wanders across China's great land."* [196] This is first of all a covert reference to a much-condemned 1981 poem by Sun Jingxuan, entitled "A Spectre is Haunting China." Sun's poem used the image of the dragon to symbolize China's tradition of despotic government, and included provocative lines such as: *"Brothers! Have you seen /The spectre prowling our land?/ ... [It] clutches with invisible claws / Silently sucks blood and marrow /Dictates every action, controls every thought;/... China, like a huge dragon, gobbles all in its path/ Like a huge vat, dyes all the same colour. .."* Yet there is another reference in this line also, to a famous tract penned in 1848, commencing with the words: *"A spectre is haunting Europe, the spectre of communism"*; this is, of course, the opening of <u>The Communist Manifesto</u> by Marx and Engels.

Part Four contains yet another example of a double allusion, one in which the second part twists the first, yielding considerable irony. After quoting several contemporary sayings describing the low esteem accorded to intellectuals nowadays, the script continues: *"Those who put the problems of the world first will be those who get rich last."* [175] "Those who put the problems of the world first," i.e., before concerns for personal gain, are China's intellectuals; the phrase alludes to the "Record of the Tower at Yueyang" by the Song writer Fan Zhongyan, who said, in praising the unselfishness of the ancient sages: *"They neither delighted in the things of the world nor were saddened on account of their own individual fate. When in high position at court, they felt concern for the people; when in exile in the country, they felt concern for their ruler; then whether in or out of office they were equally concerned. And so when did they enjoy themselves? It must be said that 'They felt concern before the rest of the world was concerned, and enjoyed themselves only after the rest of the world had enjoyed themselves.'"* This is a well-known and frequently-quoted passage. The twist comes with the second part of the phrase employed by <u>Heshang</u>, i.e., "will be those who get rich last." This alludes to the slogan proposed by Deng Xiaoping during the rural reforms, that "*to get rich is glorious*" and that, since it's obviously impossible for everyone to get rich at the same time, that it's perfectly fine for "*some people to get rich first.*" The obvious implication is that intellectuals have not gotten rich, that they have lost out.

Puns. Perhaps the best pun is on the word <u>dalu</u> whose normal meaning is 'continent,' or 'land' as opposed to 'sea.' The series frequently uses this word in reference to Hegel's distinction between sea-faring and continental peoples. Yet <u>dalu</u> also is the most common shorthand term for mainland China, or <u>Zhongguo dalu</u>. Hence when Part Two talks about the beginning of the Age of Exploration in the fifteenth century, a second meaning is possible:

For humankind as a whole, the fifteenth century was an extremely critical century. The human race began to move its gaze from the land [dalu] to the seas. History gave a fair chance, both to Orient and to Occident, to make a choice. The Pacific, Indian Ocean, and the Atlantic all opened their arms to welcome the peoples of the land [dalu]. [131]

Is this passage talking about the oceans welcoming the peoples of continental Europe in the fifteenth century, or about the oceans welcoming the surge of Chinese mainland students, scholars, and emigrants in the 1980s, in the midst of China's "craze for going overseas" [<u>chuguore</u>]?

Another use of the term <u>dalu</u> occurs in Part Six, where the text mentions the Yellow River's ultimate entrance into the sea, symbolizing China's entry into the world: "*The mud and sand it has carried thousands of <u>li</u> will collect here to form new land [xin dalu].*" [222] This would seem to say that the feudal elements of Chinese culture [the mud and sand] will be transformed peacefully and gradually into a "new mainland."

Irony. Barely-concealed irony is another mark of this style. *The Chinese hope that turmoil will never reoccur, just as they hope that the Yellow River will never again overflow.* [189] That this is really a tongue-in-cheek statement is underscored by the context. It comes immediately after a reference to the film <u>A Small Town Called Hibiscus</u> in which the character Wang Qiushe, formerly a political activist during the Cultural Revolution and now in the 1980s filling the post of village madman, continues to bang his gong down the village street calling for the beginnings of a new mass movement. Since the assumption is that the Yellow River <u>will</u> someday overflow, do the authors feel that more political turmoil is coming in future?

Systematic connections between past and present. One type of indirection in <u>Deathsong of the River</u> consists in making systematic links between past and present. Let us look first at a case where comments made about an historical event seem aimed at a current target.

After mentioning the defeat of China's navy by Japan in 1895, the script comments: *"This fact clearly proves that the inevitable defeat of a corrupt system cannot be warded off by technology."* [209] Is this sentence talking about the China of 1895, or the China of 1988?

The joining of past with present is also accomplished by attention to anniversaries. The identification of 1988 as a crucial year for China's reform takes on significance when one realizes that it is the hundredth anniversary of the birth of Stalin's victim Bukharin and the fiftieth of his death; the hundredth anniversary of the reformer Kang Yuwei's first memorial to the Guangxu emperor; the first 'dragon year' to fall after Chairman Mao's death, etc. The Cultural Revolution was also linked with past outbursts of disorder by the same means. After commenting on the disorders at the end of the Yuan dynasty [1367], the script comments: *It seems as if every six hundred years there is one turn of the Great Wheel.* [188] The Cultural Revolution broke out in 1966.

Yet another technique is to suggest an identification between an historical ruler and a contemporary one. Part Two introduces the founding emperor of the Ming dynasty, Zhu Yuanzhang, as a former 'wandering monk' whose rule held the Chinese people in bondage and suffocated movement, migration and trade. In the description of Zhu Yuanzhang as a 'wandering monk,' how many people recalled Edgar Snow's account of a conversation with Chairman Mao: *He was, he said, only a lone monk walking the world with a leaky umbrella.* [285] Similarly, Part Three moves seamlessly from remarking on the decadence of the Qing court at Yuanming yuan to that of the people's government at Zhongnanhai: *...the Chinese emperors seemed absolutely unwilling to reject Western-style enjoyments. This situation closely resembles ours at present; while some people exert their full strength to criticize western life-styles and values, yet they themselves would never refuse to enjoy those super-deluxe limousines and high-class consumer goods.* [151]

Systematic connections between the natural and the human worlds. The Confucian tradition revered the concept of the "Mandate of Heaven" [tian ming], according to which Heaven granted an individual the right to rule the empire only so long as he ruled by virtue. If he failed to rule virtuously, then Heaven would show its displeasure by causing natural disasters; and these disasters were signals to the people, who, according to Mencius, had the right to depose a ruler who was unworthy of the name of 'king.' Part Five includes a list of both natural and man-made disasters, which was censored in the second broadcast, presumably due to its sensitivity: *"As man-made disasters—such as the great forest fire in the Daxingan Range, the airplane accident at Chongqing, the trains that crashed into each other, and the epidemic of hepatitis in Shanghai occur one after the other, can we not say that our decaying social mechanism is sending us subtle warnings, over and over again?"* [197] The "social mechanism" referred to here would appear to be none other than a modern reincarnation of "Heaven."

The denial of national symbols. Heshang's treatment of the dragon, the Great Wall, and the Yellow River has already been discussed above. An important symbol so far little discussed by the critics is the color red. Just as red resides at the left side of the optical spectrum, so too does it refer to the left side of the political spectrum, indicating the politics of the Cultural Revolution, a time when red meant both revolution and spilt blood. The first clue to this level of meaning is provided by references in the script to the idea of "changing color" [gaibian yanse]:

"We cannot change the color of our skins, just as we cannot change the color of the Yellow River.[85] And yet we must rebuild the culture of the Chinese people—the structure of their minds. This will be an extremely difficult and complex piece of culturo-philosophical systems engineering." [98]

"If Hainan should succeed, it will unite with the fourteen other coastal cities and form one of the great dragons on the two shores of the Pacific. This heroic undertaking will necessarily give a new color to China's culture." [215]

The skilled reader will immediately identify both the ironic twist to the Stalinist dictum that writers are "engineers of human souls"[86] as well as the reference to Chairman Mao's Quotations, where the notion of "changing color" carries the ominous sense of abandoning socialism in favor of revisionism or capitalism:

"...if ... the enemy were able to sneak in, and if many of our workers, peasants, and intellectuals were left defenseless against both the soft and hard tactics of the enemy, then it would not take long, perhaps only several years or a decade, or several decades at most, before a counter-revolutionary

---

[85] The logic of this sentence is curiously parallel to a passage in Part Five: *"The Chinese hope that turmoil will never reoccur, just as they hope that the Yellow River will never again overflow."* [189] The irony is that they would in fact like to make the Yellow River run clear if they could.

[86] Speaking in 1934 at a Congress of Soviet Writers, Maxim Gorky declared to Stalin that *"the proletarian state must bring up thousands of excellent mechanics of culture, engineers of the soul."*

restoration on a national scale inevitably occurred, the Marxist-Leninist party would undoubtedly become a revisionist party or a fascist party, and the whole of China would change its color."[87]

Mao's concern, of course, was that China would lose the purity of its devotion to socialism, or its "redness." For the creators of Deathsong of the River, the color red has none of its original connotations in folk culture of happiness and good luck but stands rather for primitive superstition:

"Human blood is red. Almost all animals have blood that is red. Primitive religion defined the basic color of life as red. Early man daubed the corpses of the dead with red pigment from iron ore in order to summon back the life that had been lost." [203]

By implication, the redness of Maoism is the redness of a primitive religion, a redness which cannot bring the dead bones of Chinese culture back to life. This digression on redness is followed by a hymn in praise of "blueness," which is the color of our world as viewed from space, and hence is as symbolic of the modern world as red is of the primitive world. Hence the "change of color" intended by the writers of the script is not merely from the yellow of the Yellow River to the blue of the Pacific, but also from red to blue on the political spectrum.

V. Concluding Remarks

We are now ready to reconsider the question this introduction began with: What is Deathsong of the River? And what standards do we judge it by?

First of all, it is not a standard textbook history. In many ways, it is an anti-history, as it overturns many long-established opinions. Nor is it a rigorous work of scholarship, although its ability to summarize and cite the scholarship of others certainly added to its credibility. It incorporates the results of much painstaking scholarship, all of which deserves to be better known outside of China. Heshang, however, is responsible neither for their achievements nor their mistakes. Yet its critics like to find fault with it on this account. Heshang is, after all, a filmscript, a genre which permits no space for footnotes or for extended arguments.

In addition, Heshang is also an historical allegory. Its narrative of China's three thousand years of history is also a profound reflection on its past forty years. In order to understand its allegory, the reader has to regard it

---

[87] Quotations from Chairman Mao Tse-tung, Dongfang hong chubanshe, 1967, Chinese-English edition, pp. 79-81. See also pp. 518-519.

as a literary work and examine the literary techniques that it uses to develop its meaning. The result is a work of multi-layered meanings which continues to reward its audience with new insights after several readings or viewings.

Future study of <u>Heshang</u> might focus on two aspects: The film as cinematic art and the film as the product of a literary tradition. First, how do the images on the screen coordinate with the ideas in the text? How has Xia Jun developed visual symbols of the ideas in the film? How does he add to the text? How does his use of montage and editing compare with other documentary film artists? These are questions which I hope to pursue at a later date. Second, how does the filmscript compare with earlier Chinese works of a similar nature, such as Wu Han's play <u>Hai Rui Dismissed from Office</u>, Liao Mosha's <u>Notes from Three Family Village</u>, and so forth? Is there an identifiable literary style for dissidents in the Chinese literary tradition that we could identify as part of a distinctively Chinese political culture?

Indeed, the script is both a literary and a political work, a combination which is rare neither in the world nor in China. In China, these concerns link it closely with the genre of <u>baogao wenxue</u>, or "reportage literature," for which writers such as Liu Binyan and Su Xiaokang are well-known. Its creators would also see themselves in the tradition of earlier reformers, such as Kang Yuwei or Liang Qichao, who tried to awaken and enlighten [<u>qimeng</u>] the Chinese people. The strength of the controversy they have aroused proves that they have at least asked some of the right questions.

The controversy surrounding <u>Heshang</u> in itself begs for explanation. I would like to suggest three possible reasons for it. First, cognitive dissonance. For many viewers, the effect of seeing <u>Heshang</u> broadcast on national TV, on the network associated with the authority of the Party, was like the first broadcast of Orson Welles' <u>The War of the Worlds</u>. It was as if the Vatican's official organ, <u>L'Osservatore Romano</u>, had published an April 1st edition which claimed that Jesus Christ was a fraud. Second, identity crisis. Chinese both on mainland China and overseas find themselves caught between a traditional world and a modern, industrial world neither of which makes them feel at home. They have lost the certainties they used to have but have not yet found new ones. This a phenomenon not limited to China. The same sort of conflict over national identity can be seen in the controversy over Rushdie's <u>Satanic Verses</u>. Third, the shaming mechanism of Chinese society. The young child learns early in the family not to contradict his elders, no matter whether they are right or wrong; if he does contradict them, he is in for continued scoldings. The child learns to value social harmony over telling the truth. I remember vividly a skit put on by model kindergarten students on my first visit to China. The subject was a family of ducks. One day, one of the little ducklings decided to go explore on his own, but he very soon got lost and started to cry. Fortunately, Momma Duck came along and rescued him, reproving him severely never to leave the group again.

Heshang, however, was not an obedient duckling. It was an ugly duckling that grew up into a swan and flew away.

A Second Wave of Enlightenment? Or an Illusory Nirvana?

Heshang and the Intellectual Movements of the 1980s

by Pin P. Wan

Deathsong of the River is a complex work; while its overall critical tone was understood immediately by most viewers, it contains many subtleties not easy for most Chinese to comprehend, let alone the foreign reader or viewer. Two major ingredients contributing to its complexity were the high goals it set and the broad range of topics it covered. Su Xiaokang and his colleagues from the beginning had in mind a very ambitious goal, intending to make the film a "*TV film of political commentary*" and an "*all-out inquiry into our nation's history, civilization, and destiny.*" [94] Xia Jun, Heshang's young director, intended it as a vehicle to bring intellectual issues to the general public.[1] With this goal in mind, it set out to introduce a set of formidable historical, economic, and philosophic theories, reflecting the rather eclectic reading of reformist intellectuals over the decade since the end of the Cultural Revolution. To better appeal to a mass audience, the discussion of these theoretical issues was to be interwoven with topics of contemporary concern to the man in the street, including sensitive political issues[2] such as inflation, rural poverty, official corruption, the treatment of intellectuals, and the crisis in China's education.

---

[1] See Xia Jun,"Heshang chuangzuo guocheng de huigu" [A Glance Back over the Process of Creating Heshang] in Cui Wenhua, ed., Heshang lun, p. 85; and Guo Lixin, "Longnian de Heshang xianxiang— fang Heshang biandao Xia Jun" [The Dragon Year's Heshang phenomenon—an interview with Heshang's director Xia Jun] in Zhong shi wanbao, September 11th, 1988; see bibliography, items #16, #17.

[2] The pointing out of social problems was adopted by Su Xiaokang as one of his strategic approaches in designing Heshang. He calls these problems "activation points," naming as examples rafting on the Yangtze and Yellow Rivers, the worship of the dragon spirit, the plight of intellectuals, prices and the market, the student movement of 1986, democratization, the "passion for studying culture," etc. See Su Xiaokang, "Arousing the Whole Nation to Self-Questioning," p. 96 in this volume.

For the foreign reader, there are additional barriers to understanding. Perhaps the easiest pitfall for the foreign reader to fall into is to regard Heshang purely and simply as an intellectual work, without taking into account its use of language and the special environment of discourse in which it was produced; the national mood which it reflected and its makers' motives for producing it; their concept of their social role and mission; and the positive and negative responses of its audiences.

The question of Heshang's language and its environment of discourse is treated separately by my colleague Richard Bodman in his introduction. Here I would like to lay a groundwork for the non-Chinese-speaking reader to understand the other barriers listed above. What I propose is to look at Deathsong of the River from the two perspectives of the author and of society. My essay is intended to be primarily informative and descriptive rather than evaluative; it is certainly not exhaustive, for the richness and complexity of Heshang will continue to inspire new interpretations and re-interpretations.

The following discussion consists of three main sections. 1.The first section introduces the psychology of Heshang's makers: their motives, their moods and their vision of the work both before and after its broadcast. It focuses on questions such as: Why did they want to make such a film? How did they see it? And how did they approach it? 2. The second section examines the film makers' concept of the cultural crisis in contemporary China and their relation to the legacy of May Fourth, drawing on the debate over the role and values of the modern intellectual. As some scholars have pointed out, the views presented in the film are critical and iconoclastic. Hence we should ask questions such as: What concept of their roles as intellectuals led them to adopt such a cultural approach? What is their concept of China's cultural crisis? And where do their ideas derive from? 3. The third section concerns the controversy raised by the film and the reaction of conservative elements in the party and government. While the film had been praised as "a second wave of enlightenment" and as "preparatory work for the reforms," yet it still ended up being banned. Here we should ask questions such as: Are the makers of the film patriots? Is the film a work of enlightenment? Why did they choose to attack culture? Why did it become a political event, and what issues in the film particularly offended officialdom? All these are interesting sub-questions, the discussion of which may constitute an answer to the overall question, which is: what is Deathsong of the River, and how should one read it?

I. Creating a Sensation in the Dragon Year: Motive, Mood, and Vision

The series was first aired in June, 1988, via the nationwide television network. After the first broadcast, Chinese Central Television (CCTV) received an unprecedented number of letters, nearly a thousand in the first week, from people in all walks of life, including students, teachers, workers, scholars, party cadres and People's Liberation Army soldiers. In most of the letters, the writers praised the success of the film, asked for the script, and pleaded for a re-broadcast.[3] The basic tone of these letters revealed that the film series' depiction of China's cultural crisis appealed strongly to its viewers' patriotic sentiments. This overwhelmingly enthusiastic response, coupled with the Party's stated policy of non-interference with literary works, most likely made the rebroadcast in August possible.[4] Although aired only twice, we may fairly assume that it was seen by at least one hundred million viewers and perhaps by as many as several hundred million.[5]

Consequently, the series aroused deep concern and interest on the part of intellectuals; conferences and seminars were held to discuss the various issues raised by the film; and a host of articles appeared in the press. Journalists and intellectuals coined new terms: Heshang re [The Heshang craze] and Heshang xianxiang [The Heshang phenomenon]. Since the questions raised by the series were so controversial, it was not long before scholars involved in the debate split into opposing camps. The debate continued to spread and involved so many intellectuals and even some party

---

[3] See Su Xiaokang, "The Distress of a Dragon Year—Notes on Heshang" in this volume, p. 290; Guo Lixin, "Longnian de Heshang xianxiang—fang Heshang biandao Xia Jun" [The Dragon Year's Heshang Phenomenon—an interview with Heshang's director Xia Jun], in Heshang taolun ji, p. 81.

[4] For a fuller discussion of how the film series was initially approved, and how it ran into political difficulties and criticism, see "The Distress of a Dragon Year," pp. 288-299 in this volume; also W.L. Chong, "Su Xiaokang on his Film 'River Elegy'" in China Information, Leiden, vol. 4, no. 3, Winter 89/90, pp. 44-55.

[5] In 1987, China had a total of 112 million television sets and an estimated television audience of 600 million viewers. Television reached 92.5% of urban residents and 32.58% of rural residents, with a national average of 56.09%. [Zhongguo guangbo dianshi nianjian 1989, pp. 147, 321.] What percent of this audience watched Heshang is a more difficult question, as no audience surveys have been published. Though Heshang was broadcast on the national channel, it would still have had to compete for viewers, as most cities provide three channels. In addition, after the broadcast of Part One, the remaining episodes were broadcast after 10 pm at night. In July, local stations in Shanghai and Shenzhen rebroadcast the series, apparently without permission. Alice de Jong cites an article by He Yulin in Wenhui bao, September 14, 1988, which mentioned a viewing rate of 16%, presumably for the first broadcast, which would yield an audience of over 90 million, far less than the 45% rate cited for the Chinese-made Modai huangdi series. Yet the well-known public controversy over the series, plus the availability of the published script, should have made the second broadcast in August 1988 far more popular. Zhongguo qingnianbao on September 2, 1988, published a detailed questionnaire including 32 questions which it asked viewers to complete and send back; the results of the survey were to have been made into a book but do not appear to have been published.

and government cadres, that it made conservative elements in the leadership feel highly uneasy, to the point that they made a political issue of it, transforming it from the subject of an intellectual debate into a political football in the struggle between conservatives and reformers within the party. Vice-President Wang Zhen's public condemnation of the series in late September 1988 signalled the end to free discussion within China. Eventually, both the published edition of the script and the video cassette of the series were banned from the market. Yet the banning of Heshang did not dampen the climate of free expression in the press, and in the spring of 1989 many of Heshang's makers played active roles in the democracy movement. After the events of June 4, 1989 at Tian'anmen Square, the authorities accused Heshang of deliberately preparing public opinion for the students' democracy movement, and mobilized scholars to launch an ideological campaign to combat its pernicious influence. Some of the people involved in making Heshang managed to flee the country, while others were arrested.[6] However, long before 1989 this "craze" had already spread to Hong Kong, Taiwan and other countries where the debate continued amongst scholars and students in the Chinese-speaking community overseas.

To understand the motives and thinking of the film-makers, much can be learned by taking a look at what they have said themselves. Su Xiaokang, one of the principal authors of the script, gave a lecture at Leiden University in the Netherlands on November 24th, 1989, in which he stated:

However, in this lecture, I want to deal with some of the social and psychological reasons for making Heshang. Strictly speaking, it is not a theoretical or academic work. Some scholars treated it as such, and devoted much discussion and criticism to it from academic viewpoints, but they had not understood that it is a work about emotions. On the surface, it seems as if the film is about social and historical theory, but in reality, it was aimed at expressing a certain mood prevalent among the Chinese today.[7]

His statement here seems to contradict what he said in his preface to the first published edition, entitled "Arousing the Whole Nation to Self-questioning." There he states that the film was designed to *"bring information about all sorts of theories and thinking to the TV screen in large volume, endowing the film with a clear, rich and meaty awareness of the philosophy of culture..."* [95] and that for that purpose they had

---

[6] Su Xiaokang and Yuan Zhiming arrived in France in the fall of 1989, then came to the U.S. in the fall of 1990. Zhang Gang initially fled to Taiwan, where he was detained by the authorities, after which he also arrived in the U.S. Wang Luxiang was imprisoned for several months and subsequently released. Bao Zunxin was sentenced to five years in prison and Wang Juntao to thirteen years.

[7] Su Xiaokang's lecture was first published in English by W.L. Chong in his article "Su Xiaokang on His Film River Elegy," op.cit.

"invited experts and scholars in all areas to present their views succinctly on the television screen." [96] The contradiction between these two passages is so striking that it makes one wonder: which was Su Xiaokang's real motive? We have to assume that Su Xiaokang as a reportage writer had developed a keen sensitivity to the political implications of literature. Even as he and Xia Jun first wrote down their ideas in draft and planned out their goals, his professional instincts must have alerted him to the project's potential dangers. The tone of his preface reveals his pleasure and excitement about the approval of his project. He thought that they could fulfill the goals they had set, and so he used the preface to jot down his expectations. Besides, the strong support he had received from the Deputy-director of CCTV, Chen Hanyuan,[8] must have made him feel somewhat at ease. What he and Xia Jun could not know was how far the Party would let them go. But they decided to go ahead anyway, using the series as a touchstone to test the limits of free expression possible.

Su Xiaokang's lecture delivered at Leiden, however, is not about his expectations and intentions in 1988. By that time he was a dissident in exile in a foreign country; his heart was full of anger, distress, and despair.[9] And he was speaking in a very different "environment of discourse."

"What kind of mood is it that Heshang reflects? I call it a mood of anxiety (jiaolü de qingxu). In 1988-89, before the recent tempest, there was a kind of fin-de-siècle feeling pervading the country, because the reforms, during the past ten years, have come into great difficulties, and the question arose whether our people would be able to find a way out. There was a strong feeling that China's ship was about to sink.

Due to corruption and profiteering by officials, and unfair distribution, some types of jobs in the public service, like that of teachers, medical doctors, and bus drivers, had suddenly become low status. On the other hand, many traders were engaging in illegal activities, such as selling phoney cigarettes, phoney spirits, phoney medicines, and making a great deal of money. Most government officials were also greedy and corrupt, and all this gave rise to great popular resentment..." [10]

---

[8] Su later expressed his great appreciation for Chen Hanyuan, giving him all the credit for protecting the series from censorship and for allowing it to be broadcast. See Su, "The Distress of a Dragon Year," in this volume, p. 289.

[9] He expresses similar feelings in another essay written shortly after arriving in France: "Zai Bali xiangqi Caishikou—liuwang ganhuai" [Remembering Caishikou in Paris— feelings in exile], Bai xing, no. 202, October 16, 1989, pp. 3-4; bibliography item #28.

[10] W.L. Chong, op.cit., p. 45.

While Su Xiaokang's feeling of anxiety is clear, what exactly does he mean by a *"fin-de-siècle"* [shijimo de ganjue] feeling?[11] The Chinese term does not suggest anything like the artistic decadence of France at the end of the 19th century, something hardly possible under the political and economic conditions of contemporary China. Rather it indicates a deep despair and frustration, as if impending disaster threatened the downfall of the country. This mood was particularly prevalent amongst the high culture elite.[12] It was this sort of mood that impelled Su Xiaokang to make Heshang.[13] Let us now compare his account with that given by Xia Jun, Heshang's twenty-five-year-old director.

Xia Jun is the one who actually initiated the project. He was an energetic and ambitious young man who had just received his M.A. from the Central Academy of Drama in 1986 and who had long dreamed of "making a big film."[14] The "cultural craze" [wenhua re] of the years 1985-87 had had a tremendous influence on him, inspiring him to think about the issue of television culture and to express his own ideas about society and culture. He admitted that, under the influence of this debate, he had accepted the new interpretation that cultural symbols such as the dragon or the Great Wall were no longer glorious and worthy of respect. This change brought him closer to the group of "cultural luminaries" involved in the debate over traditional culture. Moreover, his participation in the shooting of the 30-part Yellow River series jointly produced by CCTV and NHK had inspired him to experiment with the idea of a film which could bring out the meaning of the Yellow River much more deeply. His first experience of seeing the Yellow River close up was rather emotional. Later, he would recall his impressions as follows:

"In the second half of 1986, as a member of the camera crew of the original Yellow River series, I travelled along part of the Yellow River. I saw it.

---

[11] Ibid.

[12] Su Xiaokang frequently refers to a shijimo de ganjue, translated here as a 'fin-de-siècle feeling.' In other passages, he uses it to express a mixture of despair, depression, fear, and uneasiness. Sometimes he calls it a 'mentality' (as in shijimo de xintai), while elsewhere it indicates a feeling or mood, as in shijimo de ganjue. See "The Distress of a Dragon Year — Notes on Heshang" in this volume, p. 273; see also his article "Shijimo de huimou: guanyu Heshang xuji de liuchan jilu" [A Glance Back at the End of the Century: Notes on the Miscarriage of Heshang's Sequel] in Wenhui yuekan, Shanghai, May, 1989, reprinted in Zhao Yaodong, et al. Heshang taolun ji, pp. 195-227.

[13] *"It was a reflection of the mood of anxiety, of deadlock, and it was against this background that we conceived the plan to make Heshang."* See W.L. Chong, op.cit., p. 46.

[14] Xia Jun, "Heshang chuangzuo guocheng de huigu" in Cui Wenhua, ed., Heshang lun, p. 83.

Before this I had often crossed the Yellow River on bridges as a traveller in a hurry. But I had never seen the Yellow River. But now I had come, I had seen it and I had felt it. The Yellow River shocked me. But it was not its grandeur, lyricized over a thousand years, that shocked me; rather it was its ugliness, its poverty, and the dangers hidden within it that shocked me. Near Huayuankou, I walked right out into the middle of the riverbed. At that time, the Yellow River was not the great rushing river that most people imagine—rather it was a swamp, a stretch of mud, a large, old, ever-changing monster. I believe that I have never been as moved, as worried, depressed, saddened or stimulated by it as I was at that time."[15]

Xia Jun's mood was thus in close accord with Su Xiaokang's feelings. They immediately proceeded to work out an outline for a trilogy on the Yellow River, whose individual parts would be called: "Ten thousand li from East to West"; "Four Thousand Years from Start to Finish"; and "A Billion People on Both Banks."[16] But they worried that the first part of the trilogy would overlap with the CCTV-NHK series. So they changed the content into six parts and gave it the tentative title of The Great Artery.[17]

While Xia Jun and Su Xiaokang's motives for making the film series both sprang from a similar mood of frustration and disquiet, this mood was heightened by their fears and worries about making the film itself. After Su Xiaokang had finished an outline of the thematic structure and logical development of the film, (which would later become the blueprint for Heshang[18]) he and Xia Jun made a formal proposal to the authorities at CCTV, who included a representative from the military. At this point they had asked Wang Luxiang to come to the meeting as an evaluator. The result of the meeting was exciting, for it was *"unanimously approved with high expectations,"* yet it was recognized that it would *"have to face potential risks."*[19] Although the series was officially approved, there was always the

---

[15] Ibid.

[16] Su Xiaokang alludes to these original titles at the beginning of his preface to the published edition; see "Arousing the Whole Nation to Self-questioning" in this volume, p. 93.

[17] The original subtitles for the six parts of the series were less ambiguous and had a stronger emotional content: "China in Search of a Dream"; "The Black Hole of Destiny"; "The Vanishing Light of the Spirit"; "The Yellow-soil Turns Blue"; "China's Sorrow"; and "Sunset over the River." Their original working title, The Great Artery, was intended to suggest an artery nourishing Chinese culture, but they later felt that it was a little too dull and stiff. The final decision on a title, Deathsong of the River [Heshang], was delegated by Xia Jun to Wang Luxiang and Xie Xuanjun. Xia Jun, op. cit., pp. 83, 85; Wang Luxiang, "Huiyi yu sikao" [Remembering and Pondering], Heshang lun, p. 95.

[18] Xia Jun, "Heshang chuangzuo guocheng de huigu," in Heshang lun, pp. 83-84.

[19] Wang Luxiang, "Huiyi yu sikao," in Heshang lun, p. 92.

threat that it could be canceled at any time before broadcast. Hence they could never feel completely free and unrestrained in producing the series.

"What made us the most apprehensive was whether or not a television piece including so many controversial topics could in the end be broadcast, and whether our labor, which we felt to be of inestimable value, could ever appear before society. This sort of apprehension was a constant influence on our creative energies and on our decisions about the form of the piece. And, throughout the whole creative process, it made us constantly cast a worried glance over our shoulder. In fact, we never really let ourselves go in writing Heshang. As a television director, how much I hoped that we could create a clear and rigorous law for television! In that case, then under its clear direction, one could create boldly, and the imagination of creators would not have to be crushed and stifled under that formless but heavy burden. Indeed, apprehension was our constant companion..."[20]

In fact, this sort of apprehension continued even after the first broadcast in June of 1988. The first broadcast had aroused both a strongly positive reaction from the public as well as a strongly negative reaction in certain academic and political circles, thus putting the network in a difficult position. In order to facilitate a rebroadcast, the leadership of CCTV asked Su Xiaokang to revise certain passages in the script; a comparison of the original text of the narrative with the narrative as revised for the August rebroadcast gives a number of clues as to which topics were sensitive and to the limits of free expression.[21]

II. Intellectuals, Cultural Crisis, and the May Fourth Legacy

Yet the question still remains: Why did they dare to express despair and anger? Further, how did they conceive of their roles as intellectuals? And why did they adopt a cultural approach, choosing Chinese culture—and the traditional Confucian bureaucratic system in particular—as the target of their criticism? These questions cannot be answered by simply attributing the cause to the film makers' temporary moods. Rather, the answer is to be sought in the concepts and ideas they expressed in their own writings and in

---

[20] See Xia Jun, "Heshang chuangzuo guocheng de huigu" in Heshang lun, p. 85.

[21] Su Xiaokang discussed the changes he had made in an interview with Mai Tianshu on the eve of the second broadcast; see Mai Tianshu, "Pipan shi zui zhongyao de jianshe — Heshang chongbo qianxi fang Su Xiaokang" [Criticism is the Most Important Contribution—an interview with Su Xiaokang on the eve of Heshang's rebroadcast], Zhongguo qingnianbao, August 16th, 1988, p. 1. The translation of the script in this volume presents the altered text of the second broadcast as footnotes to the original text. An integral text of the second broadcast of Parts Four and Six is also given on pp. 223-248 and 249-269 for the convenience of viewers of the videotape.

the theoretical works of scholarly mentors such as Jin Guantao and Bao Zunxin.

1.   First and foremost, the makers of Heshang share a collective identity in terms of their role in society. In one way or another, they all identify themselves as "intellectuals" [zhishi fenzi] and as "cultural luminaries" [wenhua jingying].[22] This identity provides the real motive driving them to take the risk of making the series. The two roles of "intellectual" and of "cultural luminary" had been major topics in the debates on culture from 1985 to 1987. While the concept of the "intellectual" had also been a key one in the May Fourth Movement, yet it was only loosely defined then. Chinese scholars, particularly those who regard Chinese culture as a culture of the elite, think that the modern intellectual derives from the shi or scholar-officials of ancient times.[23] In the late 80s, the term zhishi fenzi or "intellectual" was brought under serious scrutiny and given a clear definition. One of the film's unofficial advisors, Bao Zunxin, defined the term in a modern sense:

"Modern [Chinese] intellectuals are different from the literati and scholars in the tradition. In addition to their knowledge, they should represent the conscience of society, have a lofty sense of responsibility and sense of mission, and finally, have a highly rational and critical spirit."[24]

Bao's concept of the modern intellectual is defined in contrast to the traditional literatus, who never developed a critical spirit due to the

---

[22] In his article "Huiyi yu sikao" [Remembering and Pondering], Wang Luxiang gives a list of the intellectuals participating in the project and attributes Heshang's success to the collaboration between this group of wenhua jingying and the communications media. See Heshang lun, p. 97.

[23] A representative and typical theory of this kind can be found in Hu Qiuyuan's book, Gudai Zhongguo wenhua yu Zhongguo zhishi fenzi [Ancient Chinese Culture and China's Intellectuals], Hong Kong: Yazhou chuban she, second edition, 1957. He uses three types of intellectuals in ancient China to represent their spirit: the Confucian scholar [ru], who symbolized knowledge and morality; the knight-errant [xia], who stood for righteousness and justice; and the recluse [yin], who represented the moral integrity of the scholar who cannot serve a corrupt regime; see pp. 8-11. This conservative view has been seriously criticized by scholars in modern China; see the following discussion of Xu Jilin's ideas.

[24] See Bao Zunxin, "Zhishi fenzi yu guan xue yiti de chuantong moshi," [Intellectuals and the Traditional Pattern of the 'Identity of Office Holding and Scholarship'], in Pipan yu qimeng [Criticism and Enlightenment], Taibei: Lianjing chuban shiye gongsi, 1989, p. 161. His awareness of the crucial role of an independent personality [duli renge] for modern Chinese intellectuals is the main reason that he agrees with the New Confucianists, particularly with Du Weiming [Wei-ming Tu], in their advocacy of cultivating among Chinese intellectuals a critical self-consciousness of their group identity. For more on Bao Zunxin, see Part Six, footnote 47.

confining influence of the Confucian tradition in which the role of the scholar and of the bureaucrat were not distinguished.[25]

Xu Jilin, a scholar who also participated in the debate on culture, points out that in its entire history China had never produced a single intellectual with an independent personality, because the literati simply could not become independent under the prevailing Confucian doctrine and bureaucratic system. Their joint role as both officials and as members of the literati elite depended on the patronage of the emperor, and this very dependence prevented them from ever becoming critical and independent intellectuals. One could object that the recluse [or yinshi] and the madman [or kuangren] were two other types of traditional intellectuals that to some degree had independent personalities, and that occasionally some upright Confucian scholars had the moral integrity to criticize the emperor. Yet even this degree of independence was one based on a traditional Confucian moral consensus; it was not one which they had arrived at by independent, critical reflection. Hence, traditional Confucian society could not create truly independent intellectuals, and even those who seemed most independent exhibited a tendency to return to the tradition.[26] Echoes of this critique of the traditional intellectual are found in Heshang in several places:

"..China has never again re-enacted such a grand historical drama as the competition among the Hundred Philosophical Schools. From these large square military formations, in addition to hearing the melodies of war and dictatorship, can we not also discern the repression of individuals caused by expelling unorthodox opinions, confining people's knowledge, and forcefully unifying thought?" [141]

"A bureaucracy made up of Confucianists had an irresistible tendency to corruption, and power itself became a corrosive agent..." [196]

---

[25] When he explained why the most important quality of an independent intellectual was his critical spirit, Bao explicitly criticized the current political culture, saying *"The facts that the bureaucrats despise or even deny the independent value of scholars and take them as a flower vase or decoration for their successful policies and political achievements, and that they refuse to listen to scholars' opinions, especially opposing and critical ones, all reflect the political superiority complex of the bureaucrats. It is the manifestation of the tradition of 'the identity of office-holding and scholarship' in modern times....They confine, reform, and utilize the intellectuals. . . This is worse than the traditional 'identity of office-holding and scholarship.'"* Ibid., pp. 169-170.

[26] See Xu Jilin, "Zhishi fenzi duli renge lun" [On the Independent Personality of Intellectuals], in Xin qimeng: shidai yu xuanze,[New Enlightenment Series, No. 1: The Time and the Choice], Wang Yuanhua, ed., Hunan: Xinhua shudian, October 1988, pp. 77-91; also Bao Zunxin, "Wei wancheng de niepan" [An Incomplete Nirvana] in Bao Zunxin, Pipan yu qimeng, Taibei, Lianjing chuban shiye gongsi, August, 1989, pp. 103-139, esp. p.138.

"The tragic fate of Yan Fu and indeed of many other advanced thinkers of the early modern period such as Kang Yuwei, Liang Qichao, and Zhang Taiyan would also seem to prove that even the very best Chinese, after promoting revolution and progress for a while, would ultimately be unable to avoid retreating to the haven of Confucianism." [210]

"Chinese history did not create a bourgeoisie for the Chinese people which could hasten the victory of science and democracy; Chinese culture did not nurture a sense of citizenship. On the contrary, it taught a subject mentality... But History did give the Chinese people an entirely unique group: its intellectuals. It is very difficult for them to have economic interests in common or an independent political stance; for thousands of years they have been hangers-on. Nor can they become a solid social entity that employs a steel-hard economic strength to carry out an armed critique of the old society. Their talents can be manipulated by others, their wills can be twisted, their souls emasculated, their backbones bent, and their flesh destroyed..." [217-218]

What, then, is the "ideal type" of the modern intellectual? Xu suggests that an intellectual should (1) take his own needs, particularly his need for knowledge and truth as his priority, and not be subservient to any external social duty; (2) unyieldingly maintain a scientific, individual rationality in his methodology of thinking; and (3) have a richly critical spirit toward society.[27] He further prescribes two social roles for intellectuals: that of "cultural luminary" and that of "public conscience." As a cultural luminary, an intellectual has to pursue knowledge and truth, preserve an ultimate concern toward nature, society, and the meaning of human knowledge, and regard his pursuit of knowledge as an entirely independent and self-existing task, not subservient to any other duty. As a social conscience, an intellectual should participate in public affairs. But in addition to seeking for the interests of his social class, he should have a macroscopic vision perceiving things from the perspective of the whole society, the whole nation and the whole of mankind. In other words, an intellectual should on the one hand believe in "knowledge for knowledge's sake" in the realm of scholarship and on the other have a critical spirit which transcends all profits or interests in the realm of politics.[28] In Confucian society, all intellectuals were officials, except for a few recluses and those who did not pass the examinations. This merging of scholarship and official position made intellectuals attached to political authority [for the sake of their future careers] and made them lose their social power as a class.[29]

---

[27] See Xu Jilin, ibid., p. 78.

[28] Ibid., p. 87.

[29] Ibid., pp. 78-79.

While Western intellectuals since the Renaissance have maintained some critical independence from political power by associating themselves with the aristocracy or the universities, Chinese literati from the very beginning of the bureaucratic system in the Qin dynasty have had to depend on the monarch's patronage. The same subservient relationship to power has also held true throughout the history of the People's Republic. During the Cultural Revolution, scholarship had to serve politics, and the position of intellectuals was often tragic, with many suffering political persecution for being "Stinky Old Ninths." The persecution of intellectuals is symbolically represented by the "black cross" in the conclusion to Part Three of Heshang:

"Among the professions of mankind, no one has a greater need for a free atmosphere and unlimited space than they do. If you affixed a black cross to their spirits or weighed them down under a grey Great Wall, then the light of the spirit would never become the sun! May History never again play tricks on Chinese intellectuals. Today, this is our deepest prayer!" [156]

The concept of the independent intellectual serving as a social conscience and the need to fulfill this social responsibility would appear to have provided Su Xiaokang and his companions with the necessary motivation and courage for producing such a "television film of political commentary" as Heshang.[30]

2.   Second, it is rather ironic that these intellectuals, who have such deep concerns over social problems and who are so eager to contribute to their country, nevertheless share a subtle yet haunting sense of not belonging. While as "cultural luminaries" they identify strongly with their role as a social conscience, they have lost a feeling of generational identity and feel alienated from the rest of society. Recently, there has appeared a very popular theory of China's "four generations" [si dai ren lilun]. Wang Luxiang described these four generations as follows:

"At a gathering a young friend put forth his famous 'theory of the four generations.' He divided into four generations all those on the mainland who had received an education in communist ideology. The first generation covered a rather broad span of time; all of those party members who fought to win sovereignty belong to this first generation... In sum, all those who entered the cities dancing the yangge belong to this generation.[31]...

---

[30] See Su Xiaokang, "Shiminggan zhi wo jian" [My View of a 'Sense of Mission'], in Qiushi, no. 2, 1988, pp. 47-48. Here Su Xiaokang reveals his own thinking about how his concern for the fate of the nation is linked to a sense of mission or responsibility.

[31] The yangge, lit., "seedling songs," is a rural folk dance of north China. In 1942, in the Communist liberated areas of the northwest, a "new yangge," with revolutionary content, was introduced.

Those who participated in the building of socialism in the 1950s are the second generation. This generation has more education than the first, many of them being 'petit intellectuals'; they can dance a very standard and elegant ballroom dance... Whenever they get together they cannot help but recall the comradely feelings of their youth and the warmth of their great revolutionary family and so hum together a few Soviet songs to revive for a moment those golden days now gone forever.

The third generation are rather complicated. The representatives of this generation include both the members of the "Third National People's Congress" as well as the most fanatic and radical young generals of the Red Guards in the first period of the Cultural Revolution.[32] They can dance a very sincere "dance of loyalty." In a country such as China which lacks a religious life, they are perhaps the only group of people who in the depths of their hearts have experienced the religious emotions of worshipping a superhuman man-god and his power. Of course, they are also the generation with the strongest sense of disillusionment. In today's China, the bunch of guys making the most mischief all belong to this generation.[33] It would be hard to say, though, whether they are still rebelling on behalf of those long-gone ideals. They are constantly made into the main characters of literary works. To that period of their lives which can best represent their existence, some of them express extreme distaste, while others are not at all contrite but are rather proud that they once believed and that on behalf of those beliefs they even made sacrifices, which, though meaningless, are still worth remembering.

The fourth generation are the "anti-heroes" of the present; they can dance a very skillful "break dance" and "outer space dance" and sing "I don't have nuthin'" and "Step up bravely, baby."[34] They are ashamed to speak of ideals but pay close attention to short-lived cultural fads.

---

[32] The first Red Guard organizations are generally acknowledged to have consisted largely of the sons and daughters of Party members in power; hence they were less willing to attack the Party itself than the second wave of Red Guards, known as the zaofan pai, or red rebels.

[33] zheteng de zui huan de zhur: Here Wang Luxiang is using a Beijing dialect expression, suggesting the naughty activities of bad children.

[34] The first song, "Yi wu suo you" is a pop song sung by Cui Jian. The second, "Meimei, ni da dan de wang qian zou" is the theme song from the 1987 movie Red Sorghum directed by Zhang Yimou. In his lecture at Leiden, Su Xiaokang also discussed these songs, regarding them as reflecting a prevalent mood in the country: "*These songs were sung in a frenzied and unbridled way, like rock-and-roll. It was a reflection of the mood of anxiety, of deadlock, and it was against this background that we conceived the plan to make Heshang. Of course, as authors, we were influenced by the prevalent mood. We wanted to explain what was behind these feelings of alarm and tragedy, and in a very natural manner, we traced them back to problems of Chinese culture.*" See W.L. Chong, op.cit., p. 46.

I wonder what generation I am? I've tried very hard to think of what generation I belong to, but in the end I had to give up. ... The members of these four generations all have a sense of belonging to their own generation, and so their lives all have a home base. But as for me? And my age-mates? We have no slot to fit into, we have lost any sense of a "generation" to belong to, we have become drifters unable to find our fixed place in history on this continent [dalu]. And yet we are very numerous, for we all happened to be born in the first 'baby boom' after the founding of the People's Republic, and of that famous group who started college in 1977 and 78 we number about half. At present, a significant number of the active young intellectuals on the mainland belong to our group of generationless "historical drifters." Perhaps it is precisely the deep-rooted fear created by this sense of the loss of a historical home to belong to that has made us so active in this critical age. To lack a sense of belonging is to lack anything to rely on or to hold on to. Perhaps we were born to be critics, because we don't fit in, because we are transitional figures between generations, because History has not set aside a time for us to be builders...[35]

Wang Luxiang was not alone in feeling lost. Xie Xuanjun, co-author of Part Six of Heshang, wrote a long preface for a book entitled China's Fourth Generation. Drawing on the theory of alienation between generations popularized by Arnold Toynbee in his dialogue with Daisaku Ikeda, Xie argued that the cultural conflicts between generations in China were particularly sharp.[36]

Their feeling of being lost is in fact an existential concern. Psychologically, this generation has a strong desire to seek for recognition and identity by showing their concern for the nation. They believe that they should do something promptly, because the older generation's ideas are bankrupt and because the younger generation is not yet ready to be trusted.

Thus their alienation from other generations and their feeling of being "drifters" combine with their social conscience to generate values such as a "sense of mission" [shiming gan], "ultimate concerns" [zhongji guanhuai],

---

[35] See Wang Luxiang, "Shiqu jiayuan de piaobozhe" [Drifters Who Have Lost Their Home] in Longnian de beichuang, Hong Kong: Sanlian shudian Ltd., 1989, pp. 178-182.

[36] See Zhang Yongjie and Cheng Zhizhong, Zhongguo di sidai, Taibei: Fengyun shidai chuban gongsi, 1989. The Toynbee-Ikeda dialogues, published in English as Choose Life: A Dialogue, Richard L. Gage, ed., Oxford, 1976, were published in China under the title of Zhanwang ershiyi shiji [Looking Toward the Twenty-first Century]. The issue of alienation is discussed under the subheading of "The Establishment and the Generation Gap" in Part I, chapter 5.

and a "sense of social concern" [youhuan yishi].[37] We may say that these three new values are actually the products of their social roles.

The first two terms are quite newly minted, while the third has a long history; yet all of them are attempts to define the moral quality of the intellectual's relationship to the nation. Shiming comes from the words for "envoy" and "order"; hence when an envoy takes an order, he is on a mission. This word has a meaning close to that of the English word "mission" without sharing its specific religious and diplomatic connotations. Zhongji guanhuai is a neologism which has become popular and fashionable amongst China's modern cultural luminaries. The term has a weighty moral connotation. It refers to the highest ideals and goals of the intellectual as cultural luminary. His task on the one hand should be the pursuit of knowledge and truth, which transcends all political and personal interests; and on the other hand it should be the creation and passing on of culture.[38]

Both these terms are related in turn to youhuan yishi, which derives from a consideration of the moral duty of the scholar in traditional China. Throughout China's history, the shi or "scholar-bureaucrats" have held an honored position in society, superior to all others, whether peasant, artisan, merchant or soldier. The shi was a bureaucrat who had achieved his status through learning the Confucian classics. In fact, the Analects specified the identity of the scholar and the public servant:

"Tzu-hsia said, *The energy a man has left over after doing his duty to the State, he should devote to study; the energy that he has left after studying, he should devote to service of the State.*"[39]

He thus labored with his mind, rather than with his hands, as Mencius said.[40] The establishment of Confucianism as an intellectual orthodoxy in

---

[37] On the translation of youhuan yishi, see p. 183, fn1. Su Xiaokang's views about youhuan yishi [translated either as "sense of sorrow and worry" or as "sense of social concern"] may be found in his essay "Shiminggan zhi wo jian" ["My view of a 'sense of mission'"], in Qiu shi, 1988.1, partially translated in this volume on pp. 40-43.

[38] The term also appears in the alternative forms zhongji guanqie or zhongji yiyi [ultimate meaning]. Both Xu Jilin and Bao Zunxin define and use it in the same way, though their illustrations appear in slightly different context. See Bao, op. cit., p. 169, and Xu, op. cit., pp. 86-87.

[39] See Arthur Waley, trans., The Analects of Confucius, New York: Macmillan Company, 1939, Book XIX, verse 13, p. 227.

[40] D.C. Lau, trans., Mencius, Penguin Classics, p. 101. *"There are those who use their minds and there are those who use their muscles. The former rule; the latter are ruled. Those who rule are supported by those who are ruled."*

the Han dynasty and the commencement of the examination system under the Tang confirmed the social position of the shi. Yet the shi was also expected to accept Confucian ideology without question, and to be completely loyal both to his ruler and to the state. Gradually, a sense of loyal concern became deeply imprinted in their minds. The famous essay "On the Tower at Yueyang" by the Song dynasty writer Fan Zhongyan provided the classic definition for the term you in youhuan:

"They [the ancient sages] neither delighted in the things of the world nor were saddened on account of their own individual fate. When in high position at court, they felt concern [you] for the people; when in exile in the country, they felt concern for their ruler; then whether in or out of office they were equally concerned. And so when did they enjoy themselves? It must be said that 'they felt concern before the rest of the world was concerned, and enjoyed themselves only after the rest of the world had enjoyed themselves.'"[41]

Several centuries later, at the beginning of the Qing dynasty, the term youhuan occurs in Wang Fuzhi's Du tongjian lun in something approaching its modern sense:

"Place yourself in the situation of the past, as if you were experiencing it yourself; focus your thoughts on the concerns of the ancients, as if they were your own responsibility. When you take on the sorrow and worry [youhuan] of the ancients for the safety and peril of the altars of the state, then the way in which you can now eliminate danger and achieve peace will appear; when you take on the consideration of the fortune and misfortune of the people of the past, then you will have a way to ensure prosperity and eliminate harm in the present."[42]

The same pattern of thought certainly had its impact on Su Xiaokang also.[43] If history is indeed a mirror into which we should look for present guidance, then Heshang may be seen as a case of following Wang Fuzhi's advice to look for the solution of present problems by focussing on the past. The text of Heshang shows an abiding concern for the problems faced by China in her attempts to reform and modernize, and is constantly linking the past with the present. Although the government had started the reform process in 1978 at the famous 3rd Plenum of the 11th Party Congress, by

---

[41] See Fan Zhongyan [989-1052], "Yueyang lou ji" in Gu wen guan zhi; see also Part Four, p. 175.

[42] Wang Fuzhi, Du tongjian lun [On Reading the <Comprehensive Mirror for Aid in the Art of Government>], Beijing, Zhonghua shuju, 1975, vol. 2, p. 1114. Quoted by Bao Zunxin in Pipan yu qimeng, p. 114.

[43] Su Xiaokang, "Shiminggan zhi wo jian," p. 48.

1988 the process had apparently stagnated, while problems such as inflation, official corruption, the economic difficulties of teachers and the continuing poverty of China's interior all pointed to a single conclusion: that the system was not working. Intellectuals were particularly distressed by their meager rewards, as was reflected in a number of popular sayings: *"Those who cut open the head are not as well off as those who shave it"*[44], and *"Those who make atomic bombs are not as well off as those who sell tea eggs."*[45] Their low income in turn became the reason for many people to look down on teaching as a profession. Su Xiaokang's investigative report on the teaching profession, Shensheng yousilu [The Teacher's Lament], had revealed that teachers enjoyed low pay, low status and low morale, while fewer and fewer college students had any interest in becoming teachers after graduation.[46] Ironically, it was the very process of economic reform and the reintroduction of material incentives that had led to the intellectuals' decline in status.

3. Third, the makers of Heshang had a shared sense that it was their generation's duty to take up the legacy of the May Fourth movement of 1919 and to complete its unfinished work. Most of this generation of "cultural luminaries" are ardent champions of the May Fourth legacy. Su Xiaokang, under the influence of historians Jin Guantao and Liu Dong had in fact decided to make a sequel to Heshang which would be called Wu si [May Fourth] and which would be produced in time for the seventieth anniversary of the May Fourth movement in 1989.[47] In September 1988, he and Xia Jun had already received funding; by year's end, they had worked out a detailed script outline and had shot three thousand hours of footage in the field.[48] The project was to be far bolder in concept than Heshang but could

---

[44] Kai naolu de bu ru ti toulu de; see Part Four, p. 175.

[45] Zao yuanzi dan de bu ru mai chaye dan de.

[46] See Su Xiaokang, Shensheng yousi lu; also Part Three, p. 156.

[47] In two of his articles Su Xiaokang mentions that the idea of making a sequel to Heshang originated with Jin Guantao. Jin felt Heshang's treatment of certain issues was flawed by factual errors and a lack of clarity, and that there should be a sequel to discuss those problems in depth. See W.L. Chong, op.cit., p. 47. See also Su Xiaokang's article, "Shijimo huimou: guanyu Heshang xuji de liuchan jilu" [A Glance Back at the End of the Century: Notes on the Miscarriage of Heshang's Sequel], in Heshang taolun ji, Zhao Yaodong et al., Taibei: Fengyun shidai chuban she, 1990, pp. 195-227. Here Su described his acquaintance with Liu Dong, who wrote the outline of the script for the sequel, and their forty-day trip to do outdoor shooting at the home towns of the eminent intellectuals of the May Fourth movement, including Chairman Mao.

[48] See Su Xiaokang, ibid., p. 226, and Guo Lixin, "Longnian de Heshang xianxiang — fang Heshang biandao Xia Jun" [The Heshang Phenomenon of the Dragon Year: An

not be completed, in part because of Su Xiaokang's signing of a petition calling for an amnesty for Wei Jingshen and other political prisoners.[49] He later described the proposed film's point of view as follows:

"We felt that the reason for China's backwardness was not the traditional culture, but on the contrary, the fact that by 1840 traditional culture had been destroyed, by many factors, one of which was the impact of the West. The new culture which arose after the destruction of the old was a disastrous combination of Oriental despotism and Stalinism. What we have now in China is Communist culture, not traditional Chinese culture. Our second film was about how such a disastrous system could have arisen in China. Thus we had moved from the cultural approach of Heshang to a criticism of the Communist system."[50]

The sequel was to have been a reflection on the May Fourth movement, revolving around three major themes: First, the cyclical character of reforms in China, the fact that the reform movement since 1978 had essentially followed the same progression from the economic and technological level, to the institutional level and finally to the cultural level that had occurred between the Opium War and the May Fourth movement. Second, the lack of a new culture of science and democracy to replace the old, resulting in a cultural desert which permitted the rise of the strong man politics of Mao and Deng. And third, the problem of Chinese intellectuals, who, like the traditional shi who preceded them, had not succeeded in becoming an independent political force.[51]

Let us briefly review two major aspects of the May Fourth movement, as a national salvation movement and as a new culture movement, in order to better see how Su Xiaokang and others have interpreted its legacy. The movement got its name from a demonstration at Tian'anmen in Beijing on May 4th, 1919, when several thousand college students protested the terms of the Versailles Peace Treaty, which had assigned former German territories in Shandong to Japan. The authorities brought in police to quell the demonstration, but demonstrations soon spread to other cities with popular support from merchants and workers. A patriotic movement to "save the country" [jiu guo] from the encroachments of imperialism had erupted.

Interview with Heshang's Director Xia Jun] in Zhong shi wanbao, September 11th, 1988; reprinted in Heshang taolun ji, Taibei: Fengyun shidai chuban she, 1990, p. 82.

[49] See Su Xiaokang, "Shijimo huimou," p. 226.

[50] W.L. Chong, op. cit., p. 47.

[51] Ibid., pp. 47-48. In his interview with Guo Lixin, Xia Jun said that the title had not been decided and that the three themes were science, democracy, and the closed-door policy.

The outbreak of this political movement had been preceded, however, by a movement to change Chinese culture. Around 1917, a new generation of intellectuals trained abroad such as Hu Shih and Chen Duxiu had attacked traditional Chinese culture and Confucianism in particular, charging it with the responsibility for China's weakness. They saw their task as that of spreading a new "enlightenment" [qimeng], and in order to do so they felt they had to completely transform the consciousness of the Chinese people.[52] While Hu Shih and other liberal intellectuals called for "wholesale Westernization," they essentially stayed removed from politics and advocated education as the way to make changes. More radical intellectuals, such as Chen Duxiu, came under the influence of Marxism and Leninism and proceeded to found a political party.

The potential conflict between the political and the cultural themes of May Fourth is mentioned in Part Two of Heshang:

To save our nation from danger and destruction, we should try to keep the foreign pirates at bay beyond our country's gates; and yet to save our civilization from decline, we should also throw open our country's gates, open up to the outside, and receive the new light of science and democracy. These extremely contradictory antiphonal themes of national salvation and modernization have taken turns over the past century in writing China's abnormally-shaped history..." [134]

The perception of May Fourth as a time of cultural crisis, a crisis in which traditional culture was the principal villain, helps to explain both the cultural approach of Heshang and its decision to attack the principal symbols of tradition, such as the Great Wall, the Yellow River, and the dragon. Heshang deliberately chose to adopt the iconoclastic approach to traditional culture of the May Fourth movement. Lin Yusheng has described the cultural agenda of the May Fourth movement as follows:

"... the most crucial factor of the May Fourth iconoclasm is what I have called, for want of a more adequate term, the cultural-intellectualistic approach. The intelligentsia believed in the necessary priority of cultural and intellectual change over social, political, and economic changes and not vice-versa. The word 'intellectualistic' is needed here because the iconoclastic intellectuals either implicitly or explicitly assumed that a

---

[52] Some scholars have a somewhat broader date for the May Fourth movement. For example, Yu-sheng Lin places it within the time span from 1915 to 1927. See his The Crisis of Chinese Consciousness: Radical Antitraditionalism in the May Fourth Era, Wisconsin: The University of Wisconsin Press, 1979, p. 3.

change of basic ideas qua ideas was the most fundamental change in the sense that this change was the source of other changes."[53]

Yet while it is easy to see similarities between the iconoclasm of May Fourth and the thinking of Su Xiaokang and his colleagues, they still needed a theoretical basis from which to critique traditional culture. If the traditional culture represented by Confucianism was indeed so flawed, how had it managed to endure for so many thousands of years?

The answer to this question was provided by Jin Guantao and Liu Qingfeng and their theory that China's society possessed a "super-stable structure."[54] Their theory had caused a small sensation when it first appeared, for it attempted to explain the long persistence of China's feudal society in new terms inspired by control theory and cybernetics, and not in traditional Marxist terms. Briefly, they see society as an organic system made up of three principal subsystems—the political, the economic, and the ideological or cultural—which provide mutual feedback and balance to each other. The principal agent of this mutual feedback between the various subsystems was the shi or scholar-official of traditional times, whose command of culture [knowledge, values, communications skills] provided the glue that would normally hold society together. Whenever one of the three systems went out of alignment—as, for example, when the increasing accumulation of landed property in the hands of a privileged class threatened the state's tax revenues—then the equilibrium of the whole system was lost. This breakdown could have two possible outcomes: either the total destruction of the old society, such that a qualitative change in the system occurred, as happened during the Industrial Revolution in the West; or the canceling out of those elements causing disruption, leading to a resumption of equilibrium and the restitution of the old system, as typically happened in China. China was thus an example of a "super-stable system" which required periodic instances of disorder and disintegration in order to maintain its long-term balance. One reason why the traditional social order could be restored after the collapse of a dynasty was because of the "isomorphic unity" of its political and cultural sub-systems. That is to say, the cultural

---

[53] Yu-sheng Lin, "Radical Iconoclasm in the May Fourth Period and the Future of Chinese Liberalism," in Reflections on the May Fourth Movement: A Symposium, edited and with an introduction by Benjamin I. Schwartz, Cambridge: Harvard University Press, 1972, pp.23-58; see esp. p.29.

[54] Their theory that Chinese society was a society of "great unification" and that the reason it failed to modernize was due to its "super-stable structure" is clearly spelled out in their book Xingsheng yu weiji, [Ascendancy and Crisis], Hunan renmin chuban she, 1984. An article by Daniel Kane entitled, "Jin Guantao, Liu Qingfeng and their Historical Systems Evolution Theory" in Papers on Far Eastern History, vol. 39, 1989, pp. 45-73, does an excellent job of summarizing and introducing their ideas, and provides good translations of the many new terms they have adopted.

sub-system consisting of patriarchal clans and a system of familial ethics would survive the disintegration of a dynasty and provide the template from which a new political sub-system, i.e., a Confucian bureaucracy made up of shi or scholar-officials, could be formed. Jin and Liu's theory, while posed in a new way, thus answers the question that has long puzzled historians of culture: why did traditional Chinese civilization, once so brilliant, stagnate for so long? Why did it not evolve into industrial civilization?

But there was a price to pay for this kind of super-stability. The periodic breakdown of the political unit was due to the accumulation of what Jin and Liu call 'asystemic forces' [wuzuzhi liliang], which cause enormous destruction of life and property when they burst out of control. In his role as advisor to Heshang, Jin Guantao suggested a useful comparison between the periodic outbreak of turmoil in Chinese society and the periodic destructive floods of the Yellow River.

Jin Guantao's theory of an historical pattern of repeated cycles would seem to have had some influence on Su Xiaokang and Liu Dong's interpretation of China's attempts at modernization over the last century. Su Xiaokang summed up Liu Dong's views as follows:

"He regarded China's pre-modern history [jindai shi] as a process in which modernization repeatedly advanced and suffered repeated setbacks. The evolutionary changes in Chinese civilization under the challenge of the West followed a necessary logic, advancing in turn from the material, to the institutional, to the cultural level, and finally pressing on to the fundamental change of values. In this sort of theoretical framework, not only must we affirm the changes made by the 'self-strengthening' faction at the material level, but we should also not be surprised at the failure of the 1898 reforms and the 1911 revolution at the institutional level. While the May Fourth movement finally grasped the main theme of modernization— i.e., to combine scientific rationality and humanistic rationality with the Chinese tradition—yet, just like the ... new culture movement, it took a wrong turning on May the Fourth..."[55]

What was this wrong turning? Bao Zunxin proposes the view that the May Fourth movement was an "incomplete nirvana" [wei wancheng de niepan] in that its intellectual leaders soon lost sight of the goal of liberating the individual in face of the need to mobilize the people to resist Japanese aggression. Hence the two goals of saving the nation and of establishing a new culture came into opposition. The goal of national salvation overwhelmed that of individual liberties, leading to the modern

---

[55] See Su Xiaokang, "Shijimo hui mou — guanyu Heshang xuji liuchan de jilu" [A Glance Back at the End of the Century: Notes on the Miscarriage of Heshang's Sequel], op. cit., p. 198.

situation, in which the state was freed from the tyranny of imperialism while the individual was still subject to the tyranny of the state.[56] Perhaps it is for this reason that in Part Six of Heshang the camera pauses thoughtfully on the sculpted scene of May Fourth demonstrators outside of Mao Zedong's Memorial Hall while the narrator comments: *"Many things in China, it would seem, should all start over again from May Fourth."* [216] The need to reflect critically on the failure of the May Fourth movement is hence one of the principal reasons for making Heshang.

But the question remains: Why did Heshang choose to attack Chinese culture? And why did it choose as its targets the three cultural symbols of the dragon, the Yellow River, and the Great Wall? From the artistic and the practical point of view, television's strong point is its ability to create vivid images, and these images serve to relate the varied thematic content of the series. On a deeper level, however, we may identify three reasons: The first is the idée fixe shared by China's modern intellectuals that culture is ultimately to blame for all of modern China's social problems. Chinese have called this a wenhua fuzui gan or "feeling that culture is at fault."[57] The second is the anti-traditional bias and cultural iconoclasm inherited from the May Fourth movement. In this sense, Heshang's attack on the Great Wall can trace its origin to Lu Xun's curse on the Great Wall.[58] Lu Xun's interpretation of the Great Wall as symbolizing the confinement of the spirit is quite similar to the point made in Part Two of Heshang. Third, the attack on culture is a way of giving vent to the strong emotions of anger and despair which the authors shared with the general public. Su Xiaokang admits that because they could not confront the party and the government directly, they attacked China's ancestors instead as a form of indirect critique.[59] Later Su Xiaokang himself came to recognize and acknowledge

---

[56] See Bao Zunxin, "Wei wancheng de niepan — dui wusi de fansi" [An Incomplete Nirvana — a Meditation on May Fourth], in Pipan yu qimeng, Taibei, Lianjing chuban shiye gongsi, August, 1989, pp. 103-139.

[57] W.L. Chong, op. cit. p. 46.

[58] Lu Xun interpreted the Great Wall as not merely a physical barrier but also a psychological barrier hemming in the Chinese people: *"I am always conscious of being surrounded by a Great Wall. The stonework consists of old bricks reinforced at later times by new bricks. They have combined to make a wall hemming us in. When will we stop reinforcing the Great Wall with new bricks? A curse on this wonderful Great Wall!"* in Lu Xun, Selected Works, vol. 2, p. 167. For more on the Chinese Great Wall psychology and the problems of enlightenment, see Vera Schwartz, "A Curse on the Great Wall: The Problem of Enlightenment in Modern China," Theory and Society, May, 1984.

[59] W.L. Chong, op.cit., p.46.

the strong element of emotion in <u>Heshang</u>, one which other scholars had pointed out earlier.[60]

III. Controversy: Enlightenment, Patriotism, and Politics

As mentioned before, after the first broadcast in June, 1988, the first wave of response from <u>Heshang</u>'s viewers and critics was overwhelmingly positive. One critic writing in <u>Jiefang ribao</u> went so far as to call it the new enlightenment movement for the post-1949 period, for having once again raised the banners of "democracy" and "science."[61] Later, as the "<u>Heshang</u> fever" began to cool down, some more balanced critical assessments began to appear, pointing out some of its shortcomings. Yet it is probably fair to say that the overall reaction was still positive.

Hence we must ask: How did <u>Heshang</u> become a political issue? What controversial or sensitive issues caused it the most problems? Were its makers patriots, or rebels? Did they overstep the limits of acceptable criticism?

Most critics outside the mainland have attributed the banning of <u>Heshang</u> to China's vice-president Wang Zhen. The Hong Kong press reported extensively on the trials and tribulations of <u>Heshang</u>, revealing Wang Zhen's personal critique of the film as well as his attempts to influence the leadership to ban it. He is reported to have contacted President Yang Shangkun, ex-president Li Xiannian, and Deng Xiaoping. But each of them made excuses to turn down Wang Zhen's request.[62] Hu Qili, head of the Central Propaganda Department, continued to make public statements upholding the party's policy of non-interference in questions of literature and art,[63] while Tan Wenrui, editor-in-chief of <u>Renmin ribao</u>, diplomatically refused to print an article condemning <u>Heshang</u>.[64]

---

[60] For example, Professor Li Zehou at Beijing University said, *"This reflects a kind of emotion, an emotion to search for change. It is understandable, worthy of sympathy and respect. As a work of art and literature it reflects the needs of the audience; it lets people enjoy watching it; its cussing makes them feel happy. But in terms of scholarship, one cannot depend merely on emotions."* See Li Yi, "Ting Li Zehou Liu Shuxian tan <u>Heshang</u>" [Listening to Li Zehou and Liu Shuxian Talking about <u>Heshang</u>], <u>Jiushi niandai</u>, December, 1988, p. 90.

[61] Yi Ren in <u>Jiefang ribao</u> [<u>Liberation Daily</u>], July 30, 1988, p. 7.

[62] Wang Zhen first talked to President Yang Shangkun, but Yang replied that the Party had a new policy that leaders were not allowed to interfere with literary and artistic works. Wang then asked Li Xiannian, who simply turned down Wang saying that his eye-sight was not good. See Liu Yanying's article in <u>Jingbao</u>, November, 1988, pp. 44-45.

[63] Hu made these remarks in a talk at the Fifth Literature Conference held in Beijing in November 1988 under the auspices of the Chinese Writers' Association. See He Shaoming,

While Vice-President Wang Zhen's ultimate motives for opposing Heshang are unclear, it is undoubtedly true that he would have been offended by Heshang's portrayal of the poverty of Yan'an. After 1949, Yan'an was held up as a glorious symbol of revolution and of the Chinese people's resistance to foreign aggression, yet Heshang deliberately chose to focus on Yan'an's economic backwardness. Wang Zhen, who holds the rank of general, is a member of the generation of leaders who lived in the Yan'an base area during the anti-Japanese war. He was in personal charge of a project to transform the Nanniwan district outside of Yan'an into a productive agricultural area, and at the time there was a song praising Nanniwan for having become as fertile as the Yangtze valley. Whatever his reasons may have been, Wang Zhen went public with his criticism in the September 28th issue of Ningxia ribao. At a round-table discussion concluding Wang's visit to Ningxia to celebrate the autonomous region's thirtieth birthday, Wang described the many accomplishments of Ningxia in economic development over the past decades, after which he commented:

"But there is a TV series named Heshang which describes the great Chinese nation and our Yellow River as not having a single good quality. As I see it, this film curses the Yellow River and the Great Wall; it defames our great people and the descendants of the Yellow Emperor and Fire Emperor."

As China's Vice-President, his words carried special weight and signalled the first truly public criticism from a political official. While his talk was not reprinted elsewhere, his remarks spelled the end to public debate in the press over Heshang. Subsequently, in late 1988, Hu Qili announced that the film would not be rebroadcast and that the published script would not be reissued.[65]

However, many have suspected that Wang Zhen's opposition to Heshang may have been due to Zhao Ziyang's attempts to protect it. Zhao Ziyang is reported to have praised Heshang during a conversation with Singapore's visiting Premier Lee Kuan Yew in the late summer of 1988. He is also reported to have obtained Deng Xiaoping's consent to convene a special meeting of the Politburo and the Central Party Secretariat to reiterate the Party's policy of non-interference in literature and art and to prevent the debate over Heshang from becoming a Cultural Revolution-style witch-hunt. Zhao Ziyang's involvement in the Heshang incident thus on the one

ibid., p. 12; Zhongyang ribao, November 2, 1988; and Xu Jingen in Jiefang ribao, November 10, 1988, p. 8.

[64] He Shaoming in Zhengming, November, 1988, pp. 12-13.

[65] This report appeared in Zhongyang ribao, November 26, 1988 and in the Far Eastern Economic Review, December, 8, 1988, p. 11, respectively.

hand saved the film from being banned too soon and gave it the opportunity to be rebroadcast[66]; but on the other hand, it also caused the leadership to take sides and created a means by which the conservatives could attack Zhao Ziyang and his reform program. In this whole process, Heshang was a convenient scapegoat of the political struggle, while the political struggle over Heshang can also be seen as a precursor of the factional struggle that would erupt between Zhao and the conservatives in the following spring.

Yet Wang Zhen could not have launched his attack without some ammunition, and this ammunition could be garnered from a variety of sources: from conservative Marxist scholars who willingly pointed out Heshang's heresies; from nit-picking scholars who delighted in pointing out its errors of fact; and from overseas Chinese scholars who got passionately involved in defending the value of traditional Chinese culture against the claims of superiority for Western culture. What, then, were the objections raised against Heshang by the critics?[67]

One of the frequent themes of Heshang's academic critics was its use of an oversimplified, black-and-white dichotomy between Chinese and Western culture. Hence Chinese civilization was a "yellow" civilization, tied to the land, isolationist and conservative, while Western civilization was a "blue" civilization, liberated by sea-power, open, expansionist, and progressive. Some criticized the oversimplification inherent in such statements,[68] while others found them proof of "ethnic nihilism" [minzu xuwu zhuyi], i.e., the proposition that nothing is right about Chinese culture. A corollary of "ethnic nihilism" was the charge that Heshang was Eurocentric or that it expressed an uncritical admiration of the West. A second kind of criticism was to detect different kinds of determinism in the script: thus, Heshang's description of China's geographical environment was interpreted as geographical determinism, while its use of Jin Guantao's "super-stability theory" left it open to charges of historical fatalism. A third kind of critique, though not one employed by the conservatives, was to question Heshang's cultural approach. Hence some criticized Heshang for "whipping our ancestors" when they really should have been directly criticizing the

---

[66] See He Shaoming, ibid., p. 12; and Jiang Cong, in Zhongyang ribao, December 9, 1988, p. 4.

[67] For a more detailed account of the criticism, see Su Xiaokang, "The Distress of a Dragon Year" in this volume, esp. pp. 291-299 and "Historians in the Capital Criticize Heshang: A Summary" also in this volume, pp. 311-327.

[68] Professor Liu Shuxian of Hong Kong, in a joint discussion with mainland philosopher Li Zehou, pointed out that Heshang oversimplifies problems that are extremely complex. See Li Yi, "Ting Li Zehou Liu Shuxian tan Heshang" [Listening to Li Zehou and Liu Shuxian Talk about Heshang] in Jiushi niandai, December, 1988, p. 89.

problems of the present[69]; others criticized Heshang for still being stuck in the May Fourth mindset which saw the transformation of the Chinese people's consciousness as the most important task. Yet another kind of criticism was to fault the historical methodology and accuracy of the script. Hence Heshang was berated for its "pragmatic" quotations from authorities such as Hegel, Marx, and Toynbee; for casually taking systems theory and cybernetics out of their original context and applying them in the field of history; and for making hundreds of factual errors.[70] In general, we may see the academic critiques of Heshang, especially those published in mainland China from the summer of 1989 onwards, as attempts to discredit Heshang's credibility while maintaining the fiction of an objective, academic discussion.

Yet the academic issues raised above were not Heshang's real threat to the regime; the real threat was its advocacy of ideas that challenged the ideological foundations of the system. Let us take three examples. (1) As mentioned above, Part Five of Heshang states that the peasant rebellions of Chinese history had no revolutionary significance but only displayed a startling destruction and cruelty. This is a denial of Mao Zedong's theory of history as well as a critique of the current regime, itself brought into existence by a peasant army. Jin's "super-stability theory" would also suggest that the China of today is just as feudal as it was in the past. From the point of view of the leadership, however, the past forty years of revolution have freed China from the "three huge mountains" of feudalism, imperialism, and Kuomintang bureaucratism. Hence the China of today cannot be a repeat of the past. (2) Heshang frequently criticizes the "spectre of great unity" that still haunts China, implying that throughout its long history and even today China is a kind of "oriental despotism." Yet if Heshang criticizes "unity," it must be advocating its opposite, either disunity or diversity. Yet for the current leadership, the territorial integrity of China is fundamental, while the importance of "stability and unity" [anding tuanjie] far outweighs any putative benefits of diversity of opinion. (3) Heshang champions the process of economic reform and throws its weight behind a change in the form of ownership; Heshang's advisor on economic matters, Li Yining, is a proponent of transforming moribund state-owned industries into joint stock companies in which the government

---

[69] See for example Wang Xiaodong and Qiu Tiancao, "Jiqing de yin ying" [The Other Side of Fervor] in Cui Wenhua, ed., Heshang lun, p. 192-195; see also Su Xiaokang, "The Distress of a Dragon Year" in this volume, p. 294.

[70] From August 9th to November 19th, 1989 Beijing wanbao printed a series of short articles attacking factual errors in Heshang; these articles were subsequently reprinted in Heshang pipan [bibliography item #34] and in Li Fengxiang, ed., Heshang baimiu [bibliography item #33].

would be a partner with private shareholders.[71] Yet this challenges the basic premise that socialism is founded on collective ownership and hints of the restoration of capitalism.

IV. Concluding Remarks

Judging from the sources available to us, the makers of Heshang never had any ambition other than facilitating a broad debate in society on China's future course. They presented themselves as patriotic intellectuals on the model of the 1898 reformers, as people driven by a concern for the nation's problems, and by their social conscience. Profoundly affected by the prevailing mood of disquiet throughout the country, they hoped to repeat the "enlightenment" movement of the May Fourth period and awaken the masses. They deny that they had political ambitions or were covertly linked with a faction in the leadership. Hence it is a tragedy for the prospect of reforms in China that Heshang was banned and her makers were branded with the stigma of treason.

Despite its faults and shortcomings, Heshang achieved a remarkable success in that, using the powerful tool of television, it presented its point to a broad cross-section of China's population: that China faces a crisis, and that reform is the only way out. It probably did not reach the vast majority of peasants, but it did create a new form for television. Like the May Fourth movement seventy years previous, it was only partially successful in its task of enlightenment. If Bao Zunxin is right in calling the May Fourth movement an "incomplete Nirvana," then Heshang is also an incomplete Nirvana. But it is not an illusory one, and the Chinese people will continue in future to take up the questions it has raised.

Su Xiaokang and his colleagues deserve praise for the intellectual vision and the moral courage it took to make Heshang. They only made one mistake. They forgot that *"if the intellectuals, as in the past, go beyond the limits of independence that the party has granted them, this relative liberalization could be rescinded as quickly as it has been released."*[72]

---

[71] Li Yining was one of Heshang's two main academic advisors as well as being a member of Zhao Ziyang's brain trust. See also Part Four, "The New Era," footnotes 51, 52, and 53.

[72] Merle Goldman, Chinese Intellectuals: Advise and Dissent, Cambridge: Harvard University Press, 1981, p. 240.

Opposite: Title page of the first edition of Heshang [Deathsong of the River] in book form, published by Xiandai chubanshe, Beijing, June 1988. The birds are in blue over a yellow background, surrounding an open white space, suggesting either a tree or an empty space into which blue water is flowing. Hence the design symbolizes the merging of traditional Chinese culture (yellow) with the modern world (blue). The cover bears the following four statements:

A reflection on the destiny of China's ancient culture

An exposition of our tragic national psychology

The "blueprint" which the newspapers have competed to print

A cooperative venture among famous scholars and writers

河殤

苏晓康
王鲁湘　总撰稿

- ● 揭示悲剧性民族心态
- ● 名学者作家合作契机
- ● 反思古华夏文明命运
- ● 诸报竞相刊载之蓝本

现代出版社

Arousing the Whole Nation to Self-Questioning—A Few Words on the
Design of the Television Series <u>Deathsong of the River</u>[1]

by Su Xiaokang

The Yellow River is a broad theme, spanning ten thousand <u>li</u> from east
to west, four thousand years from start to finish, and concerning a billion
people on both its banks.[2] The Yellow River has a strong connection with
the origins, history, culture and development of the Chinese people, as well
as with East Asian civilization and even world civilization. We believe that
bringing the Yellow River to the television screen is quite different from
treating the Yangtze River, the Grand Canal or other themes. Its uniquely
deep and rich connotations[3] cannot be matched by those of the Silk Road or
the Yangtze River.[4] If we presented the Yellow River according to the old

---

[1] This article is not part of the filmscript but occurs in the first published edition by the
Xiandai chubanshe, June, 1988.

[2] Director Xia Jun revealed in an interview that <u>Heshang</u> was originally to have been a
trilogy, with parts titled: "Ten Thousand <u>Li</u> from East to West" [dong xi yi wan li], "Four
Thousand Years from Start to Finish" [shang xia siqian nian], and "A Billion People on Both
Banks" [liang an yi wan ren]. See Guo Lixin, "Longnian de <u>Heshang</u> xianxiang—fang
<u>Heshang</u> biandao Xia Jun" in <u>Heshang taolun ji</u>, pp. 75-83.

[3] Connotations translates Chinese <u>neihan</u>. Throughout the six-part series, the Yellow River
acquires enormous and varied metaphorical significance: the Yellow River valley is the
cradle of ancient Chinese civilization; its heavy burden of yellow silt suggests the heavy
burden of past culture on the present; its periodic floods suggest the periodic upheavals in
Chinese society; the direction of its flow from west to east suggests the author's contention
that China must move from being an isolationist, land-based civilization to being a
progressive, sea-faring civilization.

[4] Here Su Xiaokang refers to a whole series of television travelogues that had been made in
recent years, with titles such as "Hua shuo chang jiang" [The Story of the Yangtze], "Hua
shuo yunhe" [The Story of the Grand Canal], etc. For a brief history of television
documentaries preceding <u>Heshang</u>, see Cui Wenhua, "<u>Heshang</u> dui Zhongguo dianshi de
qishi he zai?" [What is the Lesson of <u>Heshang</u> for Chinese Television], in Cui Wenhua, ed.,
<u>Heshang lun</u>, pp. 123-142, esp. pp. 123-127. Chen Hanyuan who as assistant chief of CCTV
gave great support and encouragement to <u>Heshang</u> had been involved in many of these
earlier documentaries.

way of thinking, with old techniques and in the old style, I'm afraid we would only be able to give a mediocre view of its scenery but would be unable to bring out its broad connotations and deep significance. Moreover, in presenting the Yellow River in the present context of reform and of opening up to the outside world, we must endow this topic with clear and strong contemporary characteristics, for to make an issue of the Yellow River under the great rubric of reform will be to make the broadcast of this TV film into an all-out inquiry into our nation's history, civilization and destiny. Only in this way can we do justice to the significance of the Yellow River and accord with the demands of the times.

Based on these considerations and at the same time for the purpose of distinguishing ourselves in point of view and content from the previously broadcast thirty-part series on the Yellow River,[5] we have tentatively proposed the experiment of a TV film of political commentary,[6] dealing with the Yellow River from the angle of the philosophy of culture.[7] Based on the successful experience of past television films, we felt that this sort of film, in the design of its form, should break new ground in the following aspects:

First, it should break with the tradition by which a travel film is organized by movement through space, especially the old-fashioned design by which a river film follows the current downstream from the source;

---

[5] This was a joint production by CCTV and NHK. Xia Jun, who would later direct Heshang, was a member of its film crew; Su Xiaokang, one of Heshang's chief writers, wrote the narration for several of the episodes.

[6] dianshi zhenglun pian: This is a newly-coined term, without a precise accepted definition, but one which suggests the discussion of controversial political topics. Su Xiaokang is attempting here to suggest the definition of a new genre.

[7] wenhua zhexue yishi. This is a new term, evidently based on the underlying theme of the Philosophy of Culture book series, edited by Meng Weizai and Bao Zunxin, which attempts to grasp the essence of a culture by looking at key philosophical and cultural concepts and observing how they contrast with those of other cultures. Meng Weizai's introduction to the series says in part: *In my view, all of the 'hardware' and 'software' created by mankind up to now, his systems and polities... can all be summed up as cultural phenomena, and thus can all be analysed and discussed from historical and philosophical viewpoints.* Bao Zunxin's introduction states: *Right now in China's intellectual and cultural circles there is a tide of interest in discussing culture. Participating in this discussion are the older generation of scholars as well as middle-aged experts. What is especially stimulating is that many promising young scholars have entered the discussion. They are all pondering the problems raised by modernization. Their thoughts all concentrate on one point, namely: can China's ancient culture in modern times bring forth a new spring? Do we dare to respond to the challenge offered us by modern Western culture? Culture calls out to philosophy, and philosophy has fallen in love with culture. The philosophy of culture is becoming a field that attracts people's attention.* See the prefatory material to Xie Xuanjun, Shenhua yu minzu jingshen, Wenhua zhexue congshu, Shandong wenyi chubanshe, 1986.

rather, it should attempt to select several large themes from the rich connotations of the Yellow River, building a framework based on individual special topics. These various themes [should] all arise from the Yellow River and moreover be thought-provoking issues in social thought with contemporary relevance; and the whole film [should] have its own internal logic. Thus, on the one hand, one can avoid the unstructured form of speaking a word here and then a line there, and on the other hand avoid cutting the Yellow River into so many fragments that none of the questions to be addressed could be discussed fully or in depth.

Second, it should abandon the inflexible framework of time and space, and organize the content of each episode along the logical thread of a meditation on a particular topic, so that the frame [huamian] becomes the re-creation and expression of thought and no longer, as formerly, the passive form in which the narration explains the frame, thus assisting in thoroughly displaying and bringing out the deep connotations of the Yellow River. In terms of technique, it could thus also break out of the restrictions of the rivercourse (space) and of history(time), shooting a scene by freely striding and leaping from one end of the river to the other and from past to present, editing a version that is many-layered and pluralistic both in perspective and in direction [duo fangwei], thus enabling the language of thought to be transformed into the language of the screen and giving viewers an artistic experience that is lively, vivid, rich and inspiring.

Third, it should break away from the old concepts and patterns of the worship of our land, history and ancestors, so long taken for granted in travel documentaries, and experiment with revealing the ancient Yellow River civilization of the Chinese people as well as its modern fate from a point of view of self-conscious reflection[8]; it should propose to bring information about all sorts of theories and thinking to the TV screen in large volume, endowing the film with a clear, rich and meaty awareness of the philosophy of culture, enabling it to offer people all sorts of ideas and to create the effect of a two-way dialogue with the audience and society, in the expectation that the broadcast of Deathsong of the River will elicit broad-based concern and discussion.

This sort of design will make what used to be the most important elements in a television film—frame, music and language, etc.—retreat to a position of secondary importance, placing the element of thought in first place. Thus from the very beginning Deathsong of the River deliberately

---

[8] Here 'self-conscious reflection' is an attempt to translate the Chinese term fansi, itself a translation from Western philosophy. Originally, it translated the nachdenken of Hegel, by which Hegel meant 'thinking about the process of thinking.' Contemporary Chinese writers have taken up this concept to mean self-conscious reflection on the past, particularly on traditional culture, in order to find a solution for China's present ills.

selected as script-writers several young and middle-aged scholars known for their scholarly attainments and in its design opened up special "studio" segments, inviting experts and scholars in all areas to present their views succinctly on the television screen. One could call this an instance of cooperation between television and the world of thought, an experiment in which the finest minds of contemporary China convey theory and information through the great medium of television. And only such a vast theme as the Yellow River could provide the opportunity for such cooperation.

The participation of the world of thought has greatly raised the quality of television, enabling us to command the strategic high ground of theory in the design of particular topics. For example, Part Five, "Sorrow and Worry," from the point of view of the Yellow River can only express the problems of flood and disaster; but from the point of view of history and culture this periodic flooding is extremely similar to the periodic upheavals in Chinese society. That two such completely unrelated phenomena could overlap here in a mutually-reinforcing way has rather surprisingly achieved a strong artistic effect.

In the six-part series Deathsong of the River, each part is an extremely large and complex theoretical problem; if we let the scholars write them up, then each question could become a very large volume. A television film is unable to conduct detailed and painstaking proof and must in addition overcome the dryness and lengthiness of theory. How, then, to solve this problem? Our method has been, in each part, to latch onto the most representative and most vivid symbol in order to advance our exposition. For example, Part One "Searching for a Dream" selects the "dragon," this modern totem of the Chinese people in order to dissect the ancient cultural mind-set of the people of a great river valley. Part Two "Destiny" is tightly linked with the Great Wall, this object colored by its accretion of a thick layer of the ideological dregs of an inward-looking, defensive civilization, in order to reveal this continental people's unavoidable destiny and the historical future in which it must overcome the limits of the soil. Part Three "The Light of the Spirit," by means of a seemingly flimsy or intangible light of civilization, makes clear that only a nation which opens up to the outside and which absorbs the nourishment of foreign cultures can continue to produce creative talents. Thus, television's strong point, of creating vivid images, is given free rein.

Although there is no subject more ancient than the Yellow River, yet any telling of the Yellow River legend must adhere closely to the present age, must face the perplexities, contradictions and difficulties of today, and must be closely tied to the real problems about which the people are concerned. Perhaps while experimenting with a TV film of political commentary, which could so easily be dull and dogmatic, we should especially seek out "activation" points [ji huo dian]. For no other method could be more stimulating than directly touching on the problems that people are concerned about. Thus at the same time that we discuss some ancient and difficult-to-understand subjects, we have also introduced lots of contemporary and influential incidents and socially sensitive questions that everyone knows about and debates constantly, such as: rafting on the Yangtze and Yellow Rivers; the worship of the dragon spirit; the plight of intellectuals; prices and the market; student movements; democratization; the "passion for studying culture"[9]; and so forth. Basically speaking, all these very real questions can find answers in the deepest "cultural roots" of our nation.

Deathsong of the River is very serious. In allowing television to take up the burden of so serious an inquiry, we may not have succeeded. And yet, even if all our various experiments should fail, the serious questioning that we have proposed here is crucial. Even if we are unable to find answers, China must still find them.

Yellow soil, yellow water, a yellow-skinned people—could all these be no more than mere coincidences? This ancient oriental skin color once terrified the Occident ("The Yellow Peril"). Napoleon long ago said: *"Don't awaken the sleeping giant."* And yet, when the Orient awakened, it had already lost to the West.

From the skullbone of Lantian Man[10] down to Confucius, it seems as if we can ask another question: Why of all things did the Chinese people happen to choose such a cultural pattern as Confucianism?

This sort of culture is undoubtedly a rich legacy for the entirety of world civilization, having not only produced countless geniuses and heroes while at the same time having raised the yellow race of Chinese people to become the largest space-time entity in all humanity, having forged for them a psychological structure that sought harmony and peace, that meticulously observed reason and order, that valued traditional human relationships, while yet being closed and conservative. And yet today it has already succumbed to an irreversible decline and has collapsed. In the final analysis, is this a good or a bad thing for the Chinese people?

---

[9] "The passion for studying culture" or wenhua re principally indicates the debate over traditional Chinese culture and whether or not it can be blamed for the backwardness of China today.

[10] Lantian Man is perhaps the earliest form of homo erectus yet found in China, named after finds in Lantian, Shanxi Province, dating from ca. 700,000 years ago.

Some say that we must shatter Confucian ideas and undertake a "wholesale Westernization"[11]; there are others who say that China's only way out is to adopt "Western learning for the essential principles, with Chinese learning for practical applications"[12]; and yet others say that we must reconstruct a "third flowering of Confucian civilization."[13] In recent years, no matter whether it is the Chinese intelligentsia reflecting [fansi] on the fate of Confucianism and discussing the question of a cultural strategy, or whether it is the grand ceremonies in honor of Confucius at Qufu,[14] all of these demonstrate that the self-questioning[15] of the Chinese people has already touched on the very cutting issue of the choice of a national culture.

We cannot change the color of our skins, just as we cannot change the color of the Yellow River. And yet we must rebuild the culture of Chinese people—the structure of their minds. This will be an extremely difficult and complex piece of culturo-philosophical systems engineering.[16]

---

[11] quanpan xihua. This was the view of the famous scholar Hu Shih writing in 1929, as well as more recently that of the famous astrophysicist and dissident Fang Lizhi. See Part Six.

[12] xiti zhongyong. This is a reversal of the slogan of the Westernization movement in the latter half of the 19th century which advocated "Chinese learning for the essential principles, Western learning for practical applications." The 19th century reformers thought that China could become strong and powerful by adopting Western science and technology but without significant changes in China's traditional moral values, political system, etc. The principal advocate of "Western learning for the essential principles..." is philosopher Li Zehou whose article entitled "Man shou xiti zhongyong" may be found in Li Zehou ji published by the Heilongjiang jiaoyu chubanshe in 1988 as part of their Kaifang cong shu, pp. 331-361.

[13] The advocacy of Confucian civilization is associated with the name of Prof. Du Weiming [Weiming Tu], who holds joint appointments at Harvard and at the East-West Center, Hawaii. See Part Six.

[14] Qufu in Shandong Province is the site where Confucius' lineal descendants, the Kong clan, have their family mansion and tombs.

[15] fanxing or 'self-questioning' is closely parallel in meaning with fansi, 'self-conscious reflection' defined above.

[16] Speaking in 1934 at a Congress of Soviet Writers, Maxim Gorky declared to Stalin that *the proletarian state must bring up thousands of excellent mechanics of culture, engineers of the soul.* While ironic in tone, this statement underlines a basic theme of Heshang, that reform of the economic and political systems cannot be divorced from changes in people's psychology and cultural concepts, which are frequently quite stubborn. The discussion of suzhi in Part Four is a case in point.

The Yellow River rushes ten thousand <u>li</u> and finally flows into the sea.

In this twentieth century, what kind of courage, insight, and self-questioning shall we muster in the face of the great risks of reform?

This then is our original intention in making <u>Deathsong of the River</u>.

Part One

"Searching for a Dream"

[Music, Tenor Solo]

Tell me—
How many bends does the Yellow River make?
On those bends
How many boats are there?
On those boats,
How many poles?
and on those bends
How many boatmen
Pole those boats?

On June 13, 1987, the rafting expedition on the Yellow River that had attracted the interest of hundreds and thousands of Chinese people sent back bad news.[1] Members of two rafting teams from Luoyang and Beijing were killed when the rafts overturned at the lower part of Lajia Gorge.[2] Our heroes Lang Baoluo and Lei Jiansheng, who had previously rafted through Tiger's Leap Gorge[3] on the Yangtze River, were also swallowed up by the swift water of the Yellow River. For a while, the entire nation was engaged in heated debate.

---

[1] The screen shows the photos of two young men and has a short note saying, *Lang Baoluo, a cadre of an athletic shoe factory at Luoyang city, died in June, 1987 while rafting at Lajia Gorge on the Yellow River. Lei Jiansheng, a history teacher at the Twenty-first Middle School at Luoyang city, died in June, 1987 while rafting at Lajia Gorge.* Part One of Heshang was broadcast June 11, 1988 almost exactly one year afterwards.

[2] This gorge is near Lajia Temple in Qinghai province, about two hundred kilometers south of Qinghai Lake. On the south river bank there is a small town called Jungong.

[3] Tiger's Leap Gorge [Hu tiao xia] is located in the northwest region of Yunnan province, in the Yulong shan (Jade Dragon Mountains) range, 5936 meters above sea level.

According to the news, these young men took this great risk because they would not let the American rafter Ken Warren[4] take away their right to be the first to raft down China's rivers. Ken Warren was very puzzled by this. He said that no one would object if Chinese came to America to raft down the Mississippi River. Of course Mr. Warren could never associate today's rafting with the history of a hundred years ago when the gunboats of the Western powers sailed China's rivers in disregard of China's rights. Yet the youth of China cannot forget.[5]

Now that these rafters have tossed their lives away in the Yellow River, should we praise them for their patriotism or should we criticize them for their blind love for their country?

No matter what, what they did happened on the mother river of our nation. It was both stirring and sad in the extreme.

This sort of thing is not restricted to river rafting. Just see how wildly excited Chinese people get at sports meets!

Whenever the five-star red flag is raised, everybody jumps up and cries.

But how about when they lose? They swear, throw things, and riot.

A nation which in its heart can no longer afford to lose.[6]

China's women's volleyball team has won the championship for five years in a row. Yet, pressing down on their shoulders is a heavy responsibility to the nation and to history.[7]

---

[4] Ken Warren is a white water rafter from Tualatin, Oregon. In the Spring of 1986, he paid China Sports Services over $325,000 for the right to be the first to raft down the Yangtze River. His proposal was perceived as a threat to national pride, and several Chinese teams were quickly formed to challenge Warren's team. The contest ended tragically, with the deaths of four Chinese and one American. [See Richard Bangs and Christian Kallen, Riding the Dragon's Back, New York, Macmillan Publishing Company, 1989; also Liu Kasu, "Piao," Baogao wenxue, 1987.7, pp. 2-16.] The following year witnessed a similar tragic contest on the Yellow River.

[5] The TV screen here establishes a contrast between: (1) color footage of the American flag being raised, and of the Statue of Liberty in New York harbor; and (2) black-and-white documentary footage of foreign warships and bombers in action, no doubt intended to remind the Chinese audience of the past history of Western and Japanese aggression against China, and to elicit a nationalistic response.

[6] The screen shows the China-Hong Kong men's soccer match held in Beijing on May 19th, 1985, which China lost; then scenes of distressed fans crying; then of the crowd overturning a car. Liu Xinwu described this event in his "5-19 chang jingtou." This reference is pointed out by Tsuji Kogo, the translator of the Japanese edition of Heshang, published by Kobundo, p. 19.

[7] The screen shows the China-U.S. women's volleyball match from the 1988 Los Angeles Olympics.

What if they lose next time?

Of course, there are quite a few people who no longer worry about these things. They have been in a hurry to leave their homeland to see what's up in the outside world. At the same time, a great number of lost sheep scattered overseas have come back to their homeland to see what's happening. What is the meaning of these two tides going in opposite directions?

Has our current state of mind been created by our past century of history, in which we were always the helpless victim? Or has it been created by the poverty and backwardness of the past few decades?

Perhaps so, but not entirely. What is hidden behind these phenomena is the soul of a people in pain. Its entire pain lies in the fact that our civilization has declined.[8]

In the beginning of this century, there was a young Chinese named Chen Tianhua,[9] who, when faced with the fact that his motherland was in a dark age, committed suicide in Japan by jumping into the ocean. At that time how many Chinese could understand him?

Even today when we recall this young man Chen Tianhua, it seems as if we can infer that his deep despair was perhaps a weak sigh over the decline of our civilization. . . .

---

[8] The TV screen shows Red Guards in Tian'anmen Square attending a mass audience with Chairman Mao; they shout, shed tears, and wave Mao's Quotations. A horizontal banner urges everyone to "celebrate the success of the Cultural Revolution." Coupled with the notions of "pain" and "decline" in the accompanying narration, the effect is highly ironic. In an interview with a Taiwanese reporter, director Xia Jun described his various ideas for finding the image that would best convey the notion of decline; here, he ended up using a montage in which scenes from the Cultural Revolution are superimposed over an ox plowing the field, thus tying together the two ideas of a small-holding peasant economy and a political structure that goes awry. See Heshang taolun ji, Taibei: Fengyun shidai chubanshe, 1990, p. 81.

[9] Chen Tianhua [1875-1905] was a young man from Xinhua district in Hunan province. While studying in Japan, he threw himself into the sea in December, 1905. His suicide, according to some Chinese scholars, was not due to despair over the decline of China's civilization, but because of his patriotic motives. At that time, the Japanese government proclaimed laws to punish some of the Chinese students. Since the content of the laws was insulting, Chinese students boycotted classes in protest. Japanese newspapers in turn mocked the Chinese students. As Chen mentioned in his suicide note, his death was a symbolic protest to the Japanese government, and he encouraged his peers to work hard to repay their debt to their country. Chen wrote two books, entitled Meng hui tou [Awakening] and Jing shi zhong [A Bell Warning the World]. See Jiang Liangfu, Lidai renwu nianli beizhuan zongbiao, Hong Kong: Zhonghua shuju, 1976, p. 748; also see Heshang baimiu [Heshang's Hundred Errors], Li Fengxiang, ed., Beijing: Zhongguo wenlian chuban gongsi, 1990, p. 155.

We can no longer avoid reflecting on the fate of China's ancient civilization!

(Titles: Part One, Searching for a Dream)[10]

In the present world, whenever a people with an ancient civilization comes face to face with the challenge of western industrial civilization and with the general tendency for the merging of cultures in this world, it encounters a serious crisis, both in terms of its present situation and its tradition. The more ancient the tradition, the more serious the crisis; the more serious the crisis, the more enthusiastic the search for roots.[11]

Where are the roots of the Chinese people?[12]

For every yellow-skinned Chinese it is probably common knowledge that the Yellow River conceived and gave birth to the Chinese people.

Then, how did this great river shape the character of our people? How did it determine the fate of our civilization in history? This is probably not a question that each of us has thought about seriously.

This is truly a rather unique river in the world. Arising from the snow-covered peaks on the north slope of the Bayan Kara Mountains, after passing the yellow soil plateau on its way eastward, it becomes a river of yellow mud. It just so happened that this yellow river bred a yellow-skinned people; and this people just happened to call their first ancestor the Yellow Emperor. On the earth today one out of every five people is a descendant of the Yellow Emperor.[13]

Yellow water, yellow soil, yellow people: what a mysterious yet natural connection this is. It would appear as if the skin of this yellow people were dyed by the Yellow River.

Indeed, in the whole world there is no other natural force like the Yellow River, which played such an incalculable role in the creation of

---

[10] The image used to accompany the title "Searching for a Dream" is adopted from the U.S. television series on China entitled The Heart of the Dragon. A red dot emerges from the upper screen, gradually enlarging to form a coiled dragon whose head, with blood-red mouth wide open, fills the screen.

[11] "Searching for roots," xun gen in Chinese, alludes to a popular trend in the literature of the 1980's in both mainland China and Taiwan. The search for cultural roots led many mainland writers and later film-makers to examine China's impoverished rural areas.

[12] The TV screen reveals a mountain top, with an inscribed stone tablet and the horned skull of a yak. The inscription, in both Chinese and Tibetan, reads, *The source of the Yellow River*.

[13] Here the screen shows the inauguration of Corazon Aquino, the female president of the Republic of the Philippines, whose ethnic heritage is also Chinese.

China's civilization. On this point, we do not need to come up with painstaking archaeological proof. We can get our proof by simply looking at an idol that in China is both most visible and highly-respected.

This idol can almost be considered as the symbol of our people. Yet, have people ever wondered why the Chinese people would worship such a cruel and violent-looking monster? This year happens to be a dragon year again and research on dragon worship has become a hot topic.[14] This is doubtless an example of searching for cultural roots.

It is said that our ancestors saw in the rainbow connecting heaven and earth the magnificent image of a huge two-headed serpent sucking water from the earth. Other people said that our ancestors saw in the lightning that split the clouds a golden serpent dancing wildly in the storm.

And so they created the image of the dragon.

This is a typical dream of a river people.

(The television studio. Scholars discussing the culture of the dragon spirit.)

Cai Dacheng (a scholar of mythology): *"From our point of view, the dragon is an assemblage that primitive people put together according to certain concepts. What are its component parts? It has the head of a horse, the horns of a deer, the body of a snake, and the claws of a rooster. Its snake body embodied the concept of life of primitive people. Primitive people rarely saw a dead snake; they thought that when snakes grew old, they would grow young again after casting off their skins. A chicken claw also is a symbol of life. When an old lady goes to the market to buy chicken, she always looks first at the chicken's rear claw. If the rear claw is short, the chicken is tender. It is the same thing with horse teeth. People used to ask, 'How old is it according to its teeth?' Deer shed their antlers once a year, and*

---

[14] Mao Zedong died in 1976, and Heshang was produced in 1988; both years are dragon years. In the traditional Chinese calendar, twelve years form a cycle in which each year is represented by an animal. In his article "Longnian de beichuang," Su Xiaokang points out this coincidence, concluding that the dragon year is inauspicious. His interpretation is the opposite of the traditional Chinese view, in which most people believe that the dragon year is the most auspicious and want to have a "dragon son" or a "dragon daughter" born in that year. See Long nian de beichuang, [The Distress of a Dragon Year], Hong Kong: Joint Publishing Co., Ltd., pp. 1-3. The dragon has been criticized by some younger Chinese scholars as a symbol representing feudal oppression, one which can no longer represent the image of a new and progressive China. See "Zhongguo bu zai shi long," [China Is No Longer a Dragon], in Shijie jingji daobao [World Economic Herald], March 21, 1988, which is an interview with Yan Jiaqi by reporter Dai Qing. An abridged version of this article was published in Renmin ribao, May 23, 1988, and has been translated by David Bachman and Dali Yang in Yan Jiaqi and China's Struggle for Democracy, New York: M. E. Sharpe, 1991, pp. 77-82. Another critical reinterpretation of the dragon may be found in Xie Xuanjun's article, "Zhongguoren de Huanghe xinli" [The Yellow River mindset of the Chinese people] in Longnian de beichuang, pp. 183-191.

once a year they grow new antlers. Each year they grow a new branch; as soon as deer hunters see how many branches there are, they know how old a deer is. The shedding of antlers symbolizes death; their growing back symbolizes life and rebirth. Therefore the dragon in its cultural connotation is a symbol of life, representing the hope of people in ancient times for rebirth in the cycle of life and death." [15]

Xie Xuanjun[16] (Vice-editor of the Philosophy of Culture series): *"The worship of the dragon spirit means that people worship something inhuman—the dragon. China's rulers appointed themselves the noblest beings in the human world—even the natural world. They thought they were the embodiment of the dragon. Looking at it in this way, we can find a connection between the two: the dragon is the tyrant of the natural world, while the emperor is the tyrant of the human world. Emperors wanted to disguise themselves as something inhuman."* [17]

In short, the reason why dragon worship could originate in the Yellow River basin was exactly due to the fear and respect of this river people for its river of life. For without doubt, the Yellow River is the most brutal and most unrestrained river in the world.

Some people say that there are elements in Chinese culture that tolerate the existence of evil forces[18]; while others say that in the Chinese national character there are the fatal shortcomings of being sly and slippery, fatalistic, and submissive to oppression. If so, this is by no means accidental. For a big agricultural country with a long history, water is the lifeblood of agriculture. But water is under the charge of the dragon king. Therefore, this people love the dragon yet hate it, praise it yet also curse it. What a complex emotion this is, as complex as the image of the dragon itself.

---

[15] In the broadcast version, this paragraph is much more colloquial and the last sentence is eliminated.

[16] Xie Xuanjun has published three books: (1) Shenhua yu minzu jingshen: ji ge wenhua quan de bijiao [Myth and National Spirit: A Comparison of Several Cultural Groups], Shandong wenhua chubanshe, 1987; (2) Huangmo ganquan [A Sweet Spring in the Barren Desert], Shandong wenhua chubanshe, 1987; Kongji de shendian: Zhongguo wenhua zhi yuan [The Empty Temple: The Sources of Chinese Culture], Sichuan renmin chubanshe, 1987. He has also published an article entitled "Zhongguo ren de Huanghe xinli" [The Yellow River Mindset of the Chinese People] in Long nian de beichuang, pp. 183-191.

[17] The term bu shi ren is a pun in Chinese, meaning literally "not a human being" and figuratively "inhuman." It is a very serious insult. Therefore, Xie's comments contain a very strong condemnation of China's rulers.

[18] See for example Xie Xuanjun's article cited above, "Zhongguoren de Huanghe xinli," p. 187.

As a result, Chinese people have also become complex. On the one hand, they offer sacrifices to the dragon to make it completely satisfied and raise it to the summit of power. On the other hand, when they beat drums and gongs to celebrate the harvest, they really make fun of this old critter in order to vent their anger for having kowtowed and worshipped it in fear and trepidation throughout the previous year. (Scene of dragon dance). This truly is a marvelous sort of Chinese-style wisdom and humor. By balancing fear and mocking, people achieve a subtle psychological equilibrium.

Just as the building of the pyramids resulted in the founding of the Egyptian state, so too the struggle with the Yellow River also made China coalesce. The history of our civilization begins with Yu the Great.[19] Over the past several thousand years, the thirst for water has given the Chinese people the strength to survive. To this day, this mysterious fate still hangs over drought-stricken north China.[20]

(Scenes from the movie "Old Well."[21] The battle. Sun Wangquan jumps into the well. The well collapses.)

The story that happened in Old Well Village in the Taihang Mountains profoundly reveals both the life force and the tragic fate of the Chinese people. In a sense it can almost symbolize the entire history of our people. For this reason this film has succeeded in conducting a dialogue with the whole world. It was from the Yellow River itself that the author Zheng Yi got his inspiration.

(The television studio. An author discusses the Yellow River.)

---

[19] Yu the Great was the virtuous founding king of the legendary Xia dynasty (ca. 2205-1800 BC). His father Gun had been appointed by King Shun to control the floodwaters. Gun was executed for not fulfilling his task. His son, Yu the Great, was born from his father's stomach; he carried on his father's task and brought the flood waters under control. The Chinese flood myth is discussed in Derk Bodde, "Myths of Ancient China," in Noah Kramer, Mythologies of the Ancient World, pp. 399-400.

[20] Here the screen shows the "praying for rain" scene from the film Huang tudi [The Yellow Earth], directed by Chen Kaige. The scene depicts a crowd of peasants kneeling down before an image of the rain dragon, their heads bound with green foliage.

[21] The film script was written by Zheng Yi himself based on his novel, and the film was directed by the well-known director Wu Tianming. It won the Best Feature Film award at the Tokyo International Film Festival in 1987. Laojing [Old Well] is a tragic story about the struggles of the people in Old Well Village to fight to obtain scarce water. The village is located in the Taihang Mountains in Shanxi province. The villagers tried for three generations to find their own well and lost many lives in digging wells that collapsed. Finally in 1983 they succeeded in digging a well which provided fifty tons of water a day. The interesting thing is that in the movie the hero, Sun Wangquan, did not jump into the well; rather, he was pushed into the well in the midst of a fight between two villages over water rights.

Zheng Yi[22] (an author from Shanxi): *"Three years ago, I travelled on a bike from the Shanxi-Inner Mongolia border to Henan Province. I travelled almost ten thousand li, passing through the entire Jinshaan Canyon[23] and several dozens of towns and districts. That was a very important experience for me. Only after I had that first direct and personal experience of the Yellow River did I understand why the Yellow River is the symbol of our people. The route I travelled was the birth places and the capitals of the legendary kings Yao, Shun and Yu.[24] Later the history of the Chinese people was played out on this stretch of land in drama after vivid drama. The experience also completely changed my concept of literature. I heard a story in a small village. Once there was a whole village of farmers who made their living along the banks of the Yellow River. Later because of the decline of the shipping business and because there was not very much land for them to plow, they could no longer make a living. The government moved them to another place, giving them land and building them houses. Several years later, these people unaccountably returned one after another to the banks of the Yellow River. They found and settled down in the same cave houses[25] they had lived in before. I simply could not understand what kind of psychology this was. Later, after thinking for a long time, I realized that this was an unexplainable emotional bond between people and the land—a bond like that between flesh and blood.*

I believe this story reflects my feelings rather well. As soon as I finished my journey along the Yellow River, I knew I had found what I must write about. In these past few years I had been searching for something in literature without quite knowing what it was I was searching for. Yet as

---

[22] Zheng Yi, born in 1948, was from a well-off family and went to a prestigious middle school affiliated with Qinghua University in Beijing. Unfortunately, like millions of others, he did not finish his education but was sent down to the countryside. In 1979 he attained notoriety for publishing the short story "Maple," one of the first works to describe bloody factional fighting in the Cultural Revolution. For the text of "Maple," see Perry Link, ed., Stubborn Weeds, Indiana University Press, 1983, pp. 59-73.

[23] When the Yellow River leaves Inner Mongolia, it is blocked by the Lüliang Mountains and turns its head southward, crossing the yellow soil plateau and forming the Jinshaan Canyon along the border between Shaanxi and Shanxi provinces. This is a particularly turbulent, unnavigable stretch of river.

[24] Yao, Shun, and Yu are three sage kings in Chinese legend. Confucius and Mencius praised Yao and Shun in particular because in their old age they abdicated their thrones to a virtuous person, rather than to their own son; hence they exemplify the principle of rule by virtue. In later times, they became the model for China's emperors.

[25] A yaodong is a kind of cave house either dug into a cliff of yellow soil or excavated below the ground. Because of the strong cohesive force of the yellow soil, the cave house does not collapse.

soon as I saw the Yellow River, I immediately felt that what I wanted to write about was the Yellow River."[26]

The more difficult the environment, the stronger the positive force to stimulate the development of civilization; this is a well-known idea among Western historians.[27] They think the reason why the Yellow River became the cradle of ancient China is possibly because the natural challenges that men had to face here, in contrast with those in the south of China—the Yangtze River basin, for instance—were much more severe. People's untapped creative talents were provoked by the challenges.

The civilization nurtured by the Yellow River is indeed one that matured very early in human history. The struggle with an adverse climate and with flood ensured that the technologies of water control, the calendar system, land measurement, agricultural plowing, animal husbandry, ceramics, and metallurgy reached maturity at least one thousand years earlier than in the West. However, exactly because of this, China has followed a purely Oriental path in its historical evolution, its societal mechanisms, its political organization, and so forth.

If someone should tell you today that the long-lived despotism of oriental societies was related to water, you might think it strange. As a

---

[26] The broadcast version eliminates this paragraph.

[27] As pointed out by Heshang's critics, the theory referred to is that of Arnold J. Toynbee in his A Study of History. In Chapter V, "Challenge and Response," Toynbee writes: *If we consider next the genesis of the Sinic civilization in the lower valley of the Yellow River we shall find a human response to a challenge from physical nature which was perhaps even more severe than the challenges of the Two Rivers and of the Nile. ... The fathers of the Sinic civilization do not seem to have differed in race from the peoples occupying the vast region to the south and south-west which extends from the Yellow River to the Brahmaputra and from the Tibetan Plateau to the China Sea. If certain members of that wide-spread race created a civilization while the rest remained culturally sterile, the explanation may be that a creative faculty, latent in all alike, was evoked in those particular members, and in those only, by the presentation of a challenge to which the rest did not happen to be exposed.*—From Vol. 1, p. 74 in the two-volume abridgement of Toynbee by D.C. Somervell, Oxford Univ. Press, 1946. Compare also Chapter VII, "The Challenge of the Environment," pp. 88-89: *We have now, perhaps, established the truth that ease is inimical to civilisation... Can we say that the stimulus towards civilization grows positively stronger in proportion as the environment grows more difficult?...Let us, as a first example, consider the different degrees of difficulty presented by the lower valleys of the two great rivers of China. It seems that when man first took in hand the watery chaos of the lower valley of the Yellow River, the river was not navigable at any season; in the winter it was either frozen or choked with floating ice, and the melting of this ice every spring produced devastating floods which repeatedly changed the river's course ... The Yangtse, on the other hand, must always have been navigable, and its floods, though they occasionally assume devastating proportions, are less frequent than those of the Yellow River. In the Yangtse Valley, moreover, the winters are less severe. Nevertheless, it was on the Yellow River and not on the Yangtse that the Sinic Civilization came to birth.*

matter of fact, this view was mentioned by Marx and Engels. They thought that the natural climatic conditions in the Orient made large-scale man-made irrigation works a principal requirement for agriculture and that due to the level of production at that time, this task necessitated a highly-centralized autocratic regime to organize the thousands and tens of thousands of people required to accomplish it. This is the well-known concept of the "Asiatic Mode of Production."[28] Unfortunately, Marx and Engels did not explain this question thoroughly and clearly but left an unending debate to later generations.

In fact, no matter whether it be the pyramids of Egypt, the Grand Canal and Great Wall of China, or the pyramids of the Maya people in the jungles of South America [sic],[29] don't all these amazing feats of ancient engineering cast the same "Asiatic" dark shadow in history? Are they not all the relics of ancient empires?

---

[28] Marx's concept of Asiatic society attempted to explain two questions: why had brilliant Asian civilizations disappeared so rapidly in the past? And why had Asian society typically resisted the Western pattern of economic development? Writing in 1853, Marx emphasized the important role played by public works and especially water control in Asiatic societies: *Climate and territorial conditions, especially the vast tracts of desert... constituted artificial irrigation by canals and waterworks the basis of Oriental agriculture. ... This prime necessity of an economical and common use of water... necessitated in the Orient ... the interference of the centralizing power of government. Hence an economic function devolved upon all Asiatic government: the function of providing public works. This artificial fertilization of the soil, dependent on a central government and immediately decaying with the neglect of irrigation and drainage, explains the otherwise strange fact we now find: whole territories barren and desert that were once brilliantly cultivated...* [From "The British Rule in India," 1853.] In 1858, Marx noted the essentially static nature of Asiatic society and attributed it to the self-sufficient village commune: *The fundamental characteristic of this system was the self-sustaining unit of manufacture and agriculture within the village commune, which thus contains all the conditions for reproduction and surplus production within itself, and which therefore resisted disintegration and economic evolution more stubbornly than any other system...* [From Pre-Capitalist Economic Formations, New York, International Publishers, 1965, pp. 33-34.] Marx's ideas were in turn influential on Max Weber's concept of China as a "patrimonial state" and on Karl Wittfogel's theory of an "Oriental despotism" founded on the need for water control. A good account of these theories is provided by archaeologist K.C. Chang, who summarizes his own views by saying that: *...the theory of water control as the primary base of state power does not find support in the archaeology of the Three Dynasties. Evidence for water control is not prominent in the archaeological or inscriptional record of ancient China; the mechanisms of power evolved in other realms.* [From Art, Myth, and Ritual: The Path to Political Authority in Ancient China, Harvard Univ. Press, Cambridge, 1983, p. 126.] Another useful critique of these theories may be found in Andrew L. March, The Idea of China: Myth and Theory in Geographic Thought, Praeger, 1974.

[29] The Maya people and their civilization are found not in South America, but rather in Mexico and Central America. For the Maya-China continuum, see K. C. Chang, The Archaeology of Ancient China, pp. 419-422.

In a society of "great unification" composed of myriads of weak and insignificant individuals,[30] organized together to hold up a supreme ruler, is not the social structure very similar to a great pyramid? Therefore, it is very difficult for things such as democracy, freedom, and equality to become "Asiatic."

"Asia" is an ancient Semitic word, meaning "the place where the sun rises."[31] Where the three great continents of Europe, Asia, and Africa meet in the north temperate zone of this planet, there are several rivers originating from snow-covered mountains each of which has given birth to one of the oldest human civilizations.

The Yellow River, the Nile [sic],[32] the Tigris, the Euphrates, and the Indus are all famous rivers of the Orient that became cradles of human civilization. Thus Asia was the place of origin. The dawn of civilization rose from Asia, just as the sun rises from the east.

But five thousand years have passed, and the sun of Asia has set. The several ancient civilizations, which were the earliest to shine, have all faded out one by one.

Why is this?

(Reappearance of the title: "Searching for a Dream")

The ancient city of Babylon, which once rose above the Tigris-Euphrates Valley, has long disappeared without a trace. After the fall of Sumerian civilization eight thousand years ago, the Mesopotamian Plain was flooded by repeated conquests, empires fell one after another, and many ancient peoples successively disappeared from history. By around 300 B.C., Emperor Alexander the Great had already burnt the magnificent palaces of the Persian kings.[33]

The Great Pyramid along the bank of the Nile, too, seems like an illusion that has retreated into history, forever confused and blurred. The sorrowful Sphinx crouches here, as if unwilling to explain anything. The ancient Egyptian empire, in its course of thirty dynasties over several

---

[30] Here the screen shows rows and rows of terra-cotta warriors from the tomb of Qin Shihuang. For more on "great unification," see Part Five, p. 195.

[31] This sentence is printed on the screen over a background of a red setting sun. This image is then contrasted with the image of the blue earth seen from outer space. This blue earth is re-used in Part Six in association with the title "Blueness"; Part Six also contrasts the blue earth with a red setting sun.

[32] While the Nile is not normally considered part of the Orient or Asia, the Orient does commence on the eastern shore of the Mediterranean with what used to be the eastern Roman empire and was subsequently Byzantium.

[33] The war between Rome and Persia occurred in 333 B.C.

thousand years, was once as strong and unsurpassed as this pyramid. But long before the arrival of Alexander, it had fallen into the hands of the Persians. In the several thousand years that followed, its destiny, up to recent times, was to be conquered by others.

In the river valleys of the Indus and the Ganges, which were further to the East and even more fertile, an ancient civilization, entirely cut off from the West, had already existed for several decades[34] before Alexander's expeditions. Someone has said that there is no need to mention the word "sea" in writing India's history until the most recent four hundred years. Nevertheless, when the European pirates appeared in the Indian Ocean, this civilization could not escape its doom.

The civilization of the yellow people on the other side of the Himalayas has been unusually long-lived. This would seem to be an exception. The question why feudal society endured for so long in China has been debated for many years, and people have offered all sorts of explanations, but all of them have considered this to be a special phenomenon.

But in actuality, what is truly unusual is not the antiquity of the Orient but rather the sudden changes that occurred in Europe. Professor Zhang Guangzhi, a Chinese scholar at Harvard University in the U.S., believes that the Sumerian civilization in the Tigris-Euphrates River Valley, because it stressed factors such as economics, trade and technology, later merged with ancient Greek civilization in the Mediterranean Sea, giving rise to some new path-breaking elements of civilization, and finally moved towards modern Western industrial civilization. In the entire history of human civilization, its path was not the ordinary one.

In the process of mankind's transition from barbarism to civilization, the Oriental Asiatic Mode was actually the general and normal path in the world. Professor Zhang Guangzhi has studied the similarities between Chinese civilization and the Maya civilization of central America; he thinks that they are the products of the descendants of the same ancestors, yet at different times and places. He thinks that all the ancient civilizations of Asia, Africa, and the Americas share some similar universal characteristics.[35]

---

[34] Narrator Zhang Jiasheng here reads the character shi [ten] as qian [thousand], so that the audience hears "several thousand years." One of the first civilizations on the Indian subcontinent was the Harappan culture of ca. 2500 BC, but the first unified empire, the Mauryan dynasty, was from ca. 324 BC to 187 BC.

[35] In comparing the differences and similarities between civilizations, Zhang says, *When we do so we find that China is far from being unique—rather, its pattern is repeated within many other ancient civilizations. . .In fact, most if not all of the essential characteristics of ancient Chinese civilization are also seen in ancient Mesoamerican civilizations.* See

Therefore, it is not that Chinese civilization is particularly unique. Its long existence is just the final struggle of the entire ancient world. The challenge that Asia has encountered is a challenge from Europe to all of mankind.

Just because of this, the antiquity of their civilization has made the burden of tradition particularly heavy in Chinese people's psychology. Now that the Yellow River civilization, like Egyptian civilization and Indian civilization, has finally declined, the spirit of the Chinese people has become especially sad and pained.

Why did the large oriental country that made Marco Polo sigh with surprise, the great people that frightened European rulers into fabricating the theory of the "yellow peril," the sleeping lion that made the peerless Napoleon warn the West not to wake it up, in recent times fall into such a helpless state that others carved up its land?[36] And why is it that now, after we have finally gotten over the danger of racial and national extinction, we suddenly feel so big and strong?

In our feelings about ourselves as a nation, there is a misapprehension: we seem to think that the humiliation of the past century was merely an aberration in our long and glorious history. Since 1840,[37] there have always been people who like to use the glories and greatness of the old times to cover up the poverty and backwardness of the recent past.

Throughout the real suffering of the past century, it seems as if we have always needed an ancient and enduring tranquilizer to soothe ourselves. In every archaeological find that has startled the world, we seem able to take momentary comfort.

Yet in the final analysis, our civilization has declined.

The richness of our history and the length of our civilization are after all yesterday's stories.

No matter how rich our archaeological discoveries, how fine our cultural relics, how far we push back the origins of our civilization, don't all these things mean that our ancestors are mocking their descendants?

Kwang-chih Chang, The Archaeology of Ancient China, New Haven: Yale University, fourth edition, 1986, p. 419.

[36] Here the TV screen shows black-and-white newsreel footage of the Sino-Japanese war: fleeing Chinese soldiers die as Japanese bombers deliver their payloads overhead. The same images reappear in a montage, in which the image of a hand plucking the guzheng is superimposed over a series of scenes: the Forbidden City; a criminal in pre-war China being executed by a pistol shot to the head; crowds of refugees; children crying.

[37] The date of the Opium War between China and Great Britain.

Don't they make us feel our regret, remorse, and humiliation about the present even more deeply?

It is said that the director of an automobile plant stood one day on the wall at Tian'anmen counting the passing cars on Chang'an Boulevard one by one. When he had counted one hundred cars, he found that only three of them were made in China. All the other ninety-seven cars were imported.

This incident lets us recall the thick smoke of the opium burnt by Lin Zexu in 1840, as well as the movement to boycott Japanese goods in the 1930s.[38]

Nevertheless, history and reality are rudely mocking us. Our pride and our sorrow are often the same thing.[39]

(Zhang Mingmin wearing a long gown embroidered with dragons and singing "The Heirs of the Dragon.")[40]

What Chinese is not familiar with this song?

Do you hear a deep sigh in this song?

Yet what is the use of sighing?

(The Nine-dragon Screen. Dragon boats spurting fire. Stone pillars with coiled dragons. Dragon year postage stamps.)

---

[38] Imperial Commissioner Lin Zexu [1785-1850] forcefully confiscated and burned a great amount of opium at the Boca Tigris in 1839. His action was the immediate cause of the Opium War between China and Britain. The boycott of Japanese goods was a movement initiated by students as a response to the Mukden incident of September 18, 1931, in which officers of the Japanese Kwantung Army launched an attack on Kuomintang troops stationed at Mukden. Chinese patriotic students then initiated a movement to boycott Japanese goods, which quickly spread to the entire nation and gained the support of workers and peasants. Yet the boycott did not halt Japanese aggression, and in 1937 China finally declared war on Japan.

[39] The screen shows first, the bas-relief white marble sculpture from Mao's Memorial Hall, depicting the Opium War, then the muzzle of an antique cannon. Taken in the context of the statement that *"history and reality are rudely mocking us,"* are we perhaps being reminded of Mao's dictum that *"Political power grows out of the barrel of a gun"*?

[40] The song was written by Taiwan songwriter Hou Dejian and quickly became popular both in Taiwan and the mainland. In this song Hou uses the Yellow River and the Yangtze River as symbols to evoke Chinese people's patriotism and nationalism. Here the screen shows Zhang Mingmin singing the second stanza: (II) *In the ancient East, there is a dragon, its name is China; in the ancient East there is a people, they are all heirs of the dragon. Under the protection of the huge dragon, I grow up; after growing up, I become an heir of the dragon. Black eyes and black hair, we forever will be heirs of the dragon.* Hou Dejian moved from Taiwan to China in the 1980s and was active in the 1989 Democracy Movement.

This venerable yet frightening old image was once the embodiment of our ancestors' nightmares. Do we still want to use it to focus our current feelings of sorrow and longing for the past?

Dragon worship would seem to prove that the soul of our nation is still deeply attached to the atmosphere of that ancient culture born from the Yellow River and still stuck fast in the dark shadow of our ancestors. This soul seems to be living in a dream. Yet today the time has come to bring it fully awake.

Maybe we should not mind other people coming to raft on our Yellow River. River rafting is after all but a sport, and risking one's life to do something out of spite is not an expression of strength. Someday when we finally rediscover the real meaning of sport, and then go rafting on their Mississippi, that will be a very elegant and refined sport.

We don't have to pound our chests and stamp our feet to express our regret at losing a ball game or several championships. Olympic gold medals cannot prove we are a strong nation.[41] Our thousand-year old dream of empire already came to an end long ago in the time of Emperor Kangxi [1662—1722].[42] Now the most important thing is not to cheat ourselves any more.

Our civilization has declined,[43] but we don't have to feel sad. Without exception, all the river valley civilizations in the world have declined. The British historian Toynbee has estimated that out of twenty-one civilizations in human history, fourteen have vanished, six are in decline, while only ancient Greek civilization has been transformed into industrial civilization and has overwhelmed the entire world.[44] We should face history bravely.

---

[41] In his lengthy journalistic essay "Qiang guo meng" [The Dream of Being a Strong Nation], Zhao Yu criticizes China's nationalistic psychology as it is expressed in international athletic contests. To him the reason that Chinese cannot afford to lose athletic matches is that Chinese need victory as an outlet for the depression and shame caused by the humiliations of the past hundred years at the hands of foreigners. The subtitle of the article says, "Remember the essence of the Olympic spirit: What is important is not winning, but participating." For his article, see Liu Yangdong and Meng Chao eds, Zhongguo chongji bo: dangdai shehui wenti baogao wenxue xuan [Waves Striking China: A Selection of Contemporary Reportage on Social Problems], Beijing: Renmin daxue chuban she, 1988, pp. 145-237. Su Xiaokang describes his acquaintance with Zhao Yu in Long nian de beichuang, p. 8.

[42] For Emperor Kangxi's biographical sketch, see Arthur Hummel, Eminent Chinese of the Ch'ing Period, pp. 327-331.

[43] Here we see one of the beehive-shaped royal tombs from the Xi Xia dynasty, which are used in Part Two in association with the title "Destiny."

[44] Toynbee, ibid., pp. 42, 244-245. For a list of the 21 civilizations, see Table V.

History has proven countless times that the decline of a civilization is not caused by attack from external forces, but rather by the degeneration of its internal system.

Toynbee said that the greatest role of an outside enemy is to strike a final blow to a society that has already committed suicide, yet not drawn its last breath.[45]

For thousands of years, the Yellow River civilization was under constant attack from the outside but never fell. We have always appreciated its great power to assimilate other cultures. But today at the end of the twentieth century, even though external attacks are no longer accompanied by cannons and iron hooves, our ancient civilization can no longer resist.

It has grown old and feeble.

It needs a transfusion of new blood for its civilization.

Oh, you heirs of the dragon, what the Yellow River could give us has already been given to our ancestors. The Yellow River cannot bring forth again the civilization that our ancestors once created. What we need to create is a brand-new civilization. It cannot emerge from the Yellow River again. The dregs of the old civilization are like the sand and mud accumulated in the Yellow River; they have built up in the blood vessels of our people. We need a great tidal wave to flush them away.

This great tidal wave has already arrived. It is industrial civilization. It is summoning us!

Su Xiaokang

---

[45] The quote from Toynbee is reprinted on the screen, superimposed over the scene from the film Huo shao yuanming yuan of the burning of the Summer Palace in 1860. See Toynbee, ibid., p. 272: *We may fairly conclude from the foregoing inquiry that the cause of the breakdowns of civilizations is not to be found in loss of command over the human environment, as measured by the encroachment of alien human forces upon the life of any society whose breakdown we may be investigating. In all the cases reviewed the most that an alien enemy has achieved has been to give an expiring suicide his coup de grace. ...*

Part Two

"Destiny"

On February 2nd [sic][1], 1972, U.S. President Nixon shook the hand of Zhou Enlai[2] [1898-1976] at the Capitol Airport. Ever since the birth of New China, this was the first time that China had shaken hands with the West. Seven years later, Deng Xiaoping visited the U.S. This too was the first time in more than thirty years that China had truly gone out to encounter the West.

How difficult it was for China to take this step! Without seeking earlier examples, even in the "Cultural Revolution," didn't the "Gang of Four" keep yelling that "buying ships" [from the West] was equivalent to "selling out the country"?[3] By the time we finally announced to the whole world that we would open up to the outside and spread wide the gates of our country, how unfamiliar we were with this planet! Have we forgotten, that at the same time that we were powerfully attracted by color TV's, refrigerators, and high-class cars, how difficult it was for us to bear the sight of things such as blue jeans, shoulder-length hair, and disco?

For a country that has been isolated too long, for a people that has traditionally regarded itself as "The Middle Kingdom," to open up the nation's gates and to go out to meet the world is something that only the experience of countless disasters and embarrassments could make them realize. This was both a painful choice and an enlightened one.

---

[1] Should be February 21st, 1972.

[2] In the second broadcast, "Zhou Enlai" is changed to "Chinese premier Zhou Enlai." Zhou, as Premier of China from 1949 on, worked with Kissinger to pave the way for the Nixon visit of 1972 and the normalization of U.S.-Chinese relations.

[3] From 1971 through 1976, China purchased 250 freighters, tankers, and bulk carriers as part of an ambitious program to update its merchant fleet. Criticism of this program surfaced in 1974, when the purchase of foreign ships was characterized as "worshipping things foreign" and as "betraying the country." See Bruce Swanson, Eighth Voyage of the Dragon: A History of China's Quest for Seapower, Naval Institute Press, 1982, p. 267.

This choice, in the final analysis, was our destiny in history. When we look back on history today we can discover that the destiny which once ruled our ancestors is now forcing us to make this choice!

(Titles: Part Two: Destiny)[4]

Humankind worships the sun.

Some say that the first valuable gift that the sun gave to the Earth was its soil.

Over ten thousand years ago, after the earth's glaciers had melted, the southward moving winds swept up the fine yellow soil[5] from the glacial deposits, scattering it all over the surface of the earth's middle latitudes.

This vast thick layer of yellow soil became the homeland of the Chinese people.[6]

As one faces this cracked and fissured high plateau, it's truly hard to imagine that that ancient, fascinating and compelling legend of the Yellow Emperor's people could actually have taken place on this horizon-filling expanse of yellow soil, crisscrossed by gullies.

Scholars researching ancient culture have proposed a hypothesis, that the character di [=Emperor] in the phrase huangdi [=Yellow Emperor] is actually the same character as di meaning "earth." Hence huangdi [=Yellow Emperor] is none other than the yellow soil, equivalent to "Earth Empress" in the Chinese phrase "Sky Emperor and Earth Empress"—that is, Mother Earth.[7]

---

[4] The image on the screen associated with the title for Part Two appears to be one of the beehive-shaped tombs of the Xi Xia dynasty [ca. 1032-1227 AD], located approximately 25 kilometers west of Yinchuan in modern Ningxia. These tombs, which have been called "China's pyramids," would seem to be apt symbols of a once-powerful nation in decline.

[5] Most Western writers on China use the term loess soil to translate huang tu; here we have employed the literal translation as yellow soil in order to fit the context which emphasizes yellowness of all sorts.

[6] The yellow soil [or loess soil] plateau is a vast area in North China, covering southern Hebei, Shanxi, Shaanxi, eastern Ningxia, southern Inner Mongolia and northern Henan. The yellow soil layer is 20-30 meters deep on the average but reaches a depth of 200 meters in some places. Loess soil eroded by the Yellow River gives the river its characteristic color and name.

[7] While the two characters are both pronounced di in modern Chinese, their pronunciations were different in both archaic and ancient Chinese, nor were the written forms used interchangeably; see Bernhard Karlgren, Grammata Serica Recensa, #4b' and 877a. The alleged identity between the Yellow Emperor [huangdi] and the Earth Empress [houtu] probably relies on the statement in the Huainanzi, a text of the 1st century A.D., where the Yellow Emperor, representing the center controlling the gods of the four directions is

Looking at things this way, then, the fact that the Yellow Emperor is revered as the ancestor of the Chinese people is because he is the embodiment of the yellow soil. Of course, just look at the Chinese people on that yellow soil plateau: they are born on the yellow soil, grow up on the yellow soil, and their bodies are coated with yellow soil. What they eat is yellow millet and yellow beans [=soy beans]; what they live in are caves[8] excavated from hills of yellow soil; what they drink is muddy yellow water. In ancient times when persons rose to the highest position and became emperors, they would wear yellow robes, walk along the "yellow path,"[9] and reside in palaces covered with glazed yellow roof tiles. And after they died? They would all descend to the "Yellow Springs."[10]

Hence in worshipping the soil no other people in the world can match our ancestors for the sincerity, solemnity and depth with which the soil is imprinted in their culture and psychology.

(Beijing: the old, age-darkened foundation of the former Altar of Agriculture)

Every year, the Son of Heaven and his great ministers would come here to conduct the "Imperial Plowing." The Emperor, holding in his right hand the gilt dragon-carved plow and in his left a whip, and supported by two old men, would traverse this sacrificial altar symbolizing the land three times and thus be considered to have completed his "Imperial Plowing." And thus a rich harvest of grain could be expected.[11]

For thousands of years now, Chinese have wrested their food from the earth, facing the yellow soil, with their backs to the sky. The soil is the very root of their existence, a treasure passed from generation to generation, the entire meaning of human life.

---

paired with houtu as his assistant. The word hou in early texts means 'Lord'; only later does it acquire the sense of 'Empress.' Hence houtu should be interpreted as 'Lord Earth' and not as 'Earth Empress.' See Huainanzi, SPPY ed., ch. 3, 3ab.

[8] In the "yellow soil plateau" region of China, peasants commonly live in homes carved out of the compacted yellow soil of the cliffside.

[9] Here huang dao or "yellow path" is probably a contraction of huang dao ji ri, meaning a "propitious day in the calendar." Many of the emperor's activities would have been restricted by the traditional almanac, which listed lucky and unlucky days for travel, marriage, building a house, etc.

[10] The underworld.

[11] This description of the rite of "Imperial Plowing" is apparently borrowed from that in Ray Huang, 1587: A Year of No Significance, Yale Univ. Press, 1981, p. 6. In the Chinese edition [Wanli shiwu nian] published in Beijing in 1982 by the Zhonghua shuju, see p. 6.

Thousands of years of culture are all crystallized in this yellow soil. And so it appears very mysterious, as if it enfolded the heart and soul of the Chinese people.

(The television studio. An author discusses the Yellow River.)

Zhang Wei[12] (Shandong author): *"In the many years that the Yellow River has flowed, it has soaked many secrets into the mud of its two banks. In the spring of this year when I made a visit to the Yellow River basin, an event occurred that moved me greatly. There were two old men who in their teens had wandered to the Northeast and after several moves had forgotten where their [original] village was or even what its name was. Later, when they were in their seventies or eighties they finally thought of their old home again. They spent a lot of energy, endured frequent hardships, changed trains many times, then took boats, before with great difficulty finding their birthplace. This was a village about twenty li from the mouth of the Yellow River. Once arrived at this place the two old men were extremely excited and spent all their time poking around in the fields, doing who knows what. Having stayed for more than two weeks, they would have to go back, right? As they departed, each of them wrapped up a small packet of earth. The night before they left, the two old men hugged each other, and spent the whole night tossing and turning and crying on the kang.[13] This was all told me by their landlord. This event had a great effect on me. Even today I can't grasp why they would wrap up a packet of earth to take with them. What was there inside this packet of earth?"*

The philosophers would seem to have clarified this question somewhat.

Hegel once said that the ordinary soil, the ordinary river plain had tied mankind to the soil and enwrapped him in an unending dependency, but that the ocean had lifted up mankind and taken him far beyond those limited circles of thought and action. This sort of ocean-crossing activity, surpassing the limits of the land, is what the countries of Asia lack.[14]

---

[12] Zhang Wei is the author of the controversial novel Gu chuan [The Old Boat], first published in Dangdai, 1986; a Taiwan edition was published in 1989 by the Fengyun shidai chuban gongsi. Zhang Wei was born in 1956 in Longkou, Shandong and graduated from the Chinese department of Yantai Normal School in 1980. In 1983 he became a member of the Chinese Writers' Association. He is the author of another novel, Yuan cun [The Distant Village] and has published eight volumes of short stories, winning several national prizes.

[13] In north China, traditional houses feature a kang, a raised platform of earthen bricks heated by flues from the kitchen stove, which serves as the family bed as well as a place to sit and work during the day.

[14] Several passages in Hegel's introduction to his Lectures on the Philosophy of World History [H.B. Nisbet, trans., Cambridge Univ. Press, 1975] bear directly on this point:

China's youth today may well find fault with our ancestors: "Why is it you were so enamored of the continent[15] and were never able to overstep the limits of the land to go out and greet the ocean?"

This was our destiny in History.

An agricultural civilization was born on the banks of the Yellow River no later than about eight thousand years ago. The critical step which civilization took, from nomadic hunting to being fixed on a particular piece of land, is said to have commenced from the hand of a woman collecting seeds.

The first price paid for putting aside savagery was being firmly tied to the land. Do you think our ancestors could have chosen otherwise?

Even more beyond their power to choose was the fact that the middle and lower course of the Yellow River, this cradle of civilization, just happens to be located in an unusual geographic environment.

(The television studio. A scholar discusses the special characteristics of China's geographical environment.)

Feng Tianyu[16] (Professor of History, Hubei Univ.): *"The geographical environment is the stage and the backdrop for the great tragedy of history and culture. China's geography has the following two major characteristics: The first is that Chinese culture, which originated in the Yellow River basin, and particularly in the middle and lower courses, is relatively isolated*

Land—in the sense of broad river valleys—binds man to the soil; consequently a whole series of ties attaches him to the locality he lives in. But the sea lifts him out of these narrow confines. .... The Oriental states, splendid edifices though they are, lack this maritime outlet from their limited landbound existence, even if—as in the case of China— they are themselves situated on the sea. The sea, for them, is merely the termination of the land, and they have no positive relationship with it. The activity which the sea inspires is of a wholly peculiar nature, and it breeds a wholly peculiar character. [pp. 160-161] The second principle, that of the river plains with their agricultural existence, is the most interesting one for our present purposes. ... China, India, and Babylon have become great civilised countries in this way. But they have remained enclosed within themselves and have not developed their links with the maritime principle—at least not after their own peculiar principle had come to fruition; and if they do subsequently take to the sea, it plays no real part in their culture and civilisation. [pp. 193-194]

[15] "Continent" translates <u>da lu</u>, which can also be rendered as "mainland," a short-hand term which contemporary Chinese use to indicate the PRC since 1949. Hence an alternative interpretation of this sentence is possible: Chinese young people are asking their parents why they stayed on the mainland after 1949 and didn't go overseas.

[16] Prof. Feng's views were presented at the First International Conference on Chinese Culture held at Fudan University in Shanghai in January, 1986, in a paper entitled "Zhongguo gu wenhua de tezhi" ["The Special Characteristics of Ancient Chinese Culture"], pp. 81-99 in Fudan daxue lishi xi, ed., <u>Zhongguo chuantong wenhua de zai guji</u> [The Re-evaluation of Traditional Chinese Culture], Shanghai renmin chuban she, 1987.

from the outside world. As the core area of Chinese culture, its northern border is the difficult-to-cross Gobi desert in Mongolia, and further north, the even more impenetrable primordial Siberian forest. To the northwest are ten thousand li of yellow sand, a western region which in the past was only crossed by a small number of merchants, of court envoys on military or diplomatic missions, and of escaping criminals. And so the northwest also formed an obstacle to contact. To the southwest is the Qinghai-Tibet plateau, the tallest and most formidable in the world. Some geographers have said that of the two most difficult to cross regions in the world, one is the Sahara Desert in North Africa, and the other is the Qinghai-Tibet plateau in East Asia. In terms of land routes, the Yellow River basin has three East Asian borders that are hard to cross. To the east, it borders on the planet's greatest ocean, the Pacific, which to ancient man was hard to conquer, broad and limitless,[17] far different from the Mediterranean Sea full of archipelagoes and peninsulas. The Mediterranean Sea was relatively easy to conquer, and so seafaring was highly developed among the ancient Greeks and Romans. The Pacific Ocean also constituted a barrier to China. Looked at in this fashion, the geographical environment constituted an isolating mechanism for Chinese culture centered in the Yellow River basin. The second characteristic is that there was a relatively open area to move around in in the interior; with such a broad heartland, if there was warfare or natural disaster in the north, one could always move to the south, and vice-versa. The existence of natural barriers on the outside and of plenty of room to move around in on the inside constitute the two major characteristics of the geographical environment of Chinese civilization, which was quite different from the geographical environments of other peoples and cultures. The English, for example, had easy communications with the outside but a rather small heartland in the interior, giving rise to a sort of outwardly-expanding cultural type. On the other hand, our particular geographical environment has given rise to a cultural type that is inward-looking and which seeks stability."

And so the Chinese resemble neither the Europeans, who live around the Mediterranean Sea, nor the Americans, who live between two great oceans. Destiny gave the Chinese people this sort of space to survive in.

For thousands of years, the fertile Central Plain[18] has always faced the broad and deep Mongolian plateau; this sort of direct confrontation of plain and plateau does not exist in Europe. This has brought into being an unusual historical relationship: the herding peoples of the plateau, in a state of constant migration and without a fixed locale, have always taken the plain and the river basin as an objective to be seized, and have constantly

---

[17] In the broadcast version, the interview ends here.

[18] Western geographers commonly render zhong yuan as the North China Plain.

rushed down from the plateau in floods. Virtually the whole of China's ancient history is a history of the struggle for survival space between herders and farmers.

And for this reason, right down to the final period of feudal society, at the time of the Ming-Qing transition, the thinker Wang Fuzhi [1619-1692], was filled with a sort of cultural pride for China's agricultural civilization. He scornfully attacked the herding culture of the "Northern Barbarians" as remaining at a low stage of *"pursuing grass and water, practicing archery and hunting, forgetting the relationship of ruler and subordinate, ignoring the honors of marriage and official position and moving about without a fixed abode."* Whereas on the Central Plain, *"there were walled cities to be held, markets from which to obtain profit, lands to be plowed, taxes to be collected, and honor to be gained through marriage and examinations."*[19]

Before the appearance of industrial civilization, who could deny this progressive nature of Chinese agricultural civilization? Naturally, the people of the Central Plain had to protect it from the incursions of herding culture.

There was no better method of protection than "double ramparts."[20]

The primitive village site of Jiangzhai excavated at Lintong in Shaanxi[21] is perhaps the earliest prototype of double ramparts. See how all the doors of the houses face towards the public square in the center, and how in the whole village there is only an opening to the east.[22] This sort of layout clearly highlights the psychology of uniting towards the center.

As we take a bird's eye view of Beijing, we can discover to our surprise a certain uniformity over six thousand years.[23]

Later on, there were city walls.

---

[19] See Wang Fuzhi, Du tongjian lun, ch. 28. For his biography, see Arthur Hummel, Eminent Chinese of the Ch'ing Period, pp. 817-819.

[20] cheng kuo appears to indicate defensive fortifications consisting of both inner and outer walls.

[21] The site was excavated between 1972 and 1979. The first phase of human habitation is considered Yangshao culture, contemporaneous with that of Banbo Village near Xi'an. Jiangzhai is within the same county as the tomb of the First Emperor of Qin.

[22] See the excavation report entitled Jiang zhai—xinshiqi shidai yizhi fajue baogao [Jiang zhai—Report on the Excavation of the Neolithic Site], edited by the Xi'an Banpo Museum, the Shaanxi Provincial Archaeological Research Institute, and the Lintong County Museum, published by Wenwu chubanshe, Beijing, 1988 in 2 vols. The report reveals that the residential area of the Jiangzhai site is surrounded by defensive ditches or moats. The screen shows the map of the excavation from the published report.

[23] The screen shows a bird's-eye view of the circular enclosure of the Temple of Heaven in Beijing. The point of this sentence is to use the fiction of a continuous architectural tradition to poke fun at the Beijing government's "spirit of uniting towards the center."

By the Warring States Period [475-221 BC], city walls had been expanded to the state boundaries.[24] It's said that the first person to invent this sort of vast defensive engineering work was Duke Jian of Qin [r.414-400 BC].

Ten generations later, when his descendant Ying Zheng[25] unified the six states, a remarkable thing occurred.

If you were to extend the Great Wall of the Ming Dynasty another five hundred to a thousand Chinese li outwards, as far as the line of the Yin Shan and the He Lan Shan,[26] that then would be the Great Wall which the First Emperor of Qin ordered Meng Tian [d. 210 BC][27] to build and the same one which Meng Jiangnü[28] wailed at and cursed in legend.[29]

This is the grandest engineering feat in the history of humankind, yet the entire concept guiding this work had been invented several thousands of years earlier by the chief of the Jiangzhai Village.

With the existence of defensive walls, one could resist the attacks of herding peoples from the outside, while at the same time one could produce a sort of cohesive force on the inside, forcing the people within the walls towards the nucleus of power. Thus whoever built the Great Wall would then possess the land, the territory, and the people within it, and the Great Wall would become the wall of his family compound.

---

[24] In the second broadcast, the following text was omitted: from *"It's said that the first person... down to "as far as the line of the Yin Shan and the He Lan Shan."* The following sentence then begins: *"This, then, is the Great Wall which the First Emperor...."* This omission was perhaps motivated by criticism of the historical accuracy of this account of the history of wall building in China. For instance, in 657 B.C., the State of Chu began building its wall, over 240 years before Duke Jian of Qin [r. 414-400 B.C.].

[25] Personal name of the First Emperor of Qin.

[26] The Yin Shan mountain range extends east and west across present-day Inner Mongolia, to the north of the bend of the Yellow River. The He Lan Shan mountain range extends north-south, along the western side of the Yellow River where it bends south in modern Ningxia. Hence these two mountain ranges encapsulate the great bend of the Yellow River and the yellow-soil plateau within them.

[27] Meng Tian, one of the First Emperor's famous generals, defeated the Xiongnu in the Hetao region along the northern bend of the Yellow River and constructed the Great Wall there.

[28] In legend, a woman of the Qin period whose husband had been drafted to build the Great Wall. When she went to take him winter clothes and couldn't find him, the sound of her crying caused the Great Wall to split open, revealing his bones. The legend is based on a story first told in the Zuo zhuan and repeated in the Lie nü zhuan, about the wife of a man named Qi Liang whose crying also brought down a city wall.

[29] See Map 1, Conjectural Route of Qin Great Wall [black] Superimposed over Ming Great Wall, p. 346.

The great imagination of the First Emperor of Qin was still an imagination bounded by the land.[30]

At this same time,[31] an Emperor Alexander [356-323 BC] from the shores of the Aegean Sea in the West had already led the invincible great army of Macedon far from its homeland and had swept away the ancient empires of Europe, Asia and Africa.

Although the plateau of the Pamirs and the Himalaya Mountains stopped the iron hooves of the Macedonians, yet the incomparable Emperor Alexander could never have dreamed that even if he could have crossed that natural barrier the incomparable emperor of the orient would still have a ten-thousand li Great Wall awaiting him.[32]

In 102 A.D., the Han general Ban Chao [32-102 AD] who had pursued the Xiongnu[33] as far as the heartlands of Central Asia sent his lieutenant general Gan Ying west to cross the Persian Gulf and to spy out the strength or weakness of the Roman Empire. Yet Gan Ying was frightened into retreat by the waves.

From Alexander's eastward march to Ban Chao's advance to the west, History traversed nearly four hundred years. Due to the barriers of mountains and oceans the two great civilizations represented by the two empires of east and west twice missed the opportunity to rub shoulders in the encounter of History. The strong sparks of direct resistance and melding, of conquest and counter-conquest, of assimilation and counter-assimilation that might have been stirred up, in the end never sparkled on the great stage of History.

---

[30] The second broadcast eliminates this line, perhaps in recognition of the fact that the First Emperor had indeed sent naval expeditions into the eastern sea to seek for the isles of the immortals.

[31] The second broadcast eliminates the beginning words of this sentence and rewrites the sentence as follows: *And yet, the incomparable occidental Emperor Alexander on the shores of the Aegean Sea had already..* This change was perhaps motivated by the fact that Qin Shihuang and Alexander are not in fact contemporaries, as the published text strongly suggests.

[32] Heshang's critics have pointed out that Alexander died well before China's First Emperor, and that even if the Great Wall had existed then, he would have found himself within it upon crossing the Himalayas. The second broadcast significantly changed the text of this paragraph to read: *As if in response to Alexander's march to the east, the First Emperor of Qin also began his war against the Xiongnu. This incomparable oriental emperor was unlike Alexander who roamed in all directions; rather, relying on a mode of thinking unique to oriental monarchs, he constructed a ten-thousand li Great Wall which Alexander could not have conceived even in his wildest dreams. And yet the First Emperor of Qin's imagination was one that could not surpass the bounds of the land.*

[33] The Xiongnu (or Hsiung-nu) were a Turkic tribe on the grasslands north of the Great Wall.

(Reappearance of the title: Destiny)

For thousands of years, the Chinese have "gotten up to work at sunrise and gone home to rest at sunset"[34] on this stretch of land, and so they have developed a special sensitivity to time concepts such as the divisions of the agricultural calendar and to the seasonal cycle of spring, summer, fall and winter; yet from generation to generation their lives would seem to trace out a pattern of precise repetition. For, taking thousands of years as the time-axis of their history, the Chinese people are accustomed to seeing the pattern of rise and fall within a century as merely the blink of an eye in the long river of history. The alternation of rise and fall is like the changing of winter into spring. Even the most important social changes and human disasters seem as fugitive as clouds or smoke. In the whole world there is no people with an historical sense as strong as that of the Chinese, nor is there one which can match the Chinese in their attachment to a unique, fatalistic philosophy of life.

The Great Wall thus tightly encapsulated this peaceful, over-ripe agricultural civilization. As time passed, this civilization no longer possessed the ability to strike out aggressively which it had had in the time of the First Emperor of Qin [259-210 BC] and Emperor Wu of Han [156-87 BC].

And yet, that silent Mongolian plateau in the north could always awaken suddenly.

While the plateau was firmly sealed off from the outside and difficult to reach, nevertheless it was easy for it to send the strength and vitality it had accumulated inside itself down to the plain. Whenever there was drought, and great numbers of livestock belonging to the herders died off, they would unite and rush down off the plateau. The neighboring agricultural civilization would then be on the brink of disaster.

In the turbulent decades of the last years of the Southern Song Dynasty [1130-1279],[35] perhaps the only person to realize that a great plan was quietly being hatched on this uninviting, sparsely-populated grassland was a

---

[34] Allusion to an ancient folksong, quoted as follows in the Yuefu shiji: *The Annals of Emperors and Kings states: At the time of Emperor Yao, the world was in a state of great harmony, and the common people had no worries. Old men of eighty or ninety would work the soil and sing: "We get up and work at sunrise, go home to rest at sunset; we dig wells for drinking water and plow the fields for food. What power has the emperor over us?"* See Yuefu shiji, ch. 83; p. 1165 in Zhonghua shuju, Beijing, 1979 edition.

[35] The Song (or Sung) Dynasty is commonly divided into two periods: the Northern Song [989-1130], when the capital was at Bianliang [modern Kaifeng] in Henan; and the Southern Song [1130-1279] when the capital was at Lin'an [modern Hangzhou] in Zhejiang. The Southern Song was brought to an end by the invading Mongols.

Taoist by the name of Qiu Chuji [1148-1227].[36] This sort of short-legged Mongol horse, under the command of a great hero, would conquer half the world.[37]

By the time that Genghis Khan's [1162-1227] fierce horsemen had swept down like a tide, not even natural barriers like the Yellow River and the Yangtze, let alone the Great Wall, could stop them. And the Chinese people, despite their high level of civilization, were also powerless to resist their fate, even though they brought forth patriotic heroes such as Yue Fei [1103-1141], Wen Tianxiang [1236-1283], Lu You [1125-1210], and Xin Qiji [1140-1207].[38]

The great expanse of North China, how often it has been turned into mulberry fields![39] How often into pasture! How often the land north and south of the Great Wall has been conquered, how many bones have been left to bleach! Suddenly a lady leaves the Han Palace, a princess allies herself in marriage; suddenly a foreign king comes to court, presenting tribute, to be called a vassal. How many tragi-comedies of history have been played out before the backdrop of the Great Wall!

If one were to say that the First Emperor of Qin or Emperor Wu of Han in constructing the Great Wall expressed the strength and the spirit of Chinese civilization, then by the middle of the fifteenth century when the Ming dynasty reconstructed the Great Wall, it had become an act altogether of failure and of retreat.

The Great Wall of the Ming Dynasty, eleven thousand li in length and built of brick and stone, was naturally much stronger than the Great Wall of the Qin and Han dynasties. And yet it too exhausted the strength of the

---

[36] Qiu Chuji [Ch'iu Ch'u-chi] joined the Taoist church at age 19, studying under Wang Chongyang of the Quanzhen sect. Later, Genghis Khan summoned him to audience and honored him as an immortal. His disciple Li Zhichang wrote an account of his visit to the Khan entitled Changchun zhenren xiyou ji which Arthur Waley has translated under the title of The Travels of an Alchemist: The Journey of the Taoist Ch'ang-ch'un from China to the Hindukush at the Summons of Chingiz Khan, George Routledge, London, 1931.

[37] The second broadcast eliminates this paragraph.

[38] The second broadcast eliminates the last sentence of this paragraph, beginning with And the Chinese people, despite their high level of civilization... For biographical information, see Herbert Franke, ed., Sung Biographies, Franz Steiner Verlag, Wiesbaden, 1976, as follows: Lu You [Lu Yu], pp. 609-610; Wen Tianxiang [Wen T'ien-hsiang], pp. 1187-1201; Yue Fei [Yueh Fei], pp. 1266-1271.

[39] A legend in the Shenxian zhuan tells the story how the eastern sea was transformed into "mulberry fields" [=dry land] and then back again in quick succession; here the metaphor indicates the rapidity of change.

Ming and greatly hurt its vitality.[40] By the time the Jurchen people arose between the Long White Mountains and the Black Dragon River,[41] and their great warrior Nurhaci[42] [1559-1626] pointed his spears to the south, this ten thousand-*li* Great Wall of brick and stone could only once again record a great defeat, so that the Emperor Kangxi[43] [1654-1722] would later say,"Building the Great Wall was truly useless."[44]

The majestic section of the Great Wall at Gubeikou Pass was built by the famous general Qi Jiguang [1528-1587] when he was stationed at Jizhou.

This general, famed for spending "Three hundred and sixty days a year in the saddle with his lance" has been called the "solitary general" by historians. Not only did he reconstruct the first section of the Great Wall in the North, but he also built a Great Wall along the coast, to defend against

---

[40] Wang Luxiang later reflected on the significance of the Great Wall as follows: *"What is the Great Wall? Its most primitive prototype were double ramparts [cheng kuo]. In ancient times, due to the needs of defense, a district city would erect double ramparts to prevent their train from being stolen. By the Spring and Autumn Warring States periods, as administrative regions expanded, states would erect long walls between themselves; this too was a defensive measure. The First Emperor of Qin united all these small, equally developed agricultural states into a large state, and the enemy he faced was ... the pastoral peoples. ... That a district city should build double ramparts is understandable, but to build a great wall on such an extensive scale along the border is both a quantitative and qualitative change, and the whole idea is mistaken. ... To imagine that with one mighty effort you could create an eternal barrier is nonsense. But if you insist on building a great wall anyway, you can only exhaust your people and waste your wealth, sapping the strength of the state; hence the downfall of the Qin was a direct result of building the Great Wall. And so in fact, throughout history whenever China was strong, she never built a great wall, but only built sections. Whenever a dynasty did use a great wall to envelop its entire frontier, that was a sign that that dynasty was already unable to function. In the first place, they would have already been defeated in spirit; and when they persisted in building it, then their vitality would be greatly sapped..."* See Guan Zhizhong and Hong Shujuan, "Fang Heshang zongzhuangao Wang Luxiang," Yuan jian, Taibei, December 15, 1988, pp. 204-207

[41] The region constituting northeast China, formerly Manchuria.

[42] Founder of the Manchu or Qing dynasty. See Hummel, op. cit., pp. 594-599.

[43] Kangxi [K'ang-hsi],second Emperor of the Qing Dynasty, reigned 1654-1722. See Hummel, op. cit., under Hsuan-yeh pp.327-331. A good account is Jonathan Spence, Emperor of China: Self-portrait of K'ang-hsi.

[44] Kangxi is said to have written a poem in seven-syllable regulated verse about the Great Wall in which he appears to be addressing the Ming dynasty: *You built it for 10,000 li stretching down to the sea, but all your vast expenditures were in vain. / While at the time you exhausted the strength of the people, when did the Empire ever belong to your family?* See Zhongguo qingnian bao, August 14th, 1988, p. 6, Wang Su, "Qian nian chunqiu lun chang cheng."

the Japanese pirates: i.e., the famous sea wall of Penglai.[45] China's first naval squadron was stationed behind this wall.

Without any doubt, Qi Jiguang was the most talented military strategist of the Ming Dynasty. But he has also left us with a great regret: why was it that the pirates of an island country could cross the seas to attack China, while the Chinese could only remained stationed on the coast, unable even to conceive of going to that island country to investigate those pirates? Why was it that the Europe of that time possessed an armed navy that pursued conquest in all directions, while China could only think of rebuilding the Great Wall? And furthermore, of extending the Great Wall along the seacoast?[46]

At the outset of 1588, the general's star fell from heaven, and Qi Jiguang died amid poverty and illness. The Great Wall, following the demise of Qi Jiguang, no longer held any significance.

At this very time, the invincible Spanish Armada was about to set out to conquer England and to open up a tumultuous new page in the history of the early modern world.[47]

Does anyone still remember the old Great Wall built by the First Emperor of Qin? Today it still sleeps deeply amidst the desert. The vast moving sands nibble at it bit by bit from the north, the wild winds sculpt it, it appears to be a thousand-year-old outcast, lying in the midst of the wilderness, formed into a thought without an answer.

---

[45] Qi Jiguang, a native of Dengzhou, Shandong, came from a family with a long history of involvement in Dengzhou's coastal defenses. At the age of 16, he held his first position in charge of coastal defense at Dengzhou; in 1553, at the age of 26, he was promoted to acting assistant commissioner of the Shandong regional military commission in charge of coastal defenses. Penglai is on the north coast of Shandong opposite the Liaodong peninsula. After only two years in this position, he spent twelve years [1556-1567] suppressing Japanese pirates in Zhejiang and Fujian, followed by fifteen years in charge of the Great Wall defenses at Jizhou. Here he repaired the wall and built observation towers. For more on Qi Jiguang, see Ray Huang, 1587: A Year of No Significance, 1981, Yale University Press, esp. Chapter Six, which gives Qi the sobriquet of "solitary general"; see also Fang & Goodrich, op. cit., vol. 1, pp. 220-224. The Penglai wall and the history of the Qi family is briefly described in Shandong fengwu zhi, Shandong meishu chubanshe, Jinan, 1982, p. 197.

[46] Some of these questions are raised by Ray Huang in his preface to 1587: A Year of No Significance, where he asks: *Why could the island country of Japan attack China but China could not go and attack Japan? Why was it that Western Europe at that time had already improved its techniques of warfare with fire-arms, while China was still rebuilding the Great Wall?* [These questions appear only in the mainland China edition (p. 5) and not in the U.S. or Taiwan editions].

[47] Qi Jiguang's death and the Spanish Armada are linked in Ray Huang, 1587: A Year of No Significance, p. 188 (p. 196 in Chinese edition).

In direct contrast to the now-forgotten Great Wall of the Qin, the Great Wall of the Ming which retreated a thousand li backwards, has been the object of incomparable reverence. People pride themselves on the fact that it is the only feat of human engineering visible to astronauts on the moon. People even wish to use it as a symbol of China's strength. And yet, if the Great Wall could speak, it would very frankly tell its Chinese grandchildren that it is a great and tragic gravestone forged by historical destiny. It can by no means represent strength, initiative, and glory; it can only represent an isolationist, conservative and incompetent defence and a cowardly lack of aggression. Because of its great size and long history, it has deeply imprinted its arrogance and self-delusion in the souls of our people. Alas, O Great Wall, why do we still want to praise you?[48]

Scholars have already discovered that the Great Wall which meanders ten thousand li lies pretty much along the boundary line of fifteen inches of rainfall.[49] This rainfall line also signifies the natural boundary between agriculture and the lack of it.[50]

Today on the Great Wall at Hongshi Gorge in Shaanxi,[51] we can still see the stone tablet left by our ancestors to designate the "natural barrier between Chinese and barbarians." This truly is the last frontier of an agricultural civilization. Everything is extremely clear: our ancestors would

---

[48] Xie Xuanjun, co-author of Part Six, "Blueness," devotes part of the last chapter of his book Shenhua yu minzu jingshen [Myth and National Spirit, 1986] to the consideration of China's "great wall mentality" [chang cheng jingshen]. Like ancient Babylon and Egypt, Xie asserts, China is a "continental" civilization, quite unlike the "seafaring civilization" of ancient Greece. One of the principal themes of Chinese history is the struggle for survival space between the pastoral nomads of the grasslands and the agricultural peoples of the North China plain, a struggle fueled by progressive aridity and desertification. The Great Wall marked the dividing line between agriculture and pastoralism, but was not permanently fixed; witness its southward move between the Qin and Ming dynasties as desertification progressed in the north. From a means of defense, the Great Wall gradually assumed psychological significance as well: ..*The Great Wall became not only our physical symbol but also became the symbol of our spirit. The Great Wall spirit is characteristically long on conservatism, short on innovation; it pays attention to defensive methods but lacks the will to attack; it promotes virtue while scorning efficiency; it is content with poverty and with fate but unwilling to take risks; .. it is the complete opposite of the 'piratical spirit' of European sea-faring peoples.* [pp. 417-418]

[49] See for example Joseph Needham and Ray Huang: "The Nature of Chinese Society: A Technical Interpretation," Journal of Oriental Studies, vol. 12, nos. 1-2, 1974, pp. 1-16, esp. p. 3. The same point is made in Ray Huang's more recent work, China: A Macro-history.

[50] Here the screen shows an outline map of China indicating the 15" rainfall line and the Great Wall.

[51] The second broadcast eliminates the phrase *on the Great Wall at Hongshi Gorge in Shaanxi.*

never be able to go beyond the bounds of the soil and of agriculture. Their greatest feat of the imagination and most courageous act could only be to build the Great Wall!

Before the Qing Dynasty, and more precisely before the fifteenth century, the opposition of forces in the north was always the main tune of Chinese history. And so the southeast coastline for a long time slept undisturbed. ...[52]

For humankind as a whole, the fifteenth century was an extremely critical century. The human race began to move its gaze from the continent to the seas. History gave a fair chance, both to Orient and to Occident, to make a choice. The Pacific, Indian Ocean and the Atlantic all opened their arms to welcome the peoples of the continents [dalu].[53]

History probably never before had an emperor quite like Zhu Yuanzhang [1328-1398], the first emperor of the Ming, who tied the common people so firmly to the land. While this wandering monk[54] expelled the wandering herdsmen from the Central Plain, he seemed to share the political intuition of an oriental monarch in that he recognized the ocean as an element of freedom which constituted a potential threat to a dynasty founded on agriculture.[55] He repeatedly issued orders that "not a single match stick should set sail on the ocean." Of course this had a defensive purpose, but he also deeply understood that his dynasty would be stable only if he tied his people firmly to the land; to those who left the land he bore an extreme hate and would invariably "exile them to distant regions." The law of the Ming dynasty stipulated that anyone who left home had to carry identification, otherwise upon discovery at a frontier check-post they would be immediately sent to the authorities.

---

[52] The second broadcast eliminates this paragraph.

[53] In the second broadcast, this paragraph is moved two paragraphs down, so that it directly precedes: *Looking at the ocean from the threshold of the fifteenth century..*

[54] Zhu Yuanzhang [Chu Yuan-chang] started life as a peasant, later became a wandering Buddhist monk, and eventually rose to lead the rebels that overthrew the Mongols, founding the Ming Dynasty in 1368. See Goodrich and Fang, op. cit.,pp. 381-392. There is a possible comparison between Zhu Yuanzhang and Mao Zedong, suggested by series author Su Xiaokang who noted in Longnian de beichuang [p. 22] that Mao had described himself in a conversation with Edgar Snow as *a lone monk walking the world with a leaky umbrella.* See Edgar Snow, The Long Revolution, New York, Random House, 1971, p. 175. Both leaders came from peasant backgrounds and led rebellions to establish an authoritarian state; of both it can be said: *Movement, migration and trade were all suffocated. The land and dictatorship held the Chinese people in bondage.*

[55] The second broadcast eliminates this sentence, presumably for its allusion to Mao Zedong.

Movement, migration and trade were all suffocated. The land and dictatorship held the Chinese people in bondage. Over the course of the past several centuries, how could they still understand the meaning of freedom and of trade?

Looking at the ocean from the threshold of the fifteenth century, what kind of choice would the Chinese people make, accustomed as they were to staying on the continent?[56]

In the year 1405, a great naval fleet unmatched in the world of the fifteenth century, riding before the strong northeast monsoon, grandly set sail from Wuhumen in Fujian, and in the face of the great choice offered by history, was the first to sail towards the Pacific. Even today, people are still trying to guess the purpose of that far-sailing fleet.

Under the command of Zheng He[57] [1371-1433], this fleet sailed the Western Ocean seven times over the course of twenty-eight years, leaving its traces all across Southeast and South Asia, crossing the Indian Ocean, and reaching as far as Arabia and the east coast of Africa.

Yet human history had never before witnessed a navigation on such a grand scale yet without an economic purpose. It appeared to be a purely political demonstration[58] designed to spread the imperial grace to the many countries beyond the seas, in order to express the nominal "supreme suzerainty" of the Chinese emperor over them. How generous and kind their behaviour, worthy of the "Country of Gentlemen"![59] Hegel says that the ocean invites mankind to conquest and to trade. And yet the Chinese who answered the invitation of the Pacific were such modest gentlemen who

---

[56] These several paragraphs can also be interpreted as referring to the present, especially if one adopts the equation of "continent" da lu with mainland China. If so, then the authors are hinting at the current "passion for going overseas" [chu guo re]. Part Six "Blueness" also appears to employ the same pun on dalu as both "continent" and "mainland China."

[57] Zheng He [or Cheng Ho] was a eunuch in the service of the Ming court and rose to become commander-in-chief of the Ming naval expeditions in the early years of the 15th century. See Fang and Goodrich, op.cit., pp. 194-200. China's contacts with Africa from the time of Zheng He's voyages onwards are treated by Phillip Snow in The Star Raft: China's Encounter with Africa, Cornell University Press, Ithaca, 1988.

[58] The author appears to be making a pun on the term zhengzhi youxing, which normally applies to demonstrations by political dissidents. Heshang baimiu attacks his use of language, pointing out that Zheng He's voyages served both political and commercial ends [pp. 130-131].

[59] The "Country of Gentlemen," referred to in the satirical novel Jinghua yuan by the Qing author Li Ruzhen [1763-1830], is one where the shopkeepers adhere to fixed low prices, and customers haggle to raise the price. See the abridged translation by Lin Tai-yi, Flowers in the Mirror, Berkeley, 1965, ch. 8, or ch. 45 in the original.

"*upheld righteousness and did not scheme for profit.*"[60] Even when they reached the sea the Chinese were unable to exceed the limited circles of thought and action of the land. History chose the Chinese people, but the Chinese people were unable to choose History.

Only a few decades later, four small sailing ships under the command of the Portuguese Da Gama, representing an infant capitalism, sailed into the Indian Ocean in search of wealth and markets. By that time, Zheng He's great fleet had already entirely disappeared from the Pacific and Indian Oceans. But it was the Europeans who began the great adventure of geographical exploration.

While this was an historical coincidence, it was also historically inevitable.

Asia, this land "where the sun rises," this land where world history began, because of its failure to grasp this historical opportunity, its sun would no longer rise.

Chinese civilization, which had formerly been so far in the advance on this planet, would for this reason be forced to accept a destiny of humiliation and passivity.

Nearly five hundred years later, the Beiyang squadron in the Yellow Sea was sent to the bottom in the great sea battle of 1895 with the Japanese navy. The tragic defeats of Ding Ruchang [1836-1895] and Deng Shichang[61] [1855-1894] had actually been predetermined long ago in the time of Qi Jiguang and Zheng He.

For thousands of years, the Pacific Ocean on China's southeast had always been silent. But when the wild waves of the Pacific brought with them the navies of the western powers and — even more threatening than navies — their new thinking and new culture, the Chinese had already lost the power to resist.

This tidal wave from the West in no way resembled the nomadic culture which descended from the Mongolian plateau like a flood and then quickly retreated without a trace. What came by sea was a new sort of civilization which the ancient Chinese agricultural civilization could no longer

---

[60] From the biography of Dong Zhongshu in Han Shu ch. 56, Zhonghua shuju, p. 2524. Here, Dong Zhongshu defines the humane man as follows: *The humane man is one who upholds righteousness without seeking for profit, who understands the Way without scheming for success.*

[61] Ding Ruchang [Ting Ju-ch'ang] and Deng Shichang [Teng Shih-ch'ang]. Both were admirals of the Qing navy. Deng died in the Yellow Sea battle on Sept. 17, 1894, when his ship was hit by a torpedo. Ding was wounded in the same battle and committed suicide in the following February rather than surrender command of the port of Weihaiwei to the Japanese.

assimilate. And so a threat to our race and a crisis for our civilization broke out simultaneously.

To save our nation from danger and destruction, we should try to keep the foreign pirates at bay beyond our country's gates; and yet to save our civilization from decline, we should also throw open our country's gates, open up to the outside, and receive the new light of science and democracy.[62] These extremely contradictory antiphonal themes of national salvation and modernization have taken turns over the past century in writing China's abnormally-shaped history; as complexly intertwined as a myriad strands of hair, they can neither be trimmed by the scissors nor untangled by the comb,[63] a situation which has caused the Chinese people to pay an immeasurably heavy price!

Our ancient and yet weak agricultural civilization forced our ancestors to the point where they knew only to use an extravagant yet useless Great Wall to protect their harvest, and to the point where they could not understand trade or competition even when they did go down to the sea. This sort of shrinking back of our civilization even now is already shrinking the vitality and the creativity of the whole Chinese people, and we can no longer afford to lose a single further opportunity afforded by fate.

Today we have already become much wiser.

If we admit that China has already wasted historical opportunities, then we will never again refuse to choose.

If we admit that our destiny is not fate, then we will never again let it push us around.

We have already seen that the Yellow River flows ten thousand li to the east and finally enters the ocean.

We will never again turn down the invitation of the ocean!

Written by Wang Luxiang[64]

---

[62] Science and democracy were considered by the reformers of the May 4th movement of 1919 as the two cures for China's current problems; see also Part Six, "Blueness."

[63] Alluding to a famous ci poem by Li Yu [937-978], last Emperor of the Southern Tang, comparing the sorrow of a palace lady mourning her absent lover to a tangle of hair that can neither be cut nor combed out. Interestingly, the poetic line admits of another reading in this context, where li "to comb" can also mean "to bring order to" and luan "tangled" can also mean "in turmoil." Like the tangled hair in the poem, China is still in turmoil no matter how much one tries to put it in order. See Daniel Bryant, Lyric Poets of the Southern Tang: Feng Yen-ssu, 903-960 and Li Yu, 937-978, University of British Columbia Press, Vancouver and London, 1982, p.103.

[64] Wang Luxiang, one of Heshang's principal co-authors, was born in Jiangsu in 1956 and received his B.A. from the Chinese Dept. of Xiangtan Univ., Hunan, in 1982. He received

an M.A. from the Philosophy Dept. of Beijing Univ. in 1987, where he had studied under Ye Lang. Upon graduation he joined the faculty of the Chinese department at Beijing Normal College. He was a contributor to art journals and authored a review of Zhang Xianliang's Half of Man is Woman that Zhang is said to have praised highly. He joined the script-writing team for Heshang in the summer of 1987 and accompanied the film crew to Yan'an and Loyang. He has written two short articles, one included in Heshang lun [1988, pp. 91-97], entitled "Remembering and Pondering" [Huiyi yu sikao] in which he describes how he met Su Xiaokang and how the filmscript was written; and another, included in Longnian de beichuang [1989, pp. 178-182] entitled "A drifter without a home" [Shiqu jiayuan de piaobozhe]. He has edited a volume entitled Xiandai meixue tixi [The System of Modern Aesthetics]. He was imprisoned for several months after the crackdown on the 1989 democracy movement but has since been released.

Part Three

"The Light of the Spirit"

Humanity has already entered the space age.[1]

Those first groups of astronauts who landed on the moon were probably the celebrities of whom this age is proudest. Yet they were almost all European.

Dr. Wang Ganjun[2] was the first Chinese in the world to enter space orbit. It only took seven minutes for him to fly all the way across China in his space craft. For this, he became the pride of the Chinese people. How grand a reception his native land held for him!

Probably even the Chinese people themselves have almost forgotten that approximately five hundred years ago in the Ming dynasty, a man by the name of Wan Hu tied himself to forty-seven crude rockets, intending to fly to the sky. He was blown to pieces in an explosive bang. We should probably say his fate was just as moving and tragic as that of the space shuttle Challenger I five hundred years later. No wonder astronomers intend to name a circular mountain on the moon in Wan Hu's name.

To children in present day China, the enchantment of astronomy has always been associated with great names such as Galileo [1564-1642], Copernicus [1473-1543] and Bruno [1548-1600].[3] Yet as early as the first

---

[1] The screen shows the launching of the U. S. space shuttle and an astronaut walking in space to repair a satellite.

[2] Dr. Taylor G. Wang, a physicist at the Jet Propulsion Laboratories, was a mission specialist on the 17th Challenger flight from April 29th-May 6th, 1985. He carried with him a Chinese flag, which he later presented to Premier Zhao Ziyang on July 9th, during a visit to China. Zhao hailed him as the first person of Chinese ancestry to enter space. Born in Jiangxi province, he followed his family to Taiwan in 1952 and came to the U.S. in 1963. See Beijing Review, July 22, 1985, pp. 7-9.

[3] Galileo Galilei was an Italian physicist and astronomer; Mikotaj Kopemik a Polish astronomer; and Giordano Bruno an Italian philosopher. Chinese cosmologist Fang Lizhi, in an article entitled "A Hat, A Forbidden Zone, A Question" evaluated Italy's role in the history of astronomy: *Italy has an illustrious history when it comes to the physics of*

century B.C., Chinese had already begun to observe and record sunspots. Because of this, Westerners have recognized Chinese as the most faithful and accurate astronomical observers on this planet.[4]

About the first century A.D., there were two great astronomers existing in the East and West at the same time. Ptolemy[5] in the Roman Empire advocated his famous theory of geocentrism; Zhang Heng [78-139 A.D.], the Astronomer Royal of the Han Empire in the Orient, produced a hydraulic-powered armillary sphere, which simply transformed Ptolemy's theory into a model. But Zhang's theory of the celestial sphere[6] was still one step short of geocentrism. It is this step that the Chinese people have never been able to take.

---

heavenly bodies. Copernicus studied there; Galileo taught there; and Giordano Bruno was burned at the stake there. See Fang Lizhi, Bringing Down the Great Wall: Writings on Science, Culture, and Democracy in China, translated by James H. Williams, New York: Alfred A. Knopf, 1990, p. 56.

[4] Cf. Joseph Needham, Science and Civilization in China, vol. III, pp. 171-2: *Apart from the Babylonian records, so many of which are presumably wholly lost, those of the Chinese show that they were the most persistent and accurate observers of celestial phenomena anywhere in the world before the Arabs. ... In other cases (e.g. sunspots) phenomena were regularly observed by the Chinese for centuries, which Europeans not only ignored, but would have found inadmissible upon their cosmic preconceptions.*

[5] Ptolemy was a Greek astronomer of the second century A. D. who lived and worked in Alexandria, Egypt. Geocentrism means that the earth is the center of the universe, while the sun, moon stars, and other planets all revolve around it. His cosmology became the authoritative view in medieval times and was accepted by the Catholic church, so that Copernicus' new heliocentric cosmology was seen as heretical.

[6] Zhang Heng discusses his theories of the celestial sphere in two of his books, but the most precise description is found in his Hun i zhu: *The heavens are like a hen's egg and as round as a crossbow bullet; the earth is like the yolk of the egg, and lies alone in the centre. Heaven is large and earth small. Inside the lower part of the heavens there is water. The heavens are supported by chhi (vapour), the earth floats on the water. The circumference of the heavens is divided into 365.25°; hence half of it, 182 5/8° is above the earth, and the other half is below. This is why, of the 28 hsiu (equatorial star groups) only half are visible at one time. The two extremities of the heavens are the north and south poles, the former, in the middle of the sky, is exactly 36° above the earth, and consequently a circle with a diameter of 72° enclosed all the stars which are perpetually visible. A similar circle around the south pole encloses stars which we never see. The two poles are distant from one another 182° and a little more than half a degree. The rotation goes on like that around the axle of a chariot.* See Joseph Needham, op.cit., Volume III, pp. 217. Zhang Heng is also credited with the invention of the seismograph and the water-powered armillary sphere. Altogether he served at court as Astronomer Royal for fourteen years. He was also a well-known writer in the genre of fu, or rhymeprose; among his famous works, preserved in the Wen xuan, is the "Er jing fu" [Rhymeprose on the Two Capitals] in which he satirizes the extravagant living in the two metropolises. See also Nienhauser, ed., The Indiana Companion to Traditional Chinese Literature, pp. 211-212.

Ten years ago some Chinese airplane designers visited the famous Rolls Royce company in England. The English told them that the most advanced airplane engine in the world was based on the theory of "triaxial flow" of the Chinese engineer Wu Zhonghua.[7] The scientific principles discovered by this Professor Wu Zhonghua did not help his homeland produce new kinds of airplanes; instead, today we have to learn about this Chinese professor's theories through the achievements of the British.

Why was it that the light of Chinese civilization, which had led the way for more than a thousand years, dimmed after the seventeenth century? Why has such a smart people become so slow-witted and decrepit? What was it, after all, that we possessed yesterday yet whose loss we have only discovered today?

(Titles: Part Three: The Light of the Spirit)[8]

Six thousand years ago, not every pair of hands could make such refined and harmonious pottery.[9] Some Westerners have always tried to force a connection between the sources of Chinese civilization and the Sumerian civilization of the Tigris-Euphrates Valley, as if they were unwilling to believe that this land could give birth to a civilization.

Today it is debatable whether the Central Plain from which this pottery was excavated is the original home of Chinese civilization. In ancient times the Central Plain was both a region of conflict among the groups from east, west, north and south as well as a place where the cultures of the four directions and the hundred tribes commingled. From the very beginning, Chinese culture was a culture of fusion. As you see, we had not just one founding ancestor, but two. One wonders: why is it that the Fire Emperor[10]

---

[7] Wu Zhonghua, born 1917, well-known Chinese scientist whose work on the general theory of triaxial flow laid the groundwork for designing Boeing 747 jet engines. He came to the U.S. in 1944, earning a Ph.D. at M.I.T. in 1947 before returning to China in 1954. See Bartke, Who's Who in the People's Republic of China, 2nd. ed., p. 530.

[8] As the titles of Part Three, "The Light of the Spirit" appear, the screen also shows the sun slowly setting behind what appears to be a temple or tomb. The setting sun may be taken as representing decline and death and is here associated with the desperate plight of Chinese intellectuals.

[9] The screen shows an example of Yangshao painted pottery, noted for its black decorative designs on a red background. Yangshao culture, dating from ca. 5,000 to 3,000 BC is probably the best-known neolithic culture in China and was centered in the Wei and Fen river valleys in the yellow soil plateau. Typical sites are the villages of Banbo and Jiangzhai. See Kwang-chih Chang's The Archaeology of Ancient China, pp. 108-109, 122, 140.

[10] According to Chinese legend, the Fire Emperor [Yandi] was the leader of the Jiang tribe dwelling on the northwest yellow soil plateau. He was defeated in battle by the Yellow Emperor [Huangdi], the leader of the peoples of the Central Plain.

has been ignored, and only the Yellow Emperor, born from the northwest yellow soil plateau, has become the legitimate ancestor of the Chinese people?

When we think about it carefully, the Fire Emperor is not the only one who has been ignored. If we cannot deny the fact that Chinese culture has been nurtured and supplemented by the cultures of Chu, of Wu and Yue, of the Miao, and of the northern nomads, then we must admit that we should have still other ancestors. But where are they?

The origins of [our] civilization already lie forgotten in the midst of chaos. What we can remember is the era of the Hundred Schools in the latter part of the Spring and Autumn period [722-484 B. C.].[11] Confucius, Laozi, Mozi, Zhuangzi, Hanfeizi,[12] and so forth, the philosophers of the Hundred Schools, glittered like stars in the sky. It just so happened that sages and great philosophers appeared in both East and West at that time.

While Confucius was travelling around the feudal states, on the other side of the Himalaya Mountains, Sakyamuni founded Buddhism.

At the same time when King Xuan of Qi [r.319-301 B.C.][13] established the Jixia Academy and gathered scholars from different schools, Plato [427-347 B.C.] too founded a school in Athens on the Mediterranean, where Aristotle [384-322 B.C.] became a student.

---

[11] The Spring and Autumn Period takes its name from a chronicle, The Spring and Autumn Annals [Chunqiu] of the State of Lu, Confucius' homeland. Confucius lived at the very end of this period and was the first to teach disciples and establish a philosophical school. Many more such schools sprung up in the subsequent Warring States Period [475-256 B.C.], and these are known as the "Hundred Schools," famous for their lively and unfettered debates. In the contemporary Chinese context, the term "Hundred Schools" directly recalls Mao's "Two Hundreds Policy," i.e., "Let a hundred flowers bloom, and a hundred schools of thought contend." During the short-lived "Hundred Flowers" campaign in 1957, Mao encouraged intellectuals to speak out boldly and criticize the party and government. The response was unexpectedly critical, however, and in the subsequent "Anti-Rightist" movement, many intellectuals who had spoken out were then punished. Some remained in internal exile for twenty years.

[12] During this early period, the Confucians were one of many competing schools; Confucianism did not become a national orthodoxy until the Han dynasty. Its major contenders were the Daoist school, represented by Laozi and Chuangzi; the short-lived school of Mozi, renowned for its advocacy of "universal love" and its emphasis on frugality, pacifism, and logic; and the school of the Legalists, founded by Hanfeizi, which eventually provided the ideological basis for the autocracy of the First Emperor of Qin.

[13] King Xuan [319—301 B.C.] of the state of Qi was the grandson of the famous Duke Huan and the son of King Wei. He founded an academy at Jixia in 317 B.C., where scholars of all schools were welcome to debate freely.

Present-day philosophers call that era the "axial period" of world culture. The various philosophies produced in that era still influence mankind today.

(Scene of the tomb of the First Emperor of Qin and tomb figurines of soldiers and horses)

Ever since the First Emperor of Qin burnt the books, buried Confucian scholars alive, and banned the classics and the writings of the philosophers,[14] China has never again re-enacted such a grand historical drama as the competition among the Hundred Philosophical Schools.[15] From these large square military formations, in addition to hearing the melodies of war and dictatorship, can we not also discern the repression of individuals caused by expelling unorthodox opinions, confining people's knowledge, and forcefully unifying thought?

In contrast, judging by these Han painted wall tiles with their broad range of themes, by the unusual imagination of these paintings on silk, by the vitality of those sculptures, seemingly about to move, and by the galloping of this flying horse,[16] how could the Qin Empire which swallowed up the six directions and united the world compare with the lofty spirit and broad-mindedness of the Han?

These stone lions and winged beasts of all sizes scattered all over China, whose original forms came from Persia, started to fascinate Chinese people as early as the Han Dynasty. The interesting point is that, from the point of view of people in the Han dynasty, to embody artistically the ideal of a strong empire in the image of a beast from a foreign country did not cause the Middle Kingdom to lose face.

---

[14] In 213 B.C., the First Emperor of Qin accepted the suggestion of his prime minister Li Si and ordered that all the Confucian classics, histories of other kingdoms, and the writings of the philosophers be burned. Anyone who possessed, read, or talked about these books would be sentenced to death. The next year the Emperor buried more than four hundred and sixty Confucian scholars alive at the capital city of Xianyang. See Sima Qian, Shiji [The Historical Records], Beijing: Zhonghua shuju, 1975, Chapter 6, "Qinshihuang benji" [The Annals of the First Emperor of Qin], p. 255 and p. 258.

[15] This paragraph should also be interpreted in the context of the tragic end of Mao's "Hundred Flowers Campaign." The implied message is clear: since the Qin unification, there has never been intellectual freedom in Chinese society, including the present.

[16] The screen shows a statue of a galloping horse stepping on a swallow in flight. This cast bronze flying horse, representing the breed of 'celestial horses' from Sogdiana in Central Asia, was excavated in 1969 at Wuwei county in Gansu from a tomb dating to the 2nd century A.D. and was part of an exhibition of Chinese archaeological treasures that toured the world in 1974. See Historical Relics Unearthed in New China, p. 110; The Exposition of Archaeological Finds of the People's Republic of China, 1974, plate 222.

Via the world-famous "Silk Road,"[17] culture and art from the Western Regions,[18] and even from India and Central Asia, flowed unceasingly into China from the time of the Emperor Wu of Han [157—87 B.C.]. If the Han Empire's extremely willing spirit of openness and broad cultural tolerance had never existed, then Chinese traditional palace music and dance might have always remained the same. Although they could make Confucius forget the taste of meat for three months,[19] they absolutely could not produce the glittering and colorful song and dance performances of the Han and Tang dynasties.

In 65 A.D., a Chinese emperor[20] dreamt of Sakyamuni, and this dream led to the encounter of the two ancient civilizations on either side of the Himalayas, causing a great merging of cultures that lasted eight centuries. A western scholar once said that among the fortuitous encounters in the history of mankind, the most enchanting was probably when Greek and Indian civilizations met Chinese civilization.

(Scene of the stone sculpture of the white horse in front of the White Horse Temple)[21]

Another Chinese scholar has put it in an even more humorous way. Using dining as a metaphor to describe how Chinese culture digested Indian Buddhism, he said that this meal had lasted for a thousand years. For this

---

[17] Also called the "Silk Route," it was an important trade route linking China with the outside world. *The main route for the silk trade ran overland to the west from North China through modern Sinkiang (Xinjiang) across the Pamirs to northern Iran and on to Syria and the Mediterranean, with a branch southward to India from the upper Oxus. There was also a maritime traffic by the South China Sea and the Indian Ocean, and another commodity exported westward by the sea routes was cinnamon bark, which was produced from cultivated trees in Kwangsi.* See Raymond Dawson, ed., The Legacy of China, London: Oxford University Press, 1964, p. 347.

[18] The western regions [xiyu] is a term used as early as the official history of the Han, referring to Shaanxi, Gansu, and part of Xinjiang province in modern China.

[19] Book VII, 13 of the Analects reads, *When he was in Ch'i the Master heard the Succession, and for three months did not know the taste of meat.* The "Succession [Shao]" was a kind of court dance which "mimed the peaceful accession of the legendary Emperor Shun." See Arthur Waley, trans. The Analects of Confucius, New York: Vintage Books, 1938, Book III, p. 101, and Book VII, p. 125.

[20] Emperor Ming of the Han dynasty, r. 58-74 A.D. This story, first told in the Sutra in Forty-two Sections, has many different versions and has been proven to be fictitious. See Henri Maspero, "Le songe et l'ambassade de l'empereur Ming, étude critique des sources," BEFEO X, 1910, pp. 95-130.

[21] The White Horse Temple is located 10 km. east of Loyang city in Henan province. Founded in 68 A.D., it is said to be China's first Buddhist temple. It preserves the stone statue of a white horse which is said to have carried Buddhist sutras to China from the western regions.

reason, it is probable that today even an illiterate child in China would recognize this white horse.

(A statue of Sakyamuni standing)

This white horse carried an unfamiliar god to China. Wearing an Indian-style cassock with its right shoulder exposed, it once sat in the stone grottoes of the Aryan people on the Deccan plateau. As it travelled eastward along a route parallel to the "Silk Road," its eye sockets gradually became shallower, its nose flatter, its smile more worldly, and its garment changed into a loose Chinese-style cassock with a broad sash. The Chinese people had remolded this foreign god. At that time, our ancestors indeed had this sort of tolerance, this sort of spirit and this sort of intelligence.

(A close-up of the Vairocana Buddha at Longmen cave in Loyang)[22]

Its full and elegant face, entrancing eyes, and graceful and magnanimous manner, even now still abruptly stun those who stand before it for the first time.

This world-famous huge head with its hair in spiral curls has today almost become a symbol of Chinese Buddhist art, and even of oriental civilization. Nevertheless, according to the researches of experts, its nose is carved in the classic style of ancient Greece. And so East and West, though separated by many oceans, combined to create this masterpiece, made of different elements yet all of equal artistry.

The statue of Vairocana Buddha which sits here straight like a monarch looking down from his throne is an oriental Athena. It fully deserves to be considered a high point. Its mysterious, thoughtful smile looks like a confident smile from a people who would never reject a foreign culture. This is the high Tang spirit.[23]

(The television studio. A scholar discussing High Tang culture)

---

[22] The statue of the Vairocana Buddha is the central image among the statues in Longmen cave and is the tallest one, approximately 17 meters high. Completed in 675 A.D., it was supposedly modelled on the image of the infamous Empress Wu Zetian [625-705 A.D.], a patron of Buddhism who donated 20,000 strings of cash for its construction. The Vairocana Buddha, first described in the Avatamsaka Sutra [Hua yan jing] was considered a cosmic Buddha representing knowledge, whose light shone in all directions; the historical Buddha Sakyamuni was merely one of its manifestations. See Gong Dazhong, Longmen shi ku yishu [The Arts of the Longmen Caves], Shanghai: Shanghai remin chubanshe, 1981, esp. Chapter Nine, pp. 133-150.

[23] The language in these two paragraphs is partly derived from Su Xiaokang's article "Dongfang fodiao" [The Buddhist Sculpture of the Orient] in Renmin wenxue, 1983. 10, pp. 81-92.

Ye Lang (Professor at Beijing University and Director of the Esthetics Teaching and Research Group, Philosophy Department): *The vigor of Tang culture was closely related to its degree of openness to the outside world. The Ming dynasty dramatist Tang Xianzu [1550-1617] once compared the Ming and Tang dynasties. He said that the Tang dynasty was a 'world of feeling' while the Ming dynasty was a 'world of rule.'*[24] *The genius of Li Bai [701—762 A.D.] was closely related to his living in the 'world of feeling'; if he had lived in the 'world of rule' of the Ming dynasty, his genius would not have developed fully. What is meant by the so-called 'world of feeling' is that Tang society was suitable for the development of culture, and even more suitable for the development of human nature. The openness of Tang culture was not partial, but all-embracing. That this was true for music, painting, sculpture and literature goes without saying. In addition, philosophy and ways of thinking were also influenced by Indian philosophy. The refined philosophies of Cheng-Zhu Neo-Confucianism as well as of Wang Fuzhi*[25] *were the fruit of Buddhist influence. In observing the expression of a people's confidence, vitality and creativity, the important thing is to observe its attitude towards foreign culture, whether it is to reject it or to open up and accept it. I once saw two pieces of Tang tri-colored glazed pottery portraying noblewomen who reveal expressions full of confidence and optimism. Tang culture inspires us in two ways: First, one of its culture's truly distinguishing features was a true 'blooming of a hundred flowers'; it was not all based on a single model or played to a single tune; it was a blend of many colors, not drab and uniform. Second, how does one create a situation full of vitality in which 'a hundred flowers*

---

[24] Tang Xianzu was one of the best-known dramatists of the Ming dynasty. In writing his plays, he "prized literary quality over musical form" and was often criticized by his opponents for his "disregard of order and restraint." He also stressed *qing* (feelings) rather than *li* (reason or order). This distinction between *qing* and *li* would seem to represent the distinction between *qing* and *fa* above also. See William H. Nienhauser, Jr. ed., The Indiana Companion to Traditional Chinese Literature, Bloomington: Indiana University Press, 1986, p. 753.

[25] Neo-Confucianism represented the response of the Chinese tradition to the intellectual challenge of Buddhism and incorporated a new cosmology and metaphysics which previous Confucianism had lacked. Its major exponents were the two brothers Cheng Hao [1032-1085] and Cheng I [1033-1107] in the Northern Song and Zhu Xi [1130—1200] in the Southern Song. Zhu Xi's commentaries on the Four Books were adopted as the orthodox interpretation and were studied by candidates for the government examinations until the early 20th century. Wang Fuzhi [1619—1692], whose career spanned the end of the Ming dynasty and the beginning of the Qing, was an ardent Ming loyalist who refused to serve the Manchus. He was well-versed in both Buddhist and Taoist philosophy and was a proponent of the Song Neo-Confucian scholar Zhang Zai. His opposition to the Manchus made him a favorite of early twentieth century reformers. Wang Fuzhi's most famous work, the Du tongjian lun, is quoted in Part Two, in a passage where he expresses profound contempt for the northern nomads. On Wang Fuzhi, see Hummel, op. cit., pp. 816-819.

bloom'? A very important factor is to open up to the outside.[26] *The nourishment and stimulus provided by cultures on the outside permitted a 'hundred flowers to bloom' on the inside. If it had never had that broad absorption of nourishment afforded by opening up to the outside, then it would have been impossible to have vitality or a 'hundred flowers blooming' on the inside."*[27]

The Vairocana Buddha, unequalled in the whole world, the Vairocana Buddha which we can never finish describing, is our own miracle and source of pride. But when we face it, have we ever seriously thought: What kind of strength and spirit created its perfection and greatness? Why have we been unable to create a second one?

Even Westerners could not help but feel sorry for us.

The English writer H.G. Wells in his Outline of History, after spending a lot of ink describing the prosperity of China's Tang dynasty, immediately switches his topic and says: *"The urbanity, the culture, and the power of China under the early Tang rulers are in so vivid a contrast with the decay, disorder, and divisions of the Western world, as at once to raise some of the most interesting questions in the history of civilization. Why did not China keep this great lead she had won by her rapid return to unity and order? Why does she not to this day dominate the world culturally and politically?"*[28]

(Reappearance of the titles: The Light of the Spirit)

If we say that literature and art reached their climax in the Tang dynasty, then China's science and technology reached their maturity in the Song dynasty. In tracing the history of China's science and technology, we constantly find that discoveries and inventions were concentrated in the Song dynasty.

---

[26] "Opening up to the outside" [dui wai kaifang] has been one of the central policies of Deng Xiaoping's reform program, the other being "reviving the economy" [gaohuo jingji].

[27] In the broadcast version, this interview with Ye Lang is severely edited, eliminating the references to the policies of "letting a hundred flowers bloom" and "opening up to the outside." The remaining interview reads: *The society of the Tang dynasty was an open society in terms of culture. That is to say that Tang society was suitable to the development of culture. In observing the expression of a people's confidence, vitality and creativity, the important thing is to observe its attitude towards foreign culture, whether it is to reject it or to open up and accept it. The Tang was an open society. I once saw two pieces of Tang tri-colored glazed pottery portraying noblewomen who reveal expressions full of confidence, ease, and optimism towards life and their time. The Tang was an era full of confidence.* At this point a voice from offstage adds: *And it was a relatively free period.*

[28] H.G. Wells, The Outline of History, chapter 29, section 8. In the 1956 two-volume edition by Garden City Books, see pp. 464-465 in volume 1.

The proving ground of the first explosives in human history was the battlefield on the Central Plain of the war between the Song and the Jin. It was no later than 1000 A.D. that Chinese people were already able to use catapults to project "explosives." Yet we never would have dreamt that eight hundred years later the same Chinese people would suffer a total defeat by the iron-clad ships and fierce guns of foreigners.

In 751 A.D., China fought a large-scale battle with Arab moslems along the Talas River.[29] The Tang's crushing defeat by the moslems prevented China from ever going back to Central Asia. Yet this battle was very significant in the history of science. Tens of thousands of Tang prisoners brought the techniques of paper-making to Arabs and Westerners. Following that, movable-type printing, the compass, and gunpowder were successively transmitted from China to Europe in the darkness of its middle ages where they caused an astounding shock. The great inventions crystallized by the wisdom of the Chinese people eventually struck a fatal blow to European feudal society. "*Gunpowder blew the feudal knights[30] to bits. The compass opened up the world market and established colonies; printing technology became a tool of Protestantism. In general they became the means for a scientific renaissance.*"[31] Europe reached its second high point of technological development since the time of the Greeks. Precisely because it had reached this high point, in the seventeenth century the West far overtook China, which hitherto had been far ahead. No wonder Francis Bacon [1561-1626] said that there was not an empire, not a religion, and not

---

[29] Talas was an oasis on the western side of the Tianshan range in what is now the Kirghiz Soviet Republic. Some of the Chinese soldiers captured by the Arabs at that battle escaped and brought back to China the account of how Chinese technologies had been adopted by the Arabs in Baghdad. See Joseph Needham, op.cit., vol. I, p. 236 & III, p. 682.

[30] qishi, lit., "mounted warrior."

[31] The point made here appears to reflect the views of Joseph Needham, who in an article co-authored with Ray Huang, made a very similar point: *The strange thing is that China was able to absorb these earth-shaking discoveries and inventions while Europe was gravely affected by them, as has been shown in detail elsewhere. Gunpowder made relatively little difference to the fighting in and around China, while in Europe it ruined the feudal castle and the armoured knight. ... The magnetic compass and the axial rudder permitted Europeans to discover the Americas, but Chinese sea-captains pursued their peaceful ways in the Indian Ocean and the Pacific as of old. Printing helped to launch the Reformation and the revival of learning in the West; all it did in China (apart from preserving a host of books which would otherwise have perished) was to open civil service recruiting to a wider range of society. Perhaps there has hardly ever been so cybernetic and homeostatic a culture as that of China, but to say that is by no means to speak of 'stagnation' as so many Westerners have done.* From "The Nature of Chinese Society—A Technical Interpretation" in Journal of Oriental Studies [Hong Kong], vol. XII, nos. 1&2, 1974, pp. 1-16; esp. p. 8.

a single great person that had ever exerted more power and influence on mankind than those inventions.[32]

However, the four great inventions had a very poor fate in their own native land. The Chinese, who first lit the flame that would conquer space, did not become the first people to fly to outer space. Rockets and fireworks have remained the same for hundreds of years but are still used only for dispelling evil spirits and for celebrations. Paper and printing techniques, communication tools of immeasurable value, within a few centuries after reaching Europe, had destroyed the feudal castles. But China, a country with oceans of history books and a tradition of book collecting, even in a thousand years never succeeded in creating a knowledge "explosion," and in the end, it was the West which re-imported the technology of moveable lead type back to us. Although as early as the eleventh century Shen Kuo [1031-1095], in his Brushtalks from Dreambrook,[33] had described the compass and the phenomenon of magnetic declination, yet China was never able to become a strong sea power. On the contrary, it was the Western great powers guided by the compass who forced their way to our front door... In the final analysis, what sort of force is it that has played such tricks on the Chinese people?

(The television studio. A scholar discussing why the early modern scientific revolution did not occur in China.)

Liu Qingfeng[34] (Associate Researcher at the Chinese Academy of Sciences): *"We have done a statistical analysis of scientific achievements in*

---

[32] Francis Bacon, Novum Organum, section 129: *Again, we should notice the force, effect, and consequences of inventions, which are nowhere more conspicuous than in those three which were unknown to the ancients; namely, printing, gunpowder, and the compass. For these three have changed the appearance and state of the whole world: first in literature, then in warfare, and lastly in navigation; and innumerable changes have been thence derived, so that no empire, sect, or star, appears to have exercised a greater power and influence on human affairs than these mechanical discoveries.*

[33] The Mengqi bitan in 29 juan was a book written by the Song scholar Shen Kuo. The contents of the book reveal his broad learning, ranging from classical commentary to popular fiction and music. His specialties were astronomy, mathematics, and engineering. His book provides important early evidence of Chinese knowledge of the compass and moveable type. See Yves Hervouet, ed., A Sung Bibliography, Hong Kong: Chinese University Press, 1978, pp. 226-229.

[34] A more detailed exposition of these views may be found in an article written jointly by her husband Jin Guantao, Fan Hongye and herself, entitled "Wenhua beijing yu kexue jishu jiegou de yanbian" [The Cultural Background and the Evolution of the Structure of Science and Technology] first published in 1983 in a volume entitled Kexue chuantong yu wenhua—Zhongguo jindai kexue luohou de yuanyin [The Scientific Tradition and Culture— The Reason for the Backwardness of Chinese Early Modern Science], Shaanxi kexue jishu chubanshe. The two graphs, contrasting the development curves of science and technology

ancient China and the Western world over the past two thousand years, and as a result, we have gotten two very interesting curves. These two types of curves are very dissimilar in their forms and features. These comparative curves have destroyed the popular assumption that science and technology were rather developed in ancient China. The curves indicate that while science and technology were well-developed in ancient China, actually it was primarily technology which was well-developed. The four great inventions were all technological inventions, and not examples of run-of-the-mill technology, but rather technology related to national unification, such as communications, water conservancy, armaments, and state-run manufacturing industries. Those technologies related to national unification and suited to the feudal landlord economy were well-developed; these technologies of ours were "great unification" [35] *type technologies, of which the "four great inventions" were representatives. The technology of "great unification" put ancient China's science in chains and made it hard to transform. China's science and technology did not fall behind until early modern times. Early modern science in the West demonstrated exponential growth and quickly surpassed that of China. This is from the point of view of social structure. Furthermore, from the point of view of culture, ancient Chinese concepts such as organic naturalism, "the harmony of man and nature,"* [36] *an intuitive and inductive way of thinking, as well as an ideology of ethical centralism—i.e, that value judgments are inherent in everything— made it very difficult for the ancient Chinese to go beyond notions of right- wrong and of ethics, and to judge things based solely on objective and neutral principles. This kind of relationship between culture and science and technology is something to which we have not yet given sufficient study."* [37]

---

in China and the West, are taken from an book by Hu Juren, Li Yuese yu Zhongguo kexue [Joseph Needham and Chinese Science], Wenhua shenghuo chubanshe, Hong Kong, 1978.

[35] On the concept of "great unification" [da yitong], see the footnote to the interview with her husband, Jin Guantao, in Part Five, p. 195.

[36] The basic idea of tian ren he yi is that human society is a reflection of the cosmos, so that all human activities should imitate and be in harmony with Nature; this is particularly important for the Son of Heaven in ruling the nation. Similarly, Nature reflects the moral state of the human realm; bad rule is reflected in portents and natural disasters. The "harmony of man and nature" was advocated by the Han Confucianist Dong Zhongshu [179-104 B.C.]. See his Chunqiu fanlu [Profound Meaning of the Spring and Autumn Annals], in Sources of the Chinese Tradition: Introduction to Oriental Civilization, compiled by Wm. Theodore De Bary, Wing-tsit Chan, and Burton Watson. New York: Columbia University Press, 1960, volume I, pp. 158-9.

[37] The broadcast version edits out much of this interview. It reads: *This sort of research indicates that the development of science and technology in ancient China was primarily the development of technology [not science]. Like the well-known "four great inventions" I just mentioned, they were all technological inventions. This kind of technological invention has another characteristic: they are not run-of-the-mill technologies but are technologies divorced from [agricultural] production and related to national unification,*

Today when we think back, the sixteenth and seventeenth centuries are indeed two centuries about which Chinese people feel bitter. When Wang Yangming [1472-1528][38] was sitting there meditating on bamboo, Leonardo Da Vinci was both dissecting the human body and painting the Mona Lisa; Ferdinand Magellan had just finished the first circumnavigation of the globe; Nicolaus Copernicus was ready to publish his De revolutionibus orbium coelestium.[39] Later when Gu Yanwu [1612-1682][40] was fascinated with reconstructing the archaic pronunciation of Chinese characters, Galileo had invented the telescope, Harvey had published his magnum opus on the circulation of the blood, and Newton had invented the calculus. While Westerners were researching the planets and stars, the human body, levers, and chemical substances, Chinese were studying books, Chinese characters, and old piles of paper. Therefore, Hu Shi [1891-1962][41] said that what China's human sciences had created was more book knowledge, while western natural sciences had created a new world.

Therefore, after the seventeenth century, the "New World" would come knocking on the tightly-closed gate of the ancient East. Christianity, which abandoned the obscurantism of the Middle Ages, came from the sea full of vitality and bearing with it a brand-new civilization.[42] If we say that fifteen

---

such as communications, water conservancy, armaments, and state-run manufacturing industries. Those technologies were related to national unification and well-suited to the feudal landlord economy. Those technologies are represented by the "four great inventions"; we call them "great unification" type technologies. The fact that ancient China possessed those technologies was significant. In early modern times, they played a great role in destroying Western feudalism. Yet, at the same time they brought a serious problem. The "great unification" type technologies put ancient China's science and technology in chains and made them difficult to transform.

[38] He is also known as Wang Shouren, a native of Yuyao in modern Zhejiang province. He was the founder of the intuitionalist school of Neo-Confucianism, best known for his theory that "knowledge and action are one." See Fang and Goodrich, op. cit., pp. 1408-1416.

[39] On the revolutions of the heavenly bodies, 1543.

[40] Gu Yanwu was a late Ming philosopher who advocated a sort of primitive materialism. He is well-known for his achievements in philology and the exegesis of the Confucian classics. See Hummel, op.cit., pp. 421-426.

[41] Hu Shih was one of the pioneering leaders of China's May Fourth movement. He came to the U.S. in 1910 first to study agriculture at Cornell University and later to study philosophy at Columbia. He became a disciple of John Dewey and interpreted for him on his visit to China. Hu advocated "democracy and science," and is well-known for sayings such as: *Be bold in making hypotheses, yet careful in seeking proof* [da dan jiashe, xiaoxin qiu zheng] and *Talk more about [specific] problems and less about -isms* [duo tan xie wenti, shao tan xie zhuyi]. See Boorman and Howard, op.cit., pp. 167-174.

[42] The first Catholic missionary reached China at the end of the sixteenth century; Protestant missions did not begin until the early nineteenth century. Here the text uses

hundred years ago the Chinese emperor went out of his way to invite the eminent monks to come from India, then we would have to say that in the present time, the "eminent monks from the West" came on their own without being asked.

This man with deep-set eyes, prominent nose, and full beard, and wearing the robes of a Confucian scholar is the famous Italian missionary Matteo Ricci [1552-1610]. He came to China in 1582, died in Beijing in 1610, and his tomb is still in Beijing to this day.[43] For a rather long time in the past, we labeled him "a tool of Western cultural encroachment." Yet, since Chinese history could give the Indian missionaries Zhi Qian and Kumarajiva[44] a high position, why should we deliberately scorn this "eminent monk from the West"? It is probably because when facing this second confrontation with western culture, China had already lost the broad-mindedness and tolerance of the Han and Tang dynasties.

Matteo Ricci was the first to tell Chinese that they were not at the center of the world, but rather somewhere in the northern hemisphere. The Western scientific works he brought are still preserved in the Beijing libraries.

In the first century after the arrival of western missionaries, China adopted a relatively positive attitude towards this new civilization. Some outstanding Chinese scholar-officials converted to Catholicism, studied diligently with the western missionaries, and actively translated western scientific works, revealing a certain self-awareness of history. Even Emperor Kangxi liked astronomy and mathematics. In the Changchun Garden next to where the west gate of Beijing University stands today, he even ordered the

---

jidujiao [lit., the teaching of Christ] to indicate Christianity in general. Normally, jidujiao indicates Protestantism, while tianzhujiao indicates Catholicism.

[43] The tombs of the Catholic missionaries from the Ming and Qing period are said to be in the back courtyard of the Central Party Academy in the Haidian district of Beijing; they are not normally open to the public. This is perhaps the first publicly-released film of these tombs since 1949. The screen shows Ricci's tomb with a tablet respectfully inscribed: *The Tomb of the Missionary Li Madou*. We also see a modern plaque indicating that the cemetery is a cultural treasure under the government's protection.

[44] Zhi Qian was a Buddhist monk, a native of the Yuezhi tribe (in the area near modern Gansu and Qinghai provinces). In the second half of the 2nd century [168-189 A.D.], he came to Luoyang where he learned Chinese and translated Buddhist sutras into Chinese. His biographical sketch can be found in Huijiao, Gao seng zhuan [Biographies of Eminent Monks], Taibei: Guangwen shuju, 1976, juan 1, pp. 54-59. Kumarajiva (Jiumo luoshi in Chinese) was a eminent monk of the Later Qin, and the founder of the Three Treatise school of Buddhism. Ibid., juan 2, pp. 97-121.

establishment of a mathematics institute, which we might consider a "National Research Institute of Mathematics"![45]

(The great fountain of the Yuanming yuan.)[46]

This was once the most favorite place for Qing emperors and their empresses and concubines to come to relax. This world-famous imperial garden was designed in 1747 by the Italian Giuseppe Castiglione.[47]

The emperors and empresses, tired of oriental-style palaces and pavilions and of the artificial pastoral scenes of the imperial gardens, were happy to come here to view some western-style scenery. While the hunting dogs chased the deer in the mist from the fountain, the Chinese emperors seemed absolutely unwilling to reject western-style enjoyments. This situation closely resembles ours at present; while some people exert their full strength to criticize western life-styles and values, yet they themselves would never refuse to enjoy those super-deluxe limousines and high-class consumer goods.

The worst thing was that the Qing emperors tried to encircle the palace with high stone walls and sent soldiers from the Eight Banners Army to guard their fantasy world with huge swords and spears. They also wanted to lock the gate of the country, to close off thousands of li of coast line and trading ports, and to let big swords, spears, home-made cannons, and

---

[45] On the screen, the camera pans from the gate of Beijing University to the buildings opposite, revealing the signboard of the Changchun Restaurant. This may be an ironic comment on the value of intellectual institutions vis-à-vis the "commodity economy," as well as a comment contrasting the position of intellectuals past and present.

[46] The Yuanming yuan, or Yuanming Garden, is located at Haidian in Beijing. It was built in 1709 under the order of the Kangxi Emperor and further improved during the reigns of Yongzheng and Qianlong. In 1747, Emperor Qianlong ordered the construction of European-style fountains and buildings on the north side of the Changchun yuan, adjacent to the Yuanming yuan; the plans were the responsibility of Father Castiglione while the engineering was in the hands of Father Benoit. These gardens and the palaces in them were used as the private retreats and residences of the Qing emperors. Western visitors who saw them called them the Summer Palace. In 1860, when the allied forces of the French and the British defeated the Qing army and captured the capital, the Summer Palace was set on fire and burned to ashes. Here the screen shows a clip from a film (presumably Huo shao Yuanming yuan), in which this fountain has been recreated, showing cast metal deer and hunting dogs. In the eighteenth century Emperor Qianlong commissioned a series of copperplate engravings of these foreign buildings, which are reproduced in Carroll Brown Malone, History of the Peking Summer Palaces under the Ch'ing Dynasty, Urbana: University of Illinois, 1934. The principal fountain, the Da shui fa, is illustrated in engraving #15, Malone, p. 153.

[47] Castiglione [Chinese name: Lang Shining, 1688-1767] was a Jesuit missionary who came to Beijing in 1715. He served as court painter for two emperors, Yongzheng and Qianlong, and died in Beijing.

soldiers' flesh resist the iron-clad warships that advanced under the thunder of their guns.

In the end, their dream was destroyed.[48]

(The ruins of the grand fountain in the Yuanming yuan. The Great Wall)

Modern Chinese often like to pay a thoughtful visit to two historical sites near Beijing. Some of them, who have always regarded the Great Wall as a symbol of strength and prosperity, upon ascending the Great Wall feel proud and elated, as if the whole universe had shrunk at their feet. Yet when they come before the unbearable sight of these tumble-down stone ruins, they feel heart-broken and grind their teeth, and, of course, they resolve to wipe out the shame. My dear fellow countrymen, have you ever thought about the cause-effect connection between these two sites?

Those grand wall paintings and grand stone sculptures, once brimful with talent and alive with spirit, have now turned into knick-knacks which, though exquisite and delicate, are yet pretty and stylized. In art, excessive attention to detail and over-ornamentation foretell the decline of the creativity of a people. Vairocana has gone, never to return!

Even Wei Yuan [1749-1856], one of the most outstanding persons of his age, in his well-known book, An Illustrated Record of Maritime Countries,[49] described Catholicism using superstitious ideas from Chinese alchemy, such as "cultivating Yin and supplementing Yang" and "sucking human bone marrow." Even a superior person like Lin Zexu believed that British soldiers could not straighten their legs, and suggested to the Daoguang Emperor that *China needs only to close its doors and markets, and the English will be finished.* Their knowledge of this world had already sunk to the level preceding that of Father Matteo Ricci's arrival in China.

When the most advanced and learned persons of a people are so ignorant and when the people's soul—her intellectuals—are abandoned by the times, then what hope does this people still have? At that time, China had only one person who was fully awake, and precisely because he was awake, he felt more pain than anyone else. He said this was a decadent age in which men's hearts were stupid, in which there were no talented ministers at court,

[48] The screen shows the scene of the burning of the Summer Palace from the film Huo shao Yuanming yuan.

[49] Wei Yuan's famous Hai guo tu zhi, describing the geography of Western countries, was published in 1844, two years after China's defeat by Britain in the Opium War. Wei Yuan and Gong Zizhen were both pragmatists who advocated "learning 'barbarian' technology to subdue the barbarians." He was also the author of the Sheng wu ji in 14 juan, recording the military exploits of the Qing emperors up to Daoguang. Hummel, op. cit., pp. 850-852.

no talented commanders in the army camps, no talented scholars in the schools, no talented farmers on the land, no talented workmen building houses, no talented artisans in the workshops, no talented merchants in the markets, and not even any talented thieves and robbers. He wept aloud all day, praying for a good government for the country; when this wish proved impossible, he wept aloud all day praying that the country would descend into chaos! He was Gong Zizhen [1792-1841].[50]

What is the reason why this outstanding civilization and people, which produced Qu Yuan and Li Bai, which created the four great inventions, and which led the world for over a thousand years, has sunk to such a miserable level, that the influence of this misery has extended to the present day, and may well extend for several generations to come?

If the light of China's science, technology and culture could help the West create a new era in history, then why is it that the light of culture and science from foreign parts has always flickered on and off in China?

China is pondering.

Young people are questioning History.[51]

On the ancient Central Plain, endowed with a long-enduring civilization and rich in cultural artifacts, the sediment of history covers the landscape, and everywhere ancient spectres are roaming.

In the south-western corner of this land, there lie in eternal slumber three outstanding persons who shone in history; yet their posthumous treatment has been so varied that the degree of respect or indifference shown

---

[50] Gong Zizhen was a contemporary and a friend of both Wei Yuan and Lin Zexu. He supported Lin Zexu's harsh measures against British opium traders and proposed a variety of reform measures to strengthen the state and alleviate the burdens of the people. He was a critic of the Qing government and hence was much admired by reformers such as Kang Yuwei and Liang Qichao. The previous passage is quoted with slight changes from Gong's anthology. See Gong Zizhen, Dingan quanji, Shanghai: Dada tushu gongsi, 1938, p. 6. For his biographical sketch, see Hummel, op. cit., pp. 431-434. In a later interview, Wang Luxiang expressed his regret at leaving the impression that Wei Yuan and Lin Zexu were less far-sighted than Gong Zizhen; actually, the reverse was probably the case. See Guan Zhizhong and Hong Shujuan, "Fang Heshang zongzhuangao Wang Luxiang" [An Interview with Heshang's Main Writer Wang Luxiang], Yuan jian, Taibei, December 15, 1988, pp. 204-207.

[51] The screen shows a series of books from the Zou xiang weilai congshu [Heading Toward the Future Series, edited by Jin Guantao]: Da biandong shidai de jianshe zhe [Builders in a Time of Great Changes]; Yishu meili de tanxun [The Search for Beauty in Art]; Zuotian, jintian, mingtian [Yesterday, Today, and Tomorrow]; Xifang shehui jiegou de yanbian [The Evolution of the Structure of Western Society]; Ren de xiandaihua [The Modernization of Mankind]; Ze you fenpei yuanli [Principles of Selective Distribution].

to these three persons by Chinese history would seem to reveal to us the secrets of history itself.

On Sleeping Dragon Ridge to the west of Nanyang city, because Zhuge Liang [181-234][52] had *"peerless merits among the three divided kingdoms"*[53] and was once Prime Minister of Shu, his once small and shabby huts have now become grand and imposing. Today the Shrine of the Martial Marquis includes gates, hallways, red pavilions, covered walkways, palaces and towers, carved beams and painted rafters, green pines and cypresses, and stone tablets and inscriptions. What a grand and dignified view they make!

At Dongguan Village near Nanyang there is the Shrine of the Sage Doctor. The great physician Zhang Zhongjing[54] was once the magistrate of Changsha city and also a life-saving doctor, for which later people have paid him double respect. Yet compared to the Shrine of the Martial Marquis, the Shrine of the Sage Doctor is one grade lower. Furthermore, his official title as Magistrate of Changsha had to be carved above the title of Sage Doctor on his tomb inscription.

Among the three, the shabbiest and least-frequented is Zhang Heng's tomb to the north of Nanyang city. Zhang Heng was a great, world-class scientist and also one of the very few literary men of the Eastern Han dynasty. Today some famous foreign universities have a statue of him. But in his own homeland, he has only a reputation as an intellectual and a writer in the field of science and technology, which does not arouse any special respect from people, so that a pile of yellow soil for him was good enough—Zhang Heng's tomb even today still lies alone in the corner of a field in Stone Bridge Township of Nanyang, with only crops and weeds for company. If he had not spent a few days as a court official with the titles of Grand Historian and Grand Secretary, probably his earthen burial mound would not have lasted until today. And has anyone ever seen the tombs of

---

[52] During the Three Kingdoms period, Zhuge Liang assisted Lu Bei in founding the kingdom of Shu; his reputation is that of a master strategist and statesman.

[53] This is the first line from Du Fu's five-syllable chüeh-chü in honor of Zhuge Liang, entitled "Ba zhen tu" [The Eight Formations]. See Tang shi sanbai shou [Three Hundred Tang Poems], edited by Chu Yao, Taibei: Wenyuan shuju, 1969, p. 292; David Hawkes, A Little Primer of Du Fu, Oxford, 1967, pp. 185-187.

[54] Zhang Zhongjing was a native of Henan Province in the Eastern Han dynasty. Two books are attributed to him: On Typhus and The Essentials of Diagnosis, both considered classics in China's traditional medical science. See Zhongguo lidai mingren cidian [A Dictionary of Eminent Chinese in History], Nanjing: Nanjing daxue lishi xi, 1982, p. 87.

the two great scientists, Zu Chongzhi and Song Yingxing,[55] who spent their whole lives as commoners?[56]

Now although Chinese intellectuals in the twentieth century have finally gotten rid of the bad luck of being "Stinky Old Ninths"[57] and seem to have slightly higher social status, yet economic hardship and spiritual repression still accompany them. The sad news of their early deaths is constantly reported.[58] Their heavy burdens are wiping out the best middle-aged intellectuals in great numbers.[59]

---

[55] Zu Chongzhi [429-500] is best-known for calculating the value of π accurately to seven decimals, a feat which was not equalled until the 16th century. See Needham, op. cit., vol. III, pp. 101-102. Song Yingxing [1590-1650] was the compiler of the Tiangong kaiwu [The Exploitation of the Works of Nature], an illustrated encyclopedia of technology, published in 1637. Ibid., vol. IV.2, pp. 171-172; Hummel, op.cit., pp. 690-691.

[56] The above four paragraphs describing the tombs of the three scientists are quoted verbatim from an article in the People's Daily of November 10, 1987 by Li Gengchen, reprinted in Xinhua wenzhai, January, 1988, p. 117. Wang Luxiang has commented as follows on the significance of the comparison of these shrines and tombs: *"The comparison of the shrines and tombs of three famous historical figures in Nanyang was inspired by an article in People's Daily. Some people have criticized Heshang for not having critiqued the 'consciousness of official rank' [guan benwei yishi]. In my view, they haven't seen the conclusion of 'The Light of the Spirit.' Does not the vivid contrast of the posthumous admiration or indifference accorded to Zhuge Liang, Zhang Zhongjing and Zhang Heng express precisely our critique of 'the consciousness of official rank'?"* See Wang Luxiang, "Huiyi yu sikao," in Heshang lun, p. 95. The blue sun shown on the screen may be interpreted as a symbolic protest both against the color red, symbolic of the Chinese communist revolution, and against the red sun, symbol of Mao Zedong himself.

[57] The term for "Stinky Old Ninth" is chou lao jiu; this was a term applied to Chinese intellectuals during the Cultural Revolution. At the initial stage of the Cultural Revolution, there were five major targets: landlords, wealthy peasants, counter-revolutionaries, evildoers, and rightists, who were labelled the "Five Black Elements" [hei wu lei]. Later, another four categories were added: followers of capitalism, underground gangs, alien-class elements (bourgeoisie) and intellectuals. Anyone who fell into these categories would be the target of "class struggle." Since the end of the Cultural Revolution, intellectuals were restored to a higher social status and recognized as "part of the working class."

[58] In a piece published in 1987, Su Xiaokang reported the following figures about primary and secondary school teachers in Beijing: Out of more than 4,000 secondary school teachers in the west city district, 203 were on full sick leave, 272 were on partial sick leave; and 205 were working despite illness. In the same district in 1985 and 1986, the average age of death for teachers was in their 50s, and nearly one half had died before retirement age; this contrasts with an average age at death of over 70 for Beijing residents. See Su Xiaokang, "Shensheng yousilu" in Ziyou beiwanglu—Su Xiaokang baogao wenxue jingxuan, Hong Kong: Sanlian shudian, 1989, p. 108.

[59] This paragraph and the next one are both deleted in the second broadcast. A new paragraph is substituted, which reads: *Perhaps people today still remember the nickname "Stinky Old Ninths." That extremely leftist period when intellectuals were intensely despised is already gone. Yet the physical and mental scars caused by humiliation and*

Even more frightening is the fact that in this civilized old country, which honors the ancestral tablet of Confucius, the status of teachers has fallen to a very low position. The old generation has burned down their candles, and their oil lamps are about to die out, yet the new generation will refuse to follow in their foot-steps.[60] The educational crisis has become China's most urgent crisis. How many school teachers and intellectuals have wept sadly upon reading The Teachers' Lament![61]

These people who can transform the sparkling light of the spirit into the sun are thin and weak, their faces pinched, yet sitting in their small rooms, they are trying to imagine those new constellations in the Milky Way Galaxy of human civilizations that will belong to the Chinese people.

Among the professions of mankind, no one has a greater need for a free atmosphere and unlimited space than they do.

If you affixed a black cross[62] to their spirits or weighed them down under a grey Great Wall, then the light of the spirit would never become the sun!

---

abasement have today yielded a harvest of evil fruit. Now that their motherland and the people put the heavy burden of bringing about modernization on their shoulders, some of them have parted forever from their loved ones and their careers with infinite regret. What people worry about even more is that in this ancient civilized nation where the ancestral tablet of Confucius is worshipped highly, the social position of teachers has become less and less respected. On the other hand, the ranks of the illiterate and semi-illiterate continue to increase. Based on a partial sample survey, two-thirds of China's peasants have not managed to rid themselves of the stigma of being illiterate. While education in the advanced countries is already training talent for the next century, we are still unable even to wipe out illiteracy.

[60] Su Xiaokang quotes newspaper reports from 1986 that very few students apply to teacher's colleges [ibid., pp. 86-87].

[61] The Teachers' Lament [Shensheng you si lu] is the title of a long piece of reportage literature by Su Xiaokang and Zhang Min, first published in Renmin wenxue, September, 1987. It focuses on the crisis in China's primary and secondary schools, caused by the few numbers of students applying to teacher training colleges; the low morale and high drop-out rate of prospective teachers; the poor housing and health care afforded to teachers; and the past history of discrimination and "class struggle" directed at teachers and intellectuals in general.

[62] In his "Shensheng yousilu," Su Xiaokang metaphorically describes schoolteachers as "candles that have burnt themselves to ashes" and as suffering on the "cross" of mistreatment and discrimination. Ibid., pp. 100-101, 106. In this episode the image of the cross is presented in conjunction with the early Catholic missionaries, while the beginning of Part Five, "Sorrow and Worry," shows the startling image of a faithful Catholic nailed to the cross to reenact the crucifixion.

May History never again play tricks on Chinese intellectuals.
Today, this is our deepest prayer!

Wang Luxiang

Part Four

"The New Era"

In the middle of the nineteenth century, just as the great industries conjured up by capitalism had reached their apex, a Jew in the British Museum had already dissected its secrets and pronounced its death sentence.

As Marx [1818-1883] examined Capital, that monster whose every pore oozed blood from head to toe, his pacing feet wore ruts into the floor of the British Museum as he designed the outlines of a future society.

This great teacher was very careful. He only drew a blueprint for the future. He conceived of a communist society as one in which productive forces should be highly developed, wealth well-distributed, in which labor would no longer be a means to make a living and in which the expenditure of labor would no longer determine the price of commodities[1]; hence the bond between goods and money would exit from the stage of History.

In 1917, the sound of gunfire from the cruiser Avrora would seem to have proclaimed the appearance in Russia of that future society conceived of

---

[1] shang pin. Marxism defines commodities as products of human labor which are not consumed by their producers but which are rather exchanged for other commodities on the market through the medium of currency. A commodity economy presumes a cash, market-driven economy and a relatively high division of labor. In premodern societies peasants typically produce for themselves rather than for the market; and in the future society envisioned by Marx, productive forces would be highly developed, and the amount of wealth in society could assure that commodities would no longer have to be bought with money. Hence the commodity economy is a stage between a subsistence economy and a communist utopia. Marx's future society is described in his Critique of the Gotha Programme (1875) as follows: *In a higher phase of communist society, after the enslaving subordination of individuals under division of labor, and therewith also the antithesis between mental and physical labor, has vanished; after labor, from a mere means of life, has itself become the prime necessity of life; after the productive forces have also increased with the all-round development of the individual, and all the springs of co-operative wealth flow more abundantly—only then can the narrow horizon of bourgeois right be fully left behind and society inscribe on its banners: from each according to his ability, to each according to his needs!* From the edition by International Publishers, New York, 1938, p. 10.

159

by Marx. And yet at that time Russia was still a backwards agricultural country, with agriculture accounting for as much as 57.9% of its GNP, and industry accounting for only 7% of that of the U.S. And so it was that before the October Revolution a violent debate broke out between Plekhanov [1856-1918] and Lenin [1870-1924].[2]

Plekhanov, who has been called "the father of Russian Marxism," strongly upheld Marx's idea that history could not skip its necessary stages of development; he did not advocate the premature seizure of political power and felt that being in a hurry to achieve socialism could lead to an extremely severe economic failure.

Although Plekhanov's doubts were shattered by the success of the October Revolution, yet his challenge to Lenin was not buried by history. The great big question mark which Plekhanov sketched out, as to whether or not an economically undeveloped socialist state could successfully skip the stage of the commodity economy, has for over half a century continued to plague the socialist camp.[3]

In the 1930s, by oppressing the peasants, lowering the social level of consumption and by forcing a high rate of accumulation, iron-fisted Stalin [1879-1953] caused Soviet industry to grow at a speed that dumbfounded the whole world. For opposing these methods, Bukharin [1888-1938] was shot

---

[2] The last sentence of this paragraph is eliminated in the broadcast version. The next two paragraphs are almost entirely re-written, as follows: *Plekhanov, who did not advocate the premature seizure of political power, firmly believed that the Russia of that time could only continue to develop productive forces on the foundation of capitalism. His challenge to Lenin was shattered by the October Revolution.* [new paragraph] *Yet History seems by no means to have buried Plekhanov's doubts, for after the October Revolution, Lenin adopted a whole series of measures permitting the coexistence of various forms of economy and serving to develop a commodity economy, which would appear to constitute a step back. This would seem to mean that Lenin had by no means ignored Plekhanov's question: Can an economically undeveloped socialist state successfully skip the stage of the commodity economy?* The reason for this paragraph being changed is presumably the ominous prediction of severe economic failure in the original version.

[3] In 1987, General Secretary Zhao Ziyang outlined a theory of the socialist commodity economy, implicitly confirming that Plekhanov was right, that stages in history cannot be skipped: *Then what sort of historical stage is the preliminary stage of socialism in our country? It does not refer generally to a stage that every country must go through upon entering into socialism, but rather specifically refers to the particular stage which our country must pass through in constructing socialism, under circumstances in which productive forces are backward, and a commodity economy is not developed. From the basic completion of the transformation of privately-owned means of production in the 1950s, to the basic realization of socialist modernization will require at a minimum more than a century, all of which belongs to the preliminary stage of socialism.* From Zhao Ziyang, "Moving Ahead on the Path of Socialism with Chinese Characteristics," Zhongguo gongchandang di shisanci quanguo daibiao dahui wenjian huibian, Beijing, Renmin chubanshe, Nov. 1987, p. 12.

as an "enemy of the people."[4] But the "Stalinist model" made the Soviet Union pay a heavy price, so that after Stalin's demise, the trumpets of reform were sounded throughout the USSR.

The countries of Eastern Europe, all formerly subjected to the Stalinist model, at different times diverged from the orthodox path and proceeded with reforms. Yugoslavia on the Balkan peninsula emerged as a new force and was the first to break free of the Soviet model and seek its own path. In close succession, Hungary, Poland and Czechoslovakia all set out on the stormy path of reform. History had apparently once again raised Plekhanov's question. Not that History had gone in retreat; Man, rather, had overtaken it.

On the 18th of December, 1978 this ineluctable current of history finally swept China too into the mainstream of reform among socialist nations.[5] The problems that would have to be resolved by this country covered with scars and only recently arisen from turmoil and by this people still bearing the burden of thousands of years of tradition would be far more complex and difficult than those of the Soviet Union and Eastern Europe.

How many Chinese people are there nowadays who clearly realize that reform doesn't just mean that *"steamed wheat buns have replaced sweet potatoes,*[6] *and the bachelor gets a wife"*; that it doesn't merely mean color TVs, refrigerators and higher salaries, nor even the comfortable living standard of one thousand U.S. dollars [per annum]?[7]

---

[4] Soviet General Secretary Gorbachev, in a speech commemorating the 70th anniversary of the October Revolution, highly praised Bukharin, in effect rehabilitating him nearly fifty years after his death. Bukharin was a Soviet party theorist and economic planner, a former editor of Pravda, who opposed Stalin's methods of forced collectivization and rapid industrialization.

[5] Opening date of the Third Plenary Session of the Eleventh Central Committee of the Chinese Communist Party, at which Deng Xiaoping's leadership of his far-reaching reform program was assured, as well as his victory over the remaining proponents of Cultural Revolution policies. Among other things, he advocated greater democracy to "emancipate the mind" and to "seek truth from facts" rather than relying on traditional Maoist dogma.

[6] Dried sweet potatoes and sweet potato leaves are famine food in China; this saying optimistically describes the new face of China's countryside in the wake of rural reforms as one in which famine is banished and bachelors can find wives. Su Xiaokang ironically quotes this saying in his "Hong huang qishi lu" [1985], where he describes the aftermath of the fall 1984 floods of the Hong and Ru rivers near Zhumadian in Henan, which affected over one million mou of cropland and a population of over one million. Peasants were reduced to eating sweet potato leaves, and hundreds of thousands were forced by hunger to leave their homes to beg. The saying is attributed obliquely to Chinese sociologist Fei Xiaotong. See Ziyou beiwang lu: Su Xiaokang baogao wenxue jingxuan, Sanlian shudian, Hong Kong, 1989, which reprints "Hong huang qishi lu," esp. pp. 1 & 13.

[7] "Comfortable living standard" translates the Chinese term xiaokang shuiping. The reference comes from a speech given by Deng Xiaoping on January 16, 1980, entitled "On the Present Situation and Our Task": *Not long ago a foreign guest was talking with me and*

In the majority of cases and in its deeper sense, reform is rather a great burst of pain in which a civilization is transformed, a task fraught with danger, a difficult process which will require sacrifices from our generation and even several yet to come. Right now we are standing at a crossroads: either we can allow our ancient civilization to continue to decline, or we can force it to acquire the mechanisms of revitalization. But no matter which way we choose, we cannot shirk this historical responsibility.

(Titles: Part Four, "A New Era")[8]

Ten years ago, when we finally opened our closed bamboo curtain and once again rejoined the world, the Chinese people—who for so long had lived in the hardship of "transitional poverty" and the isolation of cultural despotism—were surprised to discover just how developed the capitalist West and Japan were and how comfortably their people lived.

Perhaps it was precisely this strong shock which caused us to pick up again a long-forgotten topic: why had Industrial Civilization with its promise of vast wealth never appeared in Chinese history?

Leaving aside strong dynasties such as the Han and Tang, even in the feeble Song dynasty [960-1279] one thousand years ago, the Chinese economy and urban commerce in particular were still the most prosperous in the whole world. At the same time that the Northern Song capital of Bianliang [=Kaifeng] and the Southern Song capital of Lin'an [=Hangzhou] were metropolises with populations numbering millions, the most prosperous commercial city in Europe numbered no more than one hundred thousand. No wonder that when the merchant of Venice Marco Polo [1254-1324] came to China he should be so happy as to forget about returning home![9]

And yet, the same Chinese civilization which evoked wonder and admiration from Marco Polo is now already in the midst of decline; while for some reason History was more sympathetic to his distant home on the Mediterranean Sea, a village that had only recently graduated from catching

---

asked, *'What do your four modernizations really mean?'* I told him that by the end of this century we would try to reach a per capita GNP of one thousand U.S. dollars, which could be considered a *'comfortable living standard.'* Note that Deng refers to per capita GNP, not income. See <u>Deng Xiaoping wenxuan (1975-1982)</u>, Renmin chubanshe, Beijing, 1983, p. 223.

[8] The image on the screen with the titles for Part Four is of newspaper headlines announcing the Third Plenum of the 11th Congress of the Communist Party in December, 1978.

[9] The reference to Marco Polo as a "merchant of Venice" is apparently deliberate irony; the Shakespeare reference is renewed below. Marco Polo stayed in China in the service of Kubilai Khan from 1275 to 1292, for a total of 17 years.

fish and evaporating salt—Venice. This was a nation without agriculture; it was not even a nation but rather a city without territory, a republic of merchants. Its government was a stock company, its leader the general manager, its senate the board of directors, and all Venetians its stockholders. And so it became the earliest birthplace of capitalist civilization.[10]

In the year 1160, the Venetian government borrowed 150,000 silver marks from the merchants of the city by issuing bonds, and so became the very first government in the whole world to be transformed into a corporation, while Venetian citizens became the government's creditors. And as the tie between goods and money became the principal tie in society and the economy, laws which protected private property could no longer be resisted. Yet even Shakespeare cursed the Venetians' commercial spirit. And so it was only a full five hundred years later that banks issuing bonds appeared in England. And for China to understand this would take perhaps eight or nine centuries.[11]

China, a large country made up of peasants with small landholdings, had never had a true concept of commodities, even though commerce had always been highly developed. Under Heaven, there was no land that was not the ruler's.[12] Through successive dynasties and generations, the Emperor was the sole private owner in all of China; he could collect taxes from the people as he pleased, draft corvée labor, and oppress the peasants without recompense and without limit.[13] Relying on the meager salaries of the

---

[10] The second broadcast eliminates the last two sentences of this paragraph, starting from: *Its government was a stock company....*

[11] The description of Venice appears to be adapted from that description given in a paper by Ray Huang [Huang Renyu] presented at the First International Conference on Chinese Culture held at Fudan University in Shanghai in January, 1986, entitled "Wo dui zibenzhuyi de renshi" [My understanding of 'capitalism'], published in the conference volume <u>Zhongguo chuantong wenhua de zai guji</u>, Shanghai renmin chubanshe, 1987, pp. 384-431, esp. pp. 404-406. While the screen shows a scene of China's new stock market, the text appears to hint that China has recently adopted the practise of issuing bonds. These treasury notes, or <u>guokujuan</u>, are bought through forced salary deductions and are quite unpopular.

[12] Alluding to the second stanza of poem #205 in the <u>Shi jing</u> [<u>Book of Songs</u>]: *Everywhere under Heaven /Is no land that is not the king's/ To the borders of those lands/ None but is the king's slave/ But the ministers are not just/ Whatever is done, I bear the brunt alone.* —Arthur Waley, trans., <u>The Book of Songs</u>, George Allen and Unwin, London, 1937, p. 320.

[13] University of Wisconsin history professor Lin Yusheng criticizes this point, saying: "*In China, after the Qin dynasty, land could be freely bought and sold, while in the medieval West, on the contrary, land was the exclusive property of the aristocracy and could not be sold.*" See Lin Yusheng, "Zhongguo yishi weiji yu chuantong to chuanzaoxing zhuanhua" [The Crisis of Chinese Consciousness and the Creative Transformation of the Tradition] in <u>Longnian de beichuang</u>, p. 46.

court, officials would naturally seek to skim off the riches of the common people either by deceit or by force. This system of centralized power, of a "great unity" built on the foundation of an agricultural civilization, became a heavy ball and chain weighing down the economy of ancient China and industrial and commercial activities in particular. For this reason, some Western scholars think that China has never had a true system of private ownership and hence one cannot even talk of the 'sprouts' of capitalism.[14]

While the Ming dynasty was enforcing its closed-door policy and the west coast of the Pacific was still undisturbed, the great world-wide commercial revolution which had been born on the shores of the Mediterranean was just in the process of spreading to the Atlantic, Indian and Pacific Oceans. Europe slowly moved towards the center of the world stage from the ignorance and barbarity of the Middle Ages. Sea-coast civilization without any hesitation seized this Heaven-sent opportunity to give free rein to its pioneering, expansive inner vitality and the superiority of its civilization.

In January, 1649, the English people defeated King Charles I.[15] The royal power faded away. A one-man dictatorship gave way to joint rule by a group of men. The success of the English capitalist revolution caused this island people to take a big step forward in human history and be the first to enter the new era of history.[16]

In 1781, Watt's double-action steam engine brought yet another "Aladdin's lamp" to the English people.[17] The wealth created by a few decades of the Industrial Revolution was equal to the total wealth

---

[14] The second broadcast eliminates this sentence. Su Xiaokang attributes the idea that China never had a true system of private ownership to historian Ray Huang. See Longnian de beichuang, p. 37.

[15] Charles I, 1600-1649, of the Stuart line and son of James I. He reigned from 1625 to 1649. He was condemned to death by Parliament in 1649 after a seven year civil war. He had opposed Parliament, repressed the Puritans, and opposed the development of industry and commerce.

[16] The "new era" mentioned here is also the "new era" of the title of Part Four. Heshang's critics have pointed out that the script calls the English revolution a "new era" but fails to give the same treatment to the revolution of 1949 that established the People's Republic. See also footnote 40.

[17] James Watt, 1736-1819, English inventor responsible for making the steam engine an important part of the Industrial Revolution. The steam engine was an "Aladdin's lamp" in the sense that, like its magic counterpart, it created great wealth. For Marx and Engels, the advent of the machine heralded a new age in history, due to an important change in the means of production. The high cost of machines kept them in the hands of wealthy capitalists; traditional handicraft and cottage industries gave way to mechanized factories, and the independent skilled craftsman was replaced by the factory worker.

accumulated by the human race over thousands of years.[18] It allowed those nations which first completed their industrialization to increase rapidly in size and strength, while those nations which were left behind would have to passively take a beating. It forced all nations either to take the path of industrialization or to be eliminated by History.

The Industrial Revolution sped up the international division of labor. Capital fed the whole world through the Machine. *"Because of the advent of machines, spinners could live in England, while weavers lived in the East Indies."*[19] The poor agricultural nations of Asia, Africa and Latin America became the sources of agricultural and mineral raw materials for the industrial countries of Europe, as well as markets for their goods. This was a sort of historical destiny.[20] Now that the world had already become a unified market, China could no longer avoid its fate of being pulled into the world-wide exchange of goods. The industrially advanced West would never willingly let go such a vast place for dumping commercial goods, for investment, and for the production of raw materials. Thus, before the great geographical discoveries at the end of the fifteenth century, and before the outbreak of conflict between China and the West, China had already lost its once-in-a-millennium chance to develop capitalism. Henceforth capitalism would never be able to develop within China, but would come to bully China from beyond the seas.

In 1895, the young Kang Youwei [1858-1927] set off a wave of petitions by students in Beijing.[21] The members of the 1898 reform party felt that to develop capitalism at that moment was the only way to save China, and they loudly called on the state to institute all-out reforms. But a

---

[18] Compare Marx and Engels, The Communist Manifesto: *The bourgeoisie, during its rule of scarce one hundred years, has created more massive and more colossal productive forces than have all preceding generations together.* [p. 489]

[19] According to Marx and Engels, the Industrial Revolution destroyed traditional handicraft industries as well as the role of the craftsman. The steam engine and other machines [for weaving, etc.] increased the division of labor, reducing the status of the worker from craftsman to machine operator; at the same time, the industrial revolution created a world market and changed the structure of production, so that different parts of the manufacturing process could be divided amongst workers in many countries. This quotation comes from Karl Marx, The Poverty of Philosophy: Answer to the <Philosophy of Poverty> of M. Proudhon, chapter two, "The Metaphysics of Political Economy," part two, written ca. 1848. See Karl Marx and Friedrich Engels, Collected Works, International Publishers, NY, 1976, vol. 6, p. 187.

[20] The second broadcast deletes this sentence.

[21] After China's defeat in the Sino-Japanese War of 1894-5, the Treaty of Peace stipulated that China cede its claims to Korea and Taiwan. Kang Yuwei organized students in Beijing who had come to take the examinations to sign a petition urging the government not to sign the treaty but to continue to fight.

mere one hundred days later, as the heads of Tan Sitong [1865-1898] and five other reformers[22] fell in the dust, China once again lost an opportunity to move towards an advanced industrial society. For the loss of this opportunity, China would doubtless continue to pay the heavy price of backwardness and exploitation for another century or two.

Why is it that capitalism, the hallmark of modern industrial civilization, should not have its fate linked with China? Why was it that the Chinese hated it so much, to the point that in the sixties and seventies of this century they were still "cutting off the tail of capitalism" on a vast scale? [23]

Fundamentally speaking, this was determined by the nature of Chinese civilization. These plateaus eroded by the Yellow River and plains built up by the same Yellow River are the survival space of the Chinese people. The green fields that squeeze themselves into every available crack of space, the farmhouses packed as tightly as cells in a honeycomb, the tightly-woven network of ditches and footpaths are the evidence of the bitter labor of countless generations of peasants. They are the skill and the persistence expressed by too many people crowded onto too little land, and of the consequent struggle of man to maintain his existence on a soil of declining strength.

In such an environment, the Chinese economy has from ancient times possessed its own path of development, of which one salient characteristic is its ability to nurture a numerous and densely-packed population. In 1800, as the West was busy grabbing overseas colonies everywhere, the Chinese soil was nurturing one third of the world's population. There are some scholars who don't feel that China is a "failed civilization" just because it didn't produce industrialization. On the contrary, they appreciate the bucolic atmosphere of this agricultural civilization with a low standard of living.

Yet the problem lies in how this civilization has nurtured the Chinese people. As late as 1980, in a rural commune forty kilometers from Lanzhou, the average per capita grain consumption was only forty to one hundred kilos; in two out of three peasant homes, the earthen kang lacked a

---

[22] In addition to Tan Sitong, the others were Yang Rui, Lin Xu, Liu Guangdi, Kang Guangren, and Yang Shenxiu. For an account of the 1898 Reform Movement, see Tan Sitong [T'an Ssu-t'ung]'s biography in Hummel, op. cit., pp. 702-705.

[23] During the Cultural Revolution, "cutting off the tail of capitalism" meant eliminating peasants' private plots and money-making opportunities. See Tsuruma Wako, Kako bunmei e no banka, p. 123.

mat; on the average, three people would share a single ragged quilt; and over sixty percent of people had no padded cotton clothes for the winter.[24]

This old peasant from northern Shaanxi told us that last year, owing to the reduction of the wheat crop due to drought, when his family had used up all their food grain, they survived solely on potatoes. Though he had passed his whole life in such poverty, he had somehow managed to have three sons and four daughters and now already had more than ten grandchildren.[25]

Due to the ever-increasing population, and even more so to such obviously unwise theories such as *"People are the greatest treasure in the world"* and *"The more people, the more strength,"*[26] scarce land has become even more valuable, and many kinds of natural resources have become increasingly hard to find. Comparatively speaking, our poor, thin soil supports an excess of healthy flesh, and the lives that clamor to be fed have become cheap and valueless. At present, the burden of population has become the most difficult problem to solve of all of China's problems. How many generations of Chinese will have to taste the bitter fruit it has borne?

Moreover, the great investment of human labor on a small area of land has made it difficult for mechanized agriculture to get started, has given surplus [lit., "liberated"] farm labor no place to go, and has caused the bitter labor of many hands to become a socially-accepted rule, so that any method to reduce labor, increase efficiency and make money is seen as the ill-gotten

---

[24] This description of rural poverty is abridged from that in Furao de pinkun: Zhongguo luohou diqu de jingji kaocha [Poverty Amidst Plenty: An Economic Investigation of China's Backwards Areas] by Wang Xiaoqiang and Bai Nanfeng, Chengdu, Sichuan renmin chubanshe, 1986, pp. 22-23.

[25] Su Xiaokang is here shown on screen interviewing the peasant. The narrator substitutes five daughters for four.

[26] In 1949, U.S. Secretary of State Dean Acheson wrote in a State Dept. white paper that the great size of China's population was the root of her poverty. Mao Zedong responded by claiming: *The large size of the Chinese population is a very good thing. No matter how many times the population should double, we could always deal with it; our solution is [increasing] production.* China's foremost population scientist, Ma Yinchu, was branded as a rightist and a Malthusian in 1957 for proposing population controls. The traditional Marxist view is that Malthus was wrong when he predicted that food resources would never increase as fast as population; this held true only for capitalist society, which required an "industrial reserve army" of the unemployed. A socialist society should be able to increase food production rapidly through the use of technology, and a large population was to be sought for. See Qiao Xiaochun et.al., Chaozai de tudi: er nan jingdi de Zhongguo renkou wenti [The Overburdened Earth: The Dilemma of the Chinese Population Problem], Qiushi chubanshe & Shenyang chubanshe, December 1989, esp. p. 25.

gains of an "upstart." Isn't it precisely for this reason that today's "red-eye disease"[27] [jealousy] is so hard to cure?[28]

Yet on the other hand the facts that wealth cannot be acquired under conditions of equal competition; and that the monopoly power of state-run enterprises and the privileged elite's power to allocate goods can damage the socialist system of ownership at will, poisoning the morality of the ruling party and of society—all this means that anyone who has the least bit of power can easily transform his power to use or to manage into the power of possession, so that what is state property is transmuted into departmental or individual property. Hasn't this point been proven by those shocking cases of corruption and bribery, of using public wealth to line private pockets, and other such decadent phenomena?[29]

The style of small-scale production has also created a whole set of values stressing setting low targets in order to keep oneself on a psychological equilibrium. Are not philosophies of life such as "being content with one's lot," "taking things as they come," "not taking risks,"

[27] hong yan bing. Xie Xuanjun, one of the series co-authors, interprets this 'red-eye disease' as a fault in the national character in his essay "Zhongguoren de Huanghe xinli" [The Yellow River mindset of the Chinese people] in Su Xiaokang et.al., Longnian de beichuang, 1989, pp. 183-191: *When we see a person succeed without having endured enough suffering, then we feel that he seems to have stolen property that wasn't his. At this point, a very common psychological reaction is to want to force him to 'pay back the debt that he owes.' That is to say, it [this attitude] views human accomplishments as a sort of reward and luxury, and moreover as a presumptuous and unearned reward. Now is the time for him to sacrifice for this reward and to 'pay the required price.'* (p. 190)

[28] The second broadcast rewrites this paragraph as follows: *Moreover, the great investment of human labor on a small area of land has made it difficult for mechanized agriculture to get started, has given surplus farm labor no place to go, and has caused the bitter labor of many hands to become a socially-accepted rule, so that those methods that rely on reducing labor, that seek profit, that seek to rake off wealth by doing business and transporting goods may all be seen as [producing] unjust wealth. And moreover it is precisely those people who lack the means to create wealth who are easily infected with 'red-eye disease.'*

[29] The second broadcast rewrites this paragraph as follows: *But on the other hand, the acquisition of wealth cannot proceed under conditions of equal competition. Today, the profiteering bureaucrats [guandao ye] that have incited so much criticism are still making use of the defects of the two-tiered price system, using the power they hold to allocate commodities, selling chits [tiaozi], approving chits, thus creating layer after layer of exploitation in highly sought-after commodities. Not only have they thrown commodity prices into chaos, they have moreover poisoned the morale of the party in power and of society at large. The union of bureaucracy and commerce is inevitably corrupt; both in past and in present, in China and abroad, there are no exceptions to this rule.* On the videotape, the narrator reads the above paragraph with increasing vehemence and anger. Presumably the reason the first version was dropped was its reference to "the privileged elite" [tequan jieceng]. Su Xiaokang discusses the reasons for making these changes in an interview with Mai Tianshu appearing in Zhongguo qingnian bao, August 16th, 1988.

and "even a bad life is better than a good death" still practiced by the great majority of people? When we asked this youth in this northern Shaanxi village why he remained at home in poverty and didn't go out to seek his fortune, he responded "*my mom and dad didn't give me the guts to do so!*"

In the vast, backwards rural areas, there are common problems in the peasant makeup[30] such as a weak spirit of enterprise, a very low ability to accept risk, a deep psychology of dependency and a strong sense of passive acceptance of fate.[31] No wonder that some scholars sigh with regret: faced

---

[30] The term suzhi, is here translated "makeup" instead of "character" or "nature." It really means something more like "quality," with especial reference to moral and educational standards. Unlike "character" or "nature," suzhi can be raised or lowered. In his essay entitled "Huiyi yu sikao" [Remembering and Reflecting] included in Heshang lun, series co-author Wang Luxiang discusses the defects of peasant character in terms of its resistance to economic or political change: *Moreover, the weakness of the impulse to enterprise amongst the people of Yan'an was startling. Of the several tens of people we interviewed in several counties, there was only one young miner in a county coal mine who clearly stated that he would go out in search of his own fortune next year, giving up the low-paying job his father and mother had found for him. Early marriage, early childbearing, and plenty of children are still common phenomena. As soon as it gets dark, to grab hold of one's woman and enter one's cave has been the ideal of life for thousands of years for the men of the locality; and in the several places that we went to we could see not a hint that this ideal had changed, nor a reason why it should. In Ansai we saw a group of young farmers who told us that in the year when the joint Sino-Japanese film crew came to shoot "The Yellow River," the county cultural office had created a thousand member waist-drumming group, which was quite magnificent. The film crew gave each person a dollar as salary, but this dollar was held back by the county. When they told us this, their tone was very flat, with only a slight degree of resentment, but nothing excessive. I was saddened. The simple and honest Chinese peasant would never be able to imagine that such shameful extortion and usury in the name of "government" could be illegal; they bear everything in silence, unable to fight back, unable to realize that this is a basic human right that must be protected and fought for. ... We next went to Henan. Mang Shan, Huayuankou, Dongbatou—here the tired, thick Yellow River resembles a mud soup. The peasants here are clearly different in their makeup from those of northern Shaanxi. In voicing their complaints their feelings run strong, and from time to time are laced with sarcasm. Towards the fact that crop prices were unreasonably low while the costs of the means of production were escalating rapidly, they were full of justified resentment. Almost all of them knew the following saying: 'I don't want your high-priced chemical fertilizer; I won't sell my low-priced wheat. As long as I've got enough to eat, f— it.' They have begun to haggle over prices with the government, they know how to make contracts with government, they know that the government too must accept duties and responsibilities—in a word, they know that agricultural production is commodity production too and no longer draft labor. This is a tremendous flying leap forward in history for the Chinese peasants. ...*

[31] Wang Xiaoqiang and Bai Nanfeng, op. cit., p. 59, give a more detailed version of how deficiencies in the psychological makeup of peasants is revealed in certain attitudes hindering economic and commercial development: *In contrast with the developed areas, the inhabitants of backwards rural areas are clearly marked by an excessive lack of enterprise and an over-attachment to the status quo. For example: their pioneering impulse is weak, and they are easily satisfied; their ability to accept risk is relatively low, they cannot resist relatively large difficulties and setbacks, so that they are unwilling to face*

with the [psychological] makeup of people such as this, not to mention the many limitations of government policy, even if a great economist like Keynes were to come back to life, what could he do about it? It's not the lack of resources, nor the level of GNP, nor the speed [of development], but rather this deficiency in the human makeup that is the essence of this so-called notion of "backwardness."[32] And the decline in the makeup of the general population is caused precisely by the rapid increases in its numbers. This truly is an agricultural civilization caught in a vicious cycle. Do we still have any reason to praise or to be infatuated with it?

This far-from-pretty bucolic atmosphere can from time to time still produce unbelievable bursts of folly. In those mad years of the Great Leap Forward [1958-1961], the fairy tale that "*the greater man's determination, the higher the level of the soil's productivity*" exaggerated the level of productivity of northern wheat up to over 7,000 jin per mou, and of southern rice up to over 50,000 jin per mou[33]; everyone, from our great leader who wrote the essay "On Practice"[34] to scientists and to the ever-practical Chinese peasants, could somehow believe this fairy tale. Throughout our land of nine million six hundred thousand square kilometers, every family for some reason or other smashed their cooking pots and closed their doors; several hundreds of millions of people all went to the communal dining halls to "eat from the public pot"[35], as if

---

danger; they are relatively deficient in independence and initiative both in production and in daily life, and they have a relatively heavy psychology of dependence and of fatalism; it is difficult to destroy tradition and custom, to accept new forms of production and modes of life, and the majority of new things and new phenomena; they lack the spirit to pursue new experiences but are content with their present situation and happy with holding on to past achievements, and so forth.

[32] These two sentences are slightly adapted from Wang Xiaoqiang and Bai Nanfeng, op.cit., p. 56.

[33] 1 jin = .5 kg or 1.1 lb; 1 mou = .066 hectares or .16 acres; hence 7,000 jin per mou of wheat is equivalent to about 52,500 kilograms per hectare [or 46,000 lbs. per acre], and 50,000 jin per mou of rice is equivalent to about 375,000 kilograms per hectare [or 330,000 lbs per acre. The United Nations Food and Agriculture Organization estimated China's 1988 wheat production at 3,017 kilograms per hectare and rice production at 5,304 kilograms per hectare. China's 1988 yields per hectare are significantly above U.S. and world average yields, and are second only to Japan's. The story of the exaggerated agricultural yields claimed during the "Great Leap Forward" is told in greater detail in Su Xiaokang's "Hong huang qishi lu" [1985] and in his Wutuobang ji [Sacrifice in Utopia], Zhongguo xinwen chubanshe, Beijing, 1988, a semi-fictionalized account of the 1959 Lushan Conference. See esp. pp. 6-10.

[34] Mao Zedong, "On Practise," July, 1937; Selected Works of Mao Tse-tung, Peking, Foreign Languages Press, 1967, vol. I, pp. 295-309.

[35] chi da guo fan,"to eat from the public pot," implies that one helps oneself freely to what the state provides, without having to earn it; everyone lives at the same low level of

communism had arrived just like that. This transition, from economic "utopia" to political crisis, leading ultimately to the historical tragedy of great social turmoil—can we not say that this is the inevitable end of an agricultural civilization?

For approximately twenty-odd years in the middle of this century, China once again faced a good opportunity for economic development. And yet locking our country's door and blindfolding our eyes we set off to "surpass England and America," never ceasing to engage in one great political movement after another, swearing that on Chinese soil *we would rather grow the weeds of socialism than the sprouts of capitalism,* so that in the end our national economy was on the brink of collapse. Once again History cold-heartedly passed us by.

Let us open our eyes and see our people's situation on this planet! The World Bank's annual reports reveal the following figures: Out of one hundred twenty-eight nations in the world, China's average per capita GNP ranks about twentieth from the bottom, in company with poor African countries such as Somalia and Tanzania. China's rate of increase in per capita GNP, the structure of her export commodities, her investment in education and public health all fail to match those of Asia's "four little dragons."[36] In 1960, China's GNP was equivalent to Japan's; by 1985, it was only one-fifth of Japan's; in 1960, U.S. GNP exceeded China by 460 billion U.S. dollars, but by 1985 it exceeded China by 3 trillion 680 billion dollars.[37]

Though we always thought we were making great strides towards progress, how little we knew that others were making far faster strides than us! If this gap should continue at present rates, some people have made a frightening comparison: that in another fifty or sixty years, China will once again be in the situation of the Opium War: that foreigners will possess foreign guns and cannon, leaving Chinese with only long knives and spears. No wonder then that someone has made an even louder appeal: that if things go wrong, China's global citizenship will be revoked![38]

---

consumption, there is no economic motivation to work, nor is there respect for public property.

[36] The four 'little dragons' are South Korea, Taiwan, Hong Kong and Singapore.

[37] Quoted from Shijie jingji daobao [World Economic Herald], February 15th, 1988, pp. 1 & 15. Current data is taken from the World Bank, 1987 World Development Report; see especially Table 1: Basic Indicators; Table 11: Structure of Merchandise Exports; Table 23: Central Government Expenditure; Table 3: Structure of Production.

[38] Ibid., p. 15. This article provoked a lengthy series of articles and letters from readers culminating in the publication of a book entitled Qiuji [Global Citizenship] by the Shanghai World Economic Herald in 1989. Mao discussed the possibility of China losing its global citizenship in an August, 1956 speech included in volume 5 of his Selected

No matter whether it was Lenin or Plekhanov, Stalin or Bukharin, Mao Zedong or his many comrades-in-arms[39]—in order to come to grips with this mysterious and invisible economic law they all had to pay a heavy price. At present Zhao Ziyang[40] is finally able to say directly and forthrightly that:

> *"The socialist economy is a planned commodity economy on the foundation of public ownership. This is the scientific conclusion our Party has drawn about the socialist economy; it is a great advance in Marxism and is the fundamental theoretical underpinning of our country's economic structural reform."*[41]

Works: *They say [socialism] is superior, but if after fifty or sixty years, you still can't overtake the U.S., then what will you look like? In that case, your global citizenship would be revoked!* Mao Zedong xuanji, 1977, vol. 5, p. 296.

[39] This would include Deng Xiaoping.

[40] Zhao Ziyang, Premier from 1980 to 1987; General Secretary of the Chinese Communist Party, 1987-1989. Zhao's predecessor as General Secretary, Hu Yaobang, was forced to resign from office in January of 1987 due to massive student demonstrations in December. Zhao was both Prime Minister and acting Party Secretary until his confirmation as the new General Secretary at the 13th Party Congress in October, 1987, at which time Li Peng took over the position of Prime Minister. During the Democracy Movement of 1989, Zhao was suspended from his duties after failing to take part in the decision to enforce martial law on May 20, and was subsequently replaced as Party Secretary by Jiang Zemin. An excellent treatment of Zhao's policies is Willy Wo-Lap Lam, The Era of Zhao Ziyang: Power Struggle in China, 1986-88, A.B. Books & Stationery, Hong Kong, 1989.

[41] The above is taken from Zhao's report to the 13th Party Congress delivered on October 25th, 1987, entitled "Moving Ahead on the Path of Socialism with Chinese Characteristics," [cited above], p.30. Zhao's complete text notes that the concept of a "planned commodity economy" derives from the decisions on economic structural reform of the 3rd plenum of the 12th Party Congress held October 20, 1984. The remainder of Zhao's report, however, includes novel ideas that give a more concrete definition to the notion of a planned commodity economy. Among these are (1) the principle of *"the State leading the market, and of the market leading enterprises"*; i.e., the State will move from direct regulation of the economy to indirect regulation via interest rates, taxes, etc.;(2) permitting the existence of private enterprise; and (3) experimentation with joint stock companies. Zhao's report addressed the concerns of proponents of political reform in two ways: (1) by proposing new regulations for public officeholders; and (2) by proposing greater consultation and dialogue in society [see Part Six, "Blueness"]. The 13th Party Congress is well summarized in Lam, op.cit., pp. 236-241; see also Shijie jingji daobao, November 2, 1987, p. 2. Heshang's critics have accused the TV series of working in league with Zhao to create favorable public opinion for his reform program. Hence his formal accession to office is heralded on the screen as the beginning of a "New Era," a term of praise which is not applied to any other previous event in the Party's history and applied only to the English bourgeois revolution. Yet the titles appear twice in this section; each time they are associated on the screen with the newspaper headline announcing the 3rd plenum of the 11th Party Congress in 1978, the one which inaugurated Deng's reform plan. The first appearance of the titles is also preceded by the scene of Deng Xiaoping

(Reappearance of the title: The New Era)

Over the past century, this vast western Pacific Ocean has uninterruptedly sent our continent both shame and hardship, while today over its stormy surface there would seem to float that vast wealth which so strongly tempts us. Japan is right now engaged in suggesting adjustments in the structure of economic relations with the U.S. and with Asia's "four small dragons."[42] The western Pacific is right now becoming the new stage for the world economy. Destiny is once again giving us a once-in-a-millennium chance. Our coastal areas, silent for centuries, this Gold Coast of the Chinese people, with an appetite long held in check, are now the first to rush towards the Pacific.

The Chinese people at this moment are more eager than ever before to enter the world market. And yet this people has been isolated for too long and is still unfamiliar with the [uncharted] seas of the commodity economy, while the actual strength with which it can participate in international competition is quite weak. This opportunity afforded by a great readjustment in the structure of world production may well be quite fleeting, while we are the late-comers whose preparations are both hasty and incomplete.

We have now finally understood that we want to have an outer-directed economy,[43] but the sole advantage still left to us is low-cost labor, and our

---

entering the 11th Congress with all present applauding. See Hua Yan, ed., Heshang pipan, Wenhua yishu chubanshe, Dec. 1989, pp. 22-23.

[42] In March, 1988 the Japan International Forum chaired by former Foreign Minister Okita Saburo made a number of important policy suggestions relating to realigning the economies of America, Japan and Asia's four small dragons, in the light of the Wall Street crash of 1987, America's huge deficit, low rate of savings, etc. The fact that the currencies of the four small dragons are tied to the U.S. dollar means that when the Japanese yen goes up in value, the exports of the four small dragons to the U.S. are much more competitive than Japanese goods; meanwhile, Japanese investment in the four small dragons has increased dramatically, so that they have experienced much more rapid growth than anticipated. America's huge budget deficit currently threatens the stability of the world economy, yet the four small dragons export principally to the U.S. In order to ensure that they not fall into a recession also, the Japanese market should replace the U.S. in absorbing the exports of the four small dragons, and in order to do so, she should open up her markets to both foreign goods and foreign labor, removing the 'invisible barriers,' and moving away from being completely self-sufficient in capital, labor and parts to being more integrated into the economy of the region. The suggestions are summarized in Shanghai's Shijie jingji daobao [World Economic Herald], March 21, 1988, p. 13.

[43] waixiangxing jingji. The "outer-directed economy" was a proposal designed to take advantage of changes in the structure of world production, in which developed countries were seeking to move manufacturing of labor-intensive goods off-shore. It was thus modeled on the development experience of Asia's newly-industrializing countries [Taiwan, Hongkong, Singapore, South Korea] by which China's coastal areas, taking advantage of their plentiful yet inexpensive labor force, would import raw materials from abroad to manufacture products for export to the developed countries, thus transforming China's

labor-intensive, low-tech processing industry is one with which it is difficult to gain an enduring competitive advantage.

We have also finally understood that we want to participate in the "Largescale International Recirculation,"[44] but at the same time that we have

---

population burden into an advantage. Capital for the importation of new technology would be raised by selling stock in state enterprises to state companies and individuals, and by auctioning off certain enterprises. A favorable investment climate would be created in the coastal regions, encouraging foreign businesses to invest in both joint ventures and wholly-owned foreign ventures in which they would also have control of management. The development of the coastal areas would then stimulate development in China's interior, while the importation of raw materials from abroad would eliminate competition for resources with China's inland provinces, which could thus concentrate on producing for the domestic market. The plan for an outer-directed economy is first mentioned in Zhao's report to the 13th Party Congress [op.cit., pp. 27-28] as part of a larger plan of development: *We must continue to consolidate and develop the nascent pattern of opening to the outside by gradual steps, from the special economic zones, to the open coastal cities, to the open coastal economic regions, to the interior. From the point of view of the entire national economy, we must correctly determine the program for the opening up and construction of special economic zones and open cities and regions, emphasize the development of an outer-directed economy, and vigorously develop horizontal economic integration with the interior in order to fully realize their roles as bases and as windows in opening up to the outside.* Zhao Ziyang visited a number of coastal cities in late 1987 and early 1988 to promote the idea of the outer-directed economy; by early March 1988, the plan had been approved by the Party Central Committee and the State Council. See Chen Yizi, Zhongguo: shi nian gaige yu bajiu minyun, Taibei, 1990, pp. 127-128; Shijie jingji daobao, Jan. 18, 1988, p. 2; Mar. 7, p. 2; March 14, p. 1; Zhongguo qingnian bao, Jan. 23, 1988, p. 2, quoting a Xinhua report of Jan. 22. For more on Zhao's strategy of economic development along the coast, see Lam, op.cit., pp. 224-226 & 247; Carol Hamrin, China and the Challenge of the Future, Westview Press, 1990, pp. 84, 169, 196. Zhao's coastal strategy is also mentioned in Part Six, "Blueness."

[44] These two concepts are summed up and clearly distinguished in an article entitled "The Coastal Development Strategy is not the same as the Large-scale International Recirculation," appearing in the first issue of Qiu shi [1988.1, p. 43], the theoretical organ of the central party school that replaced Hong qi [Red Flag]. After describing the "outer-directed economy" and making clear that it represents official policy adopted by the Central Committee and State Council, the article continues: *The theory of the 'large-scale international recirculation' is a scholarly point of view in the field of economics; scholars holding this view believe that there is a relationship of 'recirculation' between agriculture and heavy industry. They believe that to develop heavy industry at present requires capital, and that to transfer surplus labor from agriculture to the non-agricultural sector also requires capital, and that this has brought into being a contradiction in the form of a competition for capital; "this contradiction is the principal contradiction in our economic development at present." They propose using surplus agricultural labor to develop labor-intensive export commodities, which would be exchanged for foreign currency, and that this foreign currency would be used in turn to purchase equipment and technology to develop heavy industry, thus "linking up agriculture and heavy industry in a relationship of 'recirculation.'* [new paragraph] *The theory of 'Large-scale International Recirculation' emphasizes the development of labor-intensive export commodities; in this respect it is identical with the 'coastal development strategy.' But the coastal development strategy and the 'Large-scale International Recirculation' theory are not one and the same thing.*

our eyes glued on other people's markets, we keep our own markets tightly shut, always fearing that "the gravy will flow away," seeming to forget that the reason why others are willing to come to invest is precisely because they have their eyes set on our markets. If we want China to enter into the world, we must let the world enter China. Otherwise, we will lose a good opportunity once again!

These days the developing countries all have their minds set on making money off the developed countries. But as long as they lack the proper sort of internal markets, the economies of these countries will always be lopsided.

In this hospital famous for the treatment of goiters, there isn't a single doctor whose income surpasses that of the old lady selling baked sweet potatoes at the front gate. *"Those who cut open the head are not as well off as those who shave it"*; *"piano players are not as well off as piano movers"*; mental and physical labor are in an inverse relationship, so that those who *"put the problems of the world first"* will be those who *"get rich last."*[45] The source of all this unfairness is that society lacks a competitive mechanism for ensuring equality of opportunity, it lacks a common yardstick—the market. Only when we can develop a healthy market can we ensure that opportunity, equality, and competition will start to link up; yet this is precisely the thing that our people with their ancient civilization know the least about.[46]

As long as competition exists without the prerequisite of equal opportunity, then the loosening of price controls, which would seem to be

---

The former is Party and government policy; the latter is a scholarly point of view; the former explains how the coastal economy should 'develop'; the latter explains how agriculture and heavy industry 'recirculate'; the former is a policy goal which party committees and governments at all levels must carry out; the latter falls in the category of exploratory research.

[45] Adapted from the "Yueyang lou ji" of Fan Zhongyan [989-1052],substituting "getting rich" for "enjoying themselves." In praising the unselfishness of the ancient sages, he says: *They neither delighted in the things of the world nor were saddened on account of their own individual fate. When in high position at court, they felt concern [you] for the people; when in exile in the country, they felt concern for their ruler; then whether in or out of office they were equally concerned. And so when did they enjoy themselves? It must be said that 'They felt concern before the rest of the world was concerned, and enjoyed themselves only after the rest of the world had enjoyed themselves'!* ... The notion that it is the best people who "get rich last" is in ironic contrast to Deng Xiaoping's assertion during the rural reforms that it is perfectly natural for some people to get rich first.

[46] The second broadcast rewrites the opening of this paragraph as follows, both adding and deleting material: *In Beijing, a bus driver's monthly income is about 150 yuan, while a taxi driver's income can be five or six times that. In this hospital famous for the treatment of goiters, there isn't a single doctor whose income surpasses that of the old lady selling baked sweet potatoes at the front gate. Those who "put the problems of the world first" will be those who "get rich last." The source of all this unfairness...*

appropriate to the rules of a commodity economy, can actually create economic disorder and dislocation; the friction between the old structure and the new one will cancel out the positive elements on each side; the many evils such as "bureaucratism," "feudalism," the use of public power for private ends, and so forth will all seem to find their "common yardstick" and reflect themselves in society in the form of commodity prices. In a country with a long tradition of egalitarianism,[47] the loss of control over prices will necessarily make the people apprehensive, even to the point of fomenting social unrest. And if for this reason we lose the support of the majority for economic reform, then China will once again be mired in stagnation. How deep must have been the regret of Wang Anshi [1021-1086][48] eight hundred years ago and of Tan Sitong ninety years ago![49]

(The television studio. A scholar discusses economic reform.)[50]

Li Yining[51] (Beijing University professor): *"I have said before, that the failure of economic reform may come about due to the failure of price*

---

[47] pingjun zhuyi, here translated as 'egalitarianism,' in this context does not refer to equality of rights or opportunities, but rather to a social norm of behavior and of living standards;not only should everyone receive equal treatment, but also no one should be allowed to be better off than others, and no one should try to be better than others. See the subsequent discussion of 'red-eye disease.'

[48] Wang Anshi [1021-1086], Prime Minister under Emperor Shenzong of the Northern Song, was a strong advocate of 'new laws' to improve the finances and economy of the empire; his reforms were stifled by bureaucratic resistance. See Franke, op. cit., pp. 1097-1104.

[49] The second broadcast changes the beginning of this paragraph significantly: *Today, ten years of economic reform have finally arrived at their most critical and most dangerous point: the loosening of price controls. The question of prices has become a hot point of discussion on every streetcorner; everyone is distressed about them. The psychological ability of the Chinese people to accept reform has reached the point that it wavers each time a kilo of pork is put on the scales. The root cause of this danger lies in that there is not a perfected market and in that we are a people with a long tradition of egalitarianism. But this difficult step to take is precisely the narrow mountain pass which we must cross in order to progress towards a commodity economy. If indeed the meaning of reform for each person is not merely getting something but also putting something out, then the moment has now come when China must pay the price of reform. Whether or not the Chinese people can traverse this pass in step with the government will perhaps be the touchstone to test whether the Chinese people truly have the courage to reform. And if for this reason we lose ground, then China will be once again mired in stagnation...* What is presumably most sensitive in the original version is the prediction of social unrest.

[50] In the broadcast version, the interview with Li Yining is moved to the end of this section, where it is inserted following footnote 66.

[51] Li Yining is one of *Heshang*'s two principal academic advisors. Born in 1930 in Jiangsu, he graduated in December of 1948 from the high school attached to Jinling University in Nanjing. In 1951, he was admitted to the Economics Dept. of Beijing University, graduating in 1955. After graduation, he was retained by Beijing University

reform, and the success of China's economic reform will necessarily be decided by the success of reforming the system of ownership. The reform of the system of ownership must solve a key problem, which is that the system of public ownership in our minds is a traditional system of public ownership, and we must make the change from a traditional form of public ownership to a new form of public ownership."[52]

"Looking at the whole of the Yellow River basin, its reform is a matter of two levels. At one level, in terms of enterprises, it's a question of clarifying the ownership of property, and once the property ownership is clarified, of forming horizontal alliances and enterprise groups. This sort of thing can accelerate the recombination of the key elements of production. At another level, throughout the Yellow River basin the commodity economy must start to develop. The commodity economy is a natural stage of development. Once this natural stage of development has formed markets, then the state-regulated market is not an ordinary market but rather a perfected market; when the market leads enterprises, it will be a perfected

---

and eventually promoted to full professor. As of 1989, he was a member of the Standing Committee of the 7th National People's Congress, and of the Finance Committee; a member of the Economics Accreditation Group of the Academic Degrees Committee under the State Council; a member of the Committee for Sino-Japanese Friendship in the 21st Century; economic advisor to the Sichuan Provincial People's Government; economic advisor to the Beijing Railroad Bureau under the Ministry of Railways; advisor to the Beijing College of Finance; chair of the Economic Management Dept. at Beijing University; vice-editor of Beijing daxue xuebao and Zhexue shehui kexue bao; and vice-director of the Center for Management Science at Beijing University. Li Yining is the author of eleven books, including a textbook entitled Shehuizhuyi zhengzhi jingjixue [Socialist Political Economy], Beijing, Shangwu yinshuguan, 1986; Tizhi, mubiao, ren: jingjixue mianlin de tiaozhan [Structures, Goals, People: The Challenges Facing Economics, Harbin, Heilongjiang renmin chubanshe, 1986; Zhongguo jingji gaige de silu [A Guide to China Economic Reform (sic)], Beijing, Zhongguo zhanwang chubanshe, 1989. The above information comes from the latter book, pp. 334-335.

[52] Li Yining proposes that the revitalization of the urban economy depends on transforming the majority of state-owned companies into joint-stock enterprises, and that companies be further organized into enterprise groups or consortia, aiding in the economic integration of the country across provincial and local government boundaries. The formation of joint-stock companies has the advantages of greatly increasing the capital of an enterprise, while allowing the government to maintain effective control with an ownership as small as 40% of the stock; of granting complete management power to the enterprise, making it responsive to market forces and hence competitive. Furthermore, it is a policy far more attractive than price deregulation. The formation of joint stock companies can be tested out and gradually applied, while deregulation would have to be done all at once; it gives the people a specific good [just as the rural reforms gave land to the farmers], while price deregulation would threaten to take away people's purchasing power and make people suspicious of economic reform. See Li Yining, "Woguo suoyouzhi gaige de shexiang," Renmin ribao, Sept. 26, 1986, translated as "Conceiving Ownership Reform in China," Chinese Economic Studies, XXII, 2, Winter 1988-89; Zhongguo jingji gaige de silu, 1989, pp. 62-91.

market leading an flexibly-responding enterprise.[53] *In this fashion, the reform of ownership and the development of markets will be tied together, and there will be hope for the economy of the Yellow River basin."*[54]

An even greater potential problem is the extreme unevenness of economic development, which is revealing itself now in a "Matthew effect"[55] in which the backward areas get increasingly backward, and the advanced areas increasingly advanced.[56] The daily-increasing severity in the difference between poor and rich areas has given rise to the so-called division into "three worlds" within the country, has brought forth a debate over the theories of "steps" and "counter-steps,"[57] and has caused people to be greatly concerned for the homeland of our civilization—the vast yellow-soil plateau.[58] [59]

---

[53] Here Li Yining is embroidering on the policy of *"the state regulating the market, and the market leading enterprises"* announced by General Secretary Zhao Ziyang in his report to the 13th Party Congress [see above]. See also Li Yining, Zhongguo jingji gaige de silu, 1989, pp. 109-116. Indirect regulation of the market not only represents a profound policy shift, essentially abandoning the traditional command economy, but it also is intended to release the stranglehold exercised over enterprises by local and provincial governments which had resulted in local and provincial protectionism. If successfully implemented, this measure should result in greater horizontal integration of China's economy across local governmental boundaries, an improved circulation of natural resources between regions and a more efficient domestic market. The formation of enterprise groups or consortia is also intended to promote horizontal integration.

[54] The broadcast version of the interview ends after mentioning the need to find a new form of public ownership, eliminating the second paragraph entirely.

[55] Referring to the New Testament, Matthew 13:12, *For to him who has will more be given, and he will have abundance; but from him who has not, even what he has will be taken away.* Wang Xiaoqiang and Bai Nanfeng note that the "Matthew effect" is a term used in cybernetics or control theory to describe "standard feedback" [op.cit., p. 4]. They use the example of a published author to illustrate the principle of feedback: the greater his fame, the easier it is for him to publish; the more he publishes, the greater his fame; and so naturally it becomes easier and easier to publish.

[56] See Map 3, Rural Income Distribution, pp. 348-349.

[57] The tidu or 'step-by-step' approach to modernization implies first modernizing the coastal provinces, with their easy access to sea transport as well as foreign capital and know-how; then the second-tier of inland provinces, such as Sichuan; and finally, the third-tier of inland provinces, such as Xinjiang. Thus, coastal provinces would come closest to the 'first world' of developed countries, while the third tier of inland provinces would approximate the 'third world.' See Lam, op.cit., pp. 246-249. The tidu concept was developed in 1982 by Xia Yulong and He Zhongxiu.

[58] This paragraph is essentially abridged from Wang Xiaoqiang and Bai Nanfeng, op. cit., pp. 3-4. In March, 1988 a conference was held at Guiyang to discuss the problems of uneven regional development; see Shijie jingji daobao, March 14, 1988, p. 5.

[59] In the broadcast version, the interview with Wang Juntao is inserted here.

At the same time that the consumer expectations of city-dwellers in the south are fixed on the living standard of Hong Kong and Macao, there remain a considerable number of northern peasants who are still struggling to feed and clothe themselves.

At the same time that the commodity economy in the East has already penetrated the very cells of the family, there are some backwards areas in the West that are still waiting for the state to give them a "blood transfusion."[60]

(Site visit; a scholar discusses developing the Yan'an area.)[61]

Reporter: May I ask, what are Yan'an's principal problems?

Wang Juntao[62]: (Vice-director, Beijing Social and Economic Science Research Institute): They fall into three major categories, similar to other

---

[60] In other words, a hand-out. Su Xiaokang, in <u>Longnian de beichuang</u>, p. 18, writes about meeting Wang Juntao on his visit to Yan'an: *In the Yan'an Hotel, we ran into a group of young people headed by Wang Juntao from the Beijing Social and Economic Science Research Institute, who had been invited by the local party committee to advise on Yan'an's economic development. As they explained it, ever since Liberation, Yan'an had relied on a certain feeling of ancestral reverence, and so had never ceased to receive economic 'blood transfusions,' just like the old liberated areas throughout the country... Yet it was precisely this 'transfusion' mechanism which had fostered the laziness of the old liberated areas, so that there was never any internal motive force for economic development....* The problems with transfusions of economic assistance to China's backwards areas is treated in detail in Wang Xiaoqiang and Bai Nanfeng, <u>op. cit.</u>, section 4.1, entitled "Yue shuxue yue pinxue" [The more transfusions, the greater the anemia], pp. 95-119.

[61] In the broadcast version, this interview is moved to commence at the spot in the text marked by footnote 59.

[62] Wang Juntao is one of China's best-known democracy activists and a veteran of many political movements; he was sentenced in February, 1991 to 13 years in prison, charged as one of the "black hands" behind the 1989 democracy movement. Born in 1958 in Nanjing, Wang was the son of a high-ranking military officer and leading cadre of the CCP Institute of International Politics. At age 17 he participated in the April 5th, 1976 Tian'anmen Incident, gaining fame for writing one of the most strongly anti-Gang of Four poems. He was jailed in the subsequent crackdown for 8 months. In 1978, he was admitted to the Dept. of Technical Physics at Beijing University and simultaneously appointed to the Central Committee of the Communist Youth League, in recognition of his participation in the now "wholly revolutionary" Tian'anmen Incident. During the Democracy Wall Movement of 1978-81, he was associate chief editor of <u>Beijing zhi chun [Beijing Spring]</u> and had contacts within the reform wing of the CCP, including Hu Yaobang. In the fall of 1980, he ran unsuccessfully as a candidate for the district people's congress in Haidian outside of Beijing, as an independent candidate representing Beijing University; his controversial essay "On Whether Comrade Mao Zedong Was or Was Not a Marxist" influenced his defeat. After graduation from Beijing Univ. in 1981, he was assigned to the remote nuclear power research center at Fangshan as a punishment for his activism. He resigned from Fangshan in 1983 and travelled around China for some time, talking about democracy and living from hand to mouth. He was a prominent member of the Beijing Social and Economic Sciences Research Institute [SERI] founded by Chen Ziming in 1986, which was China's

backwards areas. One, the natural resources for developing an agricultural economy and various other economies are at a definite disadvantage; two, there exist drawbacks in the social structure and governmental system, such that the development of the whole society is rather uniform; three, there exists a strong sense of laziness in people's cultural concepts, which causes people to lack initiative and an awareness of diversified development.

Reporter: In other words, it can't catch up with the East and with the coastal areas?

Wang Juntao: Not only can it not catch up, but in my opinion there exists a striking contrast. During our visit this time, we have felt depressed and gloomy[63]. *In Beijing you have all probably heard of a theory known as the "stages of development." This theory states that in the pattern of human economic development, some regions will develop first, while others will still remain in a backwards state; this is the unavoidable price paid for human economic development. When is this problem finally resolved? Only when the economically advanced areas are so rich that they don't know where to spend their money will they finally invest in the backwards areas, transfer technology, and in this fashion spur the backwards areas on toward development. According to such a theory, China's east is relatively developed, while its west is relatively backwards, and so the entire western region will be left to lag twenty to fifty years behind; that is to say, one hundred million people and vast resources will be tossed out beyond the framework of China's economic development.*[64] *At present, human society has arrived at just such a pattern of development. Thus we want to issue a challenge to precisely this sort of development pattern. For, after the [implementation of] reforms in the economic system, if we wish to make use of the market system for development, then it's very possible that there might occur this sort of situation, in which the market mechanism both exerts a sort of pressure on western areas such as Yan'an while simultaneously offering it an opportunity. We feel that the Yan'an region also has its own advantages: over fifteen mou of land per capita; a superiority in energy resources; as well as many natural resources that could*

---

first privately-funded think-tank. He was one of the investigators for a nation-wide questionnaire survey on "The Political Psychology of China's Citizens" in the summer of 1987. [See Part Six. Starting in March, 1988, he served as associate chief editor of the Jingjixue zhoubao [Economics Studies Weekly] owned by SERI, in which his study of Yan'an's economy was published. He and other members of SERI played prominent roles also in the 1989 Democracy Movement. See Asia Watch, Rough Justice in Beijing, Jan. 17, 1991; Shijie ribao, Feb. 12, 1991; Shijie jingji daobao, Oct. 26, 1987; Hu Ping and Wang Juntao, Kaituo: Beida xueyun wenxian, Hongkong, Tianyuan shu'wu, 1990.

[63] The broadcast version of this interview begins immediately after this sentence, with the words: *In Beijing you have all probably heard of ...*

[64] In the broadcast version, the interview ends here.

be exploited. If it can be opened up for exploitation, then the Yan'an region can attain a relatively high degree of development.

But it has two problems. First, although the leaders at the various levels in this district clearly understand this region's problems and the technical steps needed to solve them, and although they have taken some measures, yet the results have not been great. Why this situation should arise is something we should look into. Second, in the near future the Yan'an region's markets cannot accommodate broad-scale development of resources nor the establishment of a modern industrial system; to develop these resources requires investment, human talent, technology and information, all of which the region lacks and which would have to be imported from the country at large.

The solution to Yan'an's problems can be summarized under two points: first, we must undertake comprehensive social research and come up with a program of solutions that will cause it to give birth to its own internal mechanisms; and second, in the Yan'an region we must establish mechanisms and channels linking up with and opening up to the whole country, linking up and opening up [this region to the rest of the country]; the system we have right now doesn't work.

For thousands of years, China's agricultural civilization has gradually radiated outwards from this yellow-soil plateau, heading from the Yellow River basin to the Yangtze River basin, and then on toward the southeast coast. Today, we see a radiation in exactly the opposite direction: industrial civilization is right now spreading from the coast into the Yangtze River basin, then pressing onwards to the Yellow River basin. Only when this land, which used up its milk in nurturing our people, can finally emerge from agricultural civilization, only then can the Chinese people truly enter the twenty-first century.

Today, now that there are only twelve years left till the twenty-first century, the Chinese people are indeed a little anxious; *"time is passing us by," "we should step up the pace."* But if the speed we call for is not implemented well, then we could once again step into the historical ruts of the "Great Leap Forward." How much suffering that sort of low-tech, low-quality, resource-hungry, low-efficiency wasteful model of development once caused us!

The old economic era marked by vast expenditure of cheap labor power, cheap natural resources and cheap energy has already come to a close in the second half of this century, and a new economic era, marked by scientific and technological advances and with human knowledge as the lever of progress, is already upon us. The advantages that we possess today will no longer be advantages in the future.

This is the same China which, when we let our imagination run wild, we always feel to be broad and wide and rich in resources; we are even pleased pink to be able to launch rockets for developed nations; but when we calm down and reflect, we discover that in reality it is population-rich but land-poor; short on natural resources and technologically backwards; educationally stunted and with a very low-quality labor force.

Mao Zedong put it very well once, that we really are "both poor and blank." Of course, being "poor and blank" isn't the same as a sheet of white paper that you can scribble on as you please. Being poor is due to being blank, and being blank is due to being poor.[65] We are facing the two-fold [challenge] of reform and reconstruction.[66]

This great people, which once created the most mature and brilliant agricultural civilization of mankind; this ancient people, who—precisely because this agricultural civilization was overripe—found it hard to press forward; when it stands on the threshold of industrial civilization, it may sometimes appear as naive as a child, frightened to death, unsure of what to do. But this doesn't matter, for as long as it eventually steps over that threshold and resolves to press forward, this people can once more enjoy a new spring!

Written by Zhang Gang[67] and Su Xiaokang

---

[65] This is an implicit critique of Chairman Mao, who felt that poverty and ignorance were an advantage, both causing China's people to desire change and making them easily moldable: *Apart from their other characteristics, the outstanding thing about China's 600 million people is that they are 'poor and blank.' This may seem a bad thing, but in reality it is a good thing. Poverty gives rise to the desire for change, the desire for action and the desire for revolution. On a blank sheet of paper free from any mark, the freshest and most beautiful characters can be written, the freshest and most beautiful pictures can be painted.*—Mao Zedong, "Introducing a Cooperative," April 15, 1958; Quotations from Chairman Mao Zedong, ch. 3. Mao didn't define what he meant by "blank," but presumably he meant backwardness in education, science, culture, etc.

[66] In the broadcast version, the interview with Li Yining is inserted at this point.

[67] Zhang Gang was director of the liaison office of the Institute for the Reform of the Economic System, one of ex-Party Secretary Zhao Ziyang's principal think-tanks. Born in Nanjing in 1948, he graduated from the Chinese College of Journalism. In 1979, he took part in the Democracy Wall movement with Hu Ping. In recent years, he also participated in the Research Institute of Marxism-Leninism under the Chinese Academy of Social Sciences and took part in preparation for the Jingjixue zhoubao [Economic Studies Weekly]. He was one of the first group of democracy movement activists to arrive in Taiwan after the Tian'anmen massacre of June 4th, 1989. He now lives in New York. Together with Fang Zhiyuan, he is the author of Gaige si le, gaige wansui [Reform is Dead, Long Live Reform!], Hong Kong, Tianyuan shuwu, 1990.

Part Five

"Sorrow and Worry"[1]

Nature has suddenly become a stranger to mankind.

Ranging from violent blizzards in California to huge floods in the Bengal Plain, from high heat waves overwhelming the shores of the Mediterranean Sea to the unrelenting, wide-spread drought on the African plateau, the earth shivers as if stricken by malaria, and mankind seems unexpectedly helpless, as if it had slipped back ten thousand years.

The "El Niño Phenomenon,"[2] to use a newly-coined term, roams around the world like a spectre.

In front of its Creator, human society has also become very bizarre and harder and harder to control.[3]

The death knell of capitalism long ago predicted by Karl Marx has still not sounded. Western industrial civilization, which for two hundred years has enjoyed a fairy-tale-like prosperity, still continues to readjust and renew

---

[1] The title of this part, youhuan, is difficult to translate consistently into English; hence each time it appears below, we have so indicated by putting the pinyin transcription next to the English translation. We thus render youhuan variously as "trouble," "sorrow" and "to worry." A related term, similarly difficult to translate, is youhuan yishi; this we have rendered as a "sense of social concern." This latter term has been the subject of much discussion, with some claiming that this "sense of social concern" is a distinctive characteristic of China's intellectuals, deriving ultimately from a statement by the Song writer Fan Zhongyan. See Part Four, notes; also the introductory essay by Pin P. Wan in this volume, "A Second Wave of Enlightenment? Or an Illusory Nirvana? Heshang and the Intellectual Movements of the 1980s," pp. 77-78.

[2] El Niño, originally meaning "Christ child," is a natural phenomenon occurring regularly around the Christmas season involving unusual reversals in the normal ocean currents off the shore of Peru, and causing considerable harm to the fishing industry. In this situation, the cold Peruvian current which normally hugs the shore turns west out into the open ocean, allowing the warm equatorial current from Panama to come south along the coast.

[3] The screen shows a rather graphic scene of contemporary Catholics reenacting the crucifixion.

itself in the midst of its difficulties, despite revealing all sorts of disease symptoms. The socialist countries, which, since the beginning of this century, have broken the weak shackles of imperialism, are now one after another beginning to carry out large-scale social reforms. Arms reduction talks between the U.S. and the Soviets, the Iran-Iraq war, successive political coups in Latin America and Africa, the democratic tide in East Asia, terrorist acts spreading across a wealthy Europe, the rampant spread of AIDS—all these have turned our planet into a jumble of tangled string.

Why are nature and society, these two foundations on which human civilization rests, so filled with trouble [youhuan]? Is there after all some kind of connection between these two kinds of trouble?[4]

When severe flooding occurred in the Liao River valley in Northeast China, military personnel and civilians strove to resist the flood and rescue those in danger.

Once the flood crest on the Yangtze River finally safely passed the Jingjiang dikes, and the Gezhou dam also survived its severe test, then the whole mid-China region could heave a sigh of relief.[5]

Yet the seemingly innocuous Yellow River is fraught with danger. When it was predicted that the Yellow River would have a severe flood, people all along the dikes that stretch one thousand li and throughout the whole North China Plain suddenly tensed with anxiety....

To Chinese people, no flood is more frightening than one on the Yellow River. As early as the time of the Book of Odes, the Chinese already lamented that *"Man's life is too short to see the water of the Yellow River become clear."*[6] In the entire history of civilization, the Yellow River has from the beginning been "China's Sorrow [youhuan]."

Yet now the Chinese people have an even deeper and heavier lament: Why has our feudal age lasted as long as the endless Yellow River floods?[7]

---

[4] Chinese people believe that the world of nature and society are intimately affected by the virtue of the ruling emperor. If the emperor has lost his heavenly mandate, a series of natural disasters or strange phenomena will occur to warn the emperor and people. Hence disturbances in nature herald trouble in society.

[5] This Yangtze River flood occurred in 1987. The Jingjiang dikes are near Shashi in Hubei province; Gezhou dam is located near Yichang in Sichuan province.

[6] Actually this quotation is found not in the Book of Odes [Shi jing] but rather in the Zuo zhuan. In the eighth year of Duke Xiang, when General Zi Zhen commanded his armies to attack the king of Zheng, one of his military aides quoted him this stanza. See Harvard-Yenching Institute Sinological Index Series, No. 11, Vol. 1, p. 265.

[7] Compare the first sentence in Jin Guantao and Liu Qingfeng, Xingsheng yu weiji-lun Zhonggao shehui de chaowending jiegou [Ascendancy and Crisis: on the ultra-stable

This is an even greater nightmare. It keeps oozing out from the imperial tomb at Li Mountain[8] and has spread all over, filling two thousand years of historical space. Over the past century, no matter how many times the Chinese people have tried to put it back into its tomb, it has never truly died.[9]

How slowly and how heavily the millstone of History rolls in its course. The Yellow River, too, in its bed filled with mud and sand flows just as slowly and heavily.

Will the floods come again?

Has turmoil gone forever?

We are asking the Yellow River, and also asking History.

(Titles: Part Five: Sorrow and Worry)[10]

We do not know what the Yellow River was like in ancient times. But as it unfolds before you at this moment, is the Yellow River not turbulently writhing, like a huge, fierce dragon? Here, at Hekou town in the Tuoketuo Region of Inner Mongolia, where the Yellow River is blocked by the Lüliang Mountains, the river suddenly heads south, angrily cleaves apart the yellow soil plateau, forces its way onwards, and from here on in the deep and narrow Jinshaan Canyon becomes tyrannical and unpredictable. Looking at its appearance at this moment, can you still imagine its

---

structure of Chinese feudal society], Hunan renmin chubanshe, 1983: *"What is the reason for the long persistence of Chinese feudal society? This is a question long debated amongst historians..."*

[8] Li Mountain is the tomb of the First Emperor of Qin, in Shaanxi province, about seventeen miles northwest of Xi'an and two miles east of Lintong. It symbolizes the tradition of feudal, autocratic rule which still affects China, according to the authors; it is the home of the spectre that haunts China.

[9] The screen illustrates this paragraph with scenes from China's past and present. After a rapid series of images of palaces, dragons, Li Mountain, and the first Emperor to illustrate feudalism in the past, we then see black-and-white documentary footage of student protests in the May Fourth Period; of Yuan Shikai, who attempted to install himself as emperor in the early years of the Republic; and of Red Guards waving the Little Red Book in Tian'anmen Square. Hence the nightmare of feudalism did not end with the First Emperor but has continued into the very recent past. By feudalism the author means the despotism of a strong, centralized state based on a peasant, small-holding economy. This Marxist definition of feudalism, based on the means of production [i.e., the economy], is quite at variance with the definition commonly employed by non-Marxist historians, who view feudalism as a type of political system characterized by a decentralized authority and a hereditary military aristocracy.

[10] Associated with the titles for this section, the screen shows a storm of thunder and lightning, and a river in flood.

clearness and transparency in the Yueguzonglie Basin area?[11] Can you still see its gentle, relaxed and charming manner at the Nine Bends near Hetao?[12]

Its clear waters have become muddy waves; its quiet flow has become a furious struggle; nurturing has turned into destruction; and a mother has become a tyrant.

The first Yellow River flood in recorded history happened in 602 B. C., the fifth year of King Ding of the Zhou dynasty. During the two thousand five hundred and forty year period from then until 1938 when the Kuomintang opened the dike at Huayuan kou,[13] the Yellow River has altogether broken its embankments one thousand five hundred and ninety times and made a major change of course twenty-six times—on the average breaking its dikes twice every three years and making a major change of course once a century. Among all the rivers in the world, the Yellow River is probably the most destructive one.[14]

Cyclic flooding over the past several thousand years has completely changed the face of the North China Plain, filling in lakes with silt, submerging cities and hills, making people suffer severely. Where now is Kui Hill where Duke Huan of Qi assembled the feudal lords?[15] Where now is the eight-hundred-li Liao'er swamp described in the novel <u>All Men Are Brothers</u>, the huge swamp which throughout the past the ancients compared with Dongting Lake?[16] The Eastern Capital of Bianliang,[17] once the most

---

[11] The Jinshaan Canyon is a long valley running from north to south, along the border between Shanxi and Shaanxi provinces. The Yueguzonglie Basin, in Qinghai province, is the source of the Yellow River.

[12] Hetao refers to the area at the top of the loop of the Yellow River, ranging from Dengkou to Tuoketuo in Inner Mongolia. A Chinese proverb says *"The Yellow River causes hundreds of disasters, yet only benefits the Hetao area."* [<u>Huanghe bai hai, wei fu yi tao</u>]

[13] Huayuan kou is a small town near Kaifeng city in Henan province. In June, 1938, in order to block the approaching Japanese army, the Kuomintang blew up the dike at Huayuan kou, diverting the Yellow River first into the Huai River and then into the Yangtze, so that it entered the sea south of the Shandong peninsula. In the resulting flood, 890,000 people died and 17.5 million were made homeless; much valuable farmland was covered with silt. The Yellow River was not restored to its former course until 1947.

[14] See Map 2, The Yellow River's Major Changes of Course, p. 347.

[15] The assemblage was held in 651 B.C., as recorded in the <u>Zuozhuan</u>, under the ninth year or Duke Huan of Qi. Kui Hill is near Dongren district in Henan province.

[16] The Liao'er Swamp was the place where the one hundred and eight heroes of the novel <u>Shuihu zhuan</u> assembled. At least in the Song dynasty, it was in the area of modern Shandong province. Dongting Lake is the largest lake in China, located in the northeast part of Hunan province.

prosperous in the whole world, with a population of a million people, is now submerged beneath ten meters of yellow soil—not to mention the large amounts of human life and property which were washed away in each dynasty! What other country or people in the world has had to suffer the kind of cyclic destruction that China has experienced?

What is even more frightening is that this kind of cyclic destruction is not just a natural phenomenon in China, but a socio-historical phenomenon as well. In measuring the feudal dynasties of Chinese history by a long chronological yardstick, from their founding to their rise to a peak, from the gradual emergence of crisis to the outbreak of turmoil and to collapse, they experience a violent upheaval once every two or three hundred years. The destruction of the old dynasty and the rise of a new dynasty to replace it is obviously a chronological cycle, summed up in the phrase *"What has long been divided will eventually be united; what has long been united will eventually be divided,"*[18] which like the Yellow River floods would seem to continue without end.

This kind of collapse of the social structure does not possess any "revolutionary significance," as some theories would have it.[19] No, it merely demonstrates a startling destructive force and cruelty. Usually in the last days of a dynasty, as soon as war breaks out, then for a thousand li the land is laid waste, city walls are destroyed, fields and gardens are filled with weeds, and the population is sharply reduced. In the short eight years between the Qin and Han dynasties, the population of the whole country

---

[17] Bianliang is the modern city of Kaifeng in Henan province and was the capital of the Northern Song dynasty [980-1127 A.D.].

[18] This popular proverb first appeared in a poem at the beginning of the vernacular Ming novel, The Romance of the Three Kingdoms [Sanguo yanyi].

[19] This statement clearly denies the revolutionary nature of peasant rebellions, which were an integral part of Mao's theory of history; they justified Mao's own revolution, which was based on peasants rather than on the proletariat. *The ruthless economic exploitation and political oppression of the Chinese peasants forced them into numerous uprisings against landlord rule. There were hundreds of uprisings, great and small, all of them peasant revolts or peasant revolutionary wars—from the uprisings of Chen Sheng and Wu Guang ... down to the uprising known as the War of the Taiping Heavenly Kingdom in the Ch'ing Dynasty. The scale of peasant uprisings and peasant wars in Chinese history has no parallel anywhere else. The class struggles of the peasants, the peasant uprisings and peasant wars constituted the real motive force of historical development in Chinese feudal society. For each of the major peasant uprisings and wars dealt a blow to the feudal regime of the time, and hence more or less furthered the growth of the social productive forces.* See Mao Zedong, Zhongguo geming yu Zhongguo gongchandang [The Chinese Revolution and the Chinese Communist Party], 1939, translated in Selected Works of Mao Tse-tung, Foreign Languages Press, 1967, pp. 308-309. This reference is pointed out by Huai Bing in his article, "Dui Huaxia wenming quanmian er shenke de fansi—ping dianshi pianji Heshang," Zhengming, 1988.9, pp. 62-63.

was reduced by ten million. At its height the Eastern Han [25-220 A.D.] had more than fifty million people, but after the great turmoil caused by the Yellow Turban uprising and the fight for supremacy among the Three Kingdoms,[20] there were only a little over seven million people left. Wealthy Chang'an city once had a hundred thousand households, but in two years they had "*almost entirely devoured each other.*"

These cyclical outbreaks of turmoil have time after time unfeelingly destroyed the accumulated wealth of production. Always, the more economically developed and prosperous an area is, the more severe the destruction it experiences. The Central Plain was the first area to be economically developed, but after the turmoil at the end of the Sui dynasty [581-618 A.D.], it became a place where "*the smoke of cooking fires disappeared, where chickens and dogs could no longer be heard.*" Kaifeng, a prosperous city in medieval times, had been a small town in the high Tang period; later in the Northern Song [907-1127 A.D.] it became a world-class metropolis, but by the times of disorder at the end of the Yuan dynasty [1279-1367 A.D.] it had gone back to being a small town again. It seems as if every six hundred years there is one turn of the Great Wheel.[21]

The south-pointing cart which in legend was invented at the time of the Yellow Emperor, was at the very least re-invented by Zhang Heng of the Eastern Han, yet later great scientists such as Ma Jun and Zu Chongzhi kept re-inventing it.[22] Ancient China's scientific inventions were lost over and over again in times of disorder, causing talented and capable craftsmen to exhaust their energies generation after generation.

Matteo Ricci brought from the West a fifteen-chapter edition of Euclid's Elements, of which he and Xu Guangqi [1562-1633] translated the first six chapters.[23] After the fall of the Ming Dynasty, the work of translation was interrupted for exactly two hundred years. Yet during those two hundred years, Xu Guangqi's translation was brought to Japan, where it stimulated scientific development there. The sprouts of new elements in China's civilization were thus constantly uprooted by cyclical upheavals.

---

[20] The Yellow Turban rebellion occurred between 184 A.D. and 189 A.D. towards the end of the Eastern Han; the Three Kingdoms period lasted from 221 A.D. to 264 A.D., during which time China was divided by a civil war between the Wei kingdom in the north, the Shu kingdom in the Sichuan area, and the Wu kingdom in south-east China.

[21] From the last year of the Yuan dynasty [1367] to the beginning of the Cultural Revolution [1966] is almost six hundred years.

[22] The story of the South-pointing cart is told in Needham, op.cit., Vol. IV.2, pp. 39-40 & 286-303.

[23] The translation of the first six chapters of Euclid was completed in 1607. Alexander Wylie and Li Shanlan completed the translation of the remaining chapters into Chinese in 1857. See Joseph Needham, op.cit., volume III, pp. 52 and 106.

In fact, to Chinese today, frightening social turmoil is neither remote nor unfamiliar. Although the turmoil of the "Cultural Revolution" has faded over eleven years of time, its severe scars still exist in people's hearts. But have well-intentioned people ever seriously wondered why the outbreak of that turmoil came less than two decades after the turmoil preceding Liberation [1949]? Does this mean that the cyclical pattern of social upheavals in ancient times is still continuing into the present? Have they— that horrifying prediction of "[a cultural revolution] recurring every seven or eight years"[24] and that crazy man Wang Qiushe in the movie "A Small Town Called Hibiscus"—really become past history?[25]

The Chinese hope that turmoil will never reoccur, just as they hope that the Yellow River will never again overflow.

But floods cannot be predicted. Ever since a tributary of the Huai River caused large floods in southern Henan in 1975,[26] the Yellow River Water Conservancy Committee has issued a warning: some day in the future, the Yellow River may witness the sort of flood that only occurs once in ten thousand years. Once it occurs, no matter whether it breaks the dikes on the south or on the north, it will destroy tens of billions of yuan of property, and greatly threaten China's modernization.

A Sword of Damocles is hanging high above our heads, yet we do not know when it will fall!

(Reappearance of the title: Sorrow and Worry)

---

[24] This is an unpublished statement by Mao, first quoted by Wang Hongwen in his "Report on the Revision of the Party Constitution," at the Tenth National Congress of the Communist Party of China held from August 24 to 28, 1973. Wang's report says, *In 1966 when the Great Proletarian Cultural Revolution was just rising, Chairman Mao already pointed out, 'Great disorder across the land leads to great order. And so once again every seven or eight years. Monsters and demons will jump out themselves. Determined by their own class nature, they are bound to jump out.'* See The Tenth National Congress of the Communist Party of China (Documents), Peking: Foreign Languages Press, 1973, p. 45.

[25] The movie, based on Gu Hua's novel by the same title [Furongzhen], depicts the political struggle of the Cultural Revolution as played out in Hibiscus Town. Wang Qiushe, originally an uneducated peasant, is manipulated by a woman cadre to become the local leader of the Cultural Revolution. He abuses his power to bully people and take revenge on his enemies. Yet at the end of the Cultural Revolution, he is so afraid of his enemies' revenge that he totally collapses and becomes mentally ill. The last scene of the movie shows him striking a gong as he walks down the street, yelling *It's time for a movement! It's time for a movement!*

[26] A major flood centered around Zhumadian in Henan occurred in August 1975 after prolonged rains burst several dams. While the flood was not reported in the press, the loss of life from flood and disease is said to have been extremely high.

The Yellow River is thus a strange, unpredictable river. Its most outstanding characteristic is its terrible sediment, as expressed in the saying *"a dipperful of Yellow River water is seven-tenths mud"*; among all the rivers of the world, this situation is unique.[27] If we took the 1.6 billion tons of mud and sand washed down from the yellow soil plateau every year and piled it up to form a dike one meter square in cross-section, it could circle the equator twenty-seven times. After several thousand years of erosion, the Yellow River had left above a fragmented, infertile plateau, cleft by gorges and gullies, and below a disaster-prone plain, vulnerable at any moment to the havoc of flood. Looking out only for itself, it flows into the sea, leaving behind these two heavy burdens for the Chinese people to deal with. No wonder some people describe the outflow of soil and water caused by the Yellow River as severe bleeding from the Chinese people's main artery.[28]

(Scene of Mao Zedong standing at the top of Mangshan in Henan, gazing afar at the Yellow River)

When the greatest man of contemporary China faced this huge river, what might he have been thinking? It is said that at the time he asked very worriedly, *"What if the Yellow River should rise to reach the sky?"* Mao Zedong, a man of great talent and bold vision, had said many daring things in his life, and it was only the Yellow River about which he spoke sparingly and very carefully. When he was over seventy years old, he still wanted to ride or walk to see the source of the Yellow River. He said, *"The saying goes, 'one should not stop until one reaches the Yellow River.' I am a man who would not give up even after having reached it."*[29]

For centuries, it has always been the Chinese people's wish to make the Yellow River run clear. It is like a dream that never fades. New China at

---

[27] The Yellow River carries the heaviest load of silt of all the world's rivers. In comparison to the average of 34 kilos of suspended silt in one cubic meter of Yellow River water, the Nile carries one kilo and the Colorado River ten kilos. See Charles Greer, Water Management in the Yellow River Basin of China, University of Texas Press, Austin, 1979, pp. 19-20.

[28] This metaphor recalls the original working title of the film series: Da xuemai, i.e., The Great Artery. Wang Luxiang describes the naming of the film in his essay "Huiyi yu sikao" in Heshang lun, pp. 91-98, esp. pp. 91, 95.

[29] Mao visited Mangshan in October, 1952. Mangshan is a long ridge stretching 70 kilometers from Luoyang to Zhengzhou on the south bank of the Yellow River, reaching a maximum height of 500 meters; it provides an excellent view of the river. See Tsuruma Wako, trans., Koka bunmei e no banka—Kasho to Kashoron. [An Elegy for Yellow River Civilization—Heshang and Heshang lun], Gakuseisha, Tokyo, 1990, p. 147. The popular saying quoted by Mao, *"One should not stop until one reaches the Yellow River,"* means that one should press on to the end in whatever one is doing; here, the quotation may suggest Mao's determination to press on with the Cultural Revolution despite criticism.

one point entrusted the realization of this dream to the huge dam at Sanmen Gorge. In 1955, State Council Vice-Premier Deng Zihui announced at Huairen Hall to all the representatives of the National People's Congress that *"After the Sanmen Gorge Reservoir is completed, both we gathered here as representatives and the people of the whole country can see in the lower course of the Yellow River the realization of a day that has been dreamt of by people for several thousand years—'When the Yellow River becomes clear.'"* At that solemn moment thirty-two years ago, Chinese really believed the old adage that *"When a sage is born, the Yellow River will become clear."*[30]

Yet the Yellow River did not become clear. The torrent of sediment blocked up the Sanmen Gorge dam, and the backed-up water swelled the Jing and Wei rivers, submerging eight hundred <u>li</u> of the prosperous Qinchuan region. The one thousand year long dream of our people once again burst like a bubble in the turbid yellow water.

The setback at the Sanmen Gorge dam makes us think back often on the tragic story of Gun, father of Yu the Great. In that era when flood waters reached the sky, Gun arose to lead people to control the floods, yet he failed because he used a method of "damming up the water."[31] After he was executed, his corpse was thrown into the wilderness, but it did not decay for three years. People then cut open his belly, and so Yu was born. Yu learned a lesson from his father's failure, adopted the method of "dredging deep channels," digging through mountains and making new water courses, thus eventually controlling the flood and earning a name in history.

To the Yellow River, the time it has spent in flowing from the foot of Yu down to the present seems only like a short catnap, yet in the world of man several thousands of years have passed. In those several thousand years the Chinese people have waged countless battles against the Yellow River's floods. The result of these battles is that in the end we have come to rely on two huge dikes to support the Yellow River and to channel the flood waters together with the sediment into the ocean. People often sigh with wonder at our ancestors' great strength in building the Great Wall and the Grand Canal, yet they fail to realize that these thousand-<u>li</u> long dikes are a great feat also. The Great Wall's only remaining use now is for tourism, and the Grand Canal, too, has long ago been broken up. Only these Yellow River dikes still maintain a vital connection with us even today, so that some people call them "the Great Walls by the Water."

---

[30] This quotation may be found in Li Xiaoyuan, "Yunming lun" [On Fate] in Xiao Tong's <u>Wenxuan</u>, chapter 53.

[31] The Chinese legend of the flood is also mentioned in Part One, p. 107.

The accumulation of sediment over a long time has constantly raised the river bed, broken the dikes, and changed the river's course, yet our ancestors have also unceasingly brought it back between its dikes. This kind of contest, in which *"whenever Evil grows a foot, the Good grows ten feet,"* has become the only means for the Chinese people to counter the Yellow River.

The dikes we have today were built at the beginning of the Guangxu reign [1875-1908], but in a little more than twenty years the Yellow River had already become an above-ground river again. On the average the river bed rises two millimeters every year, though in some sections it will rise twenty-two millimeters per year. Since Liberation, we have already raised and widened the dikes three times, which has provided almost forty years of security from flood—which itself is a miracle in the modern history of the Yellow River. Yet, in the final analysis, we have not freed ourselves from the passive situation of our ancestors, that *"whenever Evil grows a foot, the Good has to grow ten feet."* Look at the two banks of this "hanging river" at present: the cities, railways, petroleum fields, villages, countless facilities and countless lives, are they not all under the threat of a great disaster that could occur at any moment?

(On-site interview)

Cui Aizhong (Mayor of Kaifeng City): *"Of the eight times in history that the Yellow River has made a new exit to the sea, the two most serious ones were: first, at the end of the Ming Dynasty during Li Zicheng's uprising[32]; the Kaifeng City of that time is now buried seven meters beneath us. And second, during the Kuomintang period, when the dikes at Huayuan kou were broken, creating the Yellow River Flood Zone.[33] Of course the Yellow River has been brought under control in recent years, but the threat of flood along this section is still great. The masses have a saying that 'the Yellow River has a brass head, an iron tail, and a bean-curd waist.' The area around Kaifeng is the 'bean-curd waist' of 'bean-curd waists,' extremely soft. The reason it is extremely soft is that the river bed along this area is nine meters above ground level; it is a 'hanging river.' If it ever breaks the dikes, it will be just like pouring water from a pot, extremely serious. In the past few years that I have been mayor, this has been the greatest threat! What has worried me the most are the safety problems*

---

[32] Li Zicheng (1605?—1645) was the rebel leader who succeeded in overthrowing the Ming dynasty only to have final victory snatched from him by the invading Manchus. See Hummel, op.cit., pp. 491-493.

[33] The Yellow River Flood Zone [huang fan qu] refers to a region of 44 counties in Jiangsu, Anhui, and Henan provinces which were flooded when the Kuomintang blew up the Huayuan kou dike in June, 1938.

connected with the Yellow River; for if it should ever break its dikes, the harm it would cause people would be just too great. And in terms of history, it would be very serious too."[34]

How are we going to stop floods in the future? Is there a way to solve the problems of the Yellow River? Forty years of security have given the Chinese people a kind of psychology of indifference, as if they could almost forget its fierce face. This kind of mentality is probably similar to the fact that only after fire had already broken out in the Daxingan Range did people suddenly recall: *"Oh, that's right, there is a forest over there!"*[35]

But scholars and experts can never forget the terrible Yellow River, even when it is calm and silent. Some of them are worried, others are optimistic, and yet others are uncertain. Plans for controlling the Yellow River have always been controversial.

(In the TV studio, scholars and experts discuss strategies for controlling the Yellow River)

Wang Huayun[36] (former Vice-Minister of the Ministry of Hydroelectric Power and former Chief Director of the Yellow River Water Conservancy Committee): *"To make use of the Yellow River, we have to first make use of its flood waters before we can make use of its river water.[37] Only when we have brought the Yellow River under control will we be in a position to make use of its river water. When I reported to Prime Minister Zhao,[38] he summarized my conclusions as follows: <<Huayun, I understand your strategy for controlling the Yellow River. First, you have summed up the characteristics of the Yellow River as 'two clear seasons and one muddy season,' and you intend to make use of the 'two clear seasons' at the same time as the 'one muddy season.' Your method is none other than to 'block at the upper reaches and release at the lower reaches'; and the major projects of 'blocking at the upper reaches' are the seven reservoirs on the main stream.[39] Your specific measures are the seven reservoirs.>>"*[40]

---

[34] The broadcast version eliminates the last sentence of Cui's talk.

[35] The fire burned from May 6th to June 2nd of 1987, leaving at least 193 killed and 50,000 homeless, and devastating an area of 2.5 million acres. See Harrison Salisbury, The Great Black Dragon Fire: A Chinese Inferno, Little, Brown & Co, 1989.

[36] He is the author of an article entitled "A Nine Year Battle to Tame the Yellow River" in People's China, December 16, 1955, pp. 7-11, in which he describes the effort to restore the Yellow River to its original banks after the Huayuan kou flood of June 1938.

[37] The second broadcast deletes this sentence.

[38] Zhao Ziyang, Prime Minister from 1980 to 1987. Wang Huayun quotes Zhao as using a very familiar form of address to him, emphasizing a close relationship.

[39] The two clear seasons are spring and winter, when the dams should store clear water; the muddy season is the fall, when the dams should release the stored-up clear water to flush the

Huang Wanli (Professor at Qinghua University): *"This 'hanging river' now has a very strong advantage; being high, it can release water in several separate locations and let it flow out. Some people mistakenly think that to release water will submerge many fields. But that will not happen, because the water that is released will follow the original river-beds and low-lying land. By using this method, no matter how much water and sediment the Yellow River brings to us, it can all flow out. Moreover, we can dig the Yellow River bed deeper, so that there will never again be the danger of flood."*[41]

Zhang Hanying (Former Vice-minister of the Ministry of Water Conservancy): *"The question of whether the Yellow River might change its course in its lower reaches should be put on the agenda for the control of the Yellow River. Will it eventually change its course or not? Even if we say it will stay stable for one hundred years, how about after one hundred years is up? If it will remain stable for thirty years, then what about afterwards? If we do not consider this question today, then we are leaving the next generation a tough problem to solve."*

Chen Xiande (Vice-Director of the Yellow River Water Conservancy Committee): *"We on the Committee think first, that the Yellow River cannot be made clear, and also that there is no need to make it clear; secondly, controlling the lower reaches of the Yellow River has to be based upon the present water course; it is not necessary to change the river's course, nor should we allow it to change."*

Indeed, the control of the Yellow River is a very complex field of knowledge. Controlling the Yellow River is the toughest water conservancy problem in the world. It is an historical legacy from our ancestors that we cannot refuse; it also presents us with difficult choices from which we have to come up with a reasonable plan for the sake of generations to come. Today history and the future are tearing us apart.

(Reappearance of the title: Sorrow and Worry)[42]

---

sediment away. This technique would also prevent sediment from building up behind major dams. This interpretation is due to Tsuji Kogo's note to the Japanese translation published by Kobundo in 1989, p.121. The seven reservoirs are the seven dams (also hydroelectric power stations) at Longyang Gorge, Liujia Gorge, Yanguo Gorge, Bapan Gorge, Qingtong Gorge, Tianqiao Gorge, and Sanmen Gorge. See <u>1987 Zhongguo baike nian jian [1987 Yearbook of the Encyclopedia of China]</u>, p. 304

[40] The broadcast version deletes the last two sentences beginning with *"and the major projects. . . ."*

[41] The broadcast version eliminates the last sentence.

[42] The screen shows a waterwheel, an excellent visual symbol of cyclical change, referring both to the cyclical pattern of floods as well as to the cyclical outbreaks of turmoil in Chinese history.

The Yellow River that has nurtured us at the same time has unavoidably brought us harm. Every gain must be accompanied by a loss. It seems as if when mankind takes something away from Nature, Nature will pay us back in kind. This principle, which sounds quite absurd at first, is actually quite common in Chinese society and history.

Are not the thousand-li dikes that support the rolling Yellow River a wonderful symbol of our social structure of "great unification"?[43]

If we thumb through the world atlas of the Middle Ages, we certainly discover that Europe was fragmented into many countries, just like a "crazy quilt." Japan and India were also divided lands. Only in China in the Orient did the map show a wide and unified land; although from time to time it would split apart, yet it very soon reunited. In contrast to China, the Empire of Charlemagne in Europe, the Moslem Empire in Arabia, and even the Mongol Empire of Genghis Khan were all nothing but flashes of lightning in the long night.

What kind of tremendous power was it that bound such a big country together for more than two thousand years? The mystery of this "great unification" has stunned both Chinese and foreign scholars alike and made them rack their brains.[44]

Marx once figuratively compared a social structure built upon a feudal subsistence economy to "a bag of potatoes"; although they are all in the same bag, yet they are separated from each other. In ancient China, small-scale peasants were scattered as densely as stars in the summer sky yet were as loose as grains of sand on a plate. Confucian intellectuals, who possessed skills of social organization as well as a unified belief, very effectively knit these disunited small-scale peasants into a society.[45]

---

[43] The concept of "great unification" [da yitong] appears first in the Gongyang zhuan. The Liji [Book of Rites] defines da yitong saying, *There should be no two suns in the sky, no two kings on the earth, and no two heads in a household. It should be ruled by One man.*

[44] These two paragraphs derive from Jin Guantao's description of "The mystery of 'great unification,'" which is section 2.1 [pp. 17-20] of his book Xingsheng yu Weiji, [Ascendancy and Crisis] op.cit. Daniel Kane translates da yitong as "unitary (state)."

[45] For these ideas, see Jin Guantao, ibid., section 2.2 "Two vivid metaphors: 'potatoes' and 'mortar'" [pp. 20-23] and section 2.3 "Confucians, bureaucrats, language and communications tools" [pp. 23-27]. The quotation from Marx reads: *The small-holding peasants form a vast mass, the members of which live in similar conditions but without entering into manifold relations with each other. Their mode of production isolates them from one another instead of bringing them into mutual intercourse. ... Each individual peasant family is almost self-sufficient; it itself directly produces the major part of its consumption and thus acquires its means of life more through exchange with nature than in intercourse with society. A small holding, a peasant and his family; alongside them another small holding, another peasant and another family. A few score of these make up a*

This unique social structure once created a high degree of prosperity in China. However, even within this miracle of great unification, under the dazzling surface of an over-ripe civilization, and in the curling purple smoke of incense burned to worship the tablets of emperors, sages, elders and ancestors, the inner layer of this social structure was silently rotting away. This situation very much resembled that of the Yellow River's great dikes, which were silently being hollowed out by ants and by rats. A bureaucracy made up of Confucianists had an irresistible tendency to corruption, and power itself became a corrosive agent. And so, whenever a dynasty would reach its high point, its collapse would also be within sight.

Nevertheless, after the old dynasty had collapsed, a new one would very quickly replace it, the social structure would resume its original form and proceed towards its next collapse, just as whenever the dikes of the Yellow River would break, people would repair them and await the next rupture. Why are we always entrapped in such a cyclically-repeating fate?[46]

This mysterious super-stable structure[47] has dominated us for two thousand years. Yet today the gold imperial throne in the Forbidden City has long since become a museum-piece, and the huge bureaucratic network of Confucian scholars has vanished like ash and smoke. Yet it seems that the spectre of great unification still wanders across China's great land.[48] The

---

village, and a few score of villages make up a Department. In this way, the great mass of the French nation is formed by the simple addition of homologous magnitudes, much as potatoes in a sack form a sack of potatoes. ... In so far as there is merely a local interconnection among these small-holding peasants, and the identity of their interests begets no community... they do not form a class. They are consequently incapable of enforcing their class interest in their own name... They cannot represent themselves, they must be represented. Their representative must at the same time appear as their master, as an authority over them, as an unlimited governmental power that protects them against the other classes and sends them rain and sunshine from above. ... In other words, this type of small-holding peasant economy invites despotism. See Karl Marx, The Eighteenth Brumaire of Louis Bonaparte, International Publishers, New York, 1963, pp. 122-123.

[46] The screen shows a whirlpool slowly turning in the water. Here is a visual symbol representing the Chinese people's entrapment in a cyclically-repeating fate.

[47] The hypothesis that Chinese society is a super-stable structure is taken from Jin Guantao, who is interviewed below. This hypothesis is developed in an article written by Jin Guantao and his wife Liu Qingfeng entitled "Lishi de chensi—Zhongguo fengjian shehui jiegou ji qi changqi yanxu yuanyin de tantao" [A meditation on history—an investigation of the structure of Chinese feudal society and the reason why it has persisted so long], first published in Lishi de chensi, Sanlian shudian, 1981. A principal source of Jin's ideas is the cybernetic model advanced by William Ross Ashby in his Design for a Brain [1954, 1981] and later in his Introduction to Cybernetics [1963, 1966]. Daniel Kane translates chao wen ding jiegou as "ultra-stable structure."

[48] Bai Jieming [Geremie Barmé] points out that the "spectre haunting China's great land" is an allusion to a much-criticized poem of the same title by Sun Jingxuan, " Yige youling

nightmare of social upheaval is still fresh in people's memories. Even harder to overlook is the fact that bureaucratism, notions of privilege, and localized corruption are still doing damage to our great plan of the Four Modernizations.[49] These ancient symptoms of a sick society are very much like the sediment brought down by the Yellow River each year, which day by day silts up the river bed in its lower reaches and gradually builds up to a crisis.

As man-made disasters— such as the great forest fire in the Daxingan Range, the airplane accident at Chongqing, the trains that crashed into each other, and the epidemic of hepatitis in Shanghai occur one after the other,[50] can we not say that our decaying social mechanism is sending us subtle warnings, over and over again?[51]

Perhaps just as people are deeply concerned about the dikes that rise ever higher, should our eternal super-stability not make us worried too? Has history not given us enough food for thought already?

(In the TV studio, a scholar discusses super-stable structure)

Jin Guantao[52] (Researcher, Chinese Academy of Sciences, Chief Editor, Heading Towards the Future series): *"I think it is very appropriate to use the*

---

zai Zhongguo da di youdangzhi," which specifically uses the image of a dragon to describe despotism: *Brothers! Have you seen the spectre prowling our land? .. This spectre .. clutches with invisible claws, silently sucks blood and marrow, dictates every action, controls every thought.. China, like a huge dragon, gobbles all in its path; like a huge vat, dyes all the same color.* Sun's 1980 poem is translated in Geremie Barmé and John Minford, Seeds of Fire: Chinese Voices of Conscience, Far Eastern Economic Review, Hong Kong, 1986, pp. 121-128. See Bai Jieming, "Dianshi xilie pian Heshang ji qi qishi" [The TV series Heshang and its message], Jiushi niandai, September, 1988, pp. 98-100. A second source of this reference is, of course, The Communist Manifesto, whose first line is: *A spectre is haunting Europe, the spectre of Communism.*

[49] This sentence is attributed to Zhao Ziyang by Germie Barmé in Jiushi niandai, ibid. The Four Modernizations refer to reform in four areas: agriculture, industry, national defense, and science and technology.

[50] The forest fire in the Daxingan Range burned from May 6th to June 2nd, 1987. The airplane accident at Chongqing occurred on January 18th, 1988 when Flight 4146 crashed into a mountain causing the deaths of ninety-eight passengers and three crew members. The crash was discussed extensively at the National People's Congress in March, 1988. On January 17, 1988 two trains crashed head-on in Heilongjiang Province; and on March 24 another two trains crashed head-on at a Shanghai suburban station, causing 127 casualties. The hepatitis epidemic occurred in Shanghai in the spring of 1987, lasting for almost one year. Several thousands of people were hospitalized and the city declared a disaster area.

[51] The second broadcast deletes this paragraph, presumably due to the implied prediction of social turmoil.

[52] Jin Guantao is one of Heshang's two main scholarly advisors. Trained as chemists, he and his wife Lin Qingfeng have written extensively on the history of Chinese science and the problem of China's historical 'stagnation.' Their ideas are discussed in Daniel Kane,

"Yellow River's troubles" [huanghe youhuan] as a metaphor for China's history. In terms of the remoteness of its source and the length of its course, its vastness and the severity of its natural disasters, the Yellow River closely resembles China's history. If we take a very broad view of the two thousand years of China's feudal social history, we can discover two salient characteristics: first, that Chinese feudal society has endured for a very long time; and second, that every two or three hundred years there occurs a great cyclical upheaval and destruction in which the whole society falls apart.

We think that there is a close, inherent relationship between these two characteristics. We have presented the hypothesis that China's feudal society is a super-stable system.

Why does an instance of great social sabotage occur in China every two or three hundred years? Why did those upheavals in turn bring about the long-term stagnation of China's feudal society? Simply speaking, we may see it in this way: there is no unchangeable thing in the world, and a society is no exception. In any society, if we take a broad view to analyze the direction of its various changes, we will find two factors: one is a progressive and organizing factor, while the other is a force of disorganization, a non-constructive, destructive factor. Of the two, the growth of the force of disorganization is the factor that disintegrates society.[53]

While history is the facts of the past, I believe even more strongly that history is an endless dialogue between past and present. In this dialogue, we can create a very deep sense of social concern [youhuan yishi]. This is beneficial to the people of the present. The lesson that history gives to the Chinese people is that China must avoid destructive upheavals in the process of social change; progress and innovation must replace upheavals. As the old things fall apart, we should let new factors develop which could replace the old ones. At present I think that a sense of concern [youhuan yishi], whether for the Yellow River or for China, is a good thing. To have a sense of crisis is in itself an indication of an historical consciousness, which permits the entire people to stand on the height of history in order to sum up their past. I believe that if the Chinese people can, while reflecting on their history, truly come to understand their history, absorb its experiences, and then transform them into a kind of historical wisdom, then

---

"Jin Guantao, Liu Qingfeng and their Historical Systems Evolution Theory" in Papers on Far Eastern History, vol. 39, 1989, pp. 45-73.

[53] wu zuzhi liliang, here translated as "forces of disorganization" is translated by Daniel Kane as "asystemic forces."

the forthcoming twenty-first century will be a new starting point from which the Chinese people can head towards prosperity."[54]

Right here in that Kaifeng that lies nine meters below the bed of the Yellow River, History once played out scenes of rise and fall, of unlimited prosperity and incomparable disaster. Yet as far as the present is concerned, perhaps the stories associated with two historical figures here have impressed the Chinese people even more deeply than the Iron Pagoda and the Xiangguo Temple.[55]

This black-faced Judge Bao has not declined in fame in eight hundred years. Even though he was only an illusory idol to whom the suffering people in feudal society had no choice but to turn, yet people in Kaifeng today have nevertheless lovingly restored a grand and splendid Shrine of Judge Bao, to which travellers from the four directions flock unceasingly. Are they coming only as tourists? What does the persistence of the idea of "justice"[56] among the people tell us?

Even harder for people to forget is the fact that in an old bank building not far from the Shrine of Judge Bao, there occurred the darkest scene of the turmoil of the Cultural Revolution. In this dark and gloomy room, the President of the People's Republic of China, who had personally overseen

---

[54] Most of this interview is deleted in the broadcast version, except for the next to last paragraph. It reads: *Why does an instance of great social sabotage occur in China every two or three hundred years? Why did those upheavals in turn bring about the long-term stagnation of China's feudal society? Of course, there are many reasons, but simply speaking, we may see it in this way: there is no unchangeable thing in the world, and a social structure is no exception. Therefore we usually say there is no single empire that can exist forever. In any society, if we take a broad view to analyze the direction of its various changes, we will find two factors: one is a progressive and organizing factor, for example, the development of productivity, the development of cities, the increase of population, and the emergence of new institutions; the other is a force of disorganization, because it is a non-constructive , destructive factor, so we call it a disorganizing factor. For example, soon after the founding of a dynasty, its bureaucracy is rather young, but before long, the government starts to become corrupt, the bureaucracy starts to grow, and land ownership becomes increasingly concentrated, so that the growth of this kind of disorganizing factor begins to dissolve the original structure. If we say that the disintegration of the old society is inevitable, and it is arriving, yet no new institutions have yet emerged, then the results could definitely be tragic.*

[55] The Iron Pagoda, dating from 1049, and the frequently-rebuilt Xiangguo Temple are both in Kaifeng, Henan.

[56] "Justice" translates qingtian, literally "blue sky," the popular epithet by which Judge Bao was known. Bao Zheng [999—1062], as magistrate of Kaifeng, was renowned for his justice and kindness and for holding all people equal before the law, including the wealthy and powerful. His intervention saved many commoners from being wronged. As his exploits were taken as the subject matter of plays and stories in later generations, particularly the Ming dynasty, his image in the popular imagination became a mixture of history and fiction.

the writing of both the national and the party constitutions, was secretly imprisoned and spent the last twenty-eight days of his life. When he died, his hair had turned completely white and was fully one foot long...[57]

The fate of a President of the Republic is sufficient to represent the fate of an age. But looking at it from another angle, when the law could no longer protect an ordinary citizen, it ultimately could not even protect the President of the Republic. The white bones of Comrade Liu Shaoqi have revealed the cruelty of the turmoil and the tragedy of that time better than anything else, yet the roots of the turmoil are not something that his personal fate can show us. This was a tragedy for our entire people. If China's social structure is not renovated, if China's politics, economy, culture and thinking are not modernized, then who can ensure that this tragedy will not be re-enacted?[58]

What makes us feel delighted is that after having taken steps to carry out reforms in the economic structure, we have finally started to experiment

---

[57] Wang Luxiang explains the significance of these two sites as follows in "Huiyi yu sikao," Heshang lun, pp. 94-95: *"Kaifeng is not merely the greatest victim of the Yellow River's floods; it has also provided the stories of two persons which have become two "foci" of Part Five, "Sorrow and Worry," which provide the audience with many associations: Black-faced Judge Bao and the concept of 'justice' [qing tian] he represents; Liu Shaoqi and the strange, abnormal fate of an age and a group of people that he represents. These two persons actually illustrate a single truth: that without law there is also no justice [wu fa ye jiu wu tian]. Lacking law, the common people will thus long for a just leader [qing tian]; and without law, the asystemic forces in society will be impossible to check. And the cult of the leader is none other than the expression of a man-made increase in the asystemic forces in the political life of the party and the state. Liu Shaoqi must bear part of the responsibility for this situation himself. His tragedy was both an individual one, as well as one for the party, the nation, and even for our entire culture. The reason why we at present call out so urgently for the establishment of the rule of law and for the democratization of the political life of the state, is so that this historical tragedy will not be re-enacted. If there ever should come a day when China's simple and honest people no longer rely on a 'god of justice' [qing tian laoye] to uphold the right, but rather use the law as a weapon to protect themselves; and if law should truly become the supreme authority; then in my opinion, Judge Bao's Temple and Liu Shaoqi's death site in Kaifeng will no longer have contemporary significance for visitors but will become mere historical sites. On the other hand, if the worshippers at Judge Bao's Temple continue to hope for the appearance of people like Judge Bao in their lives and if people still come to Liu Shaoqi's death site with a certain unnameable chill, then history will be so deeply stuck in its rut that it will suffocate us. ..."* In his "Ziyou beiwanglu" [The Freedom Memorandum], Su Xiaokang had already commented on Liu Shaoqi's death as due to the lack of an adequate legal system. See Ziyou beiwanglu: Su Xiaokang baogao wenxue jingxuan, Hong Kong: Joint Publishing Co., 1989, pp. 38-39. For more on the concept of wu fa wu tian, see Su Xiaokang, "The Distress of a Dragon Year," in this volume, p. 285.

[58] During and immediately before this narration, the screen shows footage of the funeral of Liu Shaoqi, and of his wife Wang Guangmei scattering his ashes into the ocean from the deck of a boat.

with reforms in the political structure. Today, someone has finally bravely raised a hand to cast the first "no" vote in the National People's Congress; but how difficult this was![59] Who would say that this is not a kind of progress? No matter what kind of resistance and danger this reform may encounter, we can only move forward. Behind us stretch endless floods and endless turmoil. We must move forward to break through that repeating historical cycle. Perhaps we will encounter setbacks, but isn't this precisely the way in which unsuccessful Gun used his failure to pave a road of success for his son Yu the Great?

Let our generation shoulder the heavy burden of sorrow [youhuan],

So that our descendants will never again have to worry [youhuan]!

(Reappearance of title: Sorrow and Worry)[60]

Su Xiaokang

---

[59] At the Seventh National People's Congress held from March 25 to April 13, 1988, the first such "no" vote in PRC history was cast by Taiwanese representative Huang Shunxing, who was objecting to the choice of candidates for a committee on education. See the interview in Zhongguo qingnian bao, "Why I Voted 'No'—An Interview with Huang Shunxing, a Representative of the Seventh National People's Congress," March 29, 1988, p. 1. The Seventh National Political Consultative Congress [zhengxie] held at the same time also produced some lively televised speeches; Su Xiaokang reports being particularly impressed by the 30 minute speech of Qian Jiaju, interrupted by applause no fewer than 31 times, which touched on problems in education and social morale. See Su Xiaokang, "The Distress of a Dragon Year" in this volume, p. 287; Zhongguo qingnian bao, "Qian Jiaju tan shehui fengqi," March 29th, 1988, p. 2.

[60] This is an apparent error; the title does not reappear in the broadcast version.

Part Six
"Blueness"

Human blood is red.

Almost all animals have blood that is red.

Primitive religion defined the basic color of life as red. Early man daubed the corpses of the dead with red pigment from iron ore in order to summon back the life that had been lost.

The blue sky is deep and mysterious. People once firmly believed that this azure blue described the whole universe, that it was the color of the universe.

But only a little more than twenty years ago, when mankind left the earth's surface for the first time and gazed back at his home from outer space, did people discover to their surprise that amongst all the known objects of the universe, only mankind's own home, the planet Earth, was a blue planet.

(Titles: Part Six: Blueness)[1]

The planet of life is a blue planet. The atmosphere and water that permits all life on earth to survive is what makes the earth a blue planet.

The sea, which covers seventy percent of the earth's surface, is also blue.

The sea was originally the home of life. In the planet's sudden transformations, it was the sea which protected the lives of humanity's

---

[1] Here the screen shows the image of the earth viewed from outer space against a background of stars, in association with the title "Blueness." This image of the earth viewed from space may be variously interpreted as symbolizing (1) the high-tech future to which China aspires; and (2) China's aspirations for putting aside its traditional isolationism, opening up to the outside, and becoming a 'world citizen.' It stands in symbolic contrast to the image of the setting sun, which stands for the Mao Zedong era of "redness" and for the declining of Chinese civilization.

ancestors. Later, when mankind returned once again to the earth's surface[2] he was no longer suited to it. It was in the process of forcing himself to adapt to the land environment that mankind created civilization.[3]

The enigmatic stone statues on Easter Island tell us that ten thousand years ago there lived in the Pacific Ocean an ancient and energetic seafaring civilization.[4] These seafaring vessels that appear unbelievably crude and simple to us today carried mankind from the land back to the sea. What kind of faith was it that sustained early man in crossing those vast ocean routes which we still regard as dangerous to traverse? From the seafaring activities of early man to the great navigations of Columbus [1451-1506] and Magellan [1480-1521] which opened up a new era for mankind, can we not hear the grand melody of human destiny?

Precisely because of the continuing existence of seafaring life, human civilization split into two great divisions, of land-based civilization and seafaring civilization.[5]

---

[2] Here the screen shows a diagram of the evolution of life forms from the sea to the land, showing a succession of creatures crawling out of the sea, climbing the trees, and once again descending upright on the earth's surface, ending with man.

[3] While this paragraph does not make good sense from the point of view of evolution, since mankind never left the land for the sea, it does make sense as a reference to the present, taking da lu as "mainland China." In the political upheavals of this century, many Chinese have indeed fled overseas, and those who have returned to the mainland have had to *force themselves to adapt to the environment of mainland China.*

[4] While the peopling of Easter Island and the origin of its stone statues has been the source of much controversy, no western scholar has proposed a date as early as 10,000 years ago. Archaeologist Robert Suggs in his Island Civilizations of Polynesia, 1960, proposes that the Marquesas were settled by 200 BC, and that Easter Island was settled by explorers from the Marquesas soon afterwards.

[5] Xie Xuanjun, co-author of Part Six, makes this same point in his 1986 book, Shenhua yu minzu jingshen [Myth and National Spirit], Chapt. 6.2, "The ocean and the continent" [Haiyang yu neilu], pp. 267-271. The basic argument is that the use of the sea, whether for trade, fishing or piracy, stimulated an early interest in technology and mastery of nature, strengthened character traits of independence and individualism, and facilitated acceptance of a broad variety of different cultures and new ideas. Ancient Greece was the archetype of the sea-faring nation; its religion was a worship of raw power, symbolized by Zeus. The safer and easier life on land fostered a psychology of dependence and attachment to tradition; continental nations were less exposed to other cultures; their ideology emphasized ethics. This distinction between "continental" and "sea-faring" civilizations also explains the differing responses of China and Japan to the same challenge of the West. The failure of the 1898 Reform Movement in China, which was consciously modeled on the Meiji Reform Movement in Japan, shows that the path of development of an island nation such as Japan is not suited to the developmental needs of a continental nation like China.

Here is a nation poised on the Western Pacific and simultaneously perched on the eastern rim of the Eurasian continent. Its body is yellow, as is that great river which rises in its midst like a backbone.

When we see the wooden boat excavated from the Hemudu culture site[6] it's as if we were seeing sparkling blue waves dancing at the fountainhead of Chinese civilization.

And yet, even in the period of myth, the land-based culture of the yellow soil region in the middle course of the Yellow River was already unceasingly seeking to bring the lower courses of the river and the seacoast under its sway. Today, in the legends of how the Yellow Emperor defeated the Fire Emperor and Chi You[7] we can still hear the muffled sound of that distant point in history.

Later on, the conquest of the Yin-Shang dynasty [ca. 1700-1100 BC] by the Zhou dynasty [ca.1100-256 BC] proved the invincibility of this force arising from the heartland of the continent. By the late Warring States Period [475-221 BC], when Chu was defeated by Qin in an epic battle, we may fairly say that the "yellow" civilization, marked by the use of wheat as its staple food and of chariots for warfare, and influenced by nomadic peoples and Persian culture, had ultimately triumphed over the "blue" civilization, based on a staple diet of rice, understanding the art of ship- and sea-based warfare, and influenced by Southeast Asian and Pacific cultures.

This historical victory of land-based civilization was unstoppable, notwithstanding the songs of Qu Yuan which made Heaven and Earth lament or Xiang Yu's resistance which shook the earth and hills.[8]

---

[6] Hemudu is in Zhejiang Province, on the south side of Hangzhou Bay, about 25 kilometers upstream from Ningbo on the Yao River. Discovered only in 1973, the Hemudu site is an important one, showing continuous occupation between 5,000 and 3,000 B.C. and providing evidence of the earliest cultivation of rice in Asia. See Kwang-chih Chang, The Archaeology of Ancient China, 4th edition, 1986, pp. 208-220. Chongping Heshang, 1989, notes that while complete wooden oars have been excavated, indicating the existence of boats, no boats have yet been excavated. The clay models of boats excavated suggest that these boats were dugouts, constructed of single logs. [p. 269] The TV screen here does show a wooden dugout canoe in a museum case.

[7] The Chinese people take the Yellow Emperor [Huang di] as their ancestor; legend has it that he defeated the Fire Emperor [Yan di] and Chi You, leaders of other peoples who had rebelled against his authority.

[8] The names of the poet Qu Yuan [343-277 BC] and the general Xiang Yu [232-202 BC] are both associated with Chu, a large kingdom in the south of China during the Warring States period, and one of the major rivals of Qin for the mastery of China. Bordering on the Yangtze River and Dongting Lake, Chu had developed significant naval forces. Qu Yuan, a poet and courtier in the state of Chu, is said to have warned his ruler of Qin's impending invasion; his advice was ignored, and Chu was conquered by Qin as predicted. At the fall of

The retreat of "blueness" concealed within it the future destiny of this civilization to decline.

The restless blue waves of the Pacific were always silently calling to that ancient people stretched out on the continent and from time to time aroused it to action, leading its ships to the Persian Gulf and the Arabian peninsula. Yet in the end the attraction of the blue sea was no match for that of the yellow earth.

The hidden reason why the "yellow" civilization had such an enormous cohesive power was that Confucian culture had gradually attained a position of sole dominance in this land.

The Confucian system of thought expressed the norms and the ideals of land-based civilization and in the mature period of oriental feudal society was clearly rather reasonable. But this monistic ideological unity weakened the development of pluralistic thought, and so the various rich strands of seafaring civilization in ancient life, just like a few thin trickling streams flowing out onto the yellow soil of land-based civilization, vanished quickly without a trace. ...

As the land-based civilization daily increased in power in China, a "blue" sea-faring civilization was gradually arising in the Mediterranean Sea.

Long ago in ancient Greece, the democratic ideology of Athens arose contemporaneously with the growth of Athens as a sea-power, and so it was sea-power that led to a democratic revolution.

And the social precondition for the bourgeois revolution in the West was precisely this opening up of Europe's overseas trade routes. The sailing ships which roamed between sky and sea from the fifteenth century onwards both opened the curtains on an era of world trade and colonization on the one hand, and carried a cargo of hope for science and democracy as well, on the other. Thus due to these small sailing ships, "blueness" came to symbolize the destiny of the modern world.

And so, the vast markets of the Orient as well as the New World of the Americas transformed tiny Europe overnight into an upstart tycoon.

Crossing the ocean requires ships that are strong, big and finely made; making such ships requires mathematics and physics, as well as technology and science. And so, in 1636 Galileo published his Dialogue on the New Science. This "dialogue" was conducted in a shipyard.

It was England that first gained vast profit from overseas trade, accelerating both the primitive accumulation of capital as well as the

---

the short-lived Qin dynasty, Xiang Yu, the "hegemon of Western Chu" was defeated by Liu Bang who proceeded to found the Han dynasty.

popularization of liberal thinking. And hence it was in England that the bourgeois revolution first occurred, under the leadership of Cromwell [1599-1658]. In 1651, Cromwell promulgated the Navigation Acts.[9] In 1690, Locke [1632-1704] published his <u>Two Treatises of Government</u>.[10] The theory of free trade became both the catch-word and the principle of the bourgeois class.

Capitalism, by setting in motion the two wheels of the industrial revolution and of free trade, began a great flying leap, the great historical antiphonal chorus of science and democracy.

All of this was inextricably linked with the ocean.

And what was China doing at this time?

While Magellan was navigating his course around the globe, the Jiajing Emperor of the Ming Dynasty [r. 1521-1567],[11] because of fighting between Japanese tribute bearers,[12] had begun to formally "close the gates."

In 1776, Adam Smith published his famous book <u>On the Wealth of Nations</u>. In this book he declared that China's history and culture had come to a halt. He claimed that this stagnation was due to a lack of emphasis on overseas trade, and that "closing the gate" was tantamount to suicide.[13]

---

[9] The Navigation Act of 1651 was intended by the British to counter the maritime strength of the Netherlands. Essentially, they required that England's overseas trade be conducted entirely by British-owned vessels flying the national flag; the Navigation Acts were not repealed until 1849.

[10] Locke's treatises, published on the heels of the English revolution of 1688, refuted both the divine right of kings as well as absolutism in government, upholding the notion that government exists only to serve the public good and stressing the need for separation of powers. He does not, however, say anything about free trade, for which Adam Smith was the first proponent.

[11] The Jiajing Emperor, Zhu Houcong [Chu Hou-ts'ung], 1507-1567. See Fang and Goodrich, op.cit., pp. 315-322.

[12] Fighting erupted in 1523 at Ningbo between rival Japanese trade delegations, one sponsored by the Ouchi clan and the other by the Hosokawa clan; the Ming government responded by closing trade with Japan for 17 years; see Fang and Goodrich, op.cit., p. 1232.

[13] *China appears to have been long stationary, and had probably long ago acquired that full complement of riches which is consistent with the nature of its laws and institutions. But his complement may be much inferior to what, with other laws and institutions, the nature of its soil, climate, and situation might admit of. A country which neglects or despises foreign commerce, and which admits the vessels of foreign nations into one or two of its ports only, cannot transact the same quantity of business which it might do with different laws and institutions...* From Book I, Chapter 9, "Of the Profits of Stock" in Adam Smith, <u>The Wealth of Nations</u>. <u>The Wealth of Nations</u> was first translated into Chinese by the reformer Yan Fu in 1890.

How unfortunate that not a single Chinese could hear what he said in time!

Eventually, when that famous fire was lit on the docks of the Boca Tigris[14], opening the shameful chapter of China's recent history, there was already a vast gulf between the spiritual cultures of China and the West. The cultural conflict between a "blue" civilization that was expansionist and which carried on both trade and warfare all over the world, and a "yellow" civilization that clung firmly to an agricultural economy and bureaucratic government, was like that of fire and ice.

And yet, no sooner had they encountered each other, than the West's ships and guns made China's officials realize the strength of "blueness." Thus there came about the "Westernization movement"[15] as well as the notion of *"Chinese learning as the essence, western learning for practical use."*[16]

High officials of the "Westernization" faction bought formidable, iron-clad fighting ships and established one arsenal after another. The Jiangnan Arsenal in the Shanghai suburbs far surpassed Japan in its mastery of Western technology. About 1870, a Russian visited the Lanzhou arsenal in China's far northwest and was astonished by the high quality of the guns manufactured there. And when the Sino-Japanese War broke out [in 1894], China's navy outnumbered that of Japan.

Yet none of this could prevent the Qing dynasty's defeat, first by France [1885] and then by Japan [1894-5]. The most direct reason for the loss of the sea-battle in 1894 was that a corrupt contractor had filled many cannon

---

[14] The Boca Tigris [Hu men] where the Pearl River narrows downstream of Guangzhou [Canton] is where the Imperial Commissioner Lin Zexu burned the opium confiscated from Western merchants at Guangzhou in 1839. The confiscation and burning of the opium led Great Britain to declare war on China, opening a century in which China was attacked by one foreign power after another.

[15] Yangwu yundong, also called the "self-strengthening" movement. On the "self-strengthening movement," see Cambridge History of China, vol. 10, chap. 10: "Self-strengthening: the pursuit of Western technology," pp. 491-542. On the definition of yang wu and its connection with "self-strengthening," see Ibid., vol. 11, p. 167: *The self-strengthening movement was China's response to the crisis in relations with the West. .. The self-strengthening movement inevitably involved yang-wu or Western affairs. .. Gradually it came to mean government business involving relations with Westerners as well as Western methods and machines. In its narrow sense, however, the term suggested the adoption and use of Western technological knowledge. ... Although self-strengthening in theory included the reform of internal affairs, its major emphasis was actually the imitation of Western technology.*

[16] zhong ti xi yong is a contraction of zhong xue wei ti, xi xue wei yong, translating *Chinese learning as the essence, Western learning for practical use.*

shells with dirt [instead of powder]. And the Chinese fleet, which had drawn itself up into a half-moon formation, still didn't know whose orders it should obey, even on the eve of battle.[17] This fact clearly proves that the inevitable defeat brought on by a corrupt system cannot be warded off by technology.[18]

Yan Fu [1854-1921], the first student sent by the Qing government to England to study their navy, in the end never became the captain of a warship; instead, he became an enlightenment thinker.[19]

From his extensive observation of the West, Yan Fu discovered that the great achievements of European culture lay in developing the potential of the individual, thereby providing a sort of social contract. This social contract ensured that competition and all the other functions of capitalism would all play positive roles in accelerating social change.[20] And similarly he discovered that by employing the "willpower" of the individual—a sort of Faustian or Promethean strength for mankind—it was possible to create an energetic culture.

Nevertheless, just as the "Hundred Days of Reform"[21] in which Yan Fu participated were experiencing a crushing defeat, Japan's Meiji Reform, on the other hand, was succeeding. And as this great enlightenment thinker in China's recent past step by step abandoned reformist thinking under the attack of feudal forces and eventually retreated back to the embrace of Confucius and Mencius, his schoolmate at the English Naval College, Ito

---

[17] Here the screen shows scenes from the film Jiawu fengyun. For more details on the crucial battle, see Bruce Swanson, Eighth Voyage of the Dragon: A History of China's Quest for Seapower, Naval Institute Press, Annapolis, 1982, pp. 103-112.

[18] This critique applies equally well to China's present. Some of China's critics have charged that the current Four Modernizations plan, seeking to modernize China's agriculture, industry, science and technology, and defence, is no more than a revival of the philosophy of Chinese learning as the essence, Western learning for practical use. China's most famous political prisoner Wei Jingsheng, an activist in the 1979 Democracy Wall Movement, wrote a controversial essay entitled: "The Fifth Modernization: Democracy."

[19] Yan Fu studied at the Greenwich Naval College between 1877 and 1879. See also Boorman and Howard, Biographical Dictionary of Republican China, vol. IV, pp. 41-47, and Benjamin Schwartz, In Search of Wealth and Power: Yen Fu and the West, 1964.

[20] On the importance of the 'social contract,' see also "The Distress of a Dragon Year" in this volume, p. 287.

[21] Starting on June 11, 1898, the Guangxu Emperor, with the advice of radical reformers such as Kang Yuwei and Liang Qichao, issued a series of forty reform edicts, mandating changes in all aspects of society, but especially targeting the classical education system and official corruption. On Sept. 21, the Empress Dowager seized power, putting the emperor under house arrest for the remainder of his life and executing six of the reformers. It may be significant that Heshang was first broadcast on June 11th, 1988, the 90th anniversary of the 1898 reforms.

Hirobumi,[22] held the post of Prime Minister for one term after another and quickly led his island nation into the community of powerful nations.

The tragic fate of Yan Fu and indeed of many other advanced thinkers of the early modern period such as Kang Yuwei[1858-1927],[23] Liang Qichao[24] [1873-1929], and Zhang Taiyan[25] [1869-1936] would also seem to prove that even the very best Chinese, after promoting revolution and progress for a while, would ultimately be unable to avoid retreating to the haven of Confucianism.[26]

Even today in the 1980's, in the midst of our great debate stirred up by the "passion for studying Chinese culture,"[27] people still continue the century-old inconclusive argument over the strong and weak points of Chinese versus Western culture. No matter whether it is the fantasy of "wholesale Westernization"[28] or the fervent wish for a "third flowering of

---

[22] Ito's career nearly encompassed the entire Meiji period [1868-1912]. He participated in the struggle to overthrow the shogunate and restore the emperor, served four times as Prime Minister, and was principal drafter of Japan's first constitution, promulgated in 1889. In 1894, he concluded a treaty with Great Britain to abolish extraterritoriality. He was Prime Minister during Japan's successful war with China, in 1894-5. Ito visited the West several times, first in 1863 when he visited England for about five months, and later in 1882-3 when he visited Europe to study constitutional systems. There is no evidence, however, that he was ever a classmate of Yen Fu at the Greenwich Naval College. See Kodansha Encyclopedia of Japan, vol. 3, p. 353.

[23] See Boorman & Howard, op. cit., vol. II, pp 228-233.

[24] On Liang Qichao [Liang Ch'i-ch'ao], see Boorman & Howard, op.cit., pp. 346-351.

[25] His original name was Zhang Binglin [Chang Ping-lin]; see Boorman and Howard, op.cit., pp. 92-98.

[26] A very similar idea is expressed in Bao Zunxin, "Wei wancheng de niepan—dui Wusi de fansi" in Pipan yu qimeng, p. 139.

[27] The "passion for studying Chinese culture" translates zhongguo wenhua re and refers to the great upsurge of interest among intellectuals in looking at traditional Chinese culture as the source of China's backwardness; in doing so, intellectuals were consciously carrying on the spirit of the May 4th Movement of 1919, which had also criticized traditional culture. For an overview, see Joël Thoraval, "La «fièvre culturelle» chinoise: de la stratégie à la théorie" [The Chinese 'fever for culture': from strategy to theory] pp. 558-572 in Critique, vol. 45, nos. 507-508, August-September 1989; Wu Xiuyi, Zhongguo wenhua re, Shanghai renmin chubanshe, 1988; Fudan daxue lishi xi, Zhongguo chuantong wenhua de zai guji, Shanghai renmin chuban she, 1987.

[28] "Wholesale Westernization" translates the expression quanpan xihua first used by Hu Shih in his 1929 article entitled "Zhongguo jinri de wenhua chongtu" [Cultural conflict in the China of today]; more recently, the well-known Chinese cosmologist and human rights activist Fang Lizhi has used the same phrase: *Our goal at present is the thorough modernization of China. We all have a compelling sense of the need for modernization. ...We realize that grave shortcomings exist not only in our "material civilization" but also in our "spiritual civilization"—our culture, our ethical standards, our political*

Confucian civilization,"[29] it all seems to be going over the same ground as before. No wonder some young scholars say with a sigh that their tremendous cultural wealth has become a tremendous cultural burden, that their feeling of tremendous cultural superiority has become a feeling of tremendous cultural inferiority[30]; and this we cannot but admit is a tremendous psychological obstacle standing in the course of China's modernization.

---

institutions—and that these also require modernization. The question we must now ask is, what kind of modernization is required? ... I personally agree with the "complete Westernizers." What their so-called "complete Westernization" means to me is complete openness, the removal of restrictions in every sphere. We need to acknowledge that when looked at in its entirety, our culture lags far behind that of the world's most advanced societies, not in any one specific aspect but across the board... From a speech by Fang Lizhi on Nov. 18, 1986 at Tongji University, Shanghai, translated in Fang Lizhi, Bringing Down the Great Wall: Writings on Science, Culture, and Democracy in China, Knopf, New York, 1991, pp. 157-158.

[29] The suggestion of a Confucian renaissance is associated principally with Du Weiming [Weiming Tu], Prof. of Chinese History and Philosophy at Harvard University, author of Neo-Confucian Thought in Action: Wang Yang-ming's Youth, Berkeley, Univ. of California Press, 1976; Confucian Thought: Selfhood as Creative Transformation, Albany, State Univ. of New York Press, 1985. In 1985, he taught a course in Confucian philosophy at Beijing University. Subsequently he published a volume of his talks and discussions on the subject of the renaissance of Confucianism under the title: Ruxue di sanqi fazhan de qianjing wenti—dalu jiangxue, wennan he taolun [The Prospects for a Third Development of Confucianism—Lectures, Questions, and Discussions on the Mainland], Taibei. He has an article in Zhishi fenzi [The Chinese Intellectual], Autumn, 1985 entitled "Rujia chuantong de xiandai zhuanhua" [The Modern Transformation of the Confucian Tradition], pp. 90-96, in which he addresses the question of a future third flowering of Confucianism. Just as the second flowering of Confucianism came in the Song dynasty, as a response to the influx of Indian Buddhist culture and created a common philosophy throughout East Asia, so a third flowering would require Confucianism to face the various challenges of Western culture and philosophy. These would include the theological challenge of Christianity; the social, political and economic challenges of Marxism; the psychological challenge of Freud; the advocacy of science and democracy inherited from China's own May Fourth movement, as well as Western ideas of freedom and human rights. Since the second flowering of Confucianism, from the Song dynasty down to the middle of the 19th century, took 800 years, the third flowering of Confucianism, even assuming a much-accelerated pace of change, would still take at least a century. See also his review of Heshang included in this volume entitled: "Heshang: Zhongguo wenhua hechu qu" [Where is Chinese Culture Headed?].

[30] This is an apparent reference to a statement by Bang Pu, of the Chinese Academy of Social Sciences: *"The humanist spirit of Chinese culture has added luster to our people and our country yet has also erected barriers; it has passed the light of knowledge to the world while at the same time creating multiple misunderstandings in the communication between China and the outside; it is a great spiritual treasure but also a not inconsiderable cultural burden."* See his article entitled: "Zhongguo wenhua de renwen zhuyi jingshen" [The Humanist Spirit of Chinese Culture] in Zhongguo chuantong wenhua de zai guji, Shanghai renmin chubanshe, 1985, pp. 50-55.

The greatest difficulty of reform lies perhaps in that we are always worrying: "*Are the Chinese people still Chinese?*" We seem not to realize that throughout the past two or three centuries in the West, no matter whether it was the Renaissance, the Reformation, or the Enlightenment movement, Western Europeans at least never worried whether after reform they would still be Italian or German or French. Only in China is this the greatest taboo of all.

Perhaps this is precisely both the profound and the shallow point of "yellow" civilization.

Over two thousand years ago the philosopher Zhuangzi told us the following fable:

The spirit of the Yellow River, the Riverlord, found himself swollen so magnificently large at the time of the autumn floods that someone standing on one bank could no longer make out the difference between a cow and a horse on the opposite bank. He floated cockily downstream, till all of a sudden he caught sight of the sea and was struck dumb with astonishment. The ruler of the sea, the Northsea Spirit, told him: "*One can't discuss the sea with a frog in a well, because all it knows is its own tiny scrap of space, and it lacks the imagination to conceive of the vastness of the sea. And now, my dear Riverlord, you have finally left your narrow riverbed and seen the immensity of the ocean. Knowing your own limits, you have indeed attained a higher level of understanding.*"[31]

This is symbolic language. It's not talking about ancient China but rather seems to be foretelling the China of today.

Barely a century has passed since the ancient spirit of the Yellow River has clearly seen the face of the sea and recognized its vastness and strength. The long drawn-out sigh it uttered on seeing the ocean has traversed a century of history and still echoes today.

(Reappearance of the titles: Blueness)

This stretch of dirt-yellow land cannot teach us the true spirit of science.

The unruly Yellow River cannot teach us a true democratic consciousness.

Relying only on this yellow soil and this Yellow River, it is no longer possible to feed our daily-increasing population and no longer possible to

---

[31] The philosopher Zhuangzi [Chuang-tzu], together with Laozi [Lao Tzu] one of the two best-known Taoist writers of the Warring States period, is dated to the 3rd. century BC. The anecdote given here is paraphrased from ch. 17. For a translation, see Burton Watson, trans., The Complete Works of Chuang-tzu, pp. 175 on.

give birth to a new culture, for they no longer possess the nutrition and energy they once had.

Confucian culture may indeed possess all sorts of ancient and perfect "gems of wisdom," yet over these past few thousand years it has been able to create neither a national spirit of initiative, nor a legal order for the state, nor a mechanism for cultural renewal; rather on its path of decline it has created a frightening sort of suicidal mechanism,[32] which repeatedly destroys its own best talent, killing off the living elements within itself, and suffocating one generation after another of the finest flowers of our nation. Though it may possess a thousand-year's treasure hoard of gems, in today's world we may be forced to throw out the gems together with the junk.[33]

History has proven that to attempt to modernize using the style of control of a "land-based" culture, although one may be able to incorporate some of the new achievements of modern science and technology, even to the point of putting satellites in orbit and exploding atom bombs, yet it will be fundamentally impossible to infuse the whole nation with a strong, civilizing vitality.

Only when the sea-breeze of "blueness" finally turns to rain and once again moistens this stretch of parched yellow soil, only then will this awesome vitality, previously released only during the happy days of the Spring Festival,[34] be able to bring new life to the vast yellow soil plateau.

In the heartland of the yellow soil plateau—Yan'an[35]—everywhere one can see clothing stores and barber shops established by young men and women from Shanghai, Zhejiang and other coastal areas. A flood of commodities from the coast are scattered throughout the streets and lanes. Sacred, earth-grey Pagoda Mountain, to the rear of this colorful and bustling market, has gradually faded into the misty background.[36]

---

[32] The second broadcast eliminates this reference to a "frightening sort of suicidal mechanism," so that the sentence reads: *...rather on its path of decline it repeatedly destroys its own best talent, killing off the living elements within itself, and suffocating one generation after another of the finest flowers of our nation.*

[33] The second broadcast also eliminates this sentence.

[34] The Chinese lunar New Year celebration.

[35] After the Long March, Yan'an was the principal Chinese communist center in north China during the war against Japan. It is common knowledge that the old liberated areas such as Yan'an are among the poorest today. Yan'an and Pagoda Mountain hence symbolize both Mao's revolutionary tradition as well as economic backwardness.

[36] Su Xiaokang and Wang Luxiang, principal co-authors of the script, visited Yan'an during the course of the filming and both recorded their impressions in print: Wang Luxiang, "Hui yi yu sikao" [Remembering and pondering] in Heshang lun, pp. 92-93; Su Xiaokang, Longnian de beichuang, pp. 17-20. Wang writes: *Yan'an is very poor—all of the old revolutionary base areas are very poor; this common phenomenon is worth*

(Scene of a thousand people from Ansai in northern Shaanxi playing waist-drums[37])

These old men and young guys, whose ancestors once erupted from this continental heartland to conquer all of China, are now still bound to this shrunken stretch of land and with it their once magnificent energy has also diminished. It's hard to believe that these few young men are actually members of this lively team of one thousand waist-drummers. Does it mean that their vitality will forever be expended only in the frenzy of playing the waist-drums?

In 1980, the Shenzhen Special Economic Zone was established.[38] It announced to the whole world that this "land-based" civilization of several thousands of years had finally moved to the edge of the sea, and that the face which it had always kept turned to the land had turned to gaze at the distant ocean.

In 1986, fourteen coastal cities were entirely opened up to the outside. China had formally assumed a posture of challenging the sea.[39]

In 1988, Hainan Island was established as a separate province. Its short-term objective was to issue a challenge to the "four small dragons" of Asia. The ancient Asian continent had finally put aside the proud airs of a great power.[40]

---

looking into, the connection between poverty, backwardness and revolution gives much food for thought. In terms of wealth or neatness, downtown Yan'an is far behind the level of a small town south of the Yangtze. Most interesting of all is that the liveliest shopping street in all Yan'an faces the well-known Pagoda Mountain. While in the past so many romantic tales of revolution and love occurred beneath Pagoda Mountain or by the Yan'an River and the very air was filled with idealism, today all that has vanished, while fashion stores and hair-dressing salons large and small opened by southerners line the streets and alleys, bright bolts of cloth and ready-made clothes are piled by the roadside; chanted jingles selling rat-poison resonate to the sound of bamboo clappers—the commodity economy, this once unfamiliar thing, has quietly arrived in this sanctuary of the Chinese revolution.

[37] This footage is taken from the joint Sino-Japanese documentary on the Yellow River. Wang Luxiang tells the story of how the dancers were denied their pay in his essay in Heshang lun entitled "Huiyi yu sikao" [Remembering and pondering], p. 93.

[38] Shenzhen is in Guangdong Province and borders on Hong Kong, hence it is well-placed for manufacturing goods for export.

[39] The fourteen coastal cities, from north to south, are: Dalian, Qinhuangdao, Tianjin, Yantai, Qingdao, Lianyungang, Nantong, Shanghai, Ningbo, Wenzhou, Fuzhou, Guangzhou, Zhanjiang, Beihai.

[40] Translating dalu as "mainland [China]," this sentence can be interpreted as: *The ancient, Asiatic Chinese mainland has put aside the proud airs of a great power.*

If Hainan should succeed, it will unite with the fourteen other coastal cities and form one of the great dragons on the two shores of the Pacific. This historic undertaking will necessarily give a new color to China's culture.[41]

And yet, while reforms move ahead quickly, how many Chinese are consciously participating in them?

A series of reports from the Chinese Citizens Political Psychology Research Group has indicated that Chinese citizens very commonly exhibit an overly-cautious attitude towards political participation.[42] Of citizens surveyed, 62.41%[43] said that "they were very careful about discussing political issues," while 73.79% said that they either "agreed with," "basically agreed with" or "did not oppose" the statement that "It's best to minimize one's participation in politics." They continue to worry that political participation could invite trouble for them, and they continue to lack a feeling of security about political participation. The recurring wild swings of the pendulum throughout the recent decades of political movements, as well as the extreme fierceness of political oppression has made people paranoid. This will definitely constitute a serious obstacle to the progress of democracy.

---

[41] What is here described is the "coastal strategy" of development of Zhao Ziyang; for more details, see Lam, op.cit., 224-226. The metaphor of "changing color" refers to a quotation by Chairman Mao which describes a potential capitalist restoration in China as a "change of color."

[42] The summer of 1987 witnessed the appearance of the first nation-wide public opinion surveys in the history of the People's Republic, conducted by the Public Opinion Research Institute of People's Univ., Beijing; the Chinese Social Survey Network; and the Chinese Citizens Political Psychology Survey Group. This latter survey was led by Wang Juntao, Chen Xiaoping, Li Ping, Fei Yuan, Zhang Lun and Min Qi, all members of the Beijing Social and Economic Science Research Institute [SERI], a private think-tank founded by Chen Ziming in late 1986. [See Part Four under Wang Juntao]. This survey, conducted in July and August of 1987, hired 500 college students and collected 3,204 valid questionnaires with over 7.4 million items of data. Preliminary results were published as Zhongguo zhengzhi shouce [A Handbook of Chinese Politics] and reported on extensively in Shijie jingji daobao, Sept. 28th, 1987 and October 26th, 1987. Later, SERI convened a conference in Hengyang, Hunan, on the subject of China's political psychology, attended by over 30 young theorists from all over the country, including Chen Xiaoping and Min Qi from SERI. See Shijie jingji daobao, March 7, 1988. The final results of this survey were written up by Min Qi and published in February 1989 as Zhongguo zhengzhi wenhua: minzhu zhengzhi nan chan de shehui xinli yinsu [Chinese Political Culture: Socio-psychological Factors in the Delayed Birth of Democratic Politics], Yunnan renmin chubanshe.

[43] The report appearing in Shijie jingji daobao, Oct. 26, 1987, gives this percentage as 43.11%.

The May Fourth movement of 1919, for the first time and with a thoroughly uncompromising spirit, unfurled the banners of "science" and "democracy." The thought of Western culture, including Marxism, was widely disseminated throughout China.[44] But this progressive tide of culture by no means succeeded in washing away the accumulated sediment of feudalism in politics, economics, and in the moral character of individuals. Over the past several decades, from time to time this sunken sediment has resurfaced, while at other times everything has frozen solid.

Many things in China, it would seem, should all start over again from May Fourth.[45]

(The television studio. A scholar discusses democratic consciousness and East Asian industrial civilization.)[46]

Bao Zunxin[47] (Associate Researcher at the Chinese Academy of Social Sciences, editor of the Philosophy of Culture Series and of Studies on the

---

[44] For a survey of intellectual debates in this period, see Chow Tse-tsung, The May Fourth Movement: Intellectual Revolution in Modern China, Harvard Univ. Press, Cambridge, 1964; Wen-han Kiang, The Chinese Student Movement, King's Crown Press, New York, 1948; Hu Shih, The Chinese Renaissance, Univ. of Chicago Press, 1934; Tsi C. Wang, The Youth Movement in China, New Republic, New York, 1928.

[45] In other words, the past seventy years of Chinese history are a failed experiment. Here the TV screen shows the bas-relief sculpture of May 4th marchers from the Mao Zedong Memorial Hall; the implication is that Mao's political career, which began during the May Fourth period, is also in question.

[46] The broadcast version completely eliminates this interview.

[47] Bao Zunxin [1938-], a 1964 graduate of the Chinese dept. of Beijing University, intellectual disciple of Hou Wailu, student of the history of Chinese thought, and of comparative philosophy and culture, has contributed to the opening up of China's intellectual horizons through serving on the editorial boards of the book review journal Dushu and two book series: the Zouxiang weilai congshu [Heading Towards the Future] and Wenhua zhexue [Philosophy of Culture]. These editorial boards include several other contributors to Heshang, notably Jin Guantao, Liu Qingfeng, Zhang Gang, and Xie Xuanjun. He is the author of three books: Kui bu ji, Chengdu,1986;Pipan yu qimeng [Criticism and Enlightenment], Taibei, 1989; and with Zhang Zhongdong Haixia liang'an lun wusi [The Two Sides of the Taiwan Straits Discuss May 4th], Taibei, 1989. He wrote the preface to Jin Guantao and Liu Qingfeng, Xingsheng yu weiji—lun zhongguo fengjian shehui de chaowending jiegou Ascendancy and Crisis—on the Ultrastable Structure of China's Feudal Society], 1983. He wrote an article for Zhishi fenzi [The Chinese Intellectual, Winter, 1987, pp. 103-109] taking issue with Weiming Tu's proposition (cited above) that Confucianism could experience a "third flowering." [Subsequently reprinted in Pipan yu qimeng along with several other related articles.] Tu's reply to Bao Zunxin is found in Longnian de beichuang, pp. 51-61, and is reprinted in this volume. During the democracy movement of 1989, Bao Zunxin was one of the most active participants from the ranks of intellectuals. He was arrested in July of 1989, subsequently

History of Chinese Philosophy]: *"Traditional culture was established on the basis of a peasant subsistence economy which emphasized political absolutism.*[48] *We must shatter this absolutism, change traditional outlooks, establish a democratic consciousness, a national democratic spirit. The most salient characteristic of traditional culture was a pervading sense of ethics, or what one might call an "ethical centralism."*[49] *This principle of value must be smashed, and we must establish individualism.*[50] *A spirit of democracy and a spirit of science are precisely what our people most lack. Without these two spirits, the modernization of China is inconceivable. These characteristics of our people are not things that can be solved merely by exalting our tradition or by returning to our tradition. Rather the answer lies in the sort of historical creativity and the historic choice of our people in the process of bringing about modernization, as we open up to the outside, and as we bring about the collision of Chinese and Western cultures. Otherwise, even though the Yellow River rushes towards the sea, it will never be possible to change the opaque yellow color of its water. The sea will forever be the sea, and the Yellow River will still be the Yellow River. The only way out for Chinese culture is to destroy the structure of traditional culture and to establish a culture suited to the demands of socialist construction."*

Chinese history did not create a bourgeoisie for the Chinese people which could hasten the victory of science and democracy; Chinese culture did not nurture a sense of citizenship. On the contrary, it taught a subject mentality. A subject mentality can only produce obedient people who meekly submit to oppression on the one hand and madmen who act

---

charged with counter-revolutionary activities, and sentenced in January of 1991 to five years imprisonment. See Punishment Season, p. 104; "Rough Justice in Beijing," pp. 33-34; New York Times, January 27, 1991, p.3.

[48] Strictly speaking, zhengzhihua should translate as "politicization"; yet in this context, it would seem to indicate the politicization of every aspect of life under a totalitarian system. Traditional China was an agricultural subsistence economy in which the peasant was at the bottom of a vast pyramid of absolute power.

[49] lunli zhongxin zhuyi. The Chinese term lunli, translated as "ethics," refers back to the five "bonds" or lun of Confucian society, by which an individual's duty was prescribed by his or her position in that society. Hence by "ethical centralism" Bao Zunxin probably intends a social and moral code under which the individual's every action is determined by his or her position in the hierarchy and social role. Just as in Confucian society where the five bonds decreed that subjects, sons, wives, younger brothers, and friends should obey their respective rulers, fathers, husbands, elder brothers and older friends, so too in China's version of socialist society, an individual's class background is decisive in determining that person's social role.

[50] Elsewhere, Bao Zunxin talks about the need for China's intellectuals to evolve an independent, critical spirit and to overcome the tradition in which the life of scholarship was dependent on service in government. See Bao Zunxin, "Zhishi fenzi yu guan xue yiti de chuantong moshi" in Pipan yu qimeng, pp. 161-170.

recklessly on the other. But History did give the Chinese people an entirely unique group: its intellectuals.[51]

It is very difficult for them to have economic interests in common or an independent political stance; for thousands of years they have been hangers-on.

Nor can they become a solid social entity that employs a steel-hard economic strength to carry out an armed critique of the old society.

Their talents can be manipulated by others, their wills can be twisted, their souls emasculated,[52] their backbones bent, and their flesh destroyed.

And yet, they hold in their hands the weapon to destroy ignorance and superstition;

It is they who can conduct a direct dialogue with "sea-faring" civilization;[53]

It is they who can channel the "blue" sweetwater spring of science and democracy onto our yellow earth!

(The television studio. A scholar discusses the topic of intellectuals today.)

Yuan Zhiming[54] (Ph.D. candidate in Philosophy, China People's University): *"If we want to change our way of thinking[55] and change our character, then we will have to suffer a lot of pain. Those in the past who have shared this feeling most strongly have been the intellectuals. For it's always the intellectuals who first discover the faults of the tradition but lack the ability to change it. They set out full of hope to destroy tradition but always lack sufficient courage. In this present time of great changes, I believe we are also stuck in a painful crack, with the heavy burdens of*

---

[51] Here the screen shows the front cover of Zhishi fenzi [The Chinese Intellectual], a Chinese journal published in New York by Liang Heng from 1984-1990 which has served as a forum for debate by Chinese scholars from the U.S., mainland China and Taiwan. The cover photograph shows an open door. Weiming Tu, Bao Zunxin, and Ray Huang, all of whom have contributed articles to the journal, have viewpoints cited in Heshang.

[52] The second broadcast eliminates this phrase.

[53] The second broadcast eliminates this sentence.

[54] Currently in U.S. exile, Yuan Zhiming [1955-] edits the Chinese-language bimonthly journal Minzhu Zhongguo [Democratic China]. He is the author of two books: (with Xue Dezhen) Shehui yu ren [Society and Man], 1985; and Chenzhong de zhuti: Zhongguoren chuantong jiazhiguan kaocha [The Burdened Self: An Investigation of Traditional Chinese Values], Renmin chubanshe, 1987.

[55] "Way of thinking" translates xintai, a difficult term to translate, which we have rendered elsewhere as "mindset" or "psychology." It would appear to indicate habitual, culture-bound ways of thinking.

destruction and of construction weighing on our shoulders simultaneously. What can be done about it? I believe there may well be only one solution, that under the compulsion of world trends, we draw support from the pressure in the surrounding environment, and force ourselves to adapt to new surroundings, or perhaps to put up with the pain and create a new life. That's why in the conclusion to my book The Burdened Subject[56] I wrote these three lines: That China's hope lies with the world. That to make this hope into reality, we must rely on those Chinese who have been awakened by the world. That our generation is fated to endure much spiritual suffering, but that perhaps because of this we may attain greatness."

Possessing greater practical strength than these is perhaps the plain-faced, soft-spoken new breed of entrepreneurs. Even amongst the owners of these small shops, among these businessmen hurrying along the road, among these peasants who have left the land to make their living all over the country, there is building up a new social energy and a new vitality, none of which should be underestimated.

Today, the joint appeal published by Ma Shengli[57] and nine other entrepreneurs calling for a new system of enterprise management may one day be entered in the history books as a manifesto of "blueness."[58]

The student demonstrations that suddenly erupted all over the country in December 1986 and January 1987 made everyone tense, in all levels of society, high and low. Perhaps it is still premature to attempt an evaluation of this student movement. Yet the form of direct dialogue between government officials and students which was established in the course of calming down the movement in fact attained the objective of the vast majority of college students who participated in the student movement: that is, greater "transparency" in government and policy-making.[59]

---

[56] The first two of the following lines appear on the television screen: *That China's hope lies with the world. That to make this hope into reality, we must rely on those Chinese who have been awakened by the world.* This quotation comes from p. 206. Here zhuti "subject" can probably be interpreted as "self." Thanks to Prof. Edward Gunn of Cornell Univ. for information on this book and his interpretation of the title.

[57] Ma Shengli, manager of the Shijiazhuang paper factory, contracted for the management of many paper factories in other areas that were losing money or showing low profits, forming his own "Ma Shengli Enterprise Group" in January of 1988. See Shijie jingji daobao, Jan. 4, 1988; Renmin ribao, Jan. 9, 1988, p. 2, Jan. 20, p. 1, August 29th, p. 1.

[58] The second broadcast eliminates this sentence, which presumably offends by suggesting an implied contrast with the Communist Manifesto issued by Marx and Engels in 1848.

[59] The second broadcast eliminates this entire paragraph. "Transparency" or toumingdu is China's equivalent of Soviet glasnost or "openness." The 1986 student movement was effectively halted by the authorities and followed by a campaign to oppose "bourgeois liberalization" which lasted several months. As the campaign was sponsored by party

(Scene from a news conference of the 13th Party Congress.)[60]

Even in these high-level political gatherings, which used to be so solemn and serious, we can also see the appearance of a "blue" transparency. China's mass media, having taken for the first time a relatively neutral stance, are serving as a medium of dialogue between high-level policy-makers and the masses of the people.[61]

Yet for orientals with a deep tradition of despotism to really understand democracy is by no means easy. History has left us many interesting anecdotes.

At the end of 1940, Roosevelt [1882-1945] was elected to his third term as President of the U.S. Mr. Chiang Kaishek [1887-1975][62] recorded this in his diary as follows: "American democracy is really admirable. I've sent Roosevelt a special cable to congratulate him on his victory." And yet, one evening three years later, when special envoy Madame Chiang Kaishek—that is, Soong Meiling [1897-][63]—was having dinner at the White House

---

conservatives [such as Wang Zhen] and brought to an end by Zhao Ziyang, the advocate of toumingdu, this paragraph touches on the very sensitive point of inner-party struggle.

[60] The 13th Party Congress opened October 25th, 1987. General Secretary Zhao Ziyang's report to the Congress was highlighted in Part Four, "The New Era." This Congress was the first in PRC history to be completely open to both the domestic and foreign press. Zhao Ziyang's frank and informal exchanges with foreign reporters were unprecedented and aroused plenty of favorable comment in the foreign press. A second news conference was held later by officials of the Institute for Economic Structural Reform. See Shijie jingji daobao, November 2nd, 1987, p. 2 & November 9th, 1987, p. 3.

[61] Zhao Ziyang's report delivered at the 13th Congress also mentions the importance of institutionalizing consultation and dialogue; see Zhao Ziyang, op.cit., p.53. *Only when the work of leadership organs at every level is founded on listening to the complaints of the masses can it accord with actual circumstances and avoid errors. The activities of leadership organs and the difficulties they face can only be accepted by the masses if the masses understand them. The demands and appeals of the masses must have channels through which they can be constantly and smoothly reported to the top, so that there are places for them to raise their suggestions and voice their resentments. ... The basic principle behind instituting social consultation and dialogue is to promote the fine tradition of "from the masses, to the masses"; to increase the degree of openness of the activities of leadership organs, so that the people may know important issues, and that important questions may be discussed by them. ...*

[62] Chiang Kai-shek [Jiang Jieshi], succeeded Sun Yatsen as leader of the Kuomintang or Nationalist Party, and President of the Republic of China from 1927 on; after his defeat in the civil war with the Communists, Chiang removed his government and army to Taiwan. See Boorman & Howard, op. cit., Vol. I, pp. 319-338.

[63] In mainland China, images of Chiang Kaishek and his wife never appear in the press or on television; their appearance here is hence something of an event. Madame Chiang is depicted in what might be considered an undignified pose, covering her mouth with her hand in the attempt to suppress a laugh. For this reason, perhaps, Heshang cannot be

with the Roosevelts, the topic of conversation turned to strikes by American workers. Roosevelt asked Soong Meiling what the Chinese government would do if faced with such a problem in wartime.[64] Soong Meiling coolly drew a line across her throat with a long painted fingernail, elegantly signifying "off with their heads," thereby startling no end all the American dinner-guests. Afterwards, Mrs. Roosevelt said, *"Soong Meiling can talk very prettily about the democratic system, but she doesn't know how to put it into practice."*[65]

The distinguishing marks of a despotic government are secrecy, rule by an individual, and the fickleness of his temperament.[66]

The marks of a democratic government should be transparency, responsiveness to popular will, and a scientific approach.[67]

We are right now moving from opacity to transparency.

We have already moved from the closed to the open door.

The Yellow River is fated to traverse the yellow soil plateau.

The Yellow River will ultimately empty into the blue sea.

The Yellow River's suffering and its hope have made it great.

The Yellow River's greatness perhaps consists in the fact that it has created a stretch of land between the sea and the plateau.

The Yellow River has now reached its great and painful entryway into the sea.

---

broadcast in Taiwan. Madame Chiang came from a prestigious family; her sister Soong Ch'ing-ling married Sun Yatsen; her sister Ai-ling married H.H. Kung, head of the Executive Yuan; a brother T.V. Soong was Minister of Finance. She graduated from Wellesley College in the U.S. in 1917 and married Chiang Kai-shek in 1927. See Boorman & Howard, op. cit., Vol. III, pp. 146-149.

[64] The rest of the paragraph is eliminated in the Taiwan edition by the Jinfeng and Fengyun shidai chubanshe, substituting the following line: *Ms. Soong Meiling took a hard-line attitude, that it would be absolutely forbidden.*

[65] While this anecdote makes fun of Madame Chiang, it could be interpreted as applying as well to the leadership on the mainland. This account is adapted from that given in Sterling Seagrave's The Soong Dynasty, Harper & Row, New York, 1985, p. 384; translated into Chinese as Songjia wangchao, Macao, Xingguang shudian, Jan. 1988, p. 368. See also Eleanor Roosevelt, This I Remember, 1949, p. 284; and On My Own, 1958, pp. 130-131.

[66] This line of text appears on the screen overlaying the image of the Hall of Supreme Harmony in Beijing's Forbidden City, noted for its imperial yellow roof tiles. This is the ultimate symbol of "yellow culture"; clearly, the rulers of China, past and present, are being indicted as 'oriental despots.'

[67] The screen shows this line over a background scene of a steamship blowing its whistle in a cool, blue Scandinavian fjord; the two images thus present the contrast between a static, land-based culture, and a dynamic, ocean-going "blue" culture.

The mud and sand it has carried thousands of li will collect here to form new land.[68]

The surging waves of the sea will here meet head on with the Yellow River.

The Yellow River must eliminate its fear of the sea.

The Yellow River must preserve the dynamism and undaunted resolve which comes from the plateau.

The waters of life arise from the sea and flow back into the sea.

After a thousand years of solitude,[69] the Yellow River has finally seen the blue sea.

[Music. A man and woman sing a duet.]

"I know that

the Yellow River makes ninety-nine bends;

on those ninety-nine bends are ninety-nine boats

on those ninety-nine boats are ninety-nine poles

on those ninety-nine bends are ninety-nine boatmen

poling their boats along."

Written by Xie Xuanjun and Yuan Zhiming

---

[68] xin dalu, here translated as 'new land,' could also be read as 'a new mainland,' i.e., a new mainland China. The metaphor of building new land between the plateau and the sea thus suggests a gradual, peaceful accommodation between the old 'feudal' order represented by the mud and sand and the new, modern order represented by the ocean. A further implication is that the hope of transforming China lies with the new economy being developed in the open cities along China's coast.

[69] Alluding to Gabriel Marcia Marquez's novel, A Hundred Years of Solitude, translated into Chinese as Bainian gudu.

Deathsong of the River

by Su Xiaokang and Wang Luxiang

Text and Images for Part Four: "The New Era"

Note to the reader: The following is the text of Part Four, especially designed for the convenience of the viewer of the videotape. The text used is that of the second broadcast, starting on August 16th, 1988. There are a large number of differences with the narrative of the first broadcast, as represented in the published editions; these differences have been pointed out in the preceding annotated translations. Notable changes in this part include: the reversal of the order of the interviews with Wang Juntao and Li Yining; the substitution of "profiteering bureaucrats" [guandao ye] for "privileged elite" [tequan jieceng]; the elimination of hints of forthcoming social turmoil; and the toning down of the conflict between Plekhanov and Lenin. While the text has been changed, the credits at the end still say "CCTV, June, 1988."

This episode includes a number of provocative scenes. Younger viewers responded with feelings of surprise and disbelief to the scenes of Red Guards expressing their adoration for Mao [#38]. In addition, the scenes of Cultural Revolution banners critiquing "capitalist roaders" or condemning Deng Xiaoping by name could be read in a contemporary context. The close-up portrayal of General Secretary Zhao Ziyang [#42] in close association with the title "The New Era" [#44] drew the wrath of conservative critics.

There are a number of sequences of images with a strong element of satire. The images accompanying paragraph #5, describing a future communist society, are either of the advanced capitalist West, or are wry comments on the state of China: a dandelion puffball, suggesting over-ripeness and fragility; children rowing an inflatable rubber raft on dry ground, suggesting the absurdity and inevitable failure of stopgap reform measures. Interestingly, most of these images used to illustrate the society of the future come from a U.S. television series hosted by Carl Sagan called Cosmos. In a similar vein, the images accompanying the discussion of reform in paragraph #13 end with an underground nuclear explosion.

One of the principal symbols developed in this episode is the locomotive, which is first identified with the industrial revolution in the West. Since China is one of the few countries still using steam locomotives, however, the steam locomotive hence comes to stand for the current, backward state of China's industry. Hence, we see a Chinese locomotive in reverse [#46]; a locomotive heading into a setting sun [#46]; a locomotive taking a left-hand turn into a tunnel and plunging into darkness [#41]. There are also contrasts established between Chinese locomotives and foreign express trains.

Conventions: The text as read by the narrator is placed in the left-hand column. Text that is also highlighted on the screen appears in bold letters. An abridged version of the film credits is also placed in the left column, in bold letters within square brackets. For the purpose of easy reference, the text is divided into numbered sections; this is not a feature of the published text.

In the right-hand column appears a listing of the images as they appear on the screen, grouped in numbered sections corresponding to the narration. Not every single shot is listed, but an attempt has been made to identify persons and places, movies and TV programs from which material is borrowed, and to translate newspaper headlines, banners, etc. Sound effects and music are also indicated in the right-hand column.

1. [Credits, superimposed over images in #2, below]

[Deathsong of the River

six-part TV series

Advisors:	**Jin Guantao**
	Li Yining
Principal writers:	**Su Xiaokang**
	Wang Luxiang]

2. [duet]

Tell me—
How many bends does the Yellow
*   River make?*
On those bends how many boats are
*   there?*
On those boats, how many poles?
And on those bends how many
*   boatmen pole those boats?*

3. In the middle of the nineteenth century, just as the great industries conjured up by capitalism had reached their apex, a Jew in the British Museum had already dissected its secrets and pronounced its death sentence.

4. As Marx examined Capital, that monster whose every pore oozed blood from head to toe, his pacing feet wore ruts into the floor of the British Museum as he designed the outlines of a future society.

5. This great teacher was very careful. He only drew a blueprint for the future. He conceived of a communist society as one in which productive forces should be highly developed, wealth well-distributed, in which labor would no longer be a

1. [*slow drumbeats*] A series of prostrations by:

Blue-clad Chinese Buddhists;

White-capped Chinese Muslims;

Tibetan Buddhists.

[*gong*] Title appears in yellow calligraphy over blue-grey aerial view of the Yellow River at dawn, high in the mountains.

2.   Views of the Yellow River: the Yellow River in the mountains, from a height at dawn, cool blue-grey; direct overhead view of bends in muddy brown Yellow River, warm colors in strong sunlight; various shots closing in on a sailing junk, on the river near the mouth; boys in a rowboat being swept around by the swift current upstream; aerial view of the Jinshaan Canyon at dusk.

3. b&w: steam locomotive starting to move. [*huff-puff, huff-puff, toot..*] accelerating; close-up of moving wheels.

4. b&w: shipyard: a ship about to be launched; the ship slides down the ways.

5. color: [actor portraying Marx] closeup of Marx's hairy head; Marx turns to look directly at viewer.

[quick sequence of color shots:] Western couple walking hand in hand in the park; old man playing

means to make a living and in which the expenditure of labor would no longer determine the price of commodities; hence the bond between goods and money would exit from the stage of History.

chess in the park; little boys playing; oriental girl laughing; children on the swing; baton-twirler at the head of a July 4th parade; astronauts on the moon; chorus of young people from all nations singing; American and Thai Coca-Cola bottles; Moon Unit takes off from the moon; space rocket sheds a stage; close-up of twirling dandelion puffball; seagulls before a setting sun; palm tree in an American backyard: kids playing at rowing an inflated rubber raft on dry land.

6. In 1917, the sound of gunfire from the cruiser Avrora would seem to have proclaimed the appearance in Russia of that future society conceived of by Marx. And yet at that time Russia was still a backwards agricultural country, with agriculture accounting for as much as 57.9% of its GNP, and industry accounting for only 7% of that of the U.S.

6. b&w: 1917: Cruiser Avrora fires the opening shot of Russian Revolution; a Russian crowd waves flags and hats; close-up of Lenin speaking; Lenin addressing a congress; movie portrayals of Lenin seated, writing on his lap; Lenin & soldiers striding down a corridor.

7. Plekhanov, who did not advocate the premature seizure of political power, firmly believed that the Russia of that time could only continue to develop productive forces on the foundation of capitalism. His challenge to Lenin was shattered by the October Revolution.

7. b&w: photo of Plekhanov unfolds; team of horses harrowing a field; Soviet riveters; factory interior.

color: Russian peasants measuring a field.

8. Yet History seems by no means to have buried Plekhanov's doubts, for after the October Revolution, Lenin adopted a whole series of measures permitting the coexistence of various forms of economy and serving to develop a commodity economy, which would appear to constitute a step back. This would

8. b&w: Chinese poster viewed from inside a window: "The People's Democratic Dictatorship..."

b&w: movie portrayal of Lenin entering a congress; banner reads "All Power to the Soviets."

b&w: Train turning corner on

seem to mean that Lenin had by no means ignored Plekhanov's question: *Can an economically underdeveloped socialist state successfully skip the stage of the commodity economy?*

9. In the 1930s, by oppressing the peasants, lowering the social level of consumption and by forcing a high rate of accumulation, iron-fisted Stalin caused Soviet industry to grow at a speed that dumb-founded the whole world. For opposing these methods, Bukharin was shot as an "enemy of the people." But the "Stalinist model" made the Soviet Union pay a heavy price, so that after Stalin's demise, the trumpets of reform were sounded throughout the USSR.

10. The countries of Eastern Europe, all formerly subjected to the Stalinist model, at different times diverged from the orthodox path and proceeded with reforms. Yugoslavia on the Balkan peninsula emerged as a new force and was the first to break free of the Soviet model and seek its own path. In close succession, Hungary, Poland and Czechoslovakia all set out on the stormy path of reform. History had apparently once again raised Plekhanov's question. Not that History had gone in retreat; Man, rather, had overtaken it.

11. On the 18th of December, 1978 this ineluctable current of history

---

elevated track.

brown: Horses and carriages on a city street.

9. brown: Close-up of Stalin in military uniform on reviewing stand in Red Square; military parade in Red Square; close-up of marching soldiers.

photo: Bukharin smiling

color: Kremlin in winter; factory smoke stacks;

Khruschev descends from a plane; Khruschev raises a toast, downs it, holds up the glass.

10. [scenes in Eastern Europe:] bridges over a river; tourists ride in a horse-drawn carriage over cobbled streets.

brown: Marshall Tito in uniform.

color: traffic, a university, families walking in a public square; stylish young women.

speeded-up expressway traffic in modern city with skyscrapers; fish-eye lens view of skyscraper from overhead.

[*music*] New York City viewed from the Hudson.

11. [*applause*] Hua Guofeng, Deng Xiaoping enter the meeting of the

finally swept China too into the high tide of reform among socialist nations. The problems that would have to be resolved by this country covered with scars and only recently arisen from turmoil and by this people still bearing the burden of thousands of years of tradition would be far more complex and difficult than those of the Soviet Union and Eastern Europe.

12. How many Chinese people are there nowadays who clearly realize that reform doesn't just mean that *"steamed wheat buns have replaced sweet potatoes, and the bachelor gets a wife"*; that it doesn't merely mean color TVs, refrigerators and higher salaries, nor even the comfortable living standard of one thousand U.S. dollars [per annum]?

13. In the majority of cases and in its deeper sense, reform is rather a great burst of pain in which a civilization is transformed, a task fraught with danger, a difficult process which will require sacrifices from our generation and even several yet to come. Right now we are standing at a crossroads: either we can allow our ancient civilization to continue to decline, or we can force it to acquire the mechanisms of revitalization. But no matter which way we choose, we cannot shirk this historical responsibility.

14. [**Part Four, "The New Era"**]

3rd Plenum of the 11th Party Congress. Delegates give standing ovation.

b&w: student marchers with banners going to Tian'anmen Square; billboard.

color: women kneeling & praying in a temple.

12. [*music*] crowd in Beijing's Dazhalar market: chopping meat on a block; holding up crabs, frogs.

In a department store, shoppers examine electronic goods, washing machines, etc.

13. [*music builds*] Traffic circle around old belltower; a ferris wheel revolves.

A climber with modern boots and backpack climbs a vertical steel ladder; laborers carry heavy burdens up the steps at Taishan.

Close-up of clockface on Beijing telegraph tower. Old walls of a fort. Seen from a moving car: an old-fashioned building; a tall modern hotel. Underground atomic test: a cloud of debris rises.

14. [*music reaches triumphal climax*]

Color: headlines from Guangming ribao & Renmin ribao announcing 3rd Plenum of 11th Party Congress.

15. Ten years ago, when we finally opened our closed bamboo curtain and once again rejoined the world, the Chinese people—who for so long had lived in the hardship of "transitional poverty" and the isolation of cultural despotism— were surprised to discover just how developed the capitalist West and Japan were and how comfortably their people lived.

16. Perhaps it was precisely this strong shock which caused us to pick up again a long-forgotten topic: why had Industrial Civilization with its promise of vast wealth never appeared in Chinese history?

17. Leaving aside strong dynasties such as the Han and Tang, even in the feeble Song dynasty one thousand years ago, the Chinese economy and urban commerce in particular were still the most prosperous in the whole world. At the same time that the Northern Song capital of Bianliang and the Southern Song capital of Lin'an were metropolises with populations numbering millions, the most prosperous commercial city in Europe numbered no more than one hundred thousand. No wonder that when the merchant of Venice Marco Polo came to China he should be so happy as to forget about returning home!

18. And yet, the same Chinese civilization which evoked wonder

15. [*music fades*] bicyclists in a drab old city; blue-clad crowd coming downstairs; shoppers buying cloth; women on the street; a shopkeeper opens up her stall.

Sunfish sailboats; scene in a nightclub: entertainers stand on stage with white plaster replica of Statue of Liberty, with NY skyline in background.

16. [from Western TV commercials:] happy baby being bathed; smiling woman washing her face with soap; woman paddling a canoe; handsome guy in red cap smiling in the snow.

[*music*] Ultra-modern skyscrapers clad in gold and silver.

[*copter noises*] aerial view of Beijing's Forbidden City.

17. An emperor's throne room recreated with life-size statues of courtiers.

Kaifeng in the Song Dynasty: scenes from the painting <u>Qingming shang he tu</u>.

Kaifeng today: the <u>Longting</u> [Dragon Pavillion] viewed from a helicopter.

18. Outside Kaifeng: at dusk, the avenue of stone guardians ap-

and admiration from Marco Polo is now already in the midst of decline; while for some reason History was more sympathetic to his distant home on the Mediterranean Sea, a village that had only recently graduated from catching fish and evaporating salt—Venice. This was a nation without agriculture; it was not even a nation but rather a city without territory, a republic of merchants.

19. In the year 1160, the Venetian government borrowed 150,000 silver marks from the merchants of the city by issuing bonds, and so became the very first government in the whole world to be transformed into a corporation, while Venetian citizens became the government's creditors. And as the tie between goods and money became the principal tie in society and the economy, laws which protected private property could no longer be resisted. Yet even Shakespeare cursed the Venetians' commercial spirit. And so it was only a full five hundred years later that banks issuing bonds appeared in England. And for China to understand this would take perhaps eight or nine centuries.

20. China, a large country made up of peasants with small landholdings, had never had a true concept of commodities, even though commerce had always been highly developed. Under Heaven, there was no land that was not the ruler's. Through successive dynasties and generations, the Emperor was the sole private owner in all of

proaching the imperial tombs.

Venice: on a canal, passing under a bridge.

19. Gaily-decorated festival boats in Venice; feeding pigeons in the Plaza of St. Mark; Japanese tourists by a cathedral.

Portrait of Shakespeare. London.

Shanghai: the stock market reopens. [*crowd noises*] Customers crowd up to the counter; close-up of paper money being counted.

20. Peasant family plowing with a horse.

[*copter noises*] Aerial view of Maoling, tomb of Han Wudi,

China; he could collect taxes from the people as he pleased, draft corvee labor, and oppress the peasants without recompense and without limit. Relying on the meager salaries of the court, officials would naturally seek to skim off the riches of the common people either by deceit or by force. This system of centralized power, of a "great unity" built on the foundation of an agricultural civilization, became a heavy ball and chain weighing down the economy of ancient China and industrial and commercial activities in particular.

21. While the Ming dynasty was enforcing its closed-door policy and the west coast of the Pacific was still undisturbed, the great world-wide commercial revolution which had been born on the shores of the Mediterranean was just in the process of spreading to the Atlantic, Indian and Pacific Oceans. Europe slowly moved towards the center of the world stage from the ignorance and barbarity of the Middle Ages. Sea-coast civilization without any hesitation seized this Heaven-sent opportunity to give free rein to its pioneering, expansive inner vitality and the superiority of its civilization.

22. In January, 1649, the English people defeated King Charles I. The royal power faded away. A one-man dictatorship gave way to joint rule by a group of men. The success of the English capitalist revolution caused this island people to take a big step forward in human history

resembling a pyramid. Aerial view of eroded loess plateau. Aerial view of Qianling, tomb of Tang Gaozong & Wu Zetian.

21. The blue ocean. A sailing ship seen from the mast downwards, moving through the waves; lowering sails; rolling up sails.

22. color: Peasants armed with pitchforks stand beneath a royal balcony; doors open. Armed guards approaching a royal carriage; doors open on empty carriage.

[*band music*] The royal marching band. Buckingham Palace. A modern harbor. The Union Jack at

and be the first to enter the new era of history.

23. In 1781, Watt's double-action steam engine brought yet another "Aladdin's lamp" to the English people. The wealth created by a few decades of the Industrial Revolution was equal to the total wealth accumulated by the human race over thousands of years. It allowed those nations which first completed their industrialization to increase rapidly in size and strength, while those nations which were left behind would have to passively take a beating. It forced all nations either to take the path of industrialization or to be eliminated by History.

24. The Industrial Revolution sped up the international division of labor. Capital fed the whole world through the Machine. *"Because of the advent of machines, spinners could live in England, while weavers lived in the East Indies."* The poor agricultural nations of Asia, Africa and Latin America became the sources of agricultural and mineral raw materials for the industrial countries of Europe, as well as markets for their goods. Now that the world had already become a unified market, China could no longer avoid its fate of being pulled into the world-wide exchange of goods. The industrially advanced West would never willingly let go such a vast place for dumping commercial goods, for investment, and for the production of raw materials. Thus, before the

the masthead. Spherical gas storage tanks. Marching band. London doubledecker busses.

23. b&w: Early automobile being built in a workshop. Early steam locomotive; turning on an early light bulb; the Wright brothers' biplane takes off; a monoplane lands; smokestacks.

b&w: Wartime: [the invasion of Poland?] a clocktower burns; a bombed city from the air; artillery being fired in the city streets.

24. b&w: Drawing of European weaving machinery; close-up of wheels and gears. Spinning silk in a factory. Oriental woman using a handloom. Planting trees. Chinese coal mine: mining coal with a pickaxe and shovel.

b&w: Westerners relax with drinks; portly chap relaxes on a steamer deckchair.

Chinese miners pick coal from conveyor belt.

photo: The Great Wall.

photo: A naked coal miner.

Chinese hauling a boat;

Chinese stevedores unload a ship. Harbor scene.

great geographical discoveries at the end of the fifteenth century, and before the outbreak of conflict between China and the West, China had already lost its once-in-a-millennium chance to develop capitalism. Henceforth capitalism would never be able to develop within China, but would come to bully China from beyond the seas.

25. In 1895, the young Kang Youwei set off a wave of petitions by students in Beijing. The members of the 1898 reform party felt that to develop capitalism at that moment was the only way to save China, and they loudly called on the state to institute all-out reforms. But a mere one hundred days later, as the heads of Tan Sitong and five other reformers fell in the dust, China once again lost an opportunity to move towards an advanced industrial society. For the loss of this opportunity, China would doubtless continue to pay the heavy price of backwardness and exploitation for another century or two.

26. Why is it that capitalism, the hallmark of modern industrial civilization, should not have its fate linked with China? Why was it that the Chinese hated it so much, to the point that in the sixties and seventies of this century they were still "cutting off the tail of capitalism" on a vast scale?

27. Fundamentally speaking, this was determined by the nature of

25. [*music starts*]

Photo: Kang Yuwei

Bookcovers: <u>Xinxue weijing kao</u>; <u>Kongzi gaizhi kao [Confucius as a Reformer]</u>; <u>Gongju shangshu ji</u>.

line from book: *"To rule an ancient country requires new laws."*

Photo: Tan Sitong;

group photo of 1898 reformers

[Boxer rebellion?] Foreign soldiers disembarking; soldiers marching through the streets.

26. [*music builds*]

color: massive city wall seen from below, at sunset, with tiny human figures silhouetted on top.

b&w: writing big character posters: "the unrepentant capitalist roader"; "Confucius' Doctrine of the Mean and the capitalist roaders' seeking middle ground"; "thoroughly criticize the capitalist roaders' plot to oppose the critique of <u>The Water Margin</u>." [*musical climax*]

27. color: the eroded yellow soil plateau; the Yellow River plain;

Chinese civilization. These plateaus eroded by the Yellow River and plains built up by the same Yellow River are the survival space of the Chinese people. The green fields that squeeze themselves into every available crack of space, the farmhouses packed as tightly as cells in a honeycomb, the tightly-woven network of ditches and footpaths are the evidence of the bitter labor of countless generations of peasants. They are the skill and the persistence expressed by too many people crowded onto too little land, and of the consequent struggle of man to maintain his existence on a soil of declining strength.

aerial view of rice fields.

[movie?] massive labor force moving earth in wheelbarrows to rebuild Yellow River dikes; pounding earth.

28. In such an environment, the Chinese economy has from ancient times possessed its own path of development, of which one salient characteristic is its ability to nurture a numerous and densely-packed population. In 1800, as the West was busy grabbing overseas colonies everywhere, the Chinese soil was nurturing one third of the world's population. There are some scholars who don't feel that China is a "failed civilization" just because it didn't produce industrialization. On the contrary, they appreciate the bucolic atmosphere of this agricultural civilization with a low standard of living.

28. [*copter noise*] aerial view: approaching the river, zooming in on an irrigation wheel.

b&w: refugees

color: peasants driving donkey carts loaded with casks.

29. Yet the problem lies in how this civilization has nurtured the Chinese people. As late as 1980, in a rural commune forty kilometers from Lanzhou, the average per capita grain consumption was only forty to one hundred kilos; in two out of three peasant homes, the

29. poor mountain village of wooden shacks.

A mother pig leading piglets.

Camera approaches a cave-house dug beneath ground level & looks down from above.

earthen <u>kang</u> lacked a mat; on the average, three people would share a single ragged quilt; and over sixty percent of people had no padded cotton clothes for the winter.

30. [Dialogue not in script:]

Su Xiaokang: "How old are you?"

Old man: "I'm seventy-two."

30. Su Xiaokang holding the microphone, interviewing an old man in a white headcloth.

31. This old peasant from northern Shaanxi told us that last year, owing to the reduction of the wheat crop due to drought, when his family had used up all their food grain, they survived solely on potatoes. Though he had passed his whole life in such poverty, he had somehow managed to have three sons and five daughters and now already had more than ten grandchildren.

31. Close-up of peasant's face.

32. [Dialogue not in script:]

Su Xiaokang: How many daughters do you have?

Peasant: Five.

Su Xiaokang: And how many grandkids [<u>waisun</u>] do you have?

Peasant: Fourteen.

Su Xiaokang: Fourteen? He's got fourteen grandkids!

32. same

33. Due to the ever-increasing population, and even more so to such obviously unwise theories such as *"People are the greatest treasure in the world"* and *"The more people, the more strength,"* scarce land has become even more valuable, and many kinds of natural resources have become increasingly hard to find. Comparatively speak-

33. [human labor:] moving stone blocks to repair a wall; quarrying coal in an open pit mine.

scene in a crowded market: the camera slowly withdraws, revealing more & more people.

ing, our poor, thin soil supports an excess of healthy flesh, and the lives that clamor to be fed have become cheap and valueless. At present, the burden of population has become the most difficult problem to solve of all of China's problems. How many generations of Chinese will have to taste the bitter fruit it has borne?

34. Moreover,the great investment of human labor on a small area of land has made it difficult for mechanized agriculture to get started, has given surplus farm labor no place to go, and has caused the bitter labor of many hands to become a socially-accepted rule, so that those methods that rely on reducing labor, that seek profit, that seek to rake off wealth by doing business and transporting goods may all be seen as [producing] unjust wealth. And moreover it is precisely those people who lack the means to create wealth who are easily infected with 'red-eye disease.'

35. But on the other hand, the acquisition of wealth cannot proceed under conditions of equal competition. Today, the profiteering bureaucrats that have incited so much criticism are still making use of the defects of the two-tiered price system, using the power they hold to allocate commodities, sell chits, approve chits, thus creating layer after layer of exploitation in highly sought-after commodities. Not only have they thrown commodity prices into chaos, they have moreover poisoned the morale of the party in power and of society at large. The

34. Close-up of millstone going round and round, grinding grain. Camera pulls back to show donkey providing motive power. Peasants pounding earth to make a roadbed. Crowded city street.

35. Heavy city traffic

[series of TV news clips:]

"In Changsha, some work-units and individuals sublet public property."

"Hebei Province investigates serious cases of the misuse of offical power"; TV sets in a warehouse; stacks of Japanese yen.

"Xi'an investigates cases of excessive spending of public funds on medical prescriptions"; boxes of medicine in a warehouse.

"Out-dated, unwanted goods pile up in warehouses"

union of bureaucracy and commerce is inevitably corrupt; both in past and in present, in China and abroad, there are no exceptions to this rule.

36. The style of small-scale production has also created a whole set of values stressing setting low targets in order to keep oneself on a psychological equilibrium. Are not philosophies of life such as "being content with one's lot," "taking things as they come," "not taking risks," and "even a bad life is better than a good death" still practiced by the great majority of people? When we asked this youth in this northern Shaanxi village why he remained at home in poverty and didn't go out to seek his fortune, he responded *"my mom and dad didn't give me the guts to do so!"*

37. In the vast, backwards rural areas, there are common problems in the peasant makeup such as a weak spirit of enterprise, a very low ability to accept risk, a deep psychology of dependency and a strong sense of passive acceptance of fate. No wonder that some scholars sigh with regret: faced with the [psychological] makeup of people such as this, not to mention the many limitations of government policy, even if a great economist like Keynes were to come back to life, what could he do about it? It's not the lack of resources, nor the level of GNP, nor the speed [of development], but rather this deficiency in the human makeup that is the essence of this so-called notion of "backwardness." And the decline in the makeup of the general popu-

36. Chinese muslims in white caps praying. Close-ups of peasants' faces. Peasants burn spirit-money and incense.

Film crew interviews young man in green army fatigues.

37. Su Xiaokang squats to interview group of men. More interviewing in the marketplace.

Coal mine: a heavy chain hangs across the screen to stop an empty coal cart.

Pumps working at an oil well; solarized wheel image.

Irrigation pipes spraying water.

A steel tower seen from underneath as camera rotates.

Series of close-ups of peasant faces, ending with man in a blue cloth hat, with a tobacco pipe: his eyes and mouth wide open in amazement.

lation is caused precisely by the rapid increases in its numbers. This truly is an agricultural civilization caught in a vicious cycle. Do we still have any reason to praise or to be infatuated with it?

38. This far-from-pretty bucolic atmosphere can from time to time still produce unbelievable bursts of folly. In those mad years of the Great Leap Forward, the fairy tale that *"the greater man's determination, the higher the level of the soil's productivity"* exaggerated the level of productivity of northern wheat up to over 7,000 jin per mou, and of southern rice up to over 50,000 jin per mou; everyone, from our great leader who wrote the essay "On Practice" to scientists and to the ever-practical Chinese peasants, could somehow believe this fairy tale. Throughout our land of nine million six hundred thousand square kilometers, every family for some reason or other smashed their cooking pots and closed their doors; several hundreds of millions of people all went to the communal dining halls to "eat from the public pot," as if communism had arrived just like that. This transition, from economic "utopia" to political crisis, leading ultimately to the historical tragedy of great social turmoil—can we not say that this is the inevitable end of an agricultural civilization?

39. For approximately twenty-odd years in the middle of this century, China once again faced a good opportunity for economic development. And yet locking our country's door and blindfolding our eyes we

38. b&w: railroad workers swinging pickaxes, laying new track.

color: news headlines from Great Leap Forward period announcing record-making accomplishments: "210,000 jin per mou in the Jiahu Brigade" "Boyang launches a satellite in late rice"; steel production...

photo: young girl on pile of hay

color: colossal white statue of Chairman Mao on parade at Tian'anmen, surrounded by red flags.

b&w: sliding huge stone blocks downhill.

color: peasants shoulder their plows and tools, leave crowded marketplace.

Parade with banner reading: "Long Life to Chairman Mao!"

uniformed soldiers shouting & waving the little red book.

Mao & Lin Biao greet the Red Guards.

soldiers cheering; girl students crying; male students in a frenzy; schoolchildren waving the little red book.

39. b&w: [peace?] marchers with white flags; foreign soldiers on parade; Chinese & foreigners marching in a demonstration together.

set off to *"surpass England and America,"* never ceasing to engage in one great political movement after another, swearing that on Chinese soil *"we would rather grow the weeds of socialism than the sprouts of capitalism,"* so that in the end our national economy was on the brink of collapse. Once again History cold-heartedly passed us by.

Magazine headline: "Overtake England in Fifteen Years"; photos of Mao & Zhou.

Red guards with banner:"Condemn Deng Xiaoping's Crimes in Reversing Verdicts & Restoring Capitalism!"

Magazine article: "The Red Guards of Those Days Grew Up Amidst Class Struggle"

Photo of soldiers with banner: "Thoroughly Criticize Deng Xiaoping's.."

color: bulletin boards with big character posters.

b&w: Empty factory workshop; closed factory gate. Families with buckets & carrying poles lined up waiting for water.

40. [*voice becomes increasingly emphatic*] Let us open our eyes and see our people's situation on this planet! The World Bank's annual reports reveal the following figures: **Out of one hundred twenty-eight nations in the world, China's average per capita GNP ranks about twentieth from the bottom,** in company with poor African countries such as Somalia and Tanzania. China's rate of increase in per capita GNP, the structure of her export commodities, her investment in education and public health all fail to match those of Asia's "four little dragons." In 1960, China's GNP was equivalent to Japan's; **by 1985, it was only one-fifth of Japan's;** in 1960, U.S. GNP exceeded China by 460 billion U.S. dollars, but **by 1985 it exceeded China by 3 trillion 680 billion dollars.**

40. [Background for text on screen] Aerial view of a village in the yellow soil plateau.

41. Though we always thought we were making great strides towards progress, how little we knew that others were making far faster strides than us! If this gap should continue at present rates, some people have made a frightening comparison: that in another fifty or sixty years, China will once again be in the situation of the Opium War: that foreigners will possess foreign guns and cannon, leaving Chinese with only long knives and spears. No wonder then that some-one has made an even louder appeal: that if things go wrong, China's global citizenship will be revoked!

42. No matter whether it was Lenin or Plekhanov, Stalin or Bukharin, Mao Zedong or his many comrades-in-arms—in order to come to grips with this mysterious and invisible economic law they all had to pay a heavy price. At present Zhao Ziyang is finally able to say directly and forthrightly that:

43. *"The socialist economy is a planned commodity economy on the foundation of public ownership. This is the scientific conclusion our Party has drawn about the socialist economy; it is a great advance in Marxism and is the fundamental theoretical underpinning of our country's economic structural reform."*

44. **[Part Four: The New Era]**

---

41. Alternating scenes of

(1) b&w:train turns left into a dark tunnel.

(2) color: speeding through the access tunnel of a huge circular particle accelerator.

Bridge at foreign seaport; cargo ship. Dragon dance; crowds.

42. b&w: Lenin, Stalin.

photo: Mao with Liu Shaoqi, Zhou Enlai, Deng Xiaoping;many Russians standing in back rows.

b&w: younger Mao speaking to a meeting; Liu Shaoqi addressing a meeting; Zhou Enlai at the microphone.

color: close-up of General Secretary Zhao Ziyang

43. The stage of the Great Hall of the People, November, 1987, with banners proclaiming the 13th Party Congress.

Delegates at the meeting; camera zooms in on the red star in the ceiling.

44. [*music*] Newspaper headlines from Guangming ribao and Renmin ribao announcing 13th Party Congress.

45. Over the past century, this vast western Pacific Ocean has uninterruptedly sent our continent both shame and hardship, while today over its stormy surface there would seem to float that vast wealth which so strongly tempts us. Japan is right now engaged in suggesting adjustments in the structure of economic relations with the U.S. and with Asia's "four small dragons." The western Pacific is right now becoming the new stage for the world economy. Destiny is once again giving us a once-in-a-millennium chance. Our coastal areas, silent for centuries, this Gold Coast of the Chinese people, with an appetite long held in check, are now the first to rush towards the Pacific.

46. The Chinese people at this moment are more eager than ever before to enter the world market. And yet this people has been isolated for too long and is still unfamiliar with the [uncharted] seas of the commodity economy, while the actual strength with which it can participate in international competition is quite weak. This opportunity afforded by a great readjustment in the structure of world production may well be quite fleeting, while we are the late-comers whose preparations are both hasty and incomplete.

47. We have now finally understood that we want to have an outer-directed economy, but the sole advantage still left to us is low-cost labor, and our labor-intensive, low-tech processing industry is one with which it is difficult to gain an

45. The Pacific Ocean. Surf breaking on the shore.

Map of Japan. Container shipping terminal. Japanese freighter.

Aerial view of city. Beach. Oil exploration platform moored at dock. CAAC plane lands. Waves on the beach.

46. Steam locomotive backing up. Two trains whizzing past in opposite directions.

Shopkeeper opening up his shop. Young boy carrying a worn bicycle tire.

Chinese steam locomotive heading from right to left.

Bullet train heading right.

Steam locomotive heading into greenish sunset.

Locomotives lined up side by side in the railroad yard, as if waiting for a race to start.

47. Miner at the coal face with power equipment. Modern coal conveyor belt. Factory for steel truck parts. Westerners in blue construction hats visit a factory. A Chinese potter with primitive equipment; women garment workers

enduring competitive advantage.

48. We have also finally understood that we want to participate in the "Largescale International Recirculation," but at the same time that we have our eyes glued on other people's markets, we keep our own markets tightly shut, always fearing that "the gravy will flow away," seeming to forget that the reason why others are willing to come to invest is precisely because they have their eyes set on our markets. If we want China to enter into the world, we must let the world enter China. Otherwise, we will lose a good opportunity once again!

49. These days the developing countries all have their minds set on making money off the developed countries. But as long as they lack the proper sort of internal markets, the economies of these countries will always be distorted.

50. In Beijing, a bus driver's monthly income is about 150 yuan, while a taxi-driver's income can be five or six times that. In this hospital famous for the treatment of goiters, there isn't a single doctor whose income surpasses that of the old lady selling baked sweet potatoes at the front gate. Those who *put the problems of the world first* will be those who *get rich last.* The source of all this unfairness is that society lacks a competitive mechanism for ensuring equality of opportunity, it lacks a common yardstick—the market. Only when we can develop a healthy market can we ensure that opportunity, equality, and competi-

using sewing machines.

48. [*music*] Ceremony celebrating delivery of Chinese-built ship to Middle Eastern company. Oil fields in the desert. Western tourists coming toward camera. An oil tanker at sea.

49. Aerial view of Chinese city. A bridge over a river.

50. A concrete island for a traffic cop on a busy Beijing street. Close-ups of traffic.

A woman doctor feeling a patient's pulse; doctor in gauze mask; patient being slid into catscan machine.

White-bearded Zhang Hanxin, delegate at a congress.

Crowds buying stamps. Fashion show. Neon signs of Las Vegas clubs. Neon signs of Chinese restaurants, etc. Japanese dept. store

tion will start to link up; yet this is precisely the thing that our people with their ancient civilization know the least about.

51. Today, ten years of economic reform have finally arrived at their most critical and most dangerous point: the loosening of price controls. The question of prices has become a hot point of discussion on every streetcorner; everyone is distressed about them. The psychological ability of the Chinese people to accept reform has reached the point that it wavers each time a kilo of pork is put on the scales. The root cause of this danger lies in that there is not a perfected market and in that we are a people with a long tradition of egalitarianism. But this difficult step to take is precisely the narrow mountain pass which we must cross in order to progress towards a commodity economy. If indeed the meaning of reform for each person is not merely getting something but also putting something out, then the moment has now come when China must pay the price of reform. Whether or not the Chinese people can traverse this pass in step with the government will perhaps be the touchstone to test whether the Chinese people truly have the courage to reform. And if for this reason we lose ground, then China will once again be mired in stagnation. How deep must have been the regret of Wang Anshi eight hundred years ago and of Tan Sitong ninety years ago!

52. An even greater potential problem is the extreme unevenness of economic development, which is

employees bow as customer enters door.

51. [*crowd noise*] scenes at outdoor market: old lady tests red bikini underwear; customers look at shoes, clothes;

weighing meat on the scales; eating at a food stall; a watch repair booth; vegetables...

52. Aerial view of Yellow River bank, a water wheel for irrigation. Sowing seed by hand. Plows drawn

revealing itself now in a "Matthew effect" in which the backward areas get increasingly backward, and the advanced areas increasingly advanced. The daily-increasing severity in the difference between poor and rich areas has given rise to the so-called division into "three worlds" within the country, has brought forth a debate over the theories of "steps" and "counter-steps," and has caused people to be greatly concerned for the homeland of our civilization—the vast yellow-soil plateau.

by human labor.

Slopes of hills; the yellow soil plateau.

53. [**Wang Juntao, Vice-director, Beijing Social and Economic Science Research Institute**]: *In Beijing you have all probably heard of a theory known as the "stages of development." This theory states that in the pattern of human economic development, some regions will develop first, while others will still remain in a backwards state; this is the unavoidable price paid for human economic development. When is this problem finally resolved? Only when the economically advanced areas are so rich that they don't know where to spend their money will they finally invest in the backwards areas, transfer technology, and in this fashion spur the backwards areas on toward development. According to such a theory, China's east is relatively developed, while its west is relatively backwards, and so the entire western region will be left to lag twenty to fifty years behind; that is to say, one hundred million people and vast resources will be tossed*

53. Interview with Wang Juntao standing outside in a trenchcoat before a background of barren hills.

out beyond the framework of China's economic development.

54. At the same time that the consumer expectations of city-dwellers in the south are fixed on the living standard of Hong Kong and Macao, there remains a considerable number of northern peasants who are still struggling to feed and clothe themselves.

54. Miners pushing empty coal carts.

55. At the same time that the commodity economy in the East has already penetrated the very cells of the family, there are some backwards areas in the West that are still waiting for the state to give them a "blood transfusion."

55. [*Hen clucking*] In a village: six children standing outside, eating from ricebowls; their dog waits expectantly for a treat.

56. For thousands of years, China's agricultural civilization has gradually radiated outwards from this yellow-soil plateau, heading from the Yellow River basin to the Yangtze River basin, and then on toward the southeast coast. Today, we see a radiation in exactly the opposite direction: industrial civilization is right now spreading from the coast into the Yangtze River basin, then pressing onwards to the Yellow River basin. Only when this land, which used up its milk in nurturing our people, can finally emerge from agricultural civilization, only then can the Chinese people truly enter the twenty-first century.

56. Aerial views of:

yellow soil plateau;
flooded rice paddies;

the seacoast; a major city bisected by a river.

The Jinshaan Canyon in the yellow soil plateau.

57. Today, now that there are only twelve years left till the twenty-first century, the Chinese people are indeed a little anxious; *"time is passing us by," "we should step up the pace."* But if the speed we call for is not implemented well, then

57. A street crowded with bicyclists; bicyclists seen against huge chimneys or cooling towers.

Blasting in an open-pit coal mine. Carrying coal out of the pit by hand.

we could once again step into the historical ruts of the "Great Leap Forward." How much suffering that sort of low-tech, low-quality, resource-hungry, low-efficiency wasteful model of development once caused us!

58. The old economic era marked by vast expenditure of cheap labor power, cheap natural resources and cheap energy has already come to a close in the second half of this century, and a new economic era, marked by scientific and technological advances and with human knowledge as the lever of progress, is already upon us. The advantages that we possess today will no longer be advantages in the future.

59. This is the same China which, when we let our imagination run wild, we always feel to be broad and wide and rich in resources; we are even pleased pink to be able to launch rockets for developed nations; but when we calm down and reflect, we discover that in reality it is population-rich but land-poor; short on natural resources and technologically backwards; educationally stunted and with a very low-quality labor force.

60. Mao Zedong put it very well once, that we really are "both poor and blank." Of course, being "poor and blank" isn't the same as a sheet of white paper that you can scribble on as you please. Being poor is due to being blank, and being blank is due to being poor. We are facing the two-fold [challenge] of reform and reconstruction.

58. Old-fashioned mechanical loom; a board being planed in a machine; a welder welding a section of pipe. Unloading a new tractor from a ship; a bridge seen from overhead.

The West: modern office full of computers.

China: street crowded with pedestrians in winter garb, bicyclists, donkeys.

59. Dragon dancers carry dragon down the street. Setting off fire crackers.

Hauling a boat upstream; poling a boat upriver. A Tibetan Buddhist pilgrim performing prostrations.

60. A camel pulling a plow. Aerial view of yellow soil plateau.

61. [**Professor Li Yining**]: *"I have said before, that the failure of economic reform may come about due to the failure of price reform, and the success of China's economic reform will necessarily be decided by the success of reforming the system of ownership. The reform of the system of ownership must solve a key problem, which is that the system of public ownership in our minds is a traditional system of public ownership, and we must make the change from a traditional form of public ownership to a new form of public ownership."*

61. Professor Li wears a blue suit, contrasting with the yellow background.

62. This great people, which once created the most mature and brilliant agricultural civilization of mankind; this ancient people, who—precisely because this agricultural civilization was overripe— found it hard to press forward; when it stands on the threshold of industrial civilization, it may sometimes appear as naive as a child, frightened to death, unsure of what to do. But this doesn't matter, for as long as it eventually steps over that threshold and resolves to press forward, this people can once more enjoy a new spring!

62. [*music*] Aerial view of Nanjing city gates and wall.

Oil wells pumping. Boat on canal with oil wells in background. Hilltop pagoda viewed from below.

Tian'anmen Square: birds flying up; balloons being released.

63. [Ending sequence.]

[Music. A man and woman sing a duet.]

*"I know that
the Yellow River makes ninety-nine bends;
on those ninety-nine bends are ninety-nine boats
on those ninety-nine boats are ninety-nine poles*

63. A waist-drummer seen close-up, from below; his yellow costume contrasts with the blue sky. He jumps up and the frame freezes. [*cymbals*]

[Montage] Circling birds at sunset; the Yellow River rapids; aerial view of Yellow River bends; Tibetan women dancing; waist-drummers; sailing junk on the river; sailing

*on those ninety-nine bends are
        ninety-nine boatmen
poling their boats along."*

64. [credits, superimposed over montage above]

[**Director:**   **Xia Jun**

Principal writers: Zhang Gang

                    Su Xiaokang

Narration: Zhang Jiasheng]

              ....

[**Next time please tune in for Part Five, "Sorrow and Worry"**]

junks setting out to sea; red sunset over the Yellow River.

Deathsong of the River

by Su Xiaokang and Wang Luxiang

Text and Images for Part Six: "Blueness"

Note to the reader: The following is the text of Part Six, especially designed for the convenience of the viewer of the videotape. The text used is that of the second broadcast, starting on August 16th, 1988. There are some significant differences with the published edition. These differences have been pointed out in the preceding annotated translations. Noteworthy changes include the omission of the entire interview with Bao Zunxin as well as references to the student demonstrations of December, 1986.

Among the more startling images in this part are those of Generalissimo and Madame Chiang Kaishek [Soong Meiling], whose photos are never shown on the mainland. General Secretary Zhao Ziyang is shown in several instances, in a positive light. Political figures rarely seen include Pres. Roosevelt, Pres. Eisenhower, and Winston Churchill, among Westerners; and Jiang Qing and Liu Shaoqi. The anti-Deng slogans from the Cultural Revolution can be read in a contemporary context. A possibly significant juxtaposition is that of Vice-President Wang Zhen with the line that reads: *"they* [Chinese intellectuals] *hold in their hands the weapon to destroy ignorance and superstition."* [#71].

The image chosen to accompany the titles of Part Six, "Blueness," is that of the earth as seen from space. This may represent a vision of a more modern future, as well as of a future in which China becomes a full citizen of the world. The colors blue, yellow and red take on symbolic value, with blue indicating the sea and the values of modern western civilization; yellow standing for the Chinese earth, as well as for the insularity and conservatism born of an agricultural civilization; and red suggesting the Maoist era of totalitarianism, itself a product of a peasant culture.

1. [credits, superimposed over images in #2, below]

[Deathsong of the River

[six-part TV series

Advisors: **Jin Guantao**
                    Li Yining

Principal writers: Su Xiaokang
                    Wang Luxiang]

1. [*slow drumbeats*] Series of prostrations by:

Blue-clad Chinese Buddhists;

White-capped Chinese Muslims;

Tibetan Buddhists.

[*gong*] Title appears in yellow calligraphy over blue-grey aerial view of Yellow River at dawn, high in the mountains.

2. [duet]

Tell me—
How many bends does the Yellow
*   River make?*
On those bends how many boats are
*   there?*
On those boats, how many poles?
And on those bends how many
*   boatmen pole those boats?*

2. Views of Yellow River:

The Yellow River in the mountains, from a height at dawn, cool blue-grey; direct overhead view of bends in muddy brown Yellow River, warm colors in strong sunlight. various shots closing in on sailing junk, yellow sail against blue sky, near river mouth; boys in a rowboat being swept around in the swift current upstream;aerial view of Jinshaan Canyon at dusk.

3. Human blood is red.

3. Blood under microscope; blood flowing in veins

4. Almost all animals have blood that is red.

4. Contrast of red and blue: harpooning a walrus; harpooning a whale; blood in the water

5. Primitive religion defined the basic color of life as red. Early man daubed the corpses of the dead with red pigment from iron ore in order to summon back the life that had been lost.

5. Half-naked tribal people pounding food, making tools, hoeing.

6. The blue sky is deep and mysterious. People once firmly believed that this azure blue described the whole universe, that it was the color of the universe.

6. Dazzling yellow sun over blue ocean, seen from the shore;

mysterious blue sky and sea.

7. But only a little more than twenty years ago, when mankind left the earth's surface for the first time and

7. [*rocket ignition*] Yellow flames: launch of space shuttle; Jupiter red spot;

gazed back at his home from outer space, did people discover to their surprise that amongst all the known objects of the universe, only mankind's own home, the planet Earth, was a blue planet.

8. [Part Six: Blueness]

9. The planet of life is a blue planet. The atmosphere and water that permits all life on earth to survive is what makes the earth a blue planet.

10. The sea, which covers seventy percent of the earth's surface, is also blue.

11. The sea was originally the home of life. In the planet's sudden transformations, it was the sea which protected the lives of humanity's ancestors. Later, when mankind returned once again to the earth's surface he was no longer suited to it. It was in the process of forcing himself to adapt to the land environment that mankind created civilization.

12. The enigmatic stone statues on Easter Island tell us that ten thousand years ago there lived in the Pacific Ocean an ancient and energetic seafaring civilization. These seafaring vessels that appear unbelievably crude and simple to us today carried mankind from the land back to the sea. What kind of faith was it that sustained early man in crossing those vast ocean routes which we still regard as dangerous to traverse? From the seafaring activities of early man to the great navigations of Columbus and Magellan which opened up a new

[music starts] Earth from space, blue globe against black starry background.

8. The earth from outer space. [music fades]

9. Close-up of green grass backlit by sun; speeded-up plant growth.

10. [music starts] Whales swimming in blue ocean.

11. Blue: schools of dolphin, school of fish.

Orange jellyfish in blue water; dandelion puffball backlit in red light.

Sketches of evolution: reptile, rodent, monkey, ape, man, over background of sea in red sunset light.

12. Easter Island statues: stone heads.

Seen from Easter Island: a sailing ship in the distance.

Polynesian outrigger canoes, paddling out from shore to meet a sailing ship; camera at wave level.

era for mankind, can we not hear the grand melody of human destiny?

13. Precisely because of the continuing existence of seafaring life, human civilization split into two great divisions, of land-based civilization and sea-faring civilization.

13. Sailing ship seen from canoe's perspective on all sides; scenes onboard sailing ship. [*music fades*]

14. Here is a nation poised on the Western Pacific and simultaneously perched on the eastern rim of the Eurasian continent. Its body is yellow, as is that great river which rises in its midst like a backbone.

14. Map of China in yellow and green, emphasizing Yellow River

[*copter noise*] Aerial view of Yellow River bend.

15. When we see the wooden boat excavated from the Hemudu culture site it's as if we were seeing sparkling blue waves dancing at the fountainhead of Chinese civilization.

15. Dugout canoe in museum case.

[*music starts*] The ocean.

16. And yet, even in the period of myth, the land-based culture of the yellow soil region in the middle course of the Yellow River was already unceasingly seeking to bring the lower courses of the river and the seacoast under its sway. Today, in the legends of how the Yellow Emperor defeated the Fire Emperor and Chi You we can still hear the muffled sound of that distant point in history.

16. Aerial view of Yellow River entering the plains.

Han dynasty stone rubbings: ancient emperors.

17. Later on, the conquest of the Yin-Shang dynasty by the Zhou dynasty proved the invincibility of this force arising from the heartland of the continent. By the late Warring States Period, when Chu was defeated by Qin in an epic battle, we may fairly say that the "yellow" civilization, marked by the use of wheat as its staple food and of chariots for warfare, and influenced by nomadic peoples and

17. Close-up of yellow chariot wheel.

An excavated chariot, encrusted with yellow earth.

various scenes of terracotta warriors from Qin Shihuang's tomb; rubbing of ancient war chariot. [*music fades*]

Persian culture, had ultimately triumphed over the "blue" civilization, based on a staple diet of rice, understanding the art of ship- and sea-based warfare, and influenced by Southeast Asian and Pacific cultures.

[*copter noise*] Convoy of canal boats with sails.

18. This historical victory of land-based civilization was unstoppable, notwithstanding the songs of Qu Yuan which made Heaven and Earth lament or Xiang Yu's resistance which shook the earth and hills.

18. Loess-soil plateau.

Portraits: Qu Yuan
              Xiang Yu

19. The retreat of "blueness" concealed within it the future destiny of this civilization to decline.

19. Qin Great Wall, made of yellow earth, in the desert.
[*wind*] The Gobi Desert. [yellow]

20. The restless blue waves of the Pacific were always silently calling to that ancient people stretched out on the continent and from time to time aroused it to action, leading its ships to the Persian Gulf and the Arabian peninsula. Yet in the end the attraction of the blue sea was no match for that of the yellow earth.

20. [*waves*] The ocean. [blue]

Seagull over the ocean.

[*ceremonial music starts*] Confucian ceremony at Qufu.

21. The hidden reason why the "yellow" civilization had such an enormous cohesive power was that Confucian culture had gradually attained a position of sole dominance in this land.

21. Aerial view of Qufu temple, showing roof of yellow tiles.

22. The Confucian system of thought expressed the norms and the ideals of land-based civilization and in the mature period of oriental feudal society was clearly rather reasonable. But this monistic ideological unity weakened the development of pluralistic thought, and so the various rich strands of seafaring civilization in ancient life, just like

22. Rubbing of Confucius. [*music fades*]

[*clop-clop of horses' hooves; jingling of harness bells*]

Horse-drawn carriage entering gate in Qufu's thick, double city wall.

a few thin trickling streams flowing out onto the yellow soil of land-based civilization, vanished quickly without a trace. ...

23. As the land-based civilization daily increased in power in China, a "blue" sea-faring civilization was gradually arising in the Mediterranean Sea.

24. Long ago in ancient Greece, the democratic ideology of Athens arose contemporaneously with the growth of Athens as a sea-power, and so it was sea-power that led to a democratic revolution.

25. And the social precondition for the bourgeois revolution in the West was precisely this opening up of Europe's overseas trade routes. The sailing ships which roamed between sky and sea from the fifteenth century onwards both opened the curtains on an era of world trade and colonization on the one hand, and carried a cargo of hope for science and democracy as well, on the other. Thus due to these small sailing ships, "blueness" came to symbolize the destiny of the modern world.

26. And so, the vast markets of the Orient as well as the New World of the Americas transformed tiny Europe overnight into an upstart tycoon.

27. Crossing the ocean requires ships that are strong, big and finely made; making such ships requires mathematics and physics, as well as technology and science. And so, in 1636 Galileo published his <u>Dialogue on the New Science</u>. This

Horse and carriage enter dark tunnel through city wall.

23. The blue Mediterranean: approaching Venice by water.

24. [*music starts*] Horse & carriage in European city, passing through decorative stone arch.

Sailing ships.

25. Palm trees: a tropic shore.

b&w: clipper ships.

26. Scenes from a Hollywood movie:

The Jolly Rodger; pirates boarding a ship.

27. b&w: Ocean liners; modern ships in drydock. [*music fades*]

"dialogue" was conducted in a shipyard.

28. It was England that first gained vast profit from overseas trade, accelerating both the primitive accumulation of capital as well as the popularization of liberal thinking. And hence it was in England that the bourgeois revolution first occurred, under the leadership of Cromwell. In 1651, Cromwell promulgated the Navigation Acts. In 1690, Locke published his Two Treatises of Government. The theory of free trade became both the catch-word and the principle of the bourgeois class.	28. b&w: London: Houses of Parliament. The Thames. Steam locomotive coming head-on at camera; [*whistle*] view from underneath train. Portrait: Locke [*clickety-clack, toot*] b&w: steam locomotive engine rotating on turn-table; politician on train waving to crowd in station with top hat.
29. Capitalism, by setting in motion the two wheels of the industrial revolution and of free trade, began a great flying leap, the great historical antiphonal chorus of science and democracy.	29. b&w: [*whistle*] Locomotive engineer; coal for the engine. French express train [TGV]. Winston Churchill. "Ike" with hands raised in victory, with Mamie Eisenhower.
30. All of this was inextricably linked with the ocean.	30. Sailboats on the ocean.
31. And what was China doing at this time?	31. Clockwork toys from imperial collection: figures emerge from Chinese palace.
32. While Magellan was navigating his course around the globe, the Jiajing Emperor of the Ming Dynasty, because of fighting between Japanese tribute bearers, had begun to formally "close the gates."	32. Clockwork Chinese servant with moving fan. Rooves of the Forbidden City.
33. In 1776, Adam Smith published his famous book On the Wealth of	33. Portrait: Adam Smith

Nations. In this book he declared that China's history and culture had come to a halt. He claimed that this stagnation was due to a lack of emphasis on overseas trade, and that "closing the gate" was tantamount to suicide.

Bookcover of Chinese translation of On the Wealth of Nations.

b&w footage of ruined Beijing city gate,

wooden pai-lou, horse-carts.

34. How unfortunate that not a single Chinese could hear what he said in time!

34. cont'd.

35. Eventually, when that famous fire was lit on the docks of the Boca Tigris, opening the shameful chapter of China's recent history, there was already a vast gulf between the spiritual cultures of China and the West. The cultural conflict between a "blue" civilization that was expansionist and which carried on both trade and warfare all over the world, and a "yellow" civilization that clung firmly to an agricultural economy and bureaucratic government, was like that of fire and ice.

35. [*guns*] b&w: cannons firing, foreign gunboats.

Map of foreign spheres of influence in China, with cartoons: Russian bear, British bulldog, French frog, American eagle; couple drinking wine; opium smoker.
b&w photo: foreign cavalry approach Wumen in Forbidden City.

36. And yet, no sooner had they encountered each other, than the West's ships and guns made China's officials realize the strength of "blueness." Thus there came about the "Westernization movement" as well as the notion of *"Chinese learning as the essence, western learning for practical use."*

36. b&w photos: posed group portraits of foreign soldiers in Beijing

Zeng Guofan's memorials: *"Using barbarian knowhow to make cannons & ships, one can expect longlasting benefits."*
Photo of Zhang Zhidong on blue background, inscribed: *"Old learning as the essence, new learning for practical purposes."*

37. High officials of the "Westernization" faction bought formidable, iron-clad fighting ships and established one arsenal after anoth-

37. Photo: Mandarin with cannon.

Photos: Hubei arsenal

er. The Jiangnan Arsenal in the Shanghai suburbs far surpassed Japan in its mastery of Western technology. About 1870, a Russian visited the Lanzhou arsenal in China's far northwest and was astonished by the high quality of the guns manufactured there. And when the Sino-Japanese War broke out, China's navy outnumbered that of Japan.

Jiangnan arsenal

Lanzhou arsenal

Tianjin Baihe arsenal

38. Yet none of this could prevent the Qing dynasty's defeat, first by France and then by Japan. The most direct reason for the loss of the sea-battle in 1894 was that a corrupt contractor had filled many cannon shells with dirt [instead of powder]. And the Chinese fleet, which had drawn itself up into a half-moon formation, still didn't know whose orders it should obey, even on the eve of battle. This fact clearly proves that the inevitable defeat brought on by a corrupt system cannot be warded off by technology.

38. b&w: Foreign cavalry in Beijing.

[*guns*] Scenes from film: Jiawu fengyun. 1894 seabattle between Chinese & Japanese navies;

Finding an artillery shell filled with sand.

Qing navy flag on fire.

39. Yan Fu, the first student sent by the Qing government to England to study their navy, in the end never became the captain of a warship; instead, he became an enlightenment thinker.

39. Photo: Yan Fu on yellow background

Translation from J.S. Mill.

Yan's preface to Huxley.

40. From his extensive observation of the West, Yan Fu discovered that the great achievements of European culture lay in developing the potential of the individual, thereby providing a sort of social contract. This social contract ensured that competition and all the other functions of capitalism would all play positive roles in accelerating

40. Title page of Yan Fu's translation of Huxley's Evolution and Ethics.
Front view of Reichstag in Berlin, showing gilt roof.
Close-up of inscription over the door: *"Dem Deutschen Volke"* [To the German People].
b&w: Men & women in Victorian dress at RR station.

social change. And similarly he discovered that by employing the "willpower" of the individual—a sort of Faustian or Promethean strength for mankind—it was possible to create an energetic culture.

41. Nevertheless, just as the "Hundred Days of Reform" in which Yan Fu participated were experiencing a crushing defeat, Japan's Meiji Reform, on the other hand, was succeeding. And as this great enlightenment thinker in China's recent past step by step abandoned reformist thinking under the attack of feudal forces and eventually retreated back to the embrace of Confucius and Mencius, his schoolmate at the English Naval College, Ito Hirobumi, held the post of Prime Minister for one term after another and quickly led his island nation into the community of powerful nations.

42. The tragic fate of Yan Fu and indeed of many other advanced thinkers of the early modern period such as Kang Yuwei, Liang Qichao, and Zhang Taiyan would also seem to prove that even the very best Chinese, after promoting revolution and progress for a while, would ultimately be unable to avoid retreating to the haven of Confucianism.

43. Even today in the 1980's, in the midst of our great debate stirred up by the "passion for studying Chinese culture," people still continue the

Locomotive engineers in the cab.

Trains pulling away from the platform.

41. The 1898 reformers reading a proclamation at the palace (?)

Yan Fu

Mt. Fuji

Photo: Ito Hirobumi

modern Japanese ship, the Atlas Maru; a Japanese ship captain puts down his binoculars. Container cargo being loaded.

Yan Fu's translation of J.S. Mill, <u>A System of Logic</u>

42. Through a narrow alley, approaching Kang Yuwei's old home;

[*gong*] doors open.

43. Doors opening into courtyard of Confucian temple at Qufu

Inside: The Gate of the Sage

century-old inconclusive argument over the strong and weak points of Chinese versus Western culture. No matter whether it is the fantasy of "wholesale Westernization" or the fervent wish for a "third flowering of Confucian civilization," it all seems to be going over the same ground as before. No wonder some young scholars say with a sigh that their tremendous cultural wealth has become a tremendous cultural burden, that their feeling of tremendous cultural superiority has become a feeling of tremendous cultural inferiority; and this we cannot but admit is a tremendous psychological obstacle standing in the course of China's modernization.

Looking through the gate at another courtyard and gate beyond.

The steps leading up to the Temple of Confucius. Camera first focusses on the steps and on the central marble pathway reserved for the emperor, carved with dragons; then camera pans up, looking up the stairs to the yellow-tinted temple roof.

Close-up of pillars at the temple carved with bas-relief dragons; camera pulls back and changes perspective so that the row of pillars seems to close up like a wall.

44. The greatest difficulty of reform lies perhaps in that we are always worrying: *"Are the Chinese people still Chinese?"* We seem not to realize that throughout the past two or three centuries in the West, no matter whether it was the Renaissance, the Reformation, or the Enlightenment movement, Western Europeans at least never worried whether after reform they would still be Italian or German or French. Only in China is this the greatest taboo of all.

44. b&w: Manchu courtiers with a dignitary.

European women in bonnets descending from carriages;

men in top hats getting off the train.

Empress Dowager Tzu-hsi in palanquin carried by eunuchs.

45. Perhaps this is precisely both the profound and the shallow point of "yellow" civilization.

45. b&w: Tower on Great Wall; street scene, Chinese wearing the queue.

46. Over two thousand years ago the philosopher Zhuangzi told us the following fable:

46. Close-up of river surface; camera starts panning up to horizon.

47. The spirit of the Yellow River, the Riverlord, found himself swollen so magnificently large at the time of the autumn floods that someone standing on one bank could no longer make out the difference between a cow and a horse on the opposite bank. He floated cockily downstream, till all of a sudden he caught sight of the sea and was struck dumb with astonishment. The ruler of the sea, the Northsea Spirit, told him: *"One can't discuss the sea with a frog in a well, because all it knows is its own tiny scrap of space, and it lacks the imagination to conceive of the vastness of the sea. And now, my dear Riverlord, you have finally left your narrow riverbed and seen the immensity of the ocean. Knowing your own limits, you have indeed attained a higher level of understanding."*

47. the muddy river from the deck of a boat, moving rapidly at close range

[*cawing*] black birds over the river.

white gulls on the riverbank.

camera moves rapidly over river surface; the muddy river approaches the ocean.

sunset over the river from a great height

48. This is symbolic language. It's not talking about ancient China but rather seems to be foretelling the China of today.

48. a sailing junk from overhead.

49. Barely a century has passed since the ancient spirit of the Yellow River has clearly seen the face of the sea and recognized its vastness and strength. The long drawn-out sigh it uttered on seeing the ocean has traversed a century of history and still echoes today.

49. men carrying heavy wooden crates wading into the water;
scene from film [Lin Zexu?]:
Qing imperial guards drawn up in front of Wumen in the Forbidden City;
[*guns*] Qing cannons.
Machine guns & cannons.

50. [**Part Six: Blueness**]

50. [*music*] The earth from space, against a black starry background [blue]

51. This stretch of dirt-yellow land cannot teach us the true spirit of science.

51. The eroded yellow-soil plateau

52. The unruly Yellow River cannot teach us a true democratic consciousness.

53. Relying only on this yellow soil and this Yellow River, it is no longer possible to feed our daily-increasing population and no longer possible to give birth to a new culture, for they no longer possess the nutrition and energy they once had.

54. [*voice becomes angry*] Confucian culture may indeed possess all sorts of ancient and perfect "gems of wisdom," yet over these past few thousand years it has been able to create neither a national spirit of initiative, nor a legal order for the state, nor a mechanism for cultural renewal; rather on its path of decline it has repeatedly destroyed its own best talent, killing off the living elements within itself, and suffocating one generation after another of the finest flowers of our nation.

55. History has proven that to attempt to modernize using the style of control of a "land-based" culture, although one may be able to incorporate some of the new achievements of modern science and technology, even to the point of putting satellites in orbit and exploding atom bombs, yet it will be fundamentally impossible to infuse the whole nation with a strong, civilizing vitality.

56. Only when the sea-breeze of "blueness" finally turns to rain and once again moistens this stretch of parched yellow soil, only then will this awesome vitality, previously

52. Hukou Rapids in the Jinshaan Canyon; close-up of rushing yellow waters.

53. [*copter noise*] Aerial view of bend in Yellow River.

54. Inside dark Confucian temple, looking up at lofty ceiling supported by red pillars; camera pans down to ornate altar.

Row after row of carved stone tablets with the text of the Confucian classics.

[*emphatic blast of horns*]

55. [*music softens*] Close-up of Confucian quote carved in stone: *"The Master said: Gentlemen never compete."* [Analects III.7]

Photo: Hebei Jingjing Coal Mine.

Photo: Kaiping Coal Mine.

Photo: Tangshan Railroad.

b&w: moving on an old RR line.

56. [*drums*] Troupe of 1,000 waist-drummers dancing on a yellow ridge; viewed in turn from below, silhouetted against blue sky; from close-up; from helicopter.

released only during the happy days of the Spring Festival, be able to bring new life to the vast yellow soil plateau.

57. In the heartland of the yellow soil plateau—Yan'an—everywhere one can see clothing stores and barber shops established by young men and women from Shanghai, Zhejiang and other coastal areas. A flood of commodities from the coast are scattered throughout the streets and lanes. Sacred, earth-grey Pagoda Mountain, to the rear of this colorful and bustling market, has gradually faded into the misty background.

57. [*soft music*]

New shops in Yan'an: hair-dressers'

Close-up of Yan'an pagoda. Camera draws back, contrasting tiny pagoda with shopping street lined with stalls.

58. These old men and young guys, whose ancestors once erupted from this continental heartland to conquer all of China, are now still bound to this shrunken stretch of land and with it their once magnificent energy has also diminished. Its hard to believe that these few young men are actually members of this lively team of one thousand waist-drummers. Does it mean that their vitality will forever be expended only in the frenzy of playing the waist-drums?

58. Close-ups of farmers' faces

[*drums*] Aerial view of troupe of waist-drummers dancing on the ridge.

59. In 1980, the Shenzhen Special Economic Zone was established. It announced to the whole world that this "land-based" civilization of several thousands of years had finally moved to the edge of the sea, and that the face which it had always kept turned to the land had turned to gaze at the distant ocean.

59. [*music starts*] Shenzhen: new highrise buildings

Pink outline map of China, showing Shenzhen.

Gentle waves splashing on a sandy beach; birds migrating in a V.

60. In 1986, fourteen coastal cities were entirely opened up to the out-

60. Modern harbor; ship launching.

side. China had formally assumed a posture of challenging the sea.

61. In 1988, Hainan Island was established as a separate province. Its short-term objective was to issue a challenge to the "four small dragons" of Asia. The ancient Asian continent had finally put aside the proud airs of a great power.

62. If Hainan should succeed, it will unite with the fourteen other coastal cities and form one of the great dragons on the two shores of the Pacific. This historic undertaking will necessarily give a new color to China's culture.

63. And yet, while reforms move ahead quickly, how many Chinese are consciously participating in them?

64. A series of reports from the Chinese Citizens Political Psychology Research Group has indicated that Chinese citizens very commonly exhibit an overly-cautious attitude towards political participation. **Of citizens surveyed, 62.41% said that "they were very careful about discussing political issues,"** while **73.79% said that they either "agreed with," "basically agreed with" or "did not oppose" the statement that "It's best to minimize one's participation in politics."** They continue to worry that political participation could invite trouble for them, and they continue to lack a feeling of security about political participation. The recurring wild swings of the pendulum throughout the recent decades of

---

61. Dedication of Hainan Provincial Govt. building; press conference.

1st letters postmarked Haikou, Hainan.

Yellow bulldozer clearing land.

New high-rise apartments.

62. New high-rise apartment buildings.

63. Close-up of the backs of people's heads as they move forward; camera moves back to reveal narrow lane of shops, with a dense crowd of shoppers.

64. Bicyclists in heavy traffic coming toward camera.

Background for quotation on screen: bicyclists coming toward camera.

[*music fades*]

Background for quotation on screen: crowd of shoppers.

Clover-leaf intersection.
[b&w footage of Cultural Revolution:]
Jiang Qing waving the Quotations, with Kang Sheng;

Liu Shaoqi in straw hat.

political movements, as well as the extreme fierceness of political oppression has made people paranoid. This will definitely constitute a serious obstacle to the progress of democracy.

[Newspaper headlines attacking Liu & Deng:] *"Great Proletarian Cultural Revolution"; "Down with revisionism & rightist deviationism; "From bourgeois democrat to capitalist roader"; "the unrepentant capitalist roader in the Party"; "To overturn verdicts is to restore capitalism"; "Criticize the theory of the sole importance of productive forces"*

65. The May Fourth movement of 1919, for the first time and with a thoroughly uncompromising spirit, unfurled the banners of "science" and "democracy." The thought of Western culture, including Marxism, was widely disseminated throughout China. But this progressive tide of culture by no means succeeded in washing away the accumulated sediment of feudalism in politics, economics, and in the moral character of individuals. Over the past several decades, from time to time this sunken sediment has resurfaced, while at other times everything has frozen solid.

65. [*drum rolls*] b&w: May 4th movement: students marching, wearing mourning costume

contemporary newspapers announce strikes;

New Youth magazine: articles on Marx, Bakunin; Lu Xun's "Medicine."

b&w: May 4th-era students marching towards camera.

66. Many things in China, it would seem, should all start over again from May Fourth.

66. Bas-relief scene of May 4th movement carved outside Mao's Memorial Hall; a speaker addresses a rally. [*music starts*]

67. Chinese history did not create a bourgeoisie for the Chinese people which could hasten the victory of science and democracy; Chinese culture did not nurture a sense of citizenship. On the contrary, it taught a subject mentality. A

67. b&w: scene outside a factory. Workers line up, carry sacks of grain; laborers carry sacks off a boat on carrying poles; women in aprons walking; men with heavy bales on their backs.

subject mentality can only produce obedient people who meekly submit to oppression on the one hand and madmen who act recklessly on the other. But History did give the Chinese people an entirely unique group: its intellectuals.

Cover of Fall 1987 issue of The Chinese Intellectual [N.Y.], showing a door beginning to open, with light spilling in from behind.

68. It is very difficult for them to have economic interests in common or an independent political stance; for thousands of years they have been hangers-on.

68.Photos: Kang Yuwei
              Liang Qichao
              Tan Sitong

[*music fades*]

69. Nor can they become a solid social entity that employs a steel-hard economic strength to carry out an armed critique of the old society.

69.Photos: Yan Fu
              [unknown]
              Lu Xun
              [unknown]

70. Their talents can be manipulated by others, their wills can be twisted, their backbones bent, and their flesh destroyed.

70. b&w: Parade of demonstrators seen from behind an iron fence; corpses on the street.

71. And yet, they hold in their hands the weapon to destroy ignorance and superstition.

71. Meeting in Great Hall of the People to discuss 7th 5-year Plan; Wang Zhen at the mike, followed by other speakers.

72. It is they who can channel the "blue" sweetwater spring of science and democracy onto our yellow earth!

72. [*wind*] Scientists trudging thru sand dunes in the Gobi. [yellow]

73. [**Yuan Zhiming, Ph.D candidate**] The first persons to realize this contradiction, between reality and the ideal, or between tradition and the ideal, were China's intellectuals, especially from the pre-modern period onwards. They were always the first to discover the faults of the tradition. Yet they also lacked the ability to change it. Filled with high hopes they always

73. Yuan Zhiming interviewed in the studio, against a yellow background.

sought the way to destroy tradition. But they always lacked the courage. And so that's why they were always the first to feel pain in their hearts. In these circumstances, under the compulsion of world trends, and making use of the pressure in the surrounding environment, I feel our only way out is to force people to accept a new life, and to create a new life, despite the pain. That's why in the conclusion to my book, The Burdened Subject, I used three statements: **That China's hope lies with the world. That to make this hope into reality, we must rely on those Chinese who have been awakened by the world.** That our generation is fated to endure much spiritual suffering, but that perhaps because of this we may attain greatness.

74. Possessing greater practical strength than these is perhaps the plain-faced, soft-spoken new breed of entrepreneurs. Even amongst the owners of these small shops, among these businessmen hurrying along the road, among these peasants who have left the land to make their living all over the country, there is building up a new social energy and a new vitality, none of which should be underestimated.

75. Even in these high-level political gatherings, which used to be so solemn and serious, we can also see the appearance of a "blue" transparency. China's mass media having taken for the first time a relatively neutral stance are serving as a medium of dialogue between high-level policy-makers and the masses of the people.

74. [*machines whirring*] Ma Shengli [?] and workers in hard hats at paper mill.

[*crowd noise*] Watch repairman on street corner. Clothing store.

Construction workers pour concrete. Painters inside new building.

Plastic goods for sale on street corner. Women shopping. Customer pays smiling shopkeeper.

75. Press conference for 13th Party Congress [Fall 1987];

Foreign reporters with cameras;

Leadership lines up:

Zhao Ziyang, Li Peng, Qiao Shi..

Gen. Sec. Zhao offers a toast to reporters

76. Yet for orientals with a deep tradition of despotism to really understand democracy is by no means easy. History has left us many interesting anecdotes.

76. Color: Wavering reflection of an oriental palace in a pond, yellow against reflected blue sky. [Golden Temple at Amritsar]
b&w: Cadets with rifles; Chinese soldiers in straw hats marching.

77. At the end of 1940, Roosevelt was elected to his third term as President of the U.S. Mr. Chiang Kaishek recorded this in his diary as follows: *"American democracy is really admirable. I've sent Roosevelt a special cable to congratulate him on his victory."* And yet, one evening three years later, when special envoy Madame Chiang Kaishek—that is, Soong Meiling—was having dinner at the White House with the Roosevelts, the topic of conversation turned to strikes by American workers. Roosevelt asked Soong Meiling what the Chinese government would do if faced with such a problem in wartime. Soong Meiling coolly drew a line across her throat with a long painted fingernail, elegantly signifying "off with their heads," thereby startling no end all the American dinner-guests. Afterwards, Mrs. Roosevelt said, *"Soong Meiling can talk very prettily about the democratic system, but she doesn't know how to put it into practice."*

77. U.S. Capitol Building

Chiang Kaishek in uniform

b&w photo: Mme. Chiang attempting to suppress a laugh, accompanied by Chiang Kaishek and American general.

b&w: Roosevelt & Churchill at Yalta; allied soldiers marching; Japanese soldiers firing artillery.
Mme. Chiang superimposed over marching students.

b&w photo: Soong Meiling as a girl, with brothers and sisters.

Chinese soldiers arresting & shooting a suspect.

Narrow alley between high walls in Forbidden City.

78.[quotation appears on screen for several seconds before narrator reads it]

78. [*three beats of a gong as quotation appears on screen*]

Close-up on sign: Hall of Supreme Harmony.

The distinguishing marks of a despotic government are secrecy, rule by an individual, and the fickleness of his temperament.

79. The marks of a democratic government should be transparency, responsiveness to popular will, and a scientific approach.

80. We are right now moving from opacity to transparency.

81. We have already moved from the closed to the open door.

82. The Yellow River is fated to traverse the yellow soil plateau.

83. The Yellow River will ultimately empty into the blue sea.

84. The Yellow River's suffering and its hope have made it great.

85. The Yellow River's greatness perhaps consists in the fact that it has created a stretch of land between the sea and the plateau.

86. The Yellow River has now reached its great and painful entryway into the sea.

87. The mud and sand it has carried thousands of li will collect here to form new land.

88. The surging waves of the sea will here meet head on with the Yellow River.

89. The Yellow River must eliminate its fear of the sea.

Background for quotation on screen: camera pulls back to show throne hall in Forbidden City with yellow roof tiles.

79. [*whistle blast*] Background for quotation on screen: steamship in a Scandinavian fjord, blowing its whistle; blue water, blue sky and snowy hillsides. [*music starts*]

80. 13th Party Congress:

close-up of Zhao Ziyang.

81. CAAC jetliner taking off.

82. Aerial view of yellow soil plateau;

83. Close-up of Yellow River shot from back of speedboat, moving rapidly to the sea.

84. same

85. same

86. Camera moves forward towards gulls.

87. Low tide: camera moves forward over sand newly deposited by the river;

high tide: waves come in, almost covering new land.

88. same

89. Boy wading in the blue waves, hauling on a rope.

90. The Yellow River must preserve the dynamism and undaunted resolve which comes from the plateau.

90. Hukou Rapids in the Jinshaan Canyon; close-up of turbulent yellow water.

91. The waters of life arise from the sea and flow back into the sea.

91. Long shot looking out to sea; camera pulls back to reveal beach.

92. After a thousand years of solitude, the Yellow River has finally seen the blue sea.

92. Yellow River water mixing with the blue Pacific; contrast of yellow and blue.

The earth from space. [blue] [*musical climax, cut to folk song*]

93. [Ending sequence]

[Music. A man and woman sing a duet.]

*"I know that
the Yellow River makes ninety-nine
    bends;
on those ninety-nine bends are
    ninety-nine boats;
on those ninety-nine boats are
    ninety-nine poles;
on those ninety-nine bends are
    ninety-nine boatmen
poling their boats along."*

93. A waist-drummer seen close up, from below; his yellow costume contrasts with the blue sky. He jumps up and the frame freezes. [*cymbals*]

[Montage] Circling birds at sunset, Yellow River rapids; aerial view of Yellow River bends; Tibetan women dancing; waist-drummers; sailing junk on the river; sailing junks setting out to sea; sunset over the Yellow River. [*gong*]

94. [Film credits superimposed over montage, above]

[Director: **Xia Jun**

Script: **Xie Xuanjun
                 Yuan Zhiming**

Narration: **Zhang Jiasheng**]

94.

95. [CCTV 1988.6

Our broadcast of the six-part TV series Deathsong of the River is now complete.

Thank you for tuning in.

Thanks to the Political Department and the General Quartermasters Dept., People's Liberation Army]

95. Yellow sun at sunset over broad Yellow River.

"The Distress of a Dragon Year—Notes on Heshang"[1]

by Su Xiaokang

Part I: An Unlucky Year for the Chinese

On the evening of September 9th [1988], Wang Luxiang and I had gone over to Xie Xuanjun's house to chat, talking late into the night, when all of a sudden Luxiang exclaimed: "*Ai ya! Isn't today the anniversary of Mao Zedong's death?*"

The three of us fell silent all at once.

I glanced at the TV set and thought to myself: What might this evening's broadcast of "Today in History" have said? Too bad we didn't watch it. I continued to question myself: How is it that I entirely forgot this far-from-ordinary day? And how is it that after only one turn of the wheel I have forgotten that sharp stimulus together with those years and months that caused such deep pain?

Twelve years is one full turn of the cycle. Chinese had once again come to a dragon year. Twelve years previously, a star had fallen from the heavens, the northland had sunk, heaven and earth had split apart, and the black dragon had died[2]; it seemed as if the Chinese had in these great disasters and hardships fulfilled their quota of misfortune and attained release. Had the next cycle of misfortune arrived so quickly?

Chinese have always regarded a dragon year as unlucky. Whether this concept arises from the theory of the mutual interaction between man and

---

[1] This is an abridged translation of Su Xiaokang's essay entitled "Longnian de beichuang—guanyu Heshang de zhaji" as published in Wenhui yuekan [Shanghai], January, 1989. Gaps in the text are marked by [cut]. A shorter version of the same essay, dated October and missing Parts III and IV, had been published earlier in Cui Wenhua, ed., Haiwai Heshang da taolun, Harbin: Heilongjiang jiaoyu chubanshe, November, 1988, pp. 70-84. In April, 1989, the essay was published in Hongkong as the title essay of a collection of articles entitled Longnian de beichuang: Heshang zheng ming yu huiying.

[2] These are allegorical statements, probably referring to the death of Zhou Enlai, the Tangshan earthquake, and the death of Mao Zedong himself.

nature contained in the notions of Yin and Yang and the Five Elements, or whether it should be attributed to our ancestors' historical summation of their experience over thousands of years, I do not know. I only know that my wife was born in a dragon year, and whenever her birth year rolls around, she will always seek out a piece of red string to tie at her waist to avoid bad luck; as far as the Chinese of today are concerned, the disasters and hardships of that dragon year twelve years ago seem to have been a nearly pre-ordained "historical experience."

Hence the year of the dragon is to be feared.

Indeed, just as soon as it arrived in China, 1988 A.D. manifested some unlucky and unsettling phenomena that disturbed the whole country. After a series of events that alarmed the whole country, the following folk ditty appeared: *"Trains keep crashing in death kisses/ Ships keep sinking in abysses/ Airplanes tumble from the skies/ And prices reach new highs."* While the pain of last year's great forest fire still remained in people's minds, the airplane crash at Chongqing, the epidemic of hepatitis in the Yangtze region and price inflation all struck at once,[3] quickly reviving the fear deep in the Chinese people's consciousness, so that everyone more or less spontaneously started to recall the events of twelve years ago. ...

The story goes that on a dark night not long after the Spring Festival, in a provincial capital north of the Great Wall, there was a driver on the highway making his way quickly home. All of a sudden, his headlights lit up a black snake stretched across the road; he slammed on the brakes and swerved to avoid it. After he had gone a little further, he saw another snake stretched across the road and also swerved to avoid it. At this time, two women materialized into existence on the highway, stopping his car, and claimed that they were the two snakes, and that in order to thank the driver for his kindness, they would especially reveal to him a secret of Heaven: that the dragon year would have ill-luck, and that as soon as he got home he should set off a string of firecrackers to avert ill-fortune. Not long after, on a certain night this whole city resounded with the sound of firecrackers, and on the following day in greeting each other, people wished each other "Happy New Year." As soon as wind of this event reached the land within the Wall, it spread like wildfire, reaching many cities. On the night of the first day of the fifth month in the lunar calendar (June 14th), the city of Taiyuan also resounded with firecrackers, and many people didn't know why. Upon asking others, they discovered that in a dragon year, the new year has to be celebrated twice in order to avoid disaster and misfortune. Moreover, four types of canned goods were sold out in a moment: apples [ping], quail eggs

---

[3] For the events alluded to, see Part Five, p. 197

[an], peaches [tao], and pears [li], for people said that by eating them one could "safely escape [misfortune]" [ping an tao li]....

Even now I still remember very clearly that at the outset of 1976, in that unlucky spring in which Premier Zhou Enlai died,[4] everyone's faces seemed to be shrouded with a dark aura, while the weather seemed always cloudy and gloomy, and scary prophecies spread all over the country; by summer, as if foretold, Tangshan sank into the earth[5] and then Mao Zedong passed away. This ancient interaction between man and nature was so accurate, and the people were so seemingly prescient in their fearful reactions, [that I had to wonder:] were these ultimately some sort of socio-psychological phenomena whose rules could be traced, or were these really some sort of divine prophecies? No matter which, the fact that a "fin-de-siècle" mentality could occur on two [consecutive] dragon years made me believe that there may be some foundation after all to the idea that the dragon year is inauspicious.

Our Heshang was thus written in this inauspicious atmosphere.

On the last day of 1987, I began to write Part One, "Searching for a Dream."

As the dragon year quietly approached, I was seemingly totally unconscious of it. But when I went out for a walk on the streets of Beijing, I suddenly found the streets full of dragons: on the big billboards at intersections, there were dragons painted in the form of cute babies, extending their two hideous feelers and waving their hands and stamping their feet as if welcoming someone; multi-colored dragons flashed in neon lights; and especially the blue and gold old dragons magnificently coiled around the pillars at the front door of the newly-built International Hotel, opposite the railroad station, made a very deep impression... You see, 1988 had been designated the International Year of Tourism, and the symbol the Chinese had used to attract foreign guests was none other than the dragon, of all our "national cultural treasures" the most characteristic.

Wang Luxiang poked fun at it, saying, *"So this ancient totem has some practical modern use after all!"*

But I was thinking: Was there ever a clearer example of "searching for a dream"?

---

[4] Zhou Enlai died January 8th, 1976. On April 5th of that year, the traditional day for paying respect to one's ancestors, mourners gathered in Tian'anmen Square to honor him, provoking a spontaneous demonstration and bloody clash with the police that augured the impending end of the Cultural Revolution.

[5] The Tangshan earthquake, measuring 7.8 on the Richter scale, occurred on July 28th, 1976. The official toll was 242,769 dead and 164,851 seriously injured.

When, in an aerial view taken by the Yellow River[6] camera crew I saw the Yellow River under a veil of clouds and mist, I was reminded only of a blood vessel. And so the name Xia Jun and I chose for this film when we first started designing Heshang was Da xuemai [The Great Artery]. We intended to discuss the rise and fall of Yellow River civilization from the angle of the philosophy of culture; and, just like an expedition seeking out the headwaters of the Yellow River, we would seek out the wellsprings of Chinese civilization. I've only now come to realize, that from the beginning lying draped across the headwaters of that civilization there was a dragon! What's most interesting is that we captured this symbol, not from a primitive totem or bronze vessel, but on the streets of a large city!

In fact, the Yellow River is a dragon.[7] No Chinese would ever doubt this idea, just as they would never doubt that they are the heirs of the dragon. And yet, why would the Chinese people want to worship such a fierce-looking monster?[8]

It happened that just at this time Zhao Yu had come from Shanxi to Beijing to revise his Dream of Being A Strong Country.[9] I invited him to stay at the script-writing department, and every night we talked until late. That evening, he invited Luxiang, Xia Jun and I to see the film The Old Well, which was his good friend Zheng Yi's masterpiece. The unequal and nearly hopeless struggle between the people of the Taihang mountains and water made me suddenly realize the unavoidable and special civilizational significance that water holds for our people, even today. We were deeply shaken.

"You have found a 'world language' that needs no translation—water." Under Zhao Yu's urging, I wrote Zheng Yi a letter that very evening. *"In the view of Westerners—Marx saw it this way—the long-lasting despotism of the Orient was actually linked with water. The entire civilization of the great river-valley peoples was founded on the conflict between the survival strength needed for the struggle with water and the tragic destiny determined*

---

[6] The Yellow River was a 30-part television series jointly produced by China and Japan, broadcast in the spring of 1988, and from which Heshang drew considerable footage. Xia Jun was a member of the Yellow River film crew, while Su Xiaokang wrote the script for several of the episodes.

[7] See Xie Xuanjun, "Zhongguoren de Huanghe xinli" [The Yellow River Mindset of the Chinese People] in Su Xiaokang et al., Longnian de beichuang, Hong Kong, Sanlian shudian, April, 1989, pp. 183-191.

[8] Su Xiaokang asks this same question in Part One, p. 105.

[9] For more on Zhao Yu and his essay, see Part One, p. 115.

by water. The psychology and character of a people was distorted and alienated in this conflict."

The dragon is none other than the illusion and the spiritual cushion to which this distortion of the soul gives birth. The irresistible force of nature drove the Chinese to the point that they had no choice but to pool their forces in a sort of despotic centralized power in order to counter it; but this despotic centralization became in turn a kind of unchallengeable overlord and has given the Chinese a tyrant in society in addition to one in nature. The dragon has thus become a two-fold symbol.

When, in a foreign-made TV film entitled The Heart of the Dragon,[10] Xia Jun found the image of an evil dragon coming tumbling forward with its blood-red mouth wide open; and when I suddenly remembered Zhang Mingmin wearing a dragon-embroidered jacket and sadly singing "The Heirs of the Dragon"; and when, amidst a mass of archival footage we found innumerable scenes of dragon worship, dragon dances, and dragon boat races; we then made up our minds to defy public opinion and give this old critter a good scolding! [cut]

I never expected that taking a poke at this old critter would make so many people uncomfortable, such as some scholars, painters, overseas celebrities and so on who criticized us sharply, their general point being precisely that these symbols were not to be profaned, or it would undermine the vital spirit of our nation. Feeling on the contrary that our vital spirit had already suffered near maximum damage, it seemed to me difficult to revitalize it just by relying on that old dragon. I felt that if indeed as some scholars have asserted, symbols are quite complex, then there should be room for different opinions. And isn't it also somewhat one-sided to describe the Yellow River as so kind, the Great Wall as so magnificent, and the dragon as so holy? All the more so since their establishment as positive idols by no means dates from antiquity but is merely a matter of a few decades. Those who have employed the past to serve the present and imbued them with a significance in political culture would also seem to have chosen only one of the possible meanings. And so why not permit us to discuss a new interpretation from a new angle? Would that make the sky fall down? Moreover, there's one point that we needn't worry about: our own self-conscious reflection on our own totems would not go so far as to make them lose their charisma for foreigners and hence influence our foreign currency earnings.

Speaking of vitality, that young fellow Zhao Yu is very perceptive; at the beginning of the year when he was staying with us in the script-writing department revising his Dream of Being a Strong Nation, he already

---

[10] The Chinese title is given as Zhongguo zhi xin, i.e., the "Heart of China."

predicted that in the Seoul Olympics China would take a maximum of five gold medals. And unfortunately it turned out as he had predicted.[11] [cut]

And so when I read the Dream of Being a Strong Nation, I understood the psychology of Chinese today: they cannot afford to lose again.[12]

Over this past century, we have constantly lost. First we lost to the English; then to the eight allied armies; and then to the Japanese.[13] When we finally managed to send the Japanese packing, New China for a while was indeed able to make Chinese all over the world swell with pride; but who would have thought that after a mere thirty-some years, when we had awakened from a civil turmoil in which we had tried to strangle ourselves, that we would discover ourselves in the company of poor nations such as Tanzania and Zambia; that even South Korea, Singapore and Taiwan would have outpaced us[14]; and that the Japanese would have come back laughing, bearing their Toshibas, Hitachis, Toyotas, Kokans, Yamahas, and Casios? [cut]

The dragon year was indeed a troubled time: natural disasters and man-made ones; the craze for qigong; a swarm of rumors; a mad spate of panic buying; the setback at Seoul; and the thwarting of reform.[15] Broadcast in this sort of atmosphere, could Heshang possibly have good luck?

---

[11] See Zhao Yu and Lin Jiang, Bing bai Hancheng [Defeat at Seoul], Fengyun shidai chuban gongsi, Taibei, June, 1989.

[12] This same sentence is echoed in Part One, p. 102

[13] This refers to (1) the Opium War of 1839-42, with England; (2) the allied expeditionary force sent by England, the U.S., Germany, France, Russia, Japan, Italy and Austria to China in 1900 to rescue the foreign legations besieged by the Boxers in Beijing; (3) the series of Japanese incursions on Chinese territory, from the Sino-Japanese War of 1894-5 down to World War II.

[14] These comparisons are also made in Part Four, "The New Era," p. 171.

[15] Part Five mentions a list of natural disasters, accidents, etc., on p. 197. The late summer of 1988 also saw panic buying of durable goods such as refrigerators due to fears of inflation. Zhao Ziyang's reform program also received a setback that summer when at the Beidaihe conference it was decided to radically scale back state spending on major construction projects due to concern over inflation and a badly overheated economy. In the fall of 1987, Zhao had already had to give up his post as Premier in order to take the vacant position of General Secretary. Li Peng's assumption of the premiership meant that Zhao lost direct control over the day-to-day workings of government; hence his reform program could be more easily thwarted.

Part II: A God-forsaken Land

Just at this point Wang Luxiang was racking his brains to write Part Two, "Destiny."

To explain the tragic decline of an ancient country of thousands of years in a television film was obviously too difficult. We were asking Wang Luxiang to do something nearly impossible. All the more so, for to ask someone like this, who had an M.A. in Philosophy from Beijing University, a "bookworm" who had received a thorough training in abstract thinking and whose scholarly temperament had been strictly molded, to sigh eloquently and sadly, with all the airs of a poet—this was indeed an uncomfortable task. Luxiang would hide out all day in his little room, surveying mountains of books, always working until late at night, with only a few lines of writing to show for his efforts. The next day he would ask me with a pained expression: *"Don't you think that we're going to make a laughingstock of ourselves from the way we are commenting on national affairs and history?"*

Early on, when Xia Jun and I had come up with our proposal for The Great Artery, we had especially invited him to come and serve as an evaluator. He struck the table with his fist and cried, *"It's marvelous,"* giving us no end of encouragement.[16]

Before us we faced the arduous task of transforming pure scholarship into television. Now the more scholarly a person is, the more he wants to shut himself up in his ivory tower to do metaphysics; he wants to meticulously observe the principle of *"making bold hypotheses, and seeking careful proofs,"*[17] with no regard for the earth-shaking events in the real world. This perhaps is also one of the difficulties of China's enlightenment movement.

I recall that later on, after we had created the scenario, we went to call on Jin Guantao and Liu Qingfeng in order to invite them to participate. Both husband and wife wore pained expressions. They too probably feared that television was not a medium for high culture. At that point I got anxious and blurted:

"Mr. Jin, these days you are famous overseas and have published a great deal, but have you ever wondered how many people here in China know of your "super-stable structure" theory? And what would the effect be if you

---

[16] Wang Luxiang describes this meeting in his essay "Huiyi yu sikao" in Heshang lun, pp. 91-92.

[17] A famous slogan promoted by Hu Shih.

were to go on TV and say a few words yourself to an audience of several hundred millions?"

Jin Guantao's eyes sparkled with an interest that could not be concealed.

To perform a marriage of television with thought was the goal pursued by our twenty-five-year-old director Xia Jun. This M.A. graduate in literature who had come from a background in television had already as a college student grown fed up with the mediocrity of television and was interested only in "the passion for studying culture" [wenhua re]; thus he had gotten to know a large number of the famous names in the academic world in Beijing. After he graduated and was assigned to work at CCTV, he was just in time for the Sino-Japanese co-production of the Yellow River. He thought this would be a good opportunity. As a result, after he had spent over a year with the film crew, he clearly saw how a vast amount of excellent material had been treated in a mediocre fashion. The thirty-part Yellow River series was no more than a superficial travelogue of scenery and local customs. People working in television, just like those working with theories, both felt that television was not a medium for high culture and thought that this young whippersnapper was biting off more than he could chew. [cut]

This youngster was very smart. He knew that the only way to make [Wang] Luxiang and I drop our "bookishness" was for us to see the Yellow River for ourselves. And so in the depths of winter five of us flew from Beijing to Yan'an.

Wang Luxiang would later recall: *"As the plane passed over the Jinshaan Canyon, I was struck by the marks mankind had left on the earth's surface. Looking down from the plane, Shanxi's topography resembled a military map with contour lines everywhere, showing that all the hillsides had been converted into terraced fields, their summits resembling spiral-shaped pastries. I strongly appreciated the diligence of Shanxi's people and recalled Dazhai also. Yet as soon as the plane had crossed the Yellow River, the topography suddenly changed, the contour lines disappeared, and the earth's surface became unbearably ugly, with steep slopes everywhere; the loose, dried-out yellow soil seemed perched on the slopes, as if at any moment the rain might wash it away. Because of its weight, it fractures vertically, forming rows and rows of earthen pillars and pagodas, resembling the crumbling pillars remaining after the collapse of an ancient fortress, or the charred stumps left after a great forest fire. Human activity—no matter whether it was intentional or unintentional—bears an unshirkable burden of responsibility for this."*[18]

---

[18] This passage comes from Wang Luxiang's essay entitled "Huiyi yu sikao" [Remembering and Pondering] in Heshang lun, p. 92.

The aridity and barrenness of the north Shaanxi plateau, the poverty, isolation, stupidity, helplessness as well as the remarkable reproductive powers of the people living on its ridges and crags—all made us deeply aware of the exhaustion of the natural world and the hopelessness brought about when man has plundered it to the limit. This well resembles our once-splendid Chinese civilization, which, like an aging, forlorn old man, stubbornly remains in its destitute, deserted village awaiting its own death. Luxiang, born in the well-watered country south of the Yangtze, stood on a snow-covered ridge facing a lonely expanse of hills filled with the scars carved by the rains and muttered:

"This really is a God-forsaken land!"

Perhaps it was at this moment that Wang Luxiang grasped the main theme of "Destiny": the attachment of our ancestors for the land, and the tragic limitations of the continental environment that are difficult to overcome.

Encapsulating this abandoned, ancient civilization, which *"despite nine deaths still feels no regret,"*[19] is the Great Wall.

As far as our nation is concerned, it, too, like the dragon, is a great symbol that may not be profaned.

But such symbols are precisely what our television films need to make use of.

For nothing can convert abstract concepts into concrete artistic images better than they can. These are all parts of the heritage left to us by our ancestors; why should we be permitted only to revere and worship them, and not to critically reflect on them? After all, didn't our ancestors let Meng Jiangnü curse the Great Wall two thousand years ago?

We would probably have to count Xie Xuanjun as the first person to unearth the cultural meaning of the Great Wall as a symbol.[20] [cut]

Just as Wang Luxiang was busily engaged here in "forgetting his ancestors," as luck would have it, a good friend of his, a Ph.D candidate at Harvard, just happened to send him a letter, urging him not to recklessly criticize tradition. [cut]

---

[19] An allusion to the Li sao of Qu Yuan.

[20] For more on Xie Xuanjun, see Part One, footnote 16. A fascinating study of the Great Wall by a Western sinologist is Arthur Waldron's The Great Wall of China: From History to Myth, Cambridge University Press, 1990. In chapter 11, "The Wall Acquires New Meanings," Waldron assesses the relatively recent elevation of the Wall to the status of a national symbol.

"I don't deny that Chinese culture has all sorts of defects, but this is principally the fault of its carriers—the descendants of the Fire Emperor and the Yellow Emperor. This excellent culture is not at fault itself. If it really should disappear and have only the value of a museum-piece as Levenson says,[21] then that indeed is something worth mourning, and I would willingly be buried with it..."

The sound of his quiet sobs, though forcibly repressed, could still be heard on the tape.

I don't know what Luxiang's good friend would have thought if he had seen Heshang; I only feel that, having gone to the West without being assimilated by their civilization, he felt the tragedy of the abandonment of Chinese culture even more keenly, and that this had to be deeply painful. This made me think of Wang Guowei, who, at the beginning of the Republican period, committed suicide by jumping into Kunming Lake. About this the great historian Chen Yinke sadly wrote: *"The China of today has witnessed thousands of unprecedented calamities and astonishing changes; and when the calamities and changes shall have run their course, then how could those in whom the spirit of culture is crystallized not share its fate and end their lives with it?"* This sort of tremendous anguish is already very rarely seen amongst younger scholars, and so I was greatly shaken by this tape.

And yet I still feel that this is a sort of sinking into despair, the senseless crying of a child abandoned by God, the failure of nerve of Chinese intellectuals caught in a dilemma, which is of no assistance to that civilization in decline. What we need is to wake up, to re-evaluate, to criticize, to reach nirvana.[22] [cut]

Later on, when Luxiang gave the film its title of Deathsong of the River (at that point I had already gone to Hainan), was he perhaps influenced by the sad feelings of his friend?

Shang means to die young. The civilization of the Yellow River fell into stagnation precisely because it had matured early. Its stagnation was equivalent to death. To be in decline and unable to renew oneself and change is an even more painful sort of "early death," in which one is neither dead

---

[21] See Joseph R. Levenson, Confucian China and Its Modern Fate: A Trilogy, University of California Press, Berkeley, 1972, esp. p. 76. Levenson's book was translated into Chinese in the Xiandai xifang xueshu wenku [Library of Modern Western Scholarship] as Rujiao Zhongguo jiqi jindai mingyun.

[22] This is probably referring to Bao Zunxin's idea that the May Fourth movement was an 'incomplete nirvana' for China's intellectuals. See Bao Zunxin, "Wei wancheng de niepan—dui Wusi de fansi" in Pipan yu qimeng, pp. 103-139.

nor alive. It makes all of the Yellow Emperor's descendants, who are born of, raised by, and enamored of this [civilization] terribly grieved.

The suffering born of love [for one's nation or culture] is far more sacred and lofty than that sort of love which is blind and superstitious; or than numbed indifference; or than that semblance of love which actually seeks to violate it; or than that [love] which entices people to love it for its very backwardness and ugliness and even praise it, saying: *"the child does not complain of his mother's ugliness, nor a dog complain of the poverty of his house."*

But it is not enough merely to love it to the point of *"feeling angry at its failure to strive and feeling sad for its misfortune."*

Real love is to wish that it thoroughly remold itself and regain new life.

Part III: History is Hinting to Us

In November 1987, the five-man Heshang film-crew flew from Yan'an to Henan.

The impression that Yan'an had left on us was no longer holy and grand but rather poor and conservative. The Yan River had already dried up, revealing a bed of broken rocks. The pagoda seemed to have lost its holy light and stood alone and very forlorn on a barren hilltop.

The city of Yan'an was run-down and decrepit, without a single modern structure worthy of the name, its streets deserted and cold... The bridge over the Yan River had become the gathering place for peddlers' stalls of all descriptions but was only lively at night, when merchants, performers, beggars and vagabonds would mix there. Someone told us with an air of mystery that there was even some clandestine prostitution south of the city wall.

During the daytime the only lively place was the free market along a side street, filled with clothing and cloth goods brought in from the coast, interspersed with people hawking rat-poison and a few beauty-parlors opened up by southerners. This street, which to some extent breathed the atmosphere of the commodity economy of the 80s, ultimately ran right into that ancient pagoda, creating a juxtaposition not without a certain humor.

When we visited Zichang and Ansai [counties] outside Yan'an, amidst those ridges and crags, ravines and gullies which had once witnessed the grand drama of revolution, there were still the same old run-down cave dwellings, a few taciturn old men keeping a few head of sheep, women sickly from having borne too many children, children strong and healthy despite having only coarse grain[23] to fill their stomachs... The two things that cadres at both county and village levels complained of most often were the shortage of grain and the difficulty of irrigation. The year before, Yan'an had experienced a bad drought and in many places not a single kernel of grain was harvested, so that in northern Shaanxi people had mostly subsisted on potatoes. The reliance of agriculture on irrigation on this yellow soil plateau could not be changed, even over thousands of years. The "rural responsibility system" had dissolved the form of social organization here, so that there was an immediate price to pay as soon as irrigation was neglected. The spectre of Asia had once again appeared.[24]

In the Yan'an Guesthouse we ran into a group of young people headed by Wang Juntao[25] of the Beijing Social and Economic Sciences Research Institute who had come at the invitation of the local party committee to help discuss the problems of Yan'an's development. According to them, ever since Liberation, Yan'an had received uninterrupted economic "blood transfusions"[26] by relying on the support of feelings of "clan loyalty." Yet just as had happened in all the old liberated areas—such as Jiangxi, southern Anhui, Dabieshan, Yimengshan, and northern Jiangsu—this "transfusion" mechanism had of all things helped to bring about the laziness of the old liberated areas, so that there was no internal impetus for economic development. And now that those feelings of clan loyalty had faded away under the new framework of the commodity economy these days, they would never get another transfusion and so were even more forlorn. On the southeast coast where capitalism had once flourished, the main tide of industrial civilization is right now starting to rise, leaving far behind the yellow soil plateau in the northwest where revolution had once been conceived. And today, that great sense of loss, of having been abandoned by civilization and by history which we have felt in these remote mountain gullies; the plain and simple psychology of the people here; as well as that nearly-forgotten pagoda (Yan'an people say that fewer and fewer old

---

[23] zaliang, i.e., grain other than the staple diet of wheat or rice.

[24] Elsewhere, the "spectre" that Heshang refers to is the spectre of despotism, made necessary by China's agricultural economy [see Part Five]; here, the spectre appears to be the ghost of poverty that appears when the same central authority is removed. The "Asiatic Mode of Production" as defined by Marx denoted a society which relied on a strong central authority to maintain public works and water control in particular; otherwise agriculture would fail and the civilization would be doomed. While the commune system was able to mobilize vast numbers of laborers for public works projects, the new "rural responsibility system" instituted by Deng Xiaoping in the late 70s gave peasants control of their own land and allowed them to plant what they pleased. Evidently public water projects soon fell into disrepair.

[25] See Part Four, footnote 62.

[26] See also Part Four, p. 179.

comrades come to visit Yan'an)—all these would seem to be the heartless mockery of History. It was after the "old Eighth Route Army men" no longer came to Yan'an to "hold its hand" that Wang Juntao and his people, as if unable to endure this heartless mockery, had come to Yan'an in search of answers. We had originally come to Yan'an just to shoot some scenes of the topography of the yellow-soil plateau. But once having seen how Yan'an's people lived these days, we couldn't help but take some shots, such as of that old man with sixteen grandchildren; of the young fellow who stubbornly clung to his cave home, unwilling to go out to seek his fortune; and of that now drab and colorless pagoda...

After Heshang was broadcast, we heard that not a few of that older generation of revolutionaries who had come out of Yan'an were rather unhappy with what we had revealed of the backwardness of the yellow soil plateau. In particular, some of the older revolutionaries, such as Mr. Kuang Yaming of Nanjing,[27] charged that Heshang had ignored Yan'an, that center of revolution that had emerged in the middle reaches of the Yellow River, and that this was a distortion of History. We wonder whether or not these old comrades have returned to Yan'an in recent years? And if they have, then how did they feel when they saw the present state of Yan'an and the poverty of the people of northern Shaanxi? If due to such "feelings of clan loyalty" or "revolutionary enthusiasm" even someone such as I, who at first had regarded Yan'an as a revolutionary holy place, who had been filled with longing for the idealism and romanticism emanating like poetry from the banks of the Yan River, a member of the generation which had "grown up with the Republic" and served as "Red Guards," should still feel some degree of disillusioned loss and confusion, and some measure of shame and embarrassment, then should not that older generation from Yan'an feel at least a little more distressed than us? Yan'an has symbolic significance. In the past it symbolized revolution, sanctity, light; but what does it still signify today? [cut]

Before leaving Yan'an, we took a special trip to see Zaoyuan. That quiet hillside filled with fallen leaves had the feeling of a deserted house. Those long neat rows of white-washed cave homes still aroused in us a feeling of respect and admiration. But when we then looked at the great names inscribed before the caves—Mao Zedong, Zhang Wentian, Liu Shaoqi, Zhou Enlai, Zhu De, Ren Bishi and so on—and when we recalled their relationships in later days and their various ends, we started to feel gloomy and left without shooting a single scene...

---

[27] Kuang Yaming, elected vice-chairman, People's Congress of Jiangsu Province, 1979, 1983; honorary president, Nanjing University, 1982-; elected chairman of Confucius Foundation, September, 1984. See Bartke, ed., Who's Who in the People's Republic of China, 2nd ed., pp. 210-211.

When we drove into Kaifeng in Henan my heart suddenly grew heavy once again.

Several years ago as a reporter in Henan, whenever I would come to Kaifeng I would always feel an unconscious fear—an inability to forget the tragedy that had occurred here in that winter eighteen years before. It was in the middle of November also that Liu Shaoqi's corpse was carried out from that heavily-guarded old bank and transported to the crematorium in the eastern suburbs. ...

In Beijing I had said to Xia Jun, *"If we go to Henan I definitely want to find the place where Liu Shaoqi met his end and get a true taste of what despotism really is."*

By a fortunate chance, we made this request just after having listened to Mayor Cui Aizhong brief us on Kaifeng in the conference room at city hall. Mayor Cui hemmed and hawed for a moment, then said: *"All right. The place where Comrade Shaoqi passed away is right next door to this conference room."*[28]

Cameraman Cao Zhiming picked up his equipment, crewmember Huang Min picked up his tungsten lamps, and we filed into the courtyard of that old bank. It was already late at night. I craned my neck to look at the high, pitch-black wall surrounding us on all four sides and felt as if I were standing at the bottom of a well, from which it would be hard to spread one's wings and fly away.

The room where Liu Shaoqi was imprisoned was the left-hand inner room on the west side of the courtyard. His memorial portrait hung facing the door. The room still preserved everything as it had been then: there was a desk and a bed; they say the pillow on the bed was the one that he had brought with him from Beijing. Standing in front of the bed, I don't know why, but I didn't try very hard to imagine how he had suffered while lying there (I heard that his white hair was a foot long, that his nose and mouth were twisted out of shape, and that his lower jaw was covered in blood[29]); rather, I remembered the cave-home he had had on the hillside at Zaoyuan in Yan'an. It seemed as if a desk and bed were placed there too. Yet there was a sense of sanctity and sublimity there, while here the air was full of

---

[28] Mayor Cui Aizhong is interviewed in Part Five. Part Five also shows scenes of the room in which Liu Shaoqi died as well as of the ceremony years later when his widow Wang Guangmei scattered his ashes from a boat.

[29] Liu Shaoqi's death is also mentioned in Part Five, pp. 199-200. The fullest account of his death so far is that provided in Yan Jiaqi's <u>Wenge shinian shi</u> [<u>A History of the Cultural Revolution Decade</u>], which however does not include the description of Liu Shaoqi's appearance. See Chapter 10 of Part I, "Liu Shaoqi de zui hou suiyue" [Liu Shaoqi's Last Days] in the edition by the Dagong baoshe, Hong Kong, 1986, pp. 166-181.

repression and fear. I had a glimmering that the historical significance revealed in the passage from the cave house at Zaoyuan to this old bank was not the tragedy of an individual but rather the tragedy of an entire generation of communists.

During the Cultural Revolution, Mao once said to [Edgar] Snow that he was a *"lone monk wandering the world with a leaky umbrella."*[30] Snow apparently didn't understand what he meant. But what he meant actually was something that Mao liked to talk about often, particularly in his late years: [the idea of being] "lawless and godless."[31] When the Communists were resisting the control of the Kuomintang, they indeed had to be "lawless and godless." But when they themselves had become the governors, to continue to be "lawless and godless" could only bring trouble to their own regime. And so Communists such as Liu Shaoqi and Zhou Enlai must necessarily fall into the category of "rational-legal" leaders, for they put great emphasis on the establishment of a legal order for the state. In 1955, as head of the National People's Congress, Liu Shaoqi had personally drafted New China's first constitution, while Zhou Enlai was ruling the world's first large country after the fashion of a modern state. And yet they were unable to find a form of government which could prevent that even greater authority high over their heads from freely overstepping the constitutions of the nation and party according to his whim; whether in the final analysis this was an oversight or something they could do nothing about is truly worthy of serious reflection by those of us coming afterwards.

I often think that leaders are also human, and that humans have their weaknesses; when this person was endowed with supreme and unrestrainable power, how could the state and society prevent and correct his oversights, his slips, and even his pig-headedness? The history of the period from 1957 to the Cultural Revolution would appear to have proven that the party and the state were already powerless in this regard. Mao Zedong's mistakes got worse and worse, and he grew increasingly imperious and peremptory so that by the time he stood on the Gate of Heavenly Peace fueling the fanaticism of a million Red Guards, there was no one who could do anything but gape

---

[30] Edgar Snow, The Long Revolution, New York, Random House, 1971, p. 175.

[31] What Snow didn't understand is that heshang da san "a monk with an umbrella" is the first part of a xiehou yu, a comic two-part expression in which the speaker only needs to supply the first part, while his listener readily supplies the concluding part from memory. The second part of this expression is: wu fa wu tian. On the surface this means (1) that the monk has no hair [wu fa] and (2) that there is no sky [wu tian]. Buddhist monks shave their heads; and presumably their umbrellas prevent them from seeing the sky. However, fa "hair" is a homophone for fa "law," and tian can mean both "sky" and "Heaven"; hence the extended meaning of the phrase is "to be lawless and godless," which is what Mao was really talking about. For Wang Luxiang's interpretation of wu fa wutian, see Part Five, footnote 57.

helplessly in astonishment. Although the tragedies of Liu Shaoqi and Zhou Enlai were different in form, one of them dying unnaturally before his time, the other apparently enduring to meet a good end, yet as "rational-legal" leaders they were ultimately unable to resist what Max Weber has called the "charismatic" leader.[32] Since this sort of leader's power depends merely on his being able to make his followers and disciples believe in the supreme power of his spirit, he would not hesitate to break every rule in the book in order to prove his power; and so he brought a vast calamity on the whole nation. This was not merely their failure as individual revolutionaries, it was also the failure of the governing party which they had participated in creating. And how painful this failure was! In the place where Liu Shaoqi met his end, our appreciation of this point will be especially strong.

Of course, even without the roles played by her leaders, New China could have fallen into the frightful state of being "lawless and godless"; this is closely connected with the character of her people and their traditional ideas. In the ancient city of Kaifeng, we can find an excellent symbol of this point: the Temple of Judge Bao.[33] [cut]

I could easily imagine why the people of Kaifeng had wanted to rebuild such an ancient monument that had long ago ceased to exist, because in truth black-faced Judge Bao still lives in the hearts of the Chinese people, and in those of the Central Plain in particular. He is an ancient but enduring idol. As long as there is resentment in this world, as long as there is injustice and the ghosts of those who died wrongful deaths, then this idol will always possess charisma. Though he frequently appears on the opera stage and on the television screen, in fact in people's hearts he is the fairest of judges. People who have suffered wrong or false accusation in this world can all come to him to seek justice and consolation as well as a release for their anger. [cut] This Judge Bao, as honest as the blue sky, could enable the ancient Chinese concept of rule by men[34] to be balanced and to endure, so

---

[32] See for example Max Weber, The Religion of China: Confucianism and Taoism, chapter I, part 4: "The Charismatic and Pontifical Position of the Central Monarch," pp. 30-32 in the edition by Macmillan, New York, 1964. Several of Max Weber's works were translated into Chinese in the mid-80s in the Xiandai xifang xueshu wenku [Library of Modern Western Scholarship]: The Protestant Ethic and the Spirit of Capitalism, translated by Yu Xiao and Chen Weigang as Xinjiao lunli yu zibenzhuyi jingshen was published in December, 1987 by the Sanlian shudian in Beijing. Also in the same series is Rujiao he daojiao, a translation of Weber's The Religion of China: Confucianism and Taoism.

[33] See Part Five, p. 199.

[34] Contemporary Chinese intellectuals frequently contrast the two notions of ren zhi [rule by men] and fa zhi [rule by law], identifying the former with China and the latter with the West. What Su Xiaokang seems to be saying here is that while Chinese have a traditional concept of justice, as embodied in the figure of Judge Bao, this idea of justice still depends

that his virtue was sufficient to deserve a splendid new temple, even though it was not built until the 80s of the twentieth century. [cut]

To establish democracy and the rule of law in a people with almost no concept of a [social] contract is indeed like building a house on the sand.[35] It's not at all sturdy, for a single touch of wind and it will collapse in an instant. And though a people without a spirit of rule by law will be an obedient populace in times of peace, as soon as they encounter chaos they will definitely act recklessly and desperately, gather to foment turmoil, and like a river in flood destroy everything in their path. This frightening sort of social upheaval has caused China's history to go in recurring cycles, so that calamities are repeated over and over and progress is extremely slow. While Jin Guantao and Liu Qingfeng's theory of "cyclical upsets" is a brand-new view of history,[36] yet if one studied China from the point of view of law, one could reach an identical conclusion. ...

On the 7th day after the lunar new year in 1988 [February 23rd], I temporarily departed from the Heshang script-writing team and flew to Nanchang to write a long "reportage" essay on the Lushan conference of 1959.[37] [cut]

I delved in head first into the summer of 1959 at Lushan, hurriedly scribbling day and night, and only taking time off every evening at seven to watch the news on TV. Those were the days when the meetings of the Seventh National People's Congress and of the Seventh Political Consultative Conference were both being held,[38] so that the news and special reports would always carry some interesting press conferences and speeches by delegates. It was extremely lively and the atmosphere seemed to be thick with democracy. Especially so was the speech by Mr. Qian Jiaju; in thirty minutes he was interrupted by applause thirty-one times, and the problems of education and of social morale that he touched on cut to the quick of our contemporary ills, exciting everyone. [cut] And yet, as we

---

on a "great man" to be realized, and hence the principle of "rule by men" is still superior to that of "rule by law."

[35] See Part Six, p. 209.

[36] See pp. 82-83, 196.

[37] This work, written in collaboration with Chen Zheng and Luo Shixu between February and April of 1988, was published as Wutuobang ji: 1959 nian Lushan zhi xia [Sacrifice in Utopia: The Summer of 1959 at Lushan], Zhongguo xinwen chubanshe, Beijing, November, 1988. The book is a semi-fictional reconstruction of the famous meeting at which Mao dismissed Peng Dehuai and Zhang Wentian for daring to criticize the Great Leap Forward.

[38] The Seventh National People's Congress was held March 25th-April 13th, 1988; the Seventh Political Consultative Congress was convened March 24-April 10, 1988. See also Part Five, p. 201.

watched, the "transparency" of the television news gradually began to fade, and the speeches of delegates that were broadcast gradually came to lose their sharp and cutting edge, becoming more and more tasteless. I began to sense a faint "tightening of the reins." Only later did I discover that this congress was considered to have been too "lax" and reporters to have been too "active." As the time for balloting and elections drew near, disillusionment was increasingly obvious. Only now did I realize that this once again had been a case of schoolboy enthusiasm with overly high expectations, and so I once again delved into that summer of 1959.

Oh, beloved transparency, why have you become opaque again?

Oh, beloved democracy, why must you torment the Chinese people so?

Liu Shaoqi, who died in Kaifeng and was cremated under the false name of Liu Weihuang; plus Peng Dehuai, who likewise died in prison and was cremated under the false name of Wang Chuan; plus Zhang Wentian, who died while under house arrest and who likewise could only be buried under the false name of Zhang Pu—all of these go to show just to what degree of darkness China's government had once descended, and prove that as soon as transparency in government is lost, personalities on the political stage can fall to the point where even the right to die with their own names is taken away, and they don't even understand their own deaths.

Part IV. A Perspective on the "Television Spectacle"

I recall that when I first came up with the proposal to make Heshang (the title then was The Great Artery), not a few people felt that *"its melody was so rarefied that few would harmonize with it"* and that *"only those with a college education or better could understand it."* The most popular television programs in China are: cultural evenings studded with singing stars; comic dialogues; soccer matches on green playing fields; and those awful, interminable foreign soap opera series. Truly, at first we had no way to convince CCTV that a "political" or "reflective" film such as Heshang could attract an audience. Nowhere in the world had television attempted anything similar. We could only do our best to persuade the station that this was an experiment, and even if the audience rating were very low, that they should still let us have a try.

No one even dreamed that in the end Heshang would cause a sensation.

In the middle of July [1988], I was attending a writer's conference in Hainan when I suddenly received a telegram from Xia Jun: *"Situation urgent. Return immediately."* Only when I had raced back to Beijing did I discover that it had been a false alarm. Probably everyone who saw this film, whether in high or low position, all had a feeling of strangeness and of freshness. For those in authority, a literary work that requires any sort of serious thought at all is always somewhat taboo, as they always fear that it could have undesirable consequences adversely affecting "stability and unity." The suffering of the Chinese has bred in them a psychology of timidity, and so this sort of concern is only natural. But I have always felt that China's leaders have overestimated the "magic power" of literature and art; for example, when Mao Zedong proclaimed that *"To use fiction to oppose the Party is a great invention,"*[39] he was really just trying to scare himself. Why should a person who believes that *"Political power grows out of the barrel of a gun"*[40] be so jealous of a few writers playing with pen and ink? If by writing one could seize state power, then with his literary talent Mao Zedong never would have had to run off to the Jinggang hills.

From the beginning, the leadership of the Ministry of Radio, Film and TV as well as of CCTV had treated Heshang as a work of art and literature. From the examination of the scenario, to the viewing of the preliminary version, to the solicitation of opinions after broadcast, they never interfered in the slightest, but only brought in viewers and experts to criticize and discuss it. These days it's common knowledge that a work of art certainly can't be called a success if it arouses no response at all, and no one cares about it; while if everyone praises it, without a single dissenting opinion, then it can only be a mediocre work at best; the best results are only achieved when it arouses controversy, when opinions are diverse, and praise and blame equally divided. CCTV had never before had a film which had had such a broad influence and which gave rise to such fierce praise and blame. This was a mature mark of their having "stood on their own feet at the age of thirty"[41] as well as a great step towards their ultimate participation in high culture. How many viewers sent them warm, effusive thanks and congratulations on Heshang!

But if CCTV had not had a deputy station manager such as Chen Hanyuan, then there would have been no Heshang. [cut]

Chen Hanyuan appeared quite confident in entrusting Heshang to a beardless youth such as Xia Jun. He had no other instructions, but only this one word: *"If you bungle it, stay out of my sight for three years."* That day

---

[39] This statement by Mao Zedong first appeared on May 28, 1967 in Renmin ribao: *"The idea of carrying out anti-party activities through writing novels is new. The overthrow of any regime requires the preparation of public opinion, beginning with ideological work. This is true with the revolutionaries; it is also true with the reactionaries."* Translated in Jerome Ch'en, Mao Papers, London: Oxford University Press, 1970, p. 140.

[40] This quotation originally comes from Mao Zedong's "Problems of War and Strategy" of November 6, 1938, found in vol. II of his Selected Works; it was made famous by its inclusion in Mao's Quotations, where it occurs in section 5, "On War and Peace."

[41] Confucius, Analects, II.4

when he came to hear us explain our proposal to make Heshang, he found no fault with it but said only: "*You are more learned than I am; I believe young people can certainly do better than us, for otherwise China has no hope. I have no request to make of you, but only a little experience to offer for your consideration: to do television in China, you need to have a little tact, so that you can satisfy the 'two olds [er lao].' The one is the 'old comrades' at the Center; the other is the 'old hundred surnames.' If one of them is dissatisfied, then there will be trouble.*" [cut]

Chen Hanyuan loved to describe the changes in China as well as those films that had gotten into trouble with the analogy of an old maid who had gotten pregnant. "*Just think how painful it is, and how unattractive; and how bad your morning sickness is. This person congratulates you on having a boy, while that person swears it will be a girl, so that even before it is born, the debate is raging. By the time you're ready to give birth, it's even worse: your pelvis is already a set size, and the labor is drawn out; it hurts so much you feel as if you're going to die. If all goes well, you'll have a Caesarean birth; but if things go badly, then either the infant will die in the womb, or in the worst case, neither mother nor child can be saved. Anyway, it's not all that easy.*"

In the end, Heshang was born. But perhaps it had birth defects or was a preemie, for some people found it not at all pleasing to the eye, and there were many who critiqued its head and legs. But Chen Hanyuan cared for it like his own kid, unlike some leaders who looked on it as illegitimate. Despite clearly knowing that it was their own flesh and blood, they always suspected it of being some sort of bastard. Feeling fed up with it, they would always want to give it a kick or two and box its ears.

Chen Hanyuan would just silently wipe off the aspersions that had been cast on it. For he had acknowledged this unlikeable child as his own.

In truth, I had never imagined that Heshang, which at first we feared not too many viewers would enjoy, would later be such a hit. When I got back from Hainan, it had only been about a week since the broadcast had concluded, but Xia Jun gave me nearly a thousand letters from viewers. Of the "two olds," at least the "old hundred surnames" were in favor of it.

The range of the letters was very broad. From intellectuals to officials, from officers in the army and armed police to workers and young peasants, from students to old cadres, without distinction of age, occupation, or educational level, all seemed interested in Heshang. [cut]

Among the letters from high school students, the one that made the biggest impression on me was this passage written by a fifteen year old girl at the high school attached to People's University: "*When I lived through the 'Great Cultural Revolution,' I was still very, very small, and couldn't* *remember things, so that now I don't have any impression of it at all. But when I saw in <u>Heshang</u> some scenes reflecting the conditions of that time, I urgently wanted to know what the China of that time was like. When I saw some of those scenes on TV, such as: young people waving the little red book and yelling "Long Life!" upon seeing Chairman Mao, so moved that hot tears filled their eyes; or the 'fervor' of people at a criticism meeting; or the situation during the 'Great Leap Forward'—I felt I didn't understand them at all, didn't understand why they were that way."* This passage indeed shocked me far more than did those articles upbraiding <u>Heshang</u> for "historical nihilism." Though less than twenty years have passed, the children of today are as ignorant of the Cultural Revolution as if it belonged to another century; they find it extremely strange as well as inconceivable— this fact sends shivers down my spine. When I recall how I was a Red Guard myself in those days, I would have found it very hard to predict whether at any time in the future Chinese young people would ever again madly rush onto the streets under the incitement of a revolutionary slogan. Nobody is telling the next generation what the Cultural Revolution was all about; and even less are there people seriously analysing the deep social causes of that calamity and the mechanism which triggered it. On the contrary, it would seem as if we deliberately want to make people forget it. I think, could this perhaps not qualify as the only true case of "historical nihilism"? [cut]

I have much greater respect for <u>Heshang</u>'s influence amongst youth, no matter whether they approve of it or oppose it. During the summer, Wuhan organized a summer camp with <u>Heshang</u> as the main theme; young people organized speeches and an essay contest. In the fall, Guangzhou [Canton] had an "Operation Blueness" attended by a million young people, which also was to debate <u>Heshang</u>. These days, what can you use to attract the interest of so many young people?

Everyone says that 1988 was "a time to howl."

Part V. Tell Me, How Many Bends Does the Yellow River Make?

<u>Heshang</u> had the whole country in an uproar. Its various ups and downs and the struggles surrounding it became one of the hottest topics of the dragon year.

That a single TV film should be broadcast twice on national TV; reprinted in all the big newspapers; its script published and republished in book form, and copies of its video tape spreading like wildfire; discussed repeatedly by scholars and experts and debated by a million people throughout the Yangtze Valley and the South; praised by some as a "Li

Sao" or "Guo Shang"[42] and denounced by others for having "forgotten our ancestors," diametrically-opposed praise and blame more or less balancing out; reported on constantly in the Hongkong, Taiwan and overseas press; now suddenly released by the authorities and now just as suddenly banned, with the ruckus lasting altogether nearly six months before reaching the very highest councils in the land[43]—this may well be considered a grand spectacle in the world of Chinese TV.

I passed my days in a trance, stunned, as if without having stopped to count their three heads and six arms I had carelessly let some monsters out of the bottle and thus stirred up a great commotion, ultimately inviting disaster in the form of a lightning stroke of anger from above...

The "Heshang phenomenon" was so cleverly and so intangibly transformed from a phenomenon of television and of culture into a scary political phenomenon, that it in our hearts we could really never stop grumbling.

What were, then, the "monsters" that Heshang released?[44] According to director Xia Jun's original intention, this film was to bring the world of thought into television. I made a careful count, that the six-part series probably touched on the following purely scholarly viewpoints: Marx's thesis about the Asiatic mode of production[45]; Hegel's view that the natural geographic environment is the foundation of history[46]; Toynbee's view about the internal mechanisms of civilizations[47]; Joseph Needham's

---

[42] The titles of two poems by Qu Yuan, famous as the loyal minister of King Huai of Chu, who wouldn't listen to his wise advice, warning of imminent danger to the state.

[43] Heshang's critics and its supporters differ in their accounts of this inner-party struggle. According to the article by Jin Ren in Heshang pipan, Vice-President Wang Zhen tried to bring up the matter of criticizing Heshang at the meeting of the 3rd Plenum of the 13th Party Congress in late September 1988, but was rebuffed by General Secretary Zhao Ziyang. Subsequently, an article by Yi Jiayan [pseud.] entitled, "What does Heshang preach?" is said to have been suppressed on Zhao's express orders. [pp. 20-21] According to the article by He Shaoming in the December 1988 issue of Zheng ming, General Secretary Zhao Ziyang announced at a joint meeting of the Politburo and Secretariat that it was normal to have different viewpoints about Heshang, and that both sides could publish critical articles; that in this debate one should strictly avoid flaunting one's power; and that it would be strictly forbidden to engage in a "great critique" [da pipan] as had been practised in the Cultural Revolution. [p. 12]

[44] The following passage is extensively quoted and analysed in "Historians in the Capital Criticize Heshang"; see pp. 313-314.

[45] See Part One, "Searching for a Dream," p. 110.

[46] For references to Hegel, see Part Two, "Destiny," footnote 14.

[47] Presumably this refers to the view of Toynbee cited in Part One, "Searching for a Dream," that *"History has proven countless times that the decline of a civilization is not*

description of the history of China's science and technology[48]; H.G. Wells' account of Chinese history in his Outline of History[49]; Francis Bacon's description of China's four great inventions[50]; Zhang Guangzhi's comparison of Chinese and Mayan civilizations[51]; Ray Huang's proof that ancient China lacked a classical form of private ownership[52]; Deng Xiaoping's ideas about reform and opening up to the outside[53]; Zhao Ziyang's discussion of the socialist commodity economy[54]; Plekhanov's belief that the stage of the commodity economy cannot be skipped over[55]; Li Yining's proposal for structural reform of the economy[56]; Jin Guantao's "super-stable structure" theory, and so forth.[57] Herein there are Marxist classics; there are core components of Western culture which served as the origin of Marxism; there are the thoughts of famous contemporary Western scholars and overseas Chinese researchers and scholars; and there are the results of the research of contemporary Chinese scholars. No matter whether they be masters in the orthodox tradition or new persons with new theories, we have regarded each of them as an individual authority,[58] blending their

---

caused by attack from external forces, but rather by the degeneration of its internal mechanisms." See also Part One, footnote 45.

[48] Presumably this refers to Needham's statement quoted in Part Three, "The Light of the Spirit," that *"Chinese are the most faithful and accurate astronomical observers on this planet."* See footnote 4.

[49] Wells is quoted in Part Three, "The Light of the Spirit," p. 145

[50] Bacon is quoted in Part Three, "The Light of the Spirit," pp. 146-147.

[51] The views of Zhang Guangzhi [K.C. Chang] are cited in Part One, "Searching for a Dream, pp. 110, 112.

[52] This view is attributed to "some Western scholars" in Part Four, "The New Era," p. 164.

[53] The 3rd Plenum of the Eleventh Party Congress at which Deng's reform program was announced is mentioned in Part Four, "The New Era," p. 161.

[54] Zhao's speech at the 13th Party Congress in October 1987 is quoted in Part Four, "The New Era," p. 172.

[55] The disagreement between Plekhanov and Lenin is cited in Part Four, p. 160.

[56] Li Yining is known for his advocacy of reform of the system of ownership. He appears in an on-screen interview in Part Four, pp. 176-178

[57] Many of Jin Guantao's ideas are referred to in Part Five, "Sorrow and Worry"; an on-screen interview occurs on pp. 197-199.

[58] "Individual authority" translates the Chinese expression yi jia zhi yan. One of the first attacks on Heshang, entitled "Heshang xuanyang le shenme? [What has Heshang preached?] was written under the pseudonym Yi Jiayan [i.e., An Individual Authority] in the fall of 1988. According to Heshang's critics, this article was suppressed by Zhao Ziyang's express order and hence was not published until July of 1989. The article "Historians in the Capital Criticize Heshang" translated in this volume also takes issue with this statement, saying that to treat Marx as an "individual authority" is to ignore Marxism's leading role.

various parts together, to forge the strong cry of this present age that we wish to shout: Aside from modernization, China has no other way out.

In my view, no matter what sort of ugly aspersions people may cast on Heshang, they are in the final analysis profaning the strong national aspirations of modern Chinese and are defeating the Chinese nation's hopes for making itself strong and prosperous. In this sense, Heshang's hard times are hard times for China's reforms.

The first criticisms of Heshang to ooze forth were a whole string of lofty comments full of satirical "fervor," such as: "*fin-de-siècle thornbirds*"; "*a narrow view of culture*"; "*side-stepping the dangers of criticizing the status quo in order to flog our ancestors with impunity*"; "*high-class bitching*"; and so forth.[59] At that time, in the midst of the uniform praise for Heshang, this was a note of dissonance far removed from the hoi polloi. Not that our Heshang script-writers would listen only to what pleased the ear and not to what offended it; it's just that on listening to this first voice of criticism, it wasn't an open and aboveboard argument but rather gave one the feeling of being a covert attack, which really made [Wang] Luxiang and [Xie] Xuanjun feel a nagging anxiety in their hearts, and made them angry enough to want to counter-attack. I urged them not to pay any attention and to be tolerant. But I felt that a certain ulterior motive lurked in this criticism; scolding us for "*not daring to criticize the status quo*," for example, is the sort of prejudice of those who "*never tire of malicious gossip.*" Later events would prove that even "flogging our ancestors" was by no means safe. I had rather hoped that these brave critics would set us an example of "criticizing the status quo." When I thought about it later, this sort of scholar has existed in China's literary circles since ancient times; they are those who specialize in "nit-picking," "quarreling," and "serving other masters."

---

[59] These criticisms all come from one article entitled "Jiqing de yin ying" [The Other Side of Fervor] written under the pseudonyms of Wang Xiaodong and Qiu Tiancao and which first appeared in Zhongguo qingnian bao, July 10, 1988; it was reprinted in Heshang lun, pp. 192-196, to which Xie Xuanjun contributed a rebuttal article. In the first version of "Longnian de beichuang" which appeared in November, 1988, Su Xiaokang treats Qiu Tiancao with heavy sarcasm: "*The first critics of Heshang to ooze forth were some 'gentleman burglars' who are not a part of the scholarly world but who like to pass themselves off as experts. Master 'Qiu Tiancao,' who is said to be a television critic, fired the first shot. ... This first attack was quickly taken up by those in authority, who immediately placed it on the desk of the leaders of CCTV, asking that they take this criticism seriously, that this was proof that Heshang was by no means perfect and free of fault. This is truly a case of 'the crooked attacking the straight'; according to a friend, Mr. Qiu Tiancao has a habit of 'pouring cold water' on whatever is popular... if I can guess his intention, it derives from a certain 'dark horse' logic, that it is easiest to become famous by vilifying famous people.*" See "Longnian de beichuang" in Cui Wenhua, ed., Haiwai Heshang da taolun, esp. pp. 81-82.

Following on the first wave were a group of people who had already lost patience with theory and with the task of enlightenment but who couldn't bear not taking part in a ruckus. About Heshang they said such things as: *"It merely uses excessively serious language to discuss things that everyone knows, problems that are not problems"*[60]; or they called it *"historical nihilism and racial nihilism"*[61]; or they said *"it uses an anti-aircraft gun to shoot mosquitoes"*[62]; or they said: *"they are hallucinating and mentally unbalanced"*[63] and so forth. Listening to such statements made one feel as if they came from another world, from immortals in heaven watching the human comedy below, who didn't have to exert themselves like contemporary Chinese to be fed and clothed, to make money, to seek solutions and ideals. Of course, they had a little more of the air of theory about them, and they loved to use a very profound tone to dismiss Heshang as "shallow," "simple" or "alarmist." Even if I could exclude the question of the purity of their motives, at the most I could say: they want to continue with a sort of tea-party, ivory-tower scholarship and view any attempt at bringing thought to the masses as vulgar and crude. Truly, Lu Xun put it

---

[60] This criticism comes from an article by Ding Tao, entitled "Heshang de shiluo," first published in Zhongguo wenhua bao, July 31st, 1988 and reprinted in Heshang lun, pp. 175-179.

[61] When this charge was first published and by whom is unclear. The charge of "historical nihilism" [lishi xuwuzhuyi] is mentioned in an article entitled "Dianshi ju Heshang de fengbo" [The Storm Surrounding the TV film Heshang] by Huang Ertang published in the August, 1988 issue of Zheng ming: *"But it is said that there were four 'well-known professors' who, in imitation of the way in which two years previously Profs. Qian Weizhang and Fei Xiaotong had 'closed ranks with the Party,' wrote a letter to Hu Qili describing the situation, expressing their view that Heshang was not merely a work that opposed the traditional culture of our people but also that it was a seriously self-deprecating work of historical nihilism, and that 'on the ideological battlefront, it was extremely dangerous.' And so, after receiving this report, the high officials of Zhongnanhai ordered copies of the six-part series Heshang sent over for their inspection..."*

[62] The author and source of this charge is also unclear, but series co-author Yuan Zhiming took issue with it in an article published in Guangming ribao on August 18th, 1988 entitled "Heshang yu 'gaoji laosao'—xie zai Heshang chongbo zhi ji" [Heshang and 'high-class bitching'—written on the occasion of the rebroadcast of Heshang]. He says: *"When I joined in the writing of Heshang, I never imagined that the reaction to it would be so strong. Even less did I imagine that this film which advocates reform and opening up to the outside and which has made many viewers feel 'spiritually stimulated' should be deemed by some comrades as a sort of 'high-class bitching' that 'uses an anti-aircraft gun to shoot at mosquitoes.'"*

[63] The source of this criticism is from a published interview with Wang Ling and Wu Xin entitled "Heshang fanying le yi zhong shiheng xintai" [Heshang reflects an unbalanced mentality], first published in the August, 1988 issue of Zhongguo wenhua bao and reprinted in Heshang lun, pp. 180-186.

very well when he said: "*The power of the majority is great and important. If those who are determined to make reforms do not have a deep understanding of the psychology of the masses and establish means to channel it, then no matter how lofty their discourse, how romantic or classical, it will have no relation to them [the masses], and so will merely be limited to a few persons sighing in their studies and obtaining a little self-satisfaction...*"

Naturally, a work such as Heshang which boldly discusses the rise and fall of the state is rather taboo in China. Those who hide in their studies to pursue scholarship may say that we "*speak wild words and overestimate our importance*"; those who pursue office or fortune instead of scholarship may say we "*have a schoolboy's temperament, only seeking a moment's amusement*"; those who value the tradition may say that we "*have not read the Four Books and Five Classics, and so should stop talking about our ancestors*"; those who oppose tradition may say we "*have no foundation in western learning, so how do we dare to discuss culture?.*"... Actually, there's nothing wrong with such a broad discussion. I once asked Xia Jun,"*If with our limited [intellectual] capital, we try to steal the rice-bowl of the theorists, and make lofty statements on TV, aren't you afraid we'll be attacked?*" But Xia Jun said: "*That would be great! Several years ago, during the "passion for studying culture," it was precisely because the forum of discussion was too limited and the masses totally unconcerned, that there were only a few scholars arguing back and forth, and even they didn't have much enthusiasm for it.*" The original intention of Heshang was precisely to stir up a great debate, and while there was some static when the curtain went up, yet in the end everyone from ordinary people to scholars started to engage in debate...

But we never imagined that in this very changeable climate—now cloudy, now clear, now sunny, now dark, now hot, now cold—there would be a sudden sea-change: "*You vilify the Chinese nation and Chinese civilization*"; "*you want to restore capitalism*"; "*intellectuals are dangerous, if the Japanese were to invade, these associate professors and graduate students would all be on the welcoming committee*"[64]; "*if this continues, it will be the end of the Party and of the country...*"

---

[64] Su Xiaokang does not name the author of this statement, but it is attributed to Vice-President Wang Zhen by Liu Yanying in an article in the November issue of Jing bao. "It is said that on approximately September 21st [1988] Wang Zhen summoned Tan Wenrui, editor-in-chief of Renmin ribao, to his residence and launched an attack on Heshang. Wang Zhen said *I have seen Heshang ten times, and each time it makes me mad. Heshang totally denies Chinese history, so that there are no good men; but wasn't Sun Yatsen a good man?* Holding in his hand a New China News Agency report about Zhao Ziyang and [Singapore Prime Minister] Li Kuan-yew discussing Heshang, he said, *Even if the General Secretary supports Heshang; even if the Central Committee supports Heshang, I am still against it;*

As soon as Heshang became a "political problem," then all of a sudden everyone was struck dumb. Only occasionally, in the midst of silence, would a few overseas personalities utter a few moderate and reserved statements...[65] [cut]

Everyone had no choice but to shut up. [cut]

Over the past hundred years, despite all the efforts Chinese intellectuals have put into the construction of a [new] culture, it is still the case that "*a scholar in the right/ can't beat a soldier in a fight.*"[66] One day when Huaren shijie [The Chinese World] was holding a round-table discussion, Comrade Li Rui[67] of the Central Advisory Commission spoke up: "*Isn't the wide divergence of opinion on many questions today not due perhaps to a*

---

they won't take away my Party membership for that! His secretary reminded him of the sense of a Politburo resolution, that there should be no direct interference with works of literature and art. Wang said, *I will too interfere with Heshang. I've told [Deng] Xiaoping my point of view. Renmin ribao should start a critique of Heshang.* Wang Zhen also said: *Su Xiaokang was the 'black' chief-of-staff of the 'February 7th Commune' and a 'rebel Red Guard.'... Li Yining supports reform of the system of ownership, he wants to bring back capitalism. I've taken a look at their files. I fought so many years for victory, but never imagined that I had raised up such a gang of associate professors and graduate students. If the Japanese were to attack, why, they would be on the reception committee. I don't have much education; intellectuals are dangerous!* Wang Zhen also said, *... Chairman Mao was a remarkable man... Even if you say Chairman Mao is no good, I'll still hang his picture on my wall nevertheless. ... He also said, Out of two thousand delegates [to the National People's Congress] there were three hundred who opposed my becoming Vice-President, but haven't I become Vice-President all the same?*" A second account of Wang Zhen's comments is provided by He Shaoming, writing in the December 1988 issue of Zheng ming.

[65] Presumably this is a reference to the statements by Nobel laureates Yang Zhenning and Li Zhengdao. Li Zhengdao's statement, included in a speech to the student body at Nankai Univ. on October 26th, 1988, was published in both Guangming ribao and Renmin ribao on November 4th, 1988. The original source of Yang's statement is not clear. Both were reprinted in Cui Wenhua, ed., Haiwai Heshang da taolun, pp. 26-30.

[66] This may be interpreted as a lightly-veiled reference to Vice-President Wang Zhen, who holds the rank of general. Jin Ren, writing in Heshang pipan, cites this line as follows: *In October of last year [1988], in his "The Distress of a Dragon Year—notes on Heshang," Su Xiaokang unleashed a flood of invective against the correct criticism made by Wang Zhen and other comrades, saying 'a scholar who's in the right, can't beat a soldier in a fight' and went on to say that the policy of 'non-interference in questions of literature and art' would always vanish like a soap-bubble when push came to shove. [p. 24]* Only the first version of Su Xiaokang's article, published in November 1988, contains the comment about the policy of non-interference in literature.

[67] Li Rui, a former member of the Yellow River Planning Commission and the author of two books on the management of the Yellow River, was elected to the Central Advisory Commission in September, 1985. See Bartke, ed., Who's Who in the People's Republic of China, p. 240.

generation gap? I hope that young people will voluntarily seek out their elders and make contact." I think that Comrade Li Rui was entirely well-intentioned. But I feel that the struggle between the China of the young and the China of the old cannot be smoothed over. For the result of such smoothing over is always that we must endure more years in filial worship of our elders and ancestors, helpless to do anything but accept an outcome in which "*the flowers about to fade are even worse than those dead trees.*"[68] These days I've frequently been discussing China's history with Liu Dong, Li Zehou's brilliant pupil and doctoral student. [cut] He says that Chinese culture is actually a sort of aesthetic culture, which in terms of human civilization is already at a high spiritual level. Unfortunately, this sort of culture is weak and can't stand up to attack. Ever since the Opium War, we have been forced into the position of having no choice but to close ranks with Western culture or face the extinction of our nation and people. [cut] When the "self-strengthening" faction was defeated in their attempt at reform on the level of technology, the reform movement of 1898 and the 1911 revolutionaries took drastic action at the level of institutional reform, only to lose their heads and spill their blood. Reform at these two levels being insufficient to reverse China's decline, the May 4th Movement was forced to address the basic cultural level, that of concepts of value. Due to the urgent need to save our nation, however, this stirring and exciting musical passage has had to be played over from the beginning.[69] With regards to the construction of a new culture, China needs her intellectuals to bury themselves in their studies and research rooms to engage in rational criticism and in the transfer of knowledge, but this vast work of engineering requiring the cooperative efforts of several generations to complete is constantly being interrupted by crises of the present, and so there are only two possible tragic outcomes for China's intellectuals: they can either be a Hu Shih or a Chen Duxiu...[70]

---

[68] One possible interpretation is: the old leaders who aren't dead yet are worse than those already in their graves.

[69] In other words, the impetus of the May Fourth movement was lost due to the struggle to resist Japanese aggression and has only been revived in recent times.

[70] Both Hu Shih [1891-1962] and Chen Duxiu [1880-1942] were intellectuals active in the May Fourth movement. Hu Shih was best known for his advocacy of using the spoken language (bai hua) to replace the classical language; Chen Duxiu was influential through his editorship of the magazine Xin qingnian [New Youth]. Their tragedies perhaps consist in that they did not continue to have the influence in later years that should have been theirs. Hu Shih was a disciple of Dewey, but Dewey's philosophy never caught on, and Hu Shih is now remembered for his researches on Chinese literature and religion. While he never joined a political party, he did serve as China's ambassador in Washington during World War II. On mainland China, his reputation is sullied for having advocated "wholesale Westernization" and for having supported the KMT. Chen Duxiu was one of the founders of the Chinese Communist Party in 1921 and served as General Secretary until 1927. Yet he spent the last half of his life under house arrest by the Kuomintang, while as

Liu Dong chattered on. I listened to him quietly, but I couldn't help hearing that famous song from Hequ with which Heshang begins:

Tell me,
How many bends does the Yellow River make?

Indeed, to realize China's modernization, who knows how many bends must be traversed, and how many rapids; how many unavoidable repetitions of history must there be, and how many accidental mistakes; how many retreats that come in the midst of progress, and how much of a price that can never be paid off?

Drafted November, 1988 in Beijing

---

early as 1929 he was stripped of membership in the communist party on a charge of Trotskyism; to this day he has not been rehabilitated.

"Deathsong of the River: Whither Chinese Culture?"

by Tu Wei-ming[1]

We may say that the "Heshang phenomenon" is an unprecedented cultural phenomenon; that is, by presenting an essay on culture in the form of a television film, it has aroused a great debate. Within mainland China, all sorts of discussions have emerged; discussions have been lively also in Taiwan; while in North America and in Hong Kong, quite a few people have seen it and voiced their opinions as well.

Essentially, everyone would like to engage in a serious discussion of the question raised by Heshang—we may say that Heshang did not reach any conclusions but merely raised a serious and thorny question: whither Chinese culture? Basically, Heshang takes the position that if the Yellow River represents Chinese culture, then its milk has run dry. And why has China followed along the route charted by Confucianism? If it had not followed this route, wouldn't the present situation be a little better? While people regard the Yellow River as representing Chinese culture, in fact the Yellow River is "China's Sorrow," for it overflows and causes disasters.

---

[1] Tu Wei-ming [Du Weiming] is Director of the Institute of Culture and Communication at the East-West Center in Honolulu and Professor of Chinese History and Philosophy at Harvard University. This article is the substance of a conversation between the editors of the monthly magazine Dushu and Professor Tu held in the lobby of the Prince Hotel, Kowloon, Hong Kong, on Christmas Day, 1988. It was published in Chinese in Su Xiaokang, et al., Longnian de beichuang: guanyu Heshang de zhaji, Sanlian shudian, Hong Kong, 1989, pp. 51-61. The translators offer grateful thanks to Prof. Tu for permission to use his article and for elucidating several points. Words inside square brackets in the text are supplied by the translators, as are all the footnotes. Prof. Tu is known for his thesis that many elements of traditional Chinese culture and Confucianism are valuable resources as China faces the challenge of the modern world. Subsequently, Su Xiaokang responded to some of Tu Weiming's points in "Guanyu liyong chuantong ziyuan—yu Du Weiming jiaoshou zai Bali yixi tan" [On Making Use of the Resources of the Tradition—a Conversation in Paris with Prof. Tu Wei-ming] in Minzhu Zhongguo, June 1990, pp. 52-55. Tu Wei-ming's recent article: "Cultural China: The Periphery as Center" in Daedalus, Spring 1991, pp. 1-32 incorporates some of his most recent thinking.

I rather enjoy the sort of cultural approach that Heshang has taken. None of the television films I have seen in the U.S. or other countries have employed the same approach—that is, to present a scholarly essay in the form of television. Of course, they might have gotten some ideas from elsewhere, such as Japanese television's cultural inquiry into the Yellow River from ancient times to the present.[2] However, this academic essay basically starts with an idea representing the major current of thought among young people in China: that the only solution for China's problems is, if not "wholesale Westernization" [quanpan xihua], then at least "sufficient Westernization" [chongfen xihua] or "overall Westernization" [quan fangwei xihua]. People such as Bao Zunxin[3] basically hold this view. Wang Luxiang, in designing the film, suggested the concept of a "sense of social concern" [youhuan yishi], which has a strong native Chinese sense and which is quite valuable for engaging in an all-out reflection [fansi] on Chinese culture. Su Xiaokang is a writer of reportage literature and writes with a vivid style. Xie Xuanjun, a student of cultural anthropology, raised two points in Heshang: that the dragon is the evil creature of the natural world, and that the emperor is the evil tyrant of the human world. When combined, these two forces become the symbol of Chinese culture. I think this idea is too extreme, but perhaps his ideas have changed somewhat. He may well have over-simplified the cultural symbolism of the dragon for China's early people as well as its symbolic associations throughout the entire history of China's cultural development. Since the dragon is a composite totem, its shape may resemble that of a lizard; its feet, those of a goat; its body, that of a snake; its scales, those of a fish; and its claws, those of an eagle. It has many other characteristics as well, so we can say that it has represented the composite psychology of Chinese culture.

As a matter of fact, these days we have gradually discovered that the source of Chinese culture is not the Wei River Valley. Although the authors of Heshang have cited the ideas of Zhang Guangzhi[4] [K.C. Chang], they did not present his ideas very clearly. At present most archaeologists believe that China's culture did not derive from a single root or source and then slowly radiate outward, either from the Wei River Valley or the Yellow

---

[2] Referring to the joint production by CCTV and NHK of a thirty-part television documentary series entitled Huang he, released in 1988.

[3] An historian and researcher at the Chinese Academy of Social Sciences, Bao Zunxin has exchanged views with Tu Weiming in print on several occasions. An activist in the Spring of 1989, Bao Zunxin is now serving a five-year prison term. See also Part Six, pp. 216-217 and footnote 47.

[4] Prof.K.C. Chang of Harvard University is author of The Archaeology of Ancient China and many other studies of the archaeology of China's neolithic and bronze age cultures.

River Valley; rather, even before the neolithic period, China's culture was already pluralistic. The Red Mountain [Hong shan] culture recently discovered in the northeast, the black pottery culture, the colored pottery culture, even the jade-carving culture as well as those in the Shanghai area, had all appeared very early on. Very slowly, these cultures came together to form China. In the early period of its development, Chinese culture took shape under the mutual influence and impetus of agricultural and pastoral civilizations. This conflict existed a long time, from ancient times down to the Qing dynasty.

In addition, Heshang also mentioned the Confucian tradition. The authors feel that Confucianism may have done some good things in the past, but as far as the present is concerned, they use a very strange term: "auto-toxemia" [ziti zhongdu].[5] This means that whenever a system has developed to a certain point—usually we say that if a mechanism is still lively, that it is a feedback system, but that when it has reached a certain point, not only is it no longer a feedback system, but it even produces the poison to destroy itself. Hence at the very end the Confucian tradition will destroy itself. This is an idea I cannot accept.

The first three installments of Heshang are rather convincing; what is most problematic is the final conclusion. Its conclusion hints at the following sort of idea: that the life strength of everything represented by the color yellow—the yellow soil plateau and the Yellow River—has already declined; if we want to make further progress, then we must embrace "blueness" and the ocean. What the ocean represents is Western civilization, just as the Aegean Sea represents the spirit of Greek civilization. In the last installment, Heshang fails to mention exactly which ocean it is into which the Yellow River flows. It should clearly point out that it is the Pacific Ocean, and not the Atlantic. Although Bao Zunxin has said so, he was not very clear. For if indeed it does flow into the Pacific, then it must necessarily have reached Industrial East Asia, including Japan, Korea, Taiwan, Hong Kong and Singapore; and this Industrial East Asia is, as the Japanese put it, a Confucian cultural region. We believe that the present vitality of Industrial East Asia cannot be considered exclusively as a special manifestation of western civilization, but rather that it is a new sort of industrial civilization formed from the combination of many resources from the tradition of East Asian society (i.e., the Confucian cultural region). This new industrial civilization—the so-called "rise of the Pacific Rim"—even threatens Western Europe and the U.S. This is a topic which Heshang has by no means discussed sufficiently.

---

[5] This would appear to mean that Chinese civilization is suffering from an auto-immune disease.

Many people say that <u>Heshang</u> should have a sequel, but that they should not be the ones to write it. The questions they wanted to ask have already been asked, and if they were to write the sequel it would not be a success. It would be best if the sequel were written by other people and represent a different point of view.

Of the various images of Chinese culture mentioned by <u>Heshang,</u> such as the dragon, the Yellow River, and the Great Wall, they believe that the Great Wall is the symbol of the sort of closed mind that has locked up the Chinese people and prevented them from developing outward; while the flooding and disasters caused by the Yellow River mean that it is a culture that has already dried up, or that it had past glory but does not represent our future. As for the dragon, I have already discussed it above.

There's one very interesting point, which is that <u>Heshang</u>'s topics are excessively concentrated in China's northeast; this is a Beijing-centered ideology which has not faced the challenge of Shanghai, nor has it looked at Guangzhou [Canton], nor has it encountered the Yangtze River or the Pearl River. Mr. Liu Zijian [James T.C. Liu][6] once brought up the idea that one of Chinese civilization's special characteristics was that it was the product of the interaction of two river valleys. Nile River civilization, such as the cultures of Babylon [sic] and Egypt, was the product of one river valley, and was destroyed whenever it was invaded by foreign tribes. China, on the other hand, had two river valleys, and so whenever the north was invaded, they could move to the south. Many people have researched the history of the development of Chinese civilization and have discovered that its economic center and to some extent its cultural center have gradually moved from north to south. In the early period when Chinese civilization arose, it was primarily in the north. If we talk about "culture," then it was in the Shandong and Xi'an regions. Gradually, during the period of the Wei, the Jin, the Three Kingdoms, and the Northern and Southern dynasties, it moved to the Yangtze River valley. Clearly, between the Tang and the Song dynasties, the south became increasingly important. After that [Chinese civilization] gradually extended to the Pearl River Valley. Following the Opium War, revolutionaries and progressives were mostly people from Hunan, Zhejiang, and Guangdong. In contrast, northerners were comparatively few. At present, the momentum of reform is spreading from south to north. This situation is something to which <u>Heshang</u> should have devoted more attention, especially since it suggests embracing "blueness" and moving toward the Pacific.

---

[6] James T.C. Liu is Professor Emeritus in the Department of East Asian Studies at Princeton University.

There is yet another problem, which is the dilemma encountered by the young theoreticians of "sufficient Westernization" or "complete Westernization." If we may take Bao Zunxin as an example, his dilemma consists in that *"what I know best and have personally experienced are all what I do not want; that which in my opinion can save us and our people is all unfamiliar to me and even unknown to me, or at least is something I haven't personally experienced."* We may put it this way: what should have been brought in—such as democracy, freedom, and human rights—has not been brought in; what should have been kept out—such as superficial European and American fads, "bourgeois liberalization," "spiritual pollution" and so forth—has not been kept out; what should have been preserved from the tradition—such as the finest elements of Chinese culture—have not been preserved; what should have been discarded—such as the lingering effects of feudalism [fengjian liudu], the conservatism created by the small-holder farm economy, and outdated forms of social interaction [renji guanxi]—have not been discarded. In sum, what should have been preserved from the tradition has not been preserved, and what should have been discarded has not been discarded; as for Western culture, what should have been brought in has not been brought in, and what should have been kept out has not been kept out. In this sort of dilemma, they merely made an existential decision, i.e., *"I may as well just harden my heart and go ahead and embrace what I do not know, because that which I do know cannot save me, it is my 'auto-toxin.'"*

But the problem consists in that other people have already come to know that which you do not know. Many people highly sensitive to comparative cultures have done a great deal of research, both on Western and on East Asian cultures. Of course, the West has its own problems, and China has its own difficulties. The problems the West has run into are by no means smaller than the difficulties we have encountered. Nonetheless, what Heshang wants to embrace is not our future. There's no arguing that contemporary Western civilization has tapped many wellsprings of civilization for humankind, such as science, democracy, freedom, human rights, the market economy, and so forth; but Western civilization has also brought humanity to the brink of self-destruction and even to the point of destroying both mankind and the ecosystem which has taken shape over billions of years—this is a fact that's clear to anyone whose eyes are open. Quite a few outstanding thinkers in the contemporary West have begun to engage in a rather profound reflection on the principal direction of the spirit of contemporary Western civilization, and if this direction of the spirit were to be accepted by other peoples, then human civilization might change its course in a rather short time. The attitude of Bao Zunxin and people like him is that this is their [i.e. Westerners'] business, for they have already tasted the fruits of modern civilization and are already at the post-industrial stage of civilization. *"But we haven't [reached this stage], so don't tell me not to want modern civilization, for that is precisely what I do want."* That is to say, "*I clearly realize that it's awful, but I want it anyway, because I haven't had the chance to savor it yet.*"

But the problem is, if there were only one form of modernization, then you would have to have it, whether you liked it or not; there would be no other path to choose. This was the common realization of China's outstanding intellectuals in the May Fourth Period, and at that time it was correct. In the May Fourth Period, modernization was none other than Westernization; there was no other path to take. And so the most radical suggestion raised to oppose traditionalism during the May Fourth Period was to abolish Chinese characters, for the abolition of Chinese characters would be an authentic and thorough-going Westernization, because Chinese characters were the true symbol of Chinese culture. Chinese characters are not only tools of communication but also tools for identification and self-understanding. At present, even the most radical advocates of Westernization have to use Chinese characters to express their inmost feelings; on the mainland at present, you couldn't find anyone who would say, "*From now on, let's not use Chinese writing any more.*" I believe that whenever one uses Chinese writing or rather the ideas expressed by Chinese characters, then significant elements of Confucianism are present; and if this is true, then in order to "become reborn" and make a complete break with tradition, one would have to give up the Chinese written word. Yet the great majority of people would not, and could not, accept this. This means that modernization can be realized in differing cultural forms. Perhaps this was not possible in the May Fourth Period, but it is possible today. For example, we know that we can see three forms of industrial civilization nowadays: European and American, Soviet and Eastern European, and Industrial East Asian. Since modernization can be expressed through a variety of cultural forms, that means that the choice of a culture with which to realize it is up to you. What you [Bao Zunxin] have chosen is to discard all the resources of the tradition in order to embrace that which you do not know. But when you go begging for a meal [of Western civilization], what they will give you will certainly not be the best; they won't give you the choicest fish and fowl but will only give you their left-overs. In this situation, you will have lost your self-respect and self-confidence and still be unable to bring in the best things from other people [i.e. the West]; and so, you will only be able to return to the way things were before.

The dilemma faced by intellectuals in mainland China today was not caused by our long-enduring, Confucian-centered Chinese culture. It may seem very complex when we talk about it. It is the combination of the "lingering poison of feudalism" with a very complex modern form, and this very complex modern form is none other than politics. Yet politics cannot be discussed, and even if one wished to, where would one begin? Yet nevertheless we can put it this way: since the Opium War, only somewhat more than a century has passed, but its interaction with the five thousand years of development of Chinese culture has been rather complex. Yet what has most affected the hearts of Chinese intellectuals have been our traditional feelings of sorrow and anger [at the nation's predicament], a tradition in which we would sacrifice everything in order to save the nation from danger. Mr. Zhang Dainian[7] once mentioned a poem written by a youth during the anti-Japanese war: "*Four hundred million fellow country-men / Each and every one of them a bastard.*" [hundan] He brought this up in the midst of feelings of extreme anger and sorrow, in a sort of self-awareness and self-condemnation. The distorted psychological state brought about by the various humiliations people have suffered over the past hundred-odd years is understandable. From May Fourth to the present, there has constantly re-occurred a sort of vicious cycle caused by a strong desire for Westernization and a narrow nationalism. As the vicious cycle gets progressively more intense, it creates both a love and a hatred for everything foreign. Of course, this does not mean that the love of the foreign is distinct from the hatred of it, or that the hatred of the foreign is distinct from the love of it, that these represent the interaction of two separate groups of people; no, for the same group of people can both love and hate the foreign. The very same individual can love the foreign in the morning, and hate it in the afternoon; this is an extremely complex question of cultural psychology. For a rather long period of time, Chinese intellectuals have been willing to sacrifice everything; they have always believed that they should do anything, as long as it would save the country. With such a mindset as a given, many questions of culture have become politicized. And the experience of enduring this rather long period has made a one-party dictatorship the common demand and the common hope of the vast majority of intellectuals and the vast majority of the people. [They think that] having a powerful regime, a powerful party, and a powerful leader would ensure that the Chinese people—who couldn't stand up—now could stand up. They did stand up, but in the end they fell into the trap described by Lord Acton, that "*power corrupts, and absolute power corrupts absolutely.*"

But at this point we can no longer say that this absolutely corrupt authority is a special manifestation of the "lingering poison of feudalism." Rather, it is the "lingering poison of feudalism" joined with one-party dictatorship joined with a modern ideology; this sort of strong force could not have been found in traditional China. Traditional China could not have had a monarch with this sort of power; neither the First Emperor of Qin, Emperor Wu of Han, or Tang Taizong had this sort of power. It is an extremely modern form [of power]. And to tell the truth it is only somewhat

[7] Zhang Dainian is co-author with Cheng Yishan of <u>Zhongguo wenhua yu wenhua lunzheng</u> [Chinese Culture and the Cultural Debate], Beijing: Zhongguo renmin daxue chubanshe, July, 1990.

more than a decade since this modern form has passed away in China. In mainland China today, many scholars, such as Mr. Wang Yuanhua, believe that the "Cultural Revolution" was a special manifestation of the "lingering poison of feudalism." I can basically accept this statement, but it only tells half the truth. The other half is: how could the "lingering poison of feudalism" enjoy such a special manifestation? What is the mechanism? Yet this question cannot be discussed either, for it is too sensitive to discuss. It would have to touch on the "anti-rightist" movement, and so forth, and would be too complex. Under this sort of taboo, a situation has developed which can permit the "lingering remnants of feudalism" to exercise their power, and this is why it has become impossible to preserve the truly good part of our tradition. As a result, that which truly should be preserved cannot be preserved, while that which should be discarded cannot be discarded. At the time of May Fourth, one could still believe that the "lingering remnants of feudalism" were a cultural burden, like something carried on one's back, which could be thrown away. But what we never realized is that what we used to think of as a burden is now busily at work in our bloodstream. In this manner of speaking it really is a case of "auto-toxemia." I believe that, in order to cure it, if we cannot obtain fresh water from the wellspring to wash it away, but merely rely on borrowing things we don't understand from outside, then it can never be eradicated. This is an extremely large dilemma.

When Heshang got started, I believe it was because reform needed encouragement, and of course this was a good thing. But no one realized that Heshang would offend many extremely conservative forces and sensitive nerves who would employ a narrow nationalism and narrow culturalism to criticize it. The conservative forces would employ all the resources of the tradition: *"You are unpatriotic, you curse your ancestors."* This sort of criticism would be rather persuasive amongst the people, while the resources available to the Westernization faction would be much weaker, because they failed to make use of the resources of the tradition while not knowing how to employ material from the outside. What is unfortunate about the current discussion of Heshang is that although this is a rare opportunity, and we have raised serious cultural topics, yet those people who truly have the ability to reflect on these questions do not dare to express themselves, because it has been politicized. The result of not speaking up is the worst sort of vicious cycle: the thinking of the most extreme pro-Westernization faction becomes even more extreme, while the most conservative forces become even more conservative. The vast majority of people are neither extremely pro-Westernization nor extremely conservative, but when these two forces are deadlocked in a see-saw battle, they become the silent majority.

Let's take the example of the talks by Li Zhengdao [T.D. Lee] and Yang Zhenning [C.N. Yang].[8] Of course it was not the case that they got the inside dope from a certain individual and then lined up behind him; this is absolutely not the case. But when their talks were used [by the conservatives], then the opposition criticized Li and Yang as not being Chinese at all but rather as being foreign devils or even false foreign devils.[9] They would think, *"You have now left China, yet you come back to teach us a lesson; what right do you have to do so?"* This sort of argument is both ironic and absurd. Originally the point of Heshang was to embrace Western culture and to escape from a narrow nationalism; but as soon as other people criticize your views, you jump into your own "soybean paste vat,"[10] using authoritarianism and narrow nationalism to attack them. I have encountered many similar examples. Take liberalism [ziyou zhuyi], for example; it stresses the protection of the individual's right of free speech. And yet if your opinion and mine differ, then I want to curse you roundly: *"You don't even want freedom and democracy; what kind of person are you?"* I think this is really a great pity. While the original intention was to raise [the topic] to the level of a debate on culture, the result was that it got worse and worse, and all kinds of unhealthy forces came out into the open. Therefore, when we discuss Heshang, we should try our best to eliminate political interference and raise it to the level of cultural discussion.

Christmas, 1988

---

[8] T.D. Lee and C.N. Yang are both Chinese-American Nobel prize-winners in physics. T.D. Lee is now at Columbia University, while C.N. Yang is at the State University of New York at Stonybrook. In the fall of 1988 both made public statements about Heshang. One of Prof. Yang's statements was made as part of an address delivered at Nankai University. Prof. Lee's statement was dated October 26th, 1988 and was subsequently published in both Renmin ribao and Guangming ribao on November 4th, 1988. The two statements from Prof. Yang plus the one by Prof. Lee were reprinted in Cui Wenhua, ed., Haiwai Heshang da taolun, Harbin: Heilongjiang jiaoyu chubanshe, 1988, pp. 26-31.

[9] In his famous satirical story, The True Story of Ah Q, author Lu Xun mocked as "false foreign devils" those Chinese who had imitated Western fashions.

[10] A reference to a well-known metaphor developed by Taiwan writer Bo Yang [Guo Yidong], in a talk entitled "Zhongguoren yu jianggang" [The Chinese and the Soybean Paste Vat], originally delivered in New York in 1981. Bo Yang's point is that Chinese culture is hermetically sealed, like the vat, and that anything from outside that gets dropped inside is likely to change drastically. Reprinted in Choulou de Zhongguoren, Linbai chubanshe, Taibei, 1985, pp. 61-73.

"Historians in the Capital Criticize Heshang: a Summary"[1]

In order to uphold the Four Basic Principles and criticize bourgeois liberalization, the editorial departments of five journals of the Chinese Academy of Social Sciences—Lishi yanjiu [Historical Research];Shixue lilun [Historical Theory]; Zhongguo shi yanjiu [Research on Chinese History];Jindai shi yanjiu [Research on Pre-modern History]; and Shijie lishi [World History]—on September 11th, 1989 invited some historians in Beijing to engage in a special critique of Heshang. This special criticism session was chaired by Tian Jujian, editor of Historical Research. Those who spoke at the meeting included (in stroke-count order): Qi Shirong[2]; Liu Jiahe; Zhu Zongzhen; Qiao Huantian; Li Kan; Shen Yongxing; Shen Dingping[3]; Chen Zhihua; Chen Qineng; Lin Ganquan[4]; Zhao Shiyu[5]; Xia

---

[1] This is a translation of the article entitled "Shoudu bufen shixue gongzuozhe pipan Heshang jiyao" in Lishi yanjiu [Historical Research], 1989 no. 6 [Nov.-Dec.], pp. 5-12. Much of it originally appeared in Renmin ribao, Nov. 23, 1989 as well as in the overseas edition on Nov. 26th. It was reprinted in Hua Yan, ed., Heshang pipan, Wenyi chuban she, 1989, pp. 222-230. In addition, many paragraphs of this article are apparently borrowed with minor re-editing from articles by Shen Dingping, Lin Ganquan, Jiang Dachun and Qu Lindong appearing in Wenhui bao on October 23rd, 1989.

[2] Qi Shirong is the author of "Bixu zhongshi dui Heshang de pipan" [We Must Take Seriously the Critique of Heshang], which first appeared in Wenhui bao, October 23, 1989; reprinted in Heshang pipan, pp. 123-124. Qi is a member of the History dept., Beijing Normal College.

[3] Shen Dingping is the author of "Heshang lishi guan jiqi lilun laiyuan pouxi" [An Analysis of Heshang's View of History and the Origins of its Theories," from Wenhui bao, October 23rd, 1989; reprinted in Heshang pipan, pp. 114-116. Another version of this article, entitled "Heshang lishi guan pouxi" appeared in Zhongguoshi yanjiu, 1989 no. 4, pp. 155-158 in which Shen summarized his presentation at a March 1989 forum to criticize Heshang organized by the Institute of History, Chinese Academy of Social Sciences. Shen is a member of the Institute of History, Chinese Academy of Social Sciences.

[4] Lin Ganquan [1931-] is the author of "Heshang yu chaowending xitong jiashuo" [Heshang and the Super-stability System Hypothesis], first appearing in Wenhui bao, October 23, 1989; reprinted in Heshang pipan, 125-126. Lin Ganquan is a researcher at the Institute of History, Chinese Academy of Social Sciences.

Liangcai; Gong Shuduo[6]; Jiang Dachun[7]; Liao Xuesheng; Qu Lindong[8]; Wei Kaizhao, and others.

The participants first of all revealed and analyzed the reactionary role played in society by <u>Heshang</u> from its first broadcast, to the political turmoil that occurred not long ago, and even to the period of counter-revolutionary rebellion. The sinister motives of its makers were even more strongly revealed after the political storm of blood and fire of the late spring and early summer of last year. The stern facts show that <u>Heshang</u> is the collective reflection in the realm of ideology and culture of the tide of bourgeois liberal thinking over the past few years. It prepared the way ideologically and emotionally, and served to lead public opinion for the political turmoil that broke out everywhere this year and which evolved into counter-revolutionary rebellion in the capital. Its most vulnerable point[9] lies in advocating that only capitalism can save China, and that "wholesale Westernization" is the only choice that can give China hope. To use these "cultural luminaries'" own words, "*it is only when blue, seafaring civilization turns to rain over the yellow soil steeped in yellow civilization*" that China can "*once again regain vitality.*" [213] Thus, it is necessary to proceed with a far-reaching political critique of <u>Heshang</u>'s vulnerable point.

Participants at the session further pointed out that <u>Heshang</u>, this "TV film of political commentary," [94] assumed the disguise of a "scholarly, cultural film" and advocated its reactionary political goals through a so-called "*all-out inquiry into our nation's history, civilization, and destiny*"

---

[5] See his article entitled "Ping <u>Heshang</u> de lishi guannian" [Criticizing <u>Heshang</u>'s Historical Outlook] from <u>Guangming ribao</u>, August 10, 1988, reprinted in <u>Heshang lun</u>, pp. 187-191. Zhao Shiyu is a lecturer in the History Dept. at Beijing Normal University.

[6] Gong Shuduo [1929-] is the author of "Huan Zhongguo jindai shi yi benlai mianmao" [Give Modern Chinese History Back its Original Face], <u>Lishi yanjiu</u> 1990.1, pp. 13-21. He is a professor in the History Dept. of Beijing Normal University.

[7] Jiang Dachun is the author of "<u>Heshang</u> paokai le weiwu shiguan" [<u>Heshang</u> has Abandoned the Materialist View of History], which first appeared in <u>Wenhui bao</u>, October 23rd, 1989; reprinted in <u>Heshang pipan</u>, pp. 117-119. Jiang is a member of the Institute of Pre-modern History, Chinese Academy of Social Sciences.

[8] Qu Lindong [1937-] is the author of "Hua er bu shi de xuefeng" [A Flashy but Insubstantial Style of Scholarship], which first appeared in <u>Wenhui bao</u>, October 23rd, 1989; reprinted in <u>Heshang pipan</u>, pp. 120-122; and of "Ping <u>Heshang</u> de xuefeng" [Critiquing the Scholarly Style of <u>Heshang</u>] in <u>Lishi yanjiu</u>, 1990.1, pp. 22-32. Qu Lindong is a professor at the Historiography Institute at Beijing Normal University.

[9] <u>yao hai</u>, a term from Chinese martial arts, means a spot on the body where an attack could prove fatal; in other words, an Achilles' heel.

and by *"calling on the whole nation to be concerned."*[10] This was how <u>Heshang</u> succeeded in tricking and deceiving people's hearts, and this was also its makers' greatest success. Therefore, in order to extirpate <u>Heshang</u>'s odious influence on society, we must also strip off its outer robe of academic theory and thoroughly expose its pseudo-scientific substance. Based on the above understanding, participants in the meeting made a preliminary analysis of the sources of <u>Heshang</u>'s theories, its view of history, its methodology, and its style of scholarship.

I. The Sources of <u>Heshang</u>'s Ideas and Theories

One of <u>Heshang</u>'s supporters once said,*"If I had to categorize <u>Heshang</u>, I would call it a 'scholarly, cultural film.'"* *"Why do I say it is a scholarly, cultural film? Because its general nature is scholarly; and though it is not a theoretical work, it does have its own theoretical framework and scholarly point of view, and is characterized moreover by rational argument."*[11] What sort of "theoretical framework" and "scholarly point of view" is it that <u>Heshang</u> possesses? Its principal author Su Xiaokang listed thirteen items, among which are: Marx's discussion of the Asiatic mode of production; Hegel's view that natural geography is the foundation of history; Toynbee's view of the innate mechanisms of civilizations; H.G. Well's discussion of Chinese history in his <u>Outline of History</u>; Francis Bacon's discussion of China's four great inventions; Ray Huang's proof that ancient China lacked a classical system of private ownership; Plekhanov's idea that the stage of the market economy cannot be skipped over; Jin Guantao's "super-stability hypothesis," and so forth.[12] After this, he summed up: *"Herein there are Marxist classics; there is the essence of Western culture that served as the source of Marxism; there is the thought of both famous, contemporary Western scholars and of overseas Chinese researchers; there are the scholarly accomplishments of contemporary Chinese scholars. No matter whether it is a great master in the orthodox tradition, or a new person with a new theory,*

---

[10] Pp. 93-94. His critics here are misquoting the title of his essay, entitled "Huhuan quan minzu fanxing yishi" [Arousing the Whole Nation to Self-questioning]. <u>youhuan yishi</u> or "a sense of social concern" is a term occurring frequently in Part Five, "Sorrow and Worry."

[11] See Tian Benxiang's essay "<u>Heshang</u> lun" [An Essay on <u>Heshang</u>] in Cui Wenhua, ed., <u>Heshang lun</u>, p. 221.

[12] See Su Xiaokang, "Longnian de beichuang—guanyu <u>Heshang</u> de zhaji" [The Distress of a Dragon Year—Notes on <u>Heshang</u>] in <u>Longnian de beichuang</u>, Sanlian shudian, Hong Kong, 1989, p. 37; see also the translation in this volume, p. 292. His critics have omitted the following: *Joseph Needham's discussion of the history of China's science and technology; Zhang Guangzhi's comparison of Chinese civilization and Maya civilization; Deng Xiaoping's thinking on reform and opening up; Zhao Ziyang's discussion of the socialist commodity economy; and Li Yining's proposals for the reform of the economic system.*

we have treated each one as an individual authority, fusing their varied elements together to forge the loud cry of a generation that we want to shout."[13] This passage may be taken as the guiding thought of Heshang's makers, yet it happens to be very wrong.

First of all let's consider the statement *"no matter whether it is a great master in the orthodox tradition, or a new person with a new theory, we have treated each one as an individual authority, fusing their varied elements together."* On the surface this would appear to be quite fair, but in fact it denies the leading role of Marxism, degrading "the classics of Marxism" to the status of an individual authority, and not even giving them the status of an "individual authority." When one looks through Heshang one can see clearly that although its makers speak broadly of historical development and the evolution of civilization throughout its six parts, nevertheless they never say a single word about Marxism's great scientific principles of productivity and production relations, and the mutual relations of the economic base and the superstructure; what's worse, they even cross out basic principles such as the fact that human society proceeds from a primitive, classless society to a class society, and that class society takes many socio-economic forms. And even if from time to time they occasionally mention the discussions of classic Marxist authors, they either twist their interpretations or mock them. For instance, they take *"Marx and Engel's famous view of the Asiatic mode of production"* and arbitrarily interpret it as merely *"having something to do with water."* [109-110] Moreover, they make fun of Marx, saying that *"the death knell of capitalism which he predicted long ago has still not sounded"* [183]; they mock Lenin for having been unable to respond to the "challenge" of Plekhanov. [160] It can be seen that Heshang's tendencies are quite obvious: that is, what they rely on is not Marxism and what they want to spread is not Marxism either, but rather is principally an assortment of Western non-Marxist ideas and theories.

Here it's important to point out that we do not simplistically reject and deny Western ideas and theories. Rather we must absorb those elements that are reasonable and that are truly the essence of Western culture. The history of the birth and development of Marxism has repeatedly proven this point. Yet to do as Heshang does and indiscriminately give all ideas the status of *"an individual school and fuse them together"* is entirely mistaken.

Next, let's look back and ask: how does Heshang treat the ideas and theories of Western and other foreign scholars? Heshang quotes the views of many Western scholars such as Hegel, Toynbee, Wells and Bacon mentioned above. It stands to reason that if we want to employ a particular idea, we

---

[13] Ibid. The critics omit the last sentence of the paragraph, which is: *Other than modernization, China has no other way out.*

should first have a correct understanding of it before we can use it correctly. But this is not how Heshang's authors have worked. For example, in Heshang there is the passage: "*..the more difficult the environment, the stronger the positive force to stimulate the growth of civilization, this is a well-known idea among Western historians.*" [109] The view indicated here is Toynbee's theory of "challenge and response."[14] But Toynbee's original meaning was not to say that the more difficult the environment, the easier it is to produce a response. For an environment that is too awful surpasses the ability of contemporary man to respond; not only can it make it impossible for man to respond, it may even overwhelm him. Thus Toynbee believed that civilization arises in an environment that is neither too good nor too bad. Especially in the ancient world, because man's ability to transform nature was rather weak, the ocean remained a difficult environment that was hard to master. These sorts of overly challenging environments could not become places where man could successfully respond to challenge, nor could they create an advanced "blue civilization." Yet Heshang's authors recast Toynbee's view to their liking and forcefully make connections between the sea and the rise of Sumerian and Greek civilizations, which by no means had a close relationship with "a continuous maritime life," in order to reject the "yellow civilization" created by a "yellow-skinned people" on its yellow soil and water.

Again, Heshang takes the question of "*whether an economically undeveloped socialist nation can successfully skip the developmental stage of a commodity economy*" [160] which was not Plekhanov's to begin with and forcibly pins it on him, claiming that this was a great question mark that he drew. In fact, before the October Revolution Plekhanov merely believed that Russia's proletariat was a very small fraction of the total population and did not possess the necessary prerequisites for a socialist revolution, which is why he opposed the October Revolution; yet he never considered, nor could he have, the question of the development of the commodity economy in a socialist country, because he died in May of 1918. That Heshang should say so is not merely due to ignorance but even more importantly is in order to denigrate Lenin and to mock him for being unable to answer Plekhanov's challenge. And yet the facts of history are precisely the opposite; the one who sensitively brought up the question of how to use the commodity economy to establish socialism in Russia where capitalism was relatively undeveloped was none other than Lenin. That is to say, this great question mark was drawn by Lenin.

---

[14] See Toynbee, A Study of History, Book II, part V, "Challenge and Response"; also part VII, "The Challenge of the Environment." Two-volume abridged edition by D.C. Somervell, Oxford, 1946 & 1957.

Further, Heshang's "geographical determinism," according to which the Yellow River has determined the history and fate of the Chinese people, basically follows the outline of Hegel's chapter on the "Geographical Basis of History" in his Philosophy of History. Starting from a Eurocentric standpoint, he broadly discusses the differences of geographical environments and their determining roles, going so far as to say that from ancient times China had no contact with the sea, did not enjoy the advanced civilization that the sea bestowed, and thus fostered habits of isolationism and backwardness. Even some Western scholars do not agree with these views that do not fit the historical facts; the West German scholar Franke[15] has pointed out that Hegel's attitude of arrogance and contempt towards Chinese history and civilization was a classic expression of 19th-century European colonial expansionism in the intellectual sphere. Yet the authors of Heshang fail to see the true essence of Hegel's philosophy, i.e., his vast and deep dialectical thought on the historical process, and have perversely fallen in love with the dregs of his thought instead, making them one of the theoretical cornerstones of Heshang.[16]

In addition, Heshang's outworn view about the rise and fall of civilizations, that the "yellow civilization" lacks vitality, comes directly from Toynbee's A Study of History. Toynbee takes cultural entities called "civilizations" as the objects of his research, declaring that there once existed twenty-one different types of civilization (later expanded to twenty-six types), of which the great majority had already died off, while others were in decline, leaving Western Christian civilization "*as the only one which has not yet clearly fallen apart*" and which "*has a creative vitality.*"[17] Let's pass over for the moment the subjectivity of this vast system of historical philosophy so finely crafted by Toynbee and the fact that it no longer has much influence in the West at present and merely mention Toynbee's mistaken view of Chinese civilization. Indeed, in his A Study of History, he

---

[15] Shen Dingping cites an article by Franke in Chinese translation, "Heige'er he Zhongguo de lishi" [Hegel and Chinese history] which appeared in Zhexue yicong, 1982, no. 4. It's unclear which Franke this refers to.

[16] This paragraph is largely taken from Shen Dingping's October 23rd, 1989 article in Wenhui bao.

[17] See Toynbee, op. cit., Book XII, Part XXXIX: ...*in the second quarter of the twentieth century of the Christian Era, the Western civilization was the only extant representative of its species that did not show indisputable signs of being in disintegration. Of the seven others, five—namely the main body of Orthodox Christendom and its Russian offshoot, the main body of the Far Eastern civilization and its Korean and Japanese offshoot, and the Hindu civilization—had not only entered into but had passed through their universal state phase; and a scrutiny of the histories of the Iranic and Arabic Muslim civilizations revealed strong evidence that these two societies had also broken down. The Western society alone was possibly still in its growth phase.* Pp. 304 in Vol. II of the abridged edition.

did include ancient Chinese civilization amongst those civilizations that had already died. But he later abandoned this view. In a book entitled Looking Towards the Twenty-first Century published in 1974,[18] he no longer viewed Chinese civilization as isolationist but felt that in the long river of history the Chinese people had already cultivated a "world spirit" worthy of praise. He even confidently predicted that, due to her superior historical inheritance, China would play a leading role in the future inevitable process of the unification of mankind. Yet Heshang clings for dear life to Toynbee's long-discarded former view; if Toynbee in his grave were aware of it, he would certainly make a protest to Heshang's authors.[19]

Towards the development of China's premodern[20] history, the explanation of questions such as the Opium War, Heshang also takes a pragmatic[21] attitude, selecting from amongst the views of Western scholars. Regarding the reasons why China in recent history has not brought about modernization, Western scholars in general fall into two camps: one emphasizes the internal structure of Chinese society, holding that Chinese society itself was unable to give rise to capitalism and was therefore unable to destroy the original social structure, so that feudal society continued to stagnate for a long time. These types of views vary somewhat in their concrete expressions and points of emphasis, some stressing oriental despotism, others emphasizing a hydraulic society, yet others emphasizing a

---

[18] *"Eastern Asia preserves a number of historical assets that may enable it to become the geographical and cultural axis for the unification of the whole world. These assets are, as I see them: (1) the Chinese people's experience, during the last twenty-one centuries of maintaining an empire that is a regional model for a literally worldwide world-state; (2) the ecumenical spirit with which the Chinese have been imbued during this long chapter of Chinese history; (3) the humanism of the Confucian Weltanschauung; (4) the rationalism of both Confucianism and Buddhism ... It is conceivable that the future unifier of the world will not be a Western or a Westernized country but will be China. It is also conceivable that a premonition of the possible future political role of China is the cause of China's surprising present worldwide prestige..."* From Arnold Toynbee and Daisaku Ikeda, Choose Life: A Dialogue, Oxford University Press, 1976, 1989, pp. 249-250. Choose Life was translated into Chinese as Zhanwang ershiyi shiji—Tang Yinbi yu Chitian Dazuo duihua lu [Looking Towards the 21st Century—The Toynbee–Ikeda Daisaku Dialogues], Guoji chuban gongsi, 1985..

[19] Large parts of this paragraph are taken from Shen Dingping, ibid.

[20] "Premodern" translates jindai [lit., "recent period"], & usually indicates the 18th and 19th centuries.

[21] "Pragmatic" translates shiyong zhuyi. In other words, Heshang makes a non-critical selection among Western theories, choosing only those which accord with its own point of view.

"super-stable structure" or "high-level equilibrium trap."[22] These are the sort of mistaken theories that Heshang advocates. The other point of view emphasizes the external environment of Chinese society, holding that the activities of Western colonialism had a negative influence on Chinese society, forcing it to depart from its original path of development, and that therefore the West must bear the historical responsibility for the poverty of China and the whole third world since the premodern period. And yet Heshang avoids mentioning this view.

As for the Opium War, some Western scholars hold that in its broadest sense it was a sort of battle between two cultures, one of them agricultural, backwards, and Confucian, a decadent dynasty already sunk in the mud up to its waist; the other a progressive industrial society. When these two cultures met, conflict was inevitable. Heshang has also entirely accepted this point of view, saying that the Opium War was a cultural conflict between a conservative, land-based agricultural civilization and an expansionist, maritime and industrial civilization. Thus, England's responsibility for engaging in the shameful opium trade and for fomenting a war of aggression are covered over. Its conclusion is that China's gates were opened too late! China's premodern history is one in which she repeatedly missed chances; whenever foreigners came to knock on our gate, Chinese never had a positive response. This fully exposes their true faces as traitors.

These scattered bits of theory in Western thought apparently being insufficient to express Heshang's main theme, the authors also drag out the theory of "super-stable structure" originally created by their supposed advisor and "famous historian," Jin Guantao, as their principal theoretical support.[23] But this too is not an original creation and is also smuggled in from Western scholars. If one merely makes a cursory comparison of Heshang's description of "this mysterious, super-stable structure" with some of the views expressed in the book entitled Marx and the Third World by the Italian scholar Umberto Melotti,[24] then one can discover that the two are not only identical in thought but that there are surprising textual similarities as well.

---

[22] An apparent reference to the theory proposed by Mark Elvin in his book The Pattern of the Chinese Past, Stanford, 1973. See especially chapter 17.

[23] See Part Five. Two of Jin's principal concepts are that (1) China is a society of "great unification" [da yitong]; and (2) that Chinese society has a "super-stable structure" [chaowending jiegou] that returns Chinese society to equilibrium despite periodic [but non-revolutionary] upheavals.

[24] Original title: Marx e il Terzo Mondo, published by Il Saggiatore, Milano, 1972. The English translation, by Patricia Ransford, edited and with a foreword by Malcom Caldwell, was first published in 1977 as a book by the MacMillan Press Ltd. in the U.K. and the Humanities Press in the U.S.

II. The View of History and Methodology of <u>Deathsong of the River</u>

The participants in the conference felt that <u>Heshang</u> by no means possessed a complete and systematic view of history; rather the concept of history it reflected was extremely complex, a combination of historical idealism and a vulgarized historical materialism. In sum, it is roughly as follows:

With regards to the basis of historical development, <u>Heshang</u> has preached a sort of fatalistic geographical determinism. In its own words, the *"geographical environment created a sort of isolating mechanism to Chinese culture centered in the Yellow River basin,"* [122] forming a cultural type that was inner-directed, aimed at stability, and isolationist, thereby determining that this culture would necessarily decline; and that moreover the so-called European seafaring civilization which arose in the Mediterranean from the very outset possessed the characteristics of being pioneering, aggressive and expansionist, thereby determining that it would take a superior position in present and future.[25]

This sort of fatalistic geographical determinism is in complete violation of the basic principles of Marxism, nor is it in accord with the facts of history. The rise and fall of various world civilizations cannot be explained on the basis of whether their geographical environment perched on the ocean or was centered on the interior of a continent. For example, the art of seafaring was by no means highly developed in the many city states of the southern, middle and northern parts of the mainland of ancient Greece, of which Sparta is a typical example. Yet it was they who created the world-famous Greek civilization; moreover, in the extended period between then and "modern Western industrial civilization," sea-faring was not highly developed, or one might say their fate was not tied to the sea. As for the colonial expansionism and commercial activities of some Western European countries, there were profound economic and social causes, as well as scientific knowledge accumulated over a long time and the corresponding material guarantees; they were not brought about merely because they bordered on the sea. The birth, development and evolution of the whole capitalist system was the result of the mutual interaction of the economy, government and culture of all of mankind; it was a product of a definite stage of historical development; and in history there has never existed an eternal "blue civilization" determined by the geographical environment. Because the influence of the geographical environment—including climate and natural resources—on mankind is different in each stage of historical

---

[25] This paragraph is taken from Shen Dingping, <u>ibid.</u>

development, the degree of influence of the geographical environment is in an inverse relationship to the degree of development of the civilization; there does not exist by any means an eternal, unchanging influence or determining role.

As for the form taken by historical development, what Heshang has preached is a theory of an historical cycle based on a metaphysical "super-stable structure" which claims that there exists in the history and actuality of Chinese society a "mysterious super-stable structure" [196] that "governs" everything, and that up to the present the "decaying social mechanism" [197] is still powerless to "break out of the vicious circle of the repeating historical cycle."[26] [196]

In fact, the concept of a "super-stable structure" in itself is not at all mysterious; at first it was a minor concept mentioned by Ashby in his Introduction to Cybernetics.[27] Originally, in the process of "designing a brain" it was a concept used to simulate the characteristics of a structurally complex yet automatically self-balancing "internal stabilizer." The makers of Heshang in borrowing the concept second-hand took this yet-unproved hypothesis used to model the human brain and intellect as if it were an already-accepted scientific truth; they took a concept adapted to a very specific field of research as a rule with broad applications; they took knowledge belonging to the field of natural science and technology and extended it without restrictions to the field of social history and to actual life.[28]

Whether or not it is appropriate to use the concept of a "super-stable structure" in the field of social history is a question requiring a lot more research. "Super-stable structure" is founded on the premise of a "self-stabilizing structure," yet whether or not society possesses this structure still awaits scientific proof. This is because the behavior of a society is made up of the behavior of many individuals with different purposes; and the inevitable outcome of history is commonly expressed in the form of chance events. History reveals similar points, yet it cannot repeat itself. In this sense, society cannot be a self-stabilizing mechanism, and hence a "super-stable structure" cannot exist. Yet the makers of Heshang sincerely believe in the "super-stable structure hypothesis" and use it to advocate the notion

---

[26] This paragraph is taken from Shen Dingping, ibid.

[27] William Ross Ashby, An Introduction to Cybernetics, Chapman & Hall Ltd., 1956; Science Editions, 1966. Ashby uses the term "ultrastability." His first book, Design for a Brain, Chapman and Hall, 1954, focussed on the study of the brain as a cybernetic mechanism; this book emphasizes that cybernetics is a new science with broad potential applications, from the study of biological systems to that of economic and social systems.

[28] This paragraph is taken from Shen Dingping, ibid.

of an historical cycle. This sort of view of history has caused them to overlook the vast changes in Chinese society since the early modern period and even since the birth of New China, as if China could only experience change if it moved towards capitalism and only then could it break out of the "vicious circle" of the "superstable structure."[29]

As for the stages of historical development, Heshang upholds a mechanical, materialistic viewpoint featuring a vulgarized theory of productivity; and although this viewpoint is at odds in every way with Marxist historical principles, yet in order to attain their own political goals, its makers from time to time will fly the banner of Marxism. One example is citing the debate between Plekhanov and Lenin.

Heshang emphasizes that Plekhanov *"upheld Marx's idea that history could not skip its necessary stages of development; he did not advocate the premature seizure of political power."* [160] In fact, by doing so at the time, he opposed Lenin's launching of the October Revolution. Plekhanov's mistaken analysis of the state of Russian society has long been proven by the facts of history; and the reason for his mistake was that he rigidly adhered to the letter of Marx and was unable to unite the general principles of Marxism with actual conditions in Russia; still less could he—as Lenin could—creatively employ and develop Marxism, scientifically analyze the actual conditions in Russia, and realize that although Russia was not a highly-developed capitalist country that precisely for this reason the various contradictions within Russia were particularly acute and that moreover the First World War had created an advantageous situation, making Russia the weak link in the chain of imperialism, thereby preparing the objective prerequisites for a socialist revolution. At the same time, the subjective prerequisites of the Russian Revolution (such as the proletariat and its new revolutionary party, the Worker-Peasant Alliance) had to a great extent compensated for the lacks in the objective prerequisites.

The victory of the October Revolution eloquently proved that Lenin was a richly-creative Marxist. Yet Plekhanov, who had once been an outstanding Marxist, was "left behind by the times." Yet the makers of Heshang persist in employing Plekhanov's fossilized concept of Marxism, and with regard to the stages of historical development preach a vulgarized theory of productive forces and a mechanical materialism.

As for the motive force of historical development, what Heshang advocates is a theory of motivation by outside forces. Heshang basically denies that the Chinese people and its civilization possess the inherent force

---

[29] Parts of this paragraph come from Lin Ganquan, "Heshang yu chaowending xitong jiashuo" [Heshang and the Super-stable System Hypothesis], Wenhui bao, October 23rd, 1989.

for historical progress and believe that under the challenge of "Western industrial civilization, ancient Chinese civilization was already irreversibly in decline and collapse, that it was no longer able to give birth to mechanisms of cultural renewal and that China's "Yellow Civilization" could only obtain renewed life and vitality when the gentle wind and rain of "Blue Civilization" moistened the dry and cracked yellow soil, just like the Yellow River flowing into the ocean.[30] [213]

Heshang's energetic advocacy of this theory of an outside motive force; its condemnation of "Yellow Civilization"; and its lack or even loss of the most elementary self-confidence in the Chinese people and their culture is a typical reflection of the tide of irrational thought in contemporary society. This sort of thinking is generally expressed as on the one hand an unwillingness to pay the price of bitter struggle for social civilization and on the other as a rash desire to precipitously enjoy the fruits of human civilization; as a failure to consider making contributions to society, while at the same time blindly demanding one's own subjective needs from society; and whenever these needs are unsatisfied, they then blame heaven and man alike and blindly worship foreign things.

It is with just such an attitude that *Heshang* regards the history and civilization of our ancestral land. They fail to understand the objective law that historical development does not turn to suit the subjective will of individuals; and when social development fails to suit their subjective desires they then blame history and our forebears. Still less do they understand that there is an enormous price to be paid for each step in the development of world civilization. The price of the development of Western European capitalism was the enormous suffering and sacrifice of the people of Western Europe and of their vast colonies and semi-colonies; the periodic turmoil and destruction in the world that it has caused is beyond count. Not to mention the destruction of world civilization caused by the two world wars, even now the threat of atomic war is a Sword of Damocles hanging over the entire human race. Does today's China still need to be "pushed forward" by this sort of outside force? And to what point will this outside force push China?

The methodology used by *Heshang* to edit the facts of history can be summed up in a single phrase: self-serving pragmatism. More specifically, *Heshang* uses two methods which are more or less misleading: the comparative method, and the systems [*xitong*] method.[31]

---

[30] This paragraph comes from Shen Dingping, *op.cit.*

[31] Part of this paragraph comes from Jiang Dachun, "*Heshang* paokai le weiwu shiguan" [*Heshang* Has Abandoned the Materialist View of History], *Wenhui bao*, October 23rd, 1989.

Just as the use of any method entails some sort of limits, so the correct use of the historical comparative method, in addition to requiring the guidance of a scientific view of history, also requires a true understanding of the nature of the historical comparative method and the process of using it, as well as a rich knowledge and grasp of history. Yet the makers of Heshang due to their ignorance of this method and in addition to their unwillingness to expend effort in intensively studying historical events and persons with whom they are unfamiliar, are reduced to the use of hearsay, to dragging in all sorts of irrelevant matters, creating all sorts of historical anachronisms [such as Guan Gong defeating Qin Qiong] and becoming a laughing-stock.[32]

The systems method emphasizes a systemic approach to the object of study, through the interaction of individual elements within a system and between the individual elements and the system itself, as well as the interaction between the whole system and the outer environment; yet this method must be used properly.[33] The systems method is principally used in regard to a particular time or small time period; in other words when the object of study does not undergo a qualitative change due to the passage of time. The limitation of this method is that it cannot handle an historical process that undergoes multiple qualitative changes. And so, if one wishes to introduce the systems method to the long process of human history with its unending changes, it is even more crucial to have the necessary prerequisites and limitations and to proceed under the guidance of a scientific view of history, which can only be Marxist historical materialism. (Of course, Marxist historical materialism must also continue to mature and develop in connection with contemporary conditions.) Yet Heshang has betrayed and discarded historical materialism, mechanically copying Toynbee's historiography of cultural types. The distinguishing feature of this view of history, in Toynbee's own words, is as follows: *"The whole history of human society that is called civilization is in some sense parallel and simultaneous."*[34] Precisely for this reason, it is best suited to deal with the systems method of a particular time, and in the field of social history is entirely in accord with Toynbee's view of history that "all history is parallel

---

[32] This paragraph comes largely from Jiang Dachun, ibid.

[33] This paragraph is taken from Jiang Dachun, ibid; it would appear to be criticizing Jin Guantao's adaptation of Ashby's theories.

[34] Compare Toynbee, A Study of History, Ch. 3, "The Comparability of Societies," part 3, *Our civilizations may, then, be granted to be sufficiently contemporaneous with one another for our purpose"; "In fact, we maintain that our twenty-one societies should be regarded, hypothetically, as philosophically contemporaneous and philosophically equivalent.* Pp. 42-43 in 2-vol. abridgement by Somervell, Oxford Univ. Press, 1946.

and simultaneous." Yet this history, which in fact has no development and no qualitative change, is equivalent to abolishing history.[35]

III. The Style of Scholarship in <u>Deathsong of the River</u>

The participants pointed out that the theories, viewpoints and methodologies of a particular work are related to the style of scholarship of its author, and are all the outer manifestations of this or that style of scholarship. The style of scholarship revealed in <u>Heshang</u> is arrogant and shallow, flashy yet insubstantial. It is markedly revealed in the following aspects:[36]

1. Styling themselves as spokesmen of youth and as bearers of enlightenment to the nation, they willfully "interrogate" History, and arbitrarily find fault with the status quo, as if only the makers of <u>Heshang</u> were the wisest and the most clear-headed of men. This is doubtless an involuntary betrayal of their arrogance and ignorance, and the concrete manifestation of their lack of guidance by a correct view of history. Every generation has the right to study History, to explain History, and to take useful lessons from it, but no one ever has the right to torture or to flog History, for it has ever been the case that History judges Man, and not that Man judges History.[37]

<u>Heshang</u>'s so-called "sense of social concern" [<u>youhuan yishi</u>, 198] or in other words their "culturo-philosophical consciousness" [194] as the "bearer of enlightenment" to the nation, is none other than the public condemnation of the fact that Chinese civilization just happens to preserve "the final struggle of the ancient world," [113] that the Chinese people has already become *"a nation which in its heart can no longer afford to lose,"* [102] which is perhaps *"at once both the profound and the shallow point of 'yellow' civilization!"* [212] Moreover they shamelessly advocate that the solution to China's problems is to move towards "blue civilization," that *"China's hope lies with the world."* [219] These mistaken theories reveal the startling degree already attained by <u>Heshang</u>'s arrogant, ignorant and nonsensical style of scholarship.[38]

2. They refute the wise men of the past and scorn those of the present, ignoring Marx and Lenin, respecting only themselves. In order to construct their ideology as "cultural luminaries," the makers of <u>Heshang</u> act boldly

---

[35] This paragraph is taken from Jiang Dachun, <u>ibid</u>.

[36] This paragraph is taken from Qu Lindong, "Hua er bu shi de xuefeng" [A Flashy but Insubstantial Style of Scholarship], <u>Wenhui bao</u>, October 23rd, 1989.

[37] This paragraph is taken from Qu Lindong, <u>ibid</u>.

[38] This paragraph is taken from Qu Lindong, <u>ibid</u>.

and rashly, unrestrainedly distorting the facts of history, revolutionary movements, and scientific theories, thus advancing their "main theme" to a vivid point. They ridicule Confucius,[39] Zheng He[40] and Qi Jiguang[41]; they also laugh at Lin Zexu,[42] Wei Yuan,[43] and Chen Tianhua.[44] Worse, they even scorn Marx[45] and Lenin[46]; and their contempt of Mao Zedong[47] is even greater. Their rash and frivolous attitude towards national heroes, patriots and revolutionary leaders has also reached an intolerable level.[48]

3. They select their material arbitrarily and criticize people as they please; they flaunt their learning, which is flashy but lacking in substance. Heshang puts on the guise of broad learning, drawing on material from every field, from the natural world to society, from ancient mythology to current history, from China to foreign countries, touching on questions of economics, government, nationalities, military affairs, science, technology, and culture, as well as relevant historical figures. On a superficial view, it truly is wide-ranging and imposing, employing startling language and full of "philosophy," and so it really achieved a "sensational effect" for a time. Yet if one gives it even the slightest scrutiny, it is not hard to discover that Heshang's arbitrary selection of historical materials, as well as its cavalier use of historical criticism reveal the shallowness and ignorance of Heshang's makers and reflect their attempt to please the public with claptrap.[49]

For example, Heshang says that in the wooden boat from the Hemudu site [205] one can see the "blue waves" at the fountainhead of Chinese civilization; and that later on, from the story of the Yellow Emperor's

---

[39] On Confucius or Confucianism, see pp. 140, 156, 195-6, 206, 210-11, 213.

[40] On Zheng He, see p. 132.

[41] On Qi Jiguang, see pp. 128-129.

[42] On Lin Zexu, see pp. 114, 152, 208n.

[43] On Wei Yuan, see p. 152.

[44] On Chen Tianhua, see p. 103.

[45] Qu Lindong's original article is more specific: *They even ridicule Marx, saying that 'the death-knell of capitalism which he long-ago predicted had still failed to sound.'* [183]

[46] Qu Lindong's original article says: *They ridicule Lenin for being unable to respond to Plekhanov's challenge.* [160]

[47] Mao's theory of peasant rebellions as the motive force in history is criticized on page 187 as not possessing "any revolutionary significance." Qu Lindong's original article says: *...and their contempt of Mao Zedong is even greater. Their statement: 'Many things in China, it would seem, should start over from May 4th' with a single penstroke erases seventy years of China's history.* [216]

[48] This paragraph is abridged from Qu Lindong, ibid.

[49] Large parts of this paragraph are adapted from Qu Lindong, ibid.

victory over the Fire Emperor and Chi You [205] and from the history of the Zhou conquest of the Yin [Shang] dynasty, one can see the victory of the "Yellow Civilization" of a continental power [205]; while the defeat of Chu by Qin in the late Warring States period is regarded as the ultimate triumph of the Yellow Civilization over the Blue. [205] Following this logic, should not the victory of Han over Qin imply the victory of "Blue Civilization" over "Yellow"? This sort of nonsense can never stand on its feet!

As for erroneous conclusions, they are everywhere in Heshang. For example:

> "*Virtually the whole of China's ancient history is a history of the struggle for survival space between herders and farmers.*" [123]

> In Chinese history, "'*what has long been divided must unite; what has long been united must divide*'," and this, "*like the Yellow River's floods, would seem to continue without end.*" [187]

> "*A Chinese emperor's dreaming of Sakyamuni led to the encounter of two of the great ancient civilizations of mankind.*" [142]

> That before the Qing dynasty, "*China's southeast coastline for a long time slept undisturbed.*" [131][50]

... and so on and so on—the errors are so numerous that in truth they cannot be listed individually.

4. They inherit the worst faults of the tradition while appearing to oppose tradition. One of the most direct impressions that Heshang gives people is its rejection of the Chinese tradition. Yet if we investigate a bit further the methodology it uses to critique the tradition, then we will see a strange phenomenon: that some of the worst faults of the tradition occur in its style of scholarship.

As mentioned above, Heshang has in many places arbitrarily cited historical materials in order to explain questions that cannot be explained, and seemingly unrestricted by any principle. This technique is by no means the "innovation" of its makers but existed as early as the Gongyang Commentary on the Spring and Autumn Annals. The Gongyang school ignored the facts of history but "borrowed events to explain its meaning"; this technique was reenacted or replayed numerous times in feudal historiography and may be said to have become a very bad tradition in the history of Chinese historiography. What surprises us is that Heshang which claims to oppose tradition has also in the end adopted this tradition. Even if the makers of Heshang were unaware of the tradition of the Gongyang school, it does not necessarily follow that only those who know a tradition

---

[50] All four of these examples are taken from Qu Lindong, ibid.

can inherit it. But as long as people live under the influence of a tradition and are unable to recognize and analyze it with a scientific attitude, then no matter how strongly they claim to oppose tradition, in the end they still can become practitioners of the tradition. This is precisely the case with Heshang and its makers.[51]

Collated by Dong Yue and Liu Jun

---

[51] The Chunqiu [Spring and Autumn Annals], a bare and laconic chronicle of the State of Lu between 722 and 481 B.C., has gained an immense importance in traditional Chinese scholarship far beyond its value as an historical work due to its attribution to Confucius, which, if true, would make it the only one of the Five Classics to have been personally authored by the Sage. The interpretation presented in the Gongyang Commentary, one of three early commentaries on the classic, is that Confucius' choice of words as well as his decision to include or exclude mention of events and persons constituted a profound moral evaluation of the persons or events concerned. Hence in subsequent generations there have been repeated attempts to read the supposed coded messages left by Confucius. Scholarly interest in the Gongyang Commentary revived under the Qing dynasty as part of a larger movement to reevaluate the authenticity of ancient texts, using new philological and text-critical techniques. Reformers such as Gong Zizhen and Kang Yuwei were influenced by this school and sought to elicit from the classics a new vision of Confucius' social philosophy, one that could address the vital national problems of the day. Hence they interpreted Confucius as a reformer. They were, in effect, like the makers of Heshang, using a discussion of the cultural tradition as a coded text to discuss the tabooed problems of the present.

BIBLIOGRAPHY

Compiled by Richard Bodman

Note to the reader: the large volume of critical material about Heshang in newspapers and magazines is beyond the scope of this bibliography, although occasional items are mentioned in the notes to various sections. This bibliography is limited to (I) published editions of the filmscript, in Chinese; (II) articles by and interviews with Heshang's creators, in Chinese; (III) critical articles about Heshang in Chinese, collected in book form; (IV) Items in other languages, including translations and critical reviews. Chong ping Heshang [#5, below] provides a useful bibliographic survey of the debate within China in 1988 and 89. The Japanese translation by Tsuruma Wako [#45, below] provides a bibliography of over one hundred articles in Chinese and Japanese.

I. Published editions of the filmscript:

A. In newspapers and journals: [by date]

a. Renmin ribao, June 12, 1988, p. 5, Part One [abridged]
b. Guangming ribao, June 21, 1988, Part Three [abridged]
c. Guangming ribao, June 26, 1988, p. 3, Part Four [abridged]
d. Wenhui bao, June 28th, 1988, p. 3, Part Two [abridged]
e. Zhongguo qingnian bao, June 30, 1988, p. 3, Parts Five & Six [abridged]
f. Guangming ribao, July 1, 1988, p. 3, Part Five [abridged]
g. Guangming ribao, July 4, 1988, p. 4, Part Six [abridged]
h. Xinhua wenzhai, September, 1988, pp. 104-119, Parts One through Six, reprinted from above versions.
i. Zhongguo zhi chun [China Spring], New York, November, 1988; December, 1988; January, 1989. [abridged]

N.B. Beijing qingnian bao, Jingji ribao and Guoji shangbao in mainland China as well as Zhongguo shibao in Taiwan [August, 1988, Renjian supplement] are all reported to have published abridged versions of the filmscript. The abridgements for items #a-h were made by the individual newspapers on the basis of a printer's proof of the narration sent out by the authors; cuts were made presumably to fit the limited space available on the literary supplement page, as well as to avoid politically sensitive topics. Excluding the omitted sections, the text as printed in the newspapers is almost identical with the text as printed in book form.

B. In book form: [by place and date]

<u>Mainland China:</u>

1. Su Xiaokang & Wang Luxiang, <u>Heshang</u>, Xiandai chubanshe, Beijing, June 1988, 118 pp., pb. Simplified characters. ISBN 7-80028-021-7/I.003. *The fifth printing, in September of 1988, brought the total of published copies up to 490,000. This edition includes Su Xiaokang, "Huhuan quan minzu fanxing yishi" [Arousing the Whole Nation to Self-questioning], pp. 1-6; Jin Guantao, "Cong Zhongguo lishi he wenhua zhong zoulai" [Coming from China's History and Culture], pp. 113-114; and Xia Jun, "Dianshi xilie pian <u>Heshang</u> biandao hou ji" [On Having Edited the TV Series <u>Heshang</u>], pp. 115-118, dated June 11, 1988.*

2. Cui Wenhua, ed., <u>Heshang lun</u>, Dianshi wenhua congshu, Wenhua yishu chubanshe, September, 1988, 232 pp., pb. Simplified characters. ISBN 7-5039-0304-X/I.184. *The second printing brought the total number of copies of this edition up to 200,000. This edition includes the filmscript, pp. 1-80; Xia Jun, "<u>Heshang</u> chuangzuo guocheng de huigu" [A Glance Back over the Process of Creating <u>Heshang</u>], pp. 83-87; Su Xiaokang's "Arousing the Whole Nation to Self-questioning" [reprinted from item #1]; an article by Wang Luxiang entitled "Huiyi yu sikao" [Remembering and Pondering], pp. 91-98; a lengthy section of letters from viewers and readers, pp. 99-120; a long section of critical reviews, both pro and con, pp. 121-230, including Cui Wenhua, "<u>Heshang</u> dui Zhongguo dianshi de qishi he zai?" [What is the Lesson of <u>Heshang</u> for Chinese Television?], pp. 123-142; and Xie Xuanjun, "<Jiqing de yin ying> yu <yin ying> de ji qing" [The <Other Side of Fervor> and the Fervor of the <Other Side>], pp. 196-200, in which Xie replies to the critique of Wang Xiaodong & Qiu Tiancao; and Tian Benxiang, "<u>Heshang</u> lun" [An Essay on <u>Heshang</u>], pp. 217-230, discussing <u>Heshang</u>'s contribution to Chinese television.*

3. Su Xiaokang & Wang Luxiang, <u>Heshang</u>, Henan meishu chubanshe, 1988. *[unseen; referred to in bibliography of <u>Die Gelbe Kultur</u>, Item #48 below, p. 120.]*

4. Cui Wenhua, ed., <u>Haiwai Heshang da taolun</u> [Heshang: The Great Discussion Overseas], Heilongjiang jiaoyu chubanshe, Harbin, November, 1988, 197 pp., pb. ISBN 7-5316-0598-8/g.486 *Cui Wenhua's preface is dated October 20th, 1988. Only 5,000 copies were printed in the initial printing. The text of the narrative for the film series is reprinted on pp. 89-*

168. The contents include many articles in Chinese from Hong Kong, Taiwan, and overseas scholars, including Bo Yang [Taiwan]; Geremie Barme [Australia]; Univ. of Wisconsin professor Zhao Gang; and Nobel prize winners Yang Zhengning and Li Zhengdao. Of great interest is the first appearance in print of Su Xiaokang's "Longnian de beichuang—guanyu <u>Heshang</u> de zhaji" [The Distress of a Dragon Year—Notes on <u>Heshang</u>], pp. 70-84, dated October, 1988; and a long postface by Cui Wenhua entitled "<u>Heshang</u> yu xiandai wenhua qimeng—dai bianhou ji," pp. 169-197.

5. Zhong Huamin [pseud.?], <u>Chong ping Heshang</u>, Hangzhou daxue chubanshe, Nov. 1989, 299 pp., pb. Simplified characters. ISBN 7-81035-004-8/G.008. *The first printing was issued in 30,000 copies. The contents include five chapters criticizing <u>Heshang</u>, pp. 1-168; a reprint of the text of the filmscript, with interspersed critical comments, pp. 169-285; a summary of the debate over <u>Heshang</u>, pp. 286-299. This edition is prefaced with a page of comments from General Secretary Jiang Zemin.*

<u>Hongkong</u>:

6. Su Xiaokang & Wang Luxiang, <u>Heshang</u>, Sanlian shudian, Hong Kong, September, 1988, 118 pp., pb. Traditional character version. ISBN 962-04-0694-X. *Between September and November 1988, this edition sold 14,000 copies; by May 1989 it was in its third printing. It is a nearly exact reprint of the text of the first edition by the Xiandai chubanshe, published by their permission.*

7. Su Xiaokang & Wang Luxiang, <u>Heshang</u>, Zhongguo tushu kanxing she, Hong Kong, September 1988. *[unseen; referred to in Zhu Weijing, "<u>Heshang</u>: he shang?," <u>Longniang de beichuang</u>, p. 116.]*

<u>Taiwan</u>:

8. Su Xiaokang & Wang Luxiang, <u>Heshang</u>, jointly published by Jinfeng chubanshe & Fengyun shidai chubanshe, <u>Heshang</u> book series #1, Taipei, October, 1988, 247 pp., pb. [No ISBN] Traditional character version. *By September of 1989, this edition was in its 62nd printing. This edition includes a publisher's foreword, by Chen Xiaolin; Su Xiaokang's foreword to the original edition, pp. 1-6; the text of Parts One to Six, pp. 7-101; articles by film-maker Xia Jun and advisor Jin Guantao, from the original edition; a reprinting of <u>Shensheng yousi lu</u>, by Su Xiaokang & Zhang Min, on the crisis in elementary and middle-school education, pp. 109-168; a series of articles by Hong Kong and mainland critics, pp. 169-207; a series of articles by Taiwan critics, pp. 208-228; and a chronicle of the Yellow River in history, in tabular form, pp. 229-247.*

II. Articles by and interviews with Heshang's creators: [by date]

9. Su Xiaokang, "Huhuan quan minzu fanxing yishi" [Arousing the Whole Nation to Self-questioning], printed in the edition published by the Xiandai chubanshe, June, 1988. [Item #1, above]. *Reprinted in the Hong Kong edition by the Sanlian shudian and in the Taiwan edition by the Jinfeng chubanshe and Fengyun shidai chubanshe. [Items #6 & #8, above]; a Japanese translation may be found in Tsuji Kogo, Item #40, pp. 7-15; and in Tsuruma Wako, Item #45.*

10. Jin Guantao, "Cong Zhongguo lishi he wenhua zoulai" [Coming from China's History and Culture], printed in the edition published by the Xiandai chubanshe, June, 1988. [Item #1, above]. *Reprinted in the Hong Kong edition by the Sanlian shudian and in the Taiwan edition by the Jinfeng chubanshe and Fengyun shidai chubanshe. [Items #6 & #8, above] Apparently reprinted also in Wenhui bao, July 4, 1988 [unseen]. A Japanese translation appears in Tsuji Kogo, Item #40, pp. 153-155.*

11. Xia Jun, "Dianshi xilie pian Heshang biandao hou ji" [On Editing the TV Series Heshang], printed in the edition published by the Xiandai chubanshe, June, 1988. [Item #1, above.] *Reprinted in the Hong Kong edition by the Sanlian shudian and in the Taiwan edition by the Jinfeng chubanshe and Fengyun shidai chubanshe. [Items #6 & #8, above]*

12. Liu Menglan, "Huan Huanghe kuang lan yu shen si zhi zhong—fang Su Xiaokang" [Transforming the Yellow River's Wild Waves in the Midst of Deep Thought—an Interview with Su Xiaokang], Renmin ribao, July 4-5, 1988; reprinted in Heshang taolunji [Item #35, below].

13. Gao Ning, "Gan lin, qin runzhi zhe pian huang tu—fang Heshang bianchuang renyuan Xia Jun, Wang Luxiang" [Sweet Rain Moistens This Stretch of Yellow Earth—an interview with Heshang's makers Xia Jun and Wang Luxiang], Renmin ribao, July 20th and 21st, 1988.

14. Mai Tianshu, "Pipan shi zui zhongyao de jianshe—Heshang chongbo qianxi fang Su Xiaokang" [Criticism is the Most Important Contribution—an interview with Su Xiaokang on the eve of Heshang's rebroadcast], Zhongguo qingnian bao, August 16th, 1988, p. 1. *Su Xiaokang summarizes his principal historical ideas and explains the changes he made in the script before its rebroadcast.*

15. Yuan Zhiming, "Heshang yu gaoji laosao—xie zai Heshang chongbo zhi ji" [Heshang and "High-class Bitching"—written on the occasion of the rebroadcast of Heshang], Guangming ribao, August 18th, 1988, p. 3. *Yuan Zhiming responds to critics who have branded Heshang as "shooting at mosquitoes with anti-aircraft guns" or as "high-class bitching."*

16. Guo Lixin, "Longnian de Heshang xianxiang—fang Heshang biandao Xia Jun" [The Dragon Year's Heshang Phenomenon—an interview with Heshang's director Xia Jun], Zhong shi wanbao, Sept. 11, 1988; reprinted in Heshang taolunji [Item #35, below], pp. 75-83.

17. Xia Jun, "Heshang chuangzuo guocheng de huigu" [A Glance Back over the Process of Creating Heshang], in Cui Wenhua, ed., Heshang lun [Item #2, above], September 1988, pp. 83-86. *A Japanese translation occurs in Tsuruma Wako, Item #45.*

18. Wang Luxiang, "Huiyi yu sikao" [Remembering and Pondering], in Cui Wenhua, ed., Heshang lun [Item #2, above], September 1988, pp. 91-97. *Wang Luxiang here records his first meeting with Su Xiaokang, his visit with the film crew to Yenan and Loyang, the process of writing the script and naming it Heshang. He concludes with a long list of acknowledgements to individuals who helped. A Japanese translation occurs in Tsuruma Wako, Item #45.*

19. Xie Xuanjun, "<Jiqing de yinying> yu <yin ying> de jiqing" [<The Other Side of Fervor> and the Fervor of <The Other Side>], in Cui Wenhua, ed., Heshang lun [Item #2, above], September 1988, pp. 196-200. *Xie responds to the criticism of Wang Xiaodong & Qiu Tiancao, "Jiqing de yin ying" [The Other Side of Fervor] published in Zhongguo qingnian bao, July 10, 1988 & reprinted in Heshang lun.*

20. Su Xiaokang, "Longnian de beichuang —guanyu Heshang de zhaji" [The Distress of a Dragon Year—Notes on Heshang], in Cui Wenhua, ed., Haiwai Heshang da taolun [Item #4, above], pp. 70-84. *This first printing is dated October, 1988. It is shorter than the version printed in Wenhui yuekan, January 10, 1990 [see #22, below]. It lacks parts #3 and #4, "Lishi zai mingming zhong zhaoshi" and "Dianshi qiguan zhi toushi"; in section #5, "Shei xiaode tianxia Huanghe jishiji dao wan?" there is more pointed criticism of Qiu Tiancao but a long letter from the U.S. is missing.*

21. Guan Zhizhong and Hong Shujuan, "Fang Heshang zongzhuanggao Wang Luxiang" [An Interview with Heshang's Main Writer Wang Luxiang], Yuan jian [Taibei], December 15, 1988, pp. 204-207. *In this interview, Wang Luxiang replies to the charges of critics that the series favors 'wholesale Westernization'; explains that Heshang's decision to focus on traditional culture was in part because of the difficulty of saying anything about China's present problems; discusses his interpretation of the dragon and the Great Wall as symbols; and explains his regret for leaving the impression in Part Three that Lin Zexu and Wei Yuan were not as far-sighted as Gong Zizhen.*

22. Su Xiaokang, "Longnian de beichuang—guanyu Heshang de zhaji" [The Distress of a Dragon Year—Notes on Heshang], Wenhui yuekan [Encounter Monthly], Shanghai, January 10, 1989, pp. 2-12. *According to a note at the end, this was drafted in November, 1988. It contains two sections missing in the edition printed in Cui Wenhua, Haiwai Heshang da taolun [Item #20, above]. Reprinted as the title article in Su Xiaokang, et.al., Longnian de beichuang [Item #30, below], Sanlian shudian, Hong Kong, April 1989.*

23. "Women yi piping lai biaoxian aiguo" [We Express Our Patriotism Through Criticism], interview with Jin Guantao, Yazhou zhoukan, Hong Kong, January 29th, 1989, p. 29. *Jin Guantao's picture appears on the magazine cover; pp. 24-30 contain a long article summarizing the reactions of Chinese outside of the mainland to Heshang. Reprinted in Heshang taolunji [Item #35, below].*

24. "Heshang yu dong xi fang mianlin de tiaozhan—Jin Guantao he Mai Disun de duihua" [Heshang and the Challenge Faced by East and West—a dialogue between Jin Guantao and Richard Madsen], in Longnian de beichuang, April 1989, pp. 147-167. *Anthropologist Richard Madsen is a China specialist and author of a number of studies including: Morality and Power in a Chinese Village, 1984; he also contributed to Robert N. Bellah, Habits of the Heart, 1985.*

25. Su Xiaokang, "Heshang de shangzhui" [The Debate over Heshang], in Longnian de beichuang, April, 1989, pp. 168-177. *This was drafted at the end of December 1988 while visiting Hefei, Anhui. Also reprinted in Heshang ji wai ji, [Item #36, below] pp. 217-225.*

26. Wang Luxiang, "Shiqu jiayuan de piaobozhe" [A Drifter without a Home], in Longnian de beichuang, April, 1989, pp. 178-182.

27. Xie Xuanjun, "Zhongguoren de Huanghe xinli" [The Yellow River Mindset of the Chinese People], in Longnian de beichuang, April, 1989, pp. 183-191.

28. Su Xiaokang, "Zai Bali xiangqi Caishikou—liuwang ganhuai" [Remembering Caishikou in Paris—feelings in exile], Bai xing, no. 202, October 16, 1989, pp. 3-4. *Written after having escaped China in the wake of June 4th, Su Xiaokang makes allusions to the bloody suppression of the Paris commune and to the executions of the 1898 reformers at Caishikou in Beijing. He goes on to say that Heshang erred in paying too much attention to culture and not enough to the communist system.*

29. W.L. Chong, "Su Xiaokang on his film River Elegy," China Information, vol. 4, no. 3, Winter 89/90, Leiden, pp. 44-55. *Records a*

lecture and interview on November 23rd and 24th, 1989. See Item #43, below.

III. Critical articles about Heshang, collected in book form: [by date]

[N.B. Items #2,4,5 and 8 above also contain many valuable articles.]

30. Su Xiaokang, et. al., Long nian de beichuang: <Heshang> zhengming yu huiying, Sanlian shudian, Hong Kong, April, 1989, 191 pp., pb. Traditional characters. ISBN 962-04-0721-0. *This valuable collection of articles in Chinese includes Su Xiaokang, "The Distress of a Dragon Year: Notes on Heshang," pp.1-44, in which he describes how Heshang came to be written [reprinted from Wenhui yuekan, Shanghai, January, 1989]; Lin Yusheng, "The Crisis of Chinese Consciousness and the Creative Transformation of the Tradition," pp. 45-50;Weiming Tu [Du Weiming], "Deathsong of the River: Whither Chinese Culture?," pp. 51-61; Jin Yaoji, "Heshang and the Self-Questioning of the Chinese," pp. 62-75; Shen Qingsong, "My View of Heshang," pp. 76-86; Xu Jilin, "The Hope and Tragedy of a Civilization in Decline," pp. 87-101; Zhu Weijing, "What Harm is there in Heshang?," pp. 102-118; Liu Xiaogan, "Heshang and the Vogue for Westernization," pp. 119-146; "Heshang and the Challenge Faced by East and West: a Conversation between Jin Guantao and Richard Madsen," pp. 147-167; Su Xiaokang,"The Debate over Heshang," pp. 168-177, in which he responds to his critics; Wang Luxiang, "A Drifter Without a Home," pp. 178-182; Xie Xuanjun, "The Yellow River Mindset of the Chinese People," pp. 183-191.*

31. Su Xiaokang, Wang Luxiang, et.al., Long de beichuang: <Heshang> huixiang, Fengyun shidai chuban gongsi, Heshang book series # 17, Taibei, May 1989. 191 pp., pb. Traditional characters. *Essentially the same book as #30 above, in a Taiwan edition.*

32. Heshang xuanyang le shenme [What Has Heshang Preached?], Guangbo chubanshe, January, 1990. *[unseen. The title article is presumably the article by the pseudonymous Yi Jiayan published on July 17th, 1989 in Renmin ribao, p. 1, and also reprinted in Heshang bai miu, pp. 1-8 and Heshang pipan, pp. 1-7. The introductory notes to the article in Heshang pipan state that the article was written in October 1988 but could not be published at the time due to opposition from Zhao Ziyang, notwithstanding his policy of non-interference in literary matters. An English translation of Yi Jiayan's article was published in Beijing Review, August 21, 1989.[Item #42, below].*

33. Li Fengxiang, ed., Heshang bai miu [Heshang's Hundred Errors], Zhongguo wenlian chuban gongsi, Beijing, June 1990, 199 pp., pb. Simplified characters. ISBN 7-5059-1314-X/I.942. *The first printing was*

issued in an edition of 3,000 copies. This is a collection of short articles attacking one or another small facet of Heshang. These articles are reprinted from Beijing wanbao which printed a series of 101 critical articles under this title from August 9th to November 19th, 1989. [These articles are also reprinted in Heshang pipan, below.]

34. Hua Yan, ed., <Heshang> pipan [A Critique of Heshang], Wenyi chubanshe, Beijing, December 1989, 251 pp., pb. Simplified characters. ISBN 7-5039-0621-9/G.79 *The first printing was issued in an edition of 10,000 copies. It reprints a large number of newspaper articles which appeared from July, 1989 onwards. It includes, pp. 127-221, a reprint of Heshang bai miu (above). Particularly interesting is Jin Ren's article connecting Heshang with Zhao Ziyang and detailing some of Su Xiaokang's political activities, pp. 20-25.*

35. Zhao Yaodong, et. al., Heshang taolunji, Fengyun shidai chuban gongsi, Heshang book series # 16, Taibei, January, 1990, 227 pp., pb. Traditional characters. ISBN 957-9536-05-8. *This volume includes among others: an interview with Su Xiaokang by journalist Liu Menglan, from Renmin ribao, July 4-5, 1988; a reprint of an interview with director Xia Jun by journalist Guo Lixin, from Zhong shi wanbao, Sept. 11th, 1988; an interview with Jin Guantao from Yazhou zhoukan, Hong Kong, January 29th, 1989.*

36. Su Xiaokang, et.al, Heshang jiwaiji, Fengyun shidai chuban gongsi, Heshang book series #27, Taibei, January 1990, 233 pp., pb. Traditional characters. ISBN 957-9536-06-6. *This volume reprints two items from #30 above, but includes valuable new items, such as Ji Wei's article "Guanyu Heshang zuozhe Su Xiaokang" [On Heshang's Author Su Xiaokang], pp. 227-233, reprinted from Wenhui yuekan, Shanghai, May, 1988.*

IV. Items in Other Languages: [by date]

37. Geremie Barmé, "TV Requiem for the Myths of the Middle Kingdom," Far Eastern Economic Review, September 1st, 1988, pp. 40-43. *Geremie Barmé [Bai Jieming] is also the author of an article in Chinese "Dianshi xilie pian Heshang jiqi qishi" [The TV Series Heshang and its Lesson], Jiushi niandai, Hong Kong, September, 1988, pp. 98-100; reprinted in Haiwai heshang da taolun.*

38. Joint Publications Research Service, Heshang, 6 December 1988, pp. 3-37. JPRS-CAR-88-002-L. *For official use only. In two-column format. The first published translation.*

39. Frederick Wakeman, Jr., "All the Rage in China," New York Review of Books, March 2, 1989, pp. 19-21. *A valuable review of Heshang and Heshang lun. He translates the title as "River Dirge."*

40. Tsuji Kogo and Hashimoto Natsuko, trans., Kasho: chuka bunmei no hiso na suitai to konnan na saiken [Heshang: The Tragic Decline of Chinese Civilization and its Arduous Reconstruction], Kobundo, Tokyo, March 25, 1989, 188 pp., hb. ISBN 4-335-55040-5. *Second printing, June 30, 1990. Includes Su Xiaokang, preface to the Japanese edition, dated September 1988 with a postscript dated February 1989; Su Xiaokang's "Arousing the Whole Nation to Self-questioning," pp. 7-15; Jin Guantao, "Coming from Culture and History"; Tsuji Kogo, "Yakusha atogaki—Kasho to no shukkai" [Translator's Afterword: My Encounter with Heshang], pp. 157-163; Haruna Tetsu, "Kasho ni tsuite" [About Heshang], pp. 164-188. Tsuji Kogo reported for the Asahi Shimbun in Hong Kong and Beijing; since 1985 he has been a professor at Tokai Daigaku in Kanagawa-ken. His books include Bunka dai kakumei to gendai chugoku [The Cultural Revolution and Modern China], Iwanami Shoten, 1984. Hashimoto Natsuko is a lecturer at Tokai Daigaku. The translated filmscript is accompanied by marginal explanatory notes and black and white photographs.*

41. Leo Ou-fan Lee, "Towards an Azure Culture," Times Literary Supplement, April 28-May 4th, 1989, p. 454 & 458. *He translates the title as "River Elegy."*

42. Yi Jiayan [pseud.], "What does 'The River Dies Young' Advocate?," Beijing Review, August 21, 1989, pp. 14-21. *Yi Jiayan is a pseudonym meaning "the views of one person." The Chinese version, entitled "Heshang xuanyang le shenme?" was first published in Renmin ribao on July 17th, 1989, and reprinted in Heshang xuanyang le shenme?, Heshang pipan and Heshang baimiu [Items #32, #33, #34, above].*

43. Chong, W.L., "Su Xiaokang on his film River Elegy," China Information, Leiden, vol. IV, no. 3, Winter 1989/90, pp. 44-55. *This valuable piece includes a summary of a lecture given by Su Xiaokang at the Sinological Institute in Leiden, November 24th, 1989; a summary of questions from the audience; and a condensed report of an interview with Su Xiaokang carried out by W.L. Chong and Inez Kretzschmar on November 23rd, 1989 in Leiden.*

44. Alice de Jong, "The Demise of the Dragon: Backgrounds to the Chinese Film River Elegy," China Information, Leiden, vol. IV, no.3, Winter 1989/90, pp. 28-43. *Alice de Jong graduated in Sinology from Leiden Univ. in the Spring of 1989. This is a shortened and updated version of her MA thesis. Her article describes the process of making the film series, a detailed*

examination of positive and negative reactions, and an analysis of changes made in the script of the second broadcast.

45. Tsuruma Wako, trans., <u>Koka bunmei e no banka: Kasho to Kashoron</u> [An Elegy for Yellow River Civilization: Heshang and Heshang lun], Gakuseisha, Tokyo, February 28, 1990. 269 pp., hb. ISBN 4-311-60307-X. *Includes a well-annotated translation of the script, illustrated with photographs and maps; translations of ten items from <u>Heshang lun</u>, including essays by Su Xiaokang [#9], Xia Jun [#17] and Wang Luxiang [#18], an essay by the translator; and a bibliography of 105 items in Chinese and Japanese, from June 1988 to July 1989. Tsuruma Wako is a professor at Ibaraki University where he specializes in the history of the Qin and Han dynasties.*

46. Peter Zarrow, film review of <u>Heshang</u>, <u>American Historical Review</u>, vol. 95, no. 4 (October 1990), pp. 1122-1124.

47. Han Minzhu (pseud.), <u>Cries for Democracy: Writings and Speeches from the 1989 Chinese Democracy Movement</u>, Princeton Univ. Press, Princeton, 1990. *Pp. 20-22 contain excerpts from Parts One and Five of <u>Heshang</u>.*

48. Sabine Peschel (Hrsg.) und Redaktionsgruppe Heshang, <u>Die Gelbe Kultur: Der Film Heshang: Traditionskritik in China</u>, Horlemann Verlag, 1991, 165pp. ISBN 3-927905-25-9. *This is the first Western-language translation and study of <u>Heshang</u>. The contents include Udo Hoffmann: "Von der <Kulturellen Begeisterung> bis zu den <Hundert Fehlern von Heshang>" [From "Culture Fever" to "<u>Heshang's Hundred Errors</u>"], pp. 7-15; an annotated translation of the filmscript by Sabine Peschel, liberally illustrated with black and white photographs of scenes from the film, pp. 16-108; W.L. Chong, "Su Xiaokang zu seinem Film Heshang [partial translation into German of item #41 above], pp. 109-116; norBert Rozowski, Gabi Schneider, Jacob Eyferth, "Die gelbe Bilderflut" [The Yellow Image Stream], a discussion of <u>Heshang</u> as cinema, pp. 117-120; "Schnitt: Vier Minuten im Film" [Cut: Four Minutes of the Film], reconstruction of a second-by-second shooting script, including parallel columns for time, text, screen image, sound, and camera technique; the section incorporates the last four minutes of Part Two, "Destiny," starting from "Asia, this land where the sun rises...," pp. 121-128; Goat-koei Lang-Tan, "Die Mach des Drachen—Kulturkritik und Identitatsuche in Heshang" [The Power of the Dragon—Cultural Criticism and the Search for Identity in <u>Heshang</u>], pp. 129-140; Peter M. Kuhfus, "Die Weltgesischte ist nicht der Boden des Glucks" [World History is not a Garden of Delights], pp. 141-161; a chronological table of dynasties, pp. 162-163; and biographical sketches of the authors, commentators and translators, pp. 164-165.*

河殇书目

【编者按：河殇问世仅仅三年，而有关河殇的文章已不可胜数矣。此乃仅以上文第1-36 条用汉字书写，详细情况请看上文。中文书目分三类，即：(1) 河殇解说词的版本；(2) 河殇编导人员自己发表的文章，以及记者访问；(3) 有关河殇之论文集。外文书目请看上文第37-48 条。】

I. 河殇解说词版本：

A. 见于报刊者：【按出版年月排列】

a.人民日报，1988年 6月12日。第1 集 寻梦
b.光明日报，1988年 6月21日。第3 集 灵光
c.光明日报，1988年 6月26日。第4 集 新纪元
d.文汇报， 1988年 6月28日。第2 集 命运
e.中国青年报，1988年 6月30日。第5-6 集
f.光明日报，1988 年 7月 1日。第5 集 忧患
g.光明日报，1988 年 7月 4日。第6 集 蔚蓝色
h.新华文摘，1988年 9月第104-119 页第1-6 集
i.中国之春，【纽约】1988年 11 月【上】；12 月【中】；1989 年 1月【下】。

【注：以上的版本都节略。】

B. 单行本：【按出版地点及年月排列】

中国大陆：

1.苏晓康及王鲁湘，河殇，北京：现代出版，1988年 6月。
2.崔文华编，河殇论，电视文化丛书，北京：文化艺术出版社，1988年 9月。

3.苏晓康及王鲁湘，河殇解说词和图片集，河南美术出版社，1988   。【未见】
4.崔文华编，海外河殇大讨论，哈尔滨：黑龙江教育出版社，1988年 11 月。【第89-168 页】
5.钟华民，重评《河殇》，杭州：杭州大学出版社，1988年 11 月。【第169-285 页】

香港：

6.苏晓康及王鲁湘，河殇，三联书店，1988年 12月。繁体字。
7.苏晓康及王鲁湘，河殇，中国图书刊行社，1988年 9月。【未见】

台湾：

8.苏晓康及王鲁湘，河殇，河殇系列丗1 ，台北：金枫出版社及风云时代出版社1988年10月。繁体字。

II. 河殇编导者文章以及记者访问： 【按年月排列】

9.苏晓康，"呼唤全民族反省意识"【1988年 6月】。收于北京现代出版社，香港三联书店以及台北金枫／风云时代出版社之河殇版本中。
10. 金观涛，"从中国历史和文化走来"【1988年 6 月】收于北京现代出版社，香港三联书店以及台北金枫／风云时代出版社之河殇版本中。
11. 夏骏，"电视系列片河殇编导后记"【1988年 6 月】收于北京现代出版社，香港三联书店以及台北金枫／风云时代出版社之河殇版本中。
12. 刘梦岚，"挽黄河狂澜于沈思之中 -- 访苏晓康，" 人民日报，1988年 7月4-5 日，亦见于河殇讨论集，第37-44页。

13．高宁，"甘霖，浸润着这片黄土 —— 访河殇编创人员夏骏，王鲁湘，"人民日报，1988年7月20-21日。

14．麦天枢，"批判是最重要的建设，河殇重播前夕访苏晓康，"见于中国青年报，1988年8月16日。

15．远志明，"河殇与高级牢骚 —— 写在河殇重播之际，"光明日报，1988年8月18日。

16．郭力昕，"龙年的河殇现象 —— 访河殇编导夏骏，"中时晚报，【台北】1988年9月11日。亦收于河殇讨论集，第75-83页。

17。夏骏，"河殇创作过程的回顾，"收于崔文华编，河殇论，1988年9月，第83-86页。

18．王鲁湘，"回忆与思考，"收于崔文华编，河殇论，第91-97页。

19．谢选骏，"《激情的阴影》与《阴影》的激情，"收于崔文华编，河殇论，第196-200页。

20．苏晓康，"龙年的悲怆 —— 关于河殇的札记"【1988年10月】。收于崔文华编，海外河殇大讨论，第70-84页。【内容缺少 "历史在冥冥中昭示""《电视奇观》之透视"，见下文第22条】

21．管执中及洪淑娟，"访河殇总撰稿王鲁湘"远见【台北】，1989年1月。

22．苏晓康，"龙年的悲怆 —— 关于河殇的札记，"文汇月刊【上海】，1989年1月，第2-12页。亦收于苏晓康等，龙年的悲怆，香港，三联书店【下文第30条】。

23．"我们以批评来表现爱国，"亚洲周刊【香港】，1989年1月29日。

24．"河殇与东西方面临的挑战 —— 金观涛与麦迪逊对话，"【1989年4月】收于龙年的悲怆，第147-167页。

25. 苏晓康，"河殇的商榷，"【1989年 4月】收于苏晓康等，龙年的悲怆，第168-177 页， 亦收于河殇集外集，第217-225 页。
26. 王鲁湘，"失去家园的飘泊者，" 【1989年 4 月】收于龙年的悲怆， 第178-182 页。
27. 谢选骏，"中国人的黄河心理，"【1989年 4 月】收于龙年的悲怆，第183-191 页。
28. 苏晓康，"在巴黎想起菜市口，流亡感怀，"百姓 【香港】，1989 年 10 月 6日，第3-4 页。
29。【这是1989 年11月 23-24 日 荷兰学者向苏晓康的访问， 用英文发表，请见第廾43 条】

III. 关于河殇的论文集：【按年月排列】

【按：上文第廾2 ，4 ，5 ，8 条亦包括有关文章。】

30. 苏晓康等，龙年的悲怆：河殇争鸣与回应，香港：三联书店，1989年 4月。繁体字。
31. 苏晓康，王鲁湘等，龙的悲怆：河殇回响，河殇系列廾17 ，台北：风云时代出版公司，1989年 5 月。繁体字。【与廾30 一样】
32. 河殇宣扬了什么，广播出版社，1990年。【未见】
33. 李凤祥编，河殇百谬， 北京：中国文联出版公司，1990年 6月。
34. 华严编，河殇批判， 北京：文艺出版社，1989年 12 月。
35. 赵耀东等，河殇讨论集，台北：风云时代出版公司，河殇系列廾16 ，1990年 1月。繁体字。
36. 苏晓康等，河殇集外集，台北：风云时代出版公司， 河殇系列廾27 ，1990年 1月。繁体字。

Chinese Historical Chronology

PALEOLITHIC CULTURE

700,000 BC   Lantian Man
                    Peking Man

NEOLITHIC CULTURES

4,000 BC   Jiangzhai
                    Hemudu

BRONZE & EARLY IRON AGE CULTURES

1766–1122 BC   Shang\Yin dynasty

1122– 256 BC   Zhou [Chou] dynasty
1122– 770 BC   Western Zhou
 770– 256 BC   Eastern Zhou
 722– 481 BC   "Spring & Autumn" period
 403– 221 BC   "Warring States" period

EARLY EMPIRE

 221– 206 BC   Qin [Ch'in] dynasty

 206– 220 AD   Han dynasty
 206–   8 AD   Former Han
  25– 220 AD   Later Han

PERIOD OF DIVISION

 221– 264 AD   Three Kingdoms
 265– 311 AD   Western Jin [Chin]
 311– 580 AD   Northern and Southern Dynasties

MIDDLE EMPIRE

 589– 617 AD   Sui dynasty
 618– 906 AD   Tang [T'ang] dynasty

 907– 959 AD   Five dynasties and Ten Kingdoms

LATER EMPIRE

960–1275 AD	Song [Sung] dynasty
960–1126 AD	Northern Song
1127–1275 AD	Jin/ Mongol rule in north
	Southern Song in south
1276–1367 AD	Yuan dynasty [Mongols]
1368–1644 AD	Ming dynasty
1645–1911 AD	Qing dynasty [Manchus]

MODERN PERIOD

1912–	Republic of China
1949–	People's Republic of China

Maps

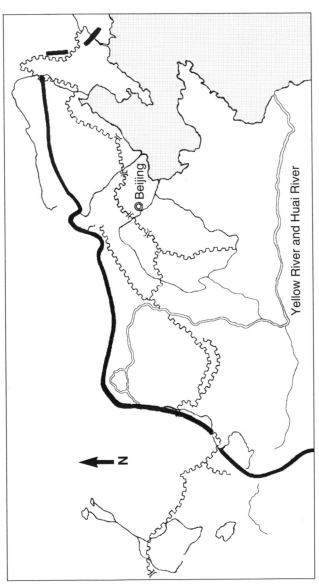

Map 1: Conjectural Route of Qin Great Wall [black]
Superimposed over Ming Great Wall

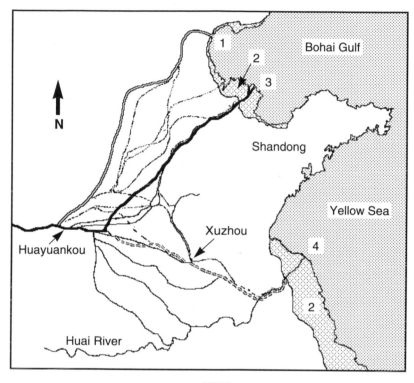

KEY

1   Yellow River mouth before 602 BC

2   New land added since ca. 1400

3   Exit of Yellow River 1947–present; 1855–1938; before 1100

4   Exit of Yellow River combined with Huai 1938–1947; ca. 1100–1855.

Map 2: The Yellow River's Major Changes of Course

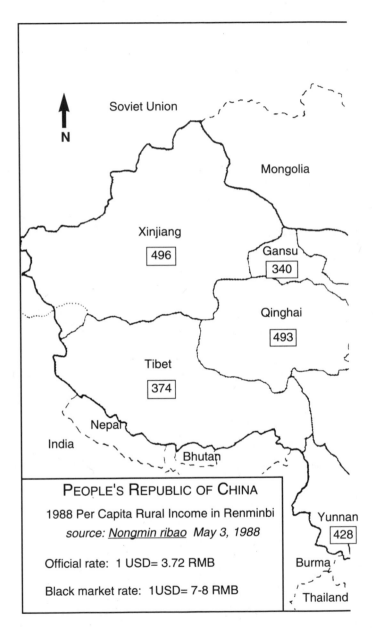

Map 3: Rural Income Distribution

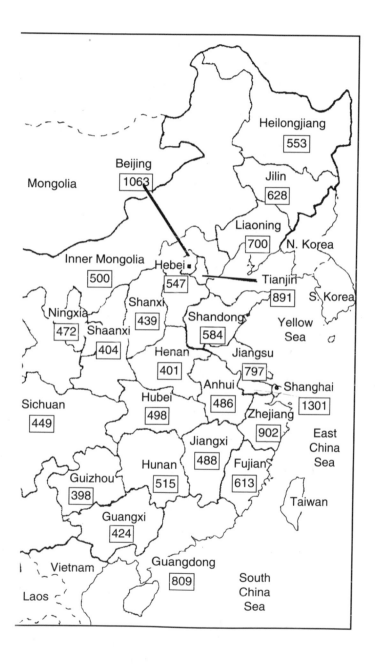

Heilongjiang
553

Beijing
1063

Mongolia

Jilin
628

Liaoning
700   N. Korea

Inner Mongolia
500   Hebei
547   Tianjin
891   S. Korea

Shanxi
439   Shandong
584   Yellow
Sea

Ningxia
472   Shaanxi
404   Henan
401   Jiangsu
797

Sichuan
449   Hubei
498   Anhui
486   Shanghai
1301

Zhejiang
902   East
China
Sea

Jiangxi
488   Fujian
613

Hunan
515

Guizhou
398

Taiwan

Guangxi
424

Vietnam   Guangdong
809   South
China
Sea

Laos

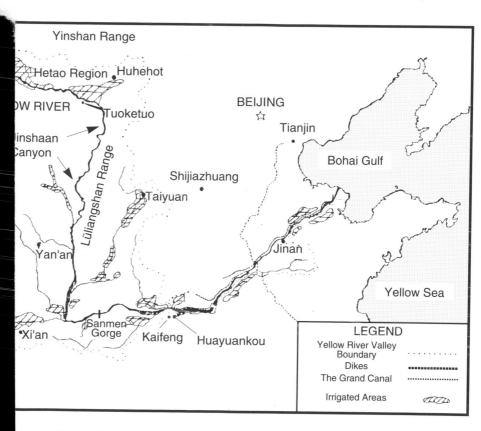

of the Yellow River

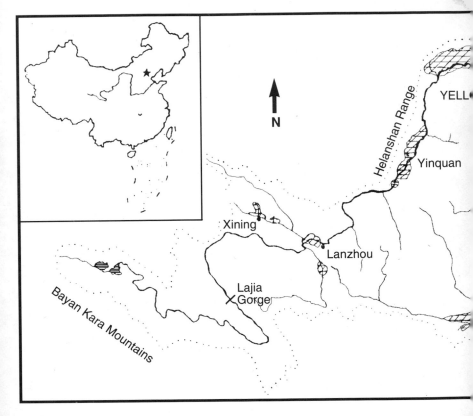

Map 4: Sketch M

CORNELL EAST ASIA SERIES

For information on ordering the preceding publications and videotapes, please write to:

CORNELL EAST ASIA SERIES
East Asia Program
Cornell University
140 Uris Hall
Ithaca, NY 14853-7601

3-92/.6M/BB